MW00636284

Special Report 245

EXPANDING
METROPOLITAN
HIGHWAYS

Implications for
Air Quality and Energy Use

Committee for Study of Impacts of
Highway Capacity Improvements on
Air Quality and Energy Consumption

TRANSPORTATION RESEARCH BOARD
National Research Council

National Academy Press
Washington, D.C. 1995

Transportation Research Board Special Report 245

Subscriber Categories
IA planning and administration
IB energy and environment

Transportation Research Board publications are available by ordering directly from TRB. They may also be obtained on a regular basis through organizational or individual affiliation with TRB; affiliates or library subscribers are eligible for substantial discounts. For further information, write to the Transportation Research Board, National Research Council, 2101 Constitution Avenue, N.W., Washington, D.C. 20418.

NOTICE: The project that is the subject of this report was approved by the Governing Board of the National Research Council, whose members are drawn from the councils of the National Academy of Sciences, the National Academy of Engineering, and the Institute of Medicine. The members of the committee responsible for the report were chosen for their special competencies and with regard for appropriate balance.

This report has been reviewed by a group other than the authors according to the procedures approved by a Report Review Committee consisting of members of the National Academy of Sciences, the National Academy of Engineering, and the Institute of Medicine.

The study was sponsored by the Transportation Research Board, the American Association of State Highway and Transportation Officials, the Federal Highway Administration of the U.S. Department of Transportation, and the Environmental Protection Agency. Transportation Research Board funds came from unrestricted contributions of the Association of American Railroads, the UPS Foundation, Norfolk Southern Corporation, and Consolidated Rail Corporation.

Library of Congress Cataloging-in-Publication Data

Expanding metropolitan highways : implications for air quality and
    energy use / Committee for a Study of the Impacts of Highway
    Capacity Improvements on Air Quality and Energy Consumption.
        p.   cm.—(Special report : 245)
    Includes bibliographical references.
    ISBN 0-309-06107-5
    1. Highway capacity—United States.   2. Traffic flow—United
    States.   3. Air—Pollution—Economic aspects—United States.
    4. Energy consumption—United States.   I. National Research Council
    (U.S.).   Transportation Research Board.   Committee for a Study of
    the Impacts of Highway Capacity Improvements on Air Quality and
    Energy Consumption.   II. Series : Special report (National Research
    Council (U.S.). Transportation Research Board) : 245.
    HE336.H48E95   1995
    388.4'13142'0973—dc20   95-4464
                                                                    CIP

Cover design: Karen L. White

Committee for Study of Impacts of Highway Capacity Improvements on Air Quality and Energy Consumption

Preface

The Clean Air Act Amendments of 1990 (CAAA) raised the importance of air quality as a goal for the transportation sector alongside the more traditional goals of mobility and safety. Transportation agencies face an enormous challenge to provide a transportation system that meets these multiple goals. In particular, highway projects—the backbone of traditional transportation programs—have come under intense scrutiny. Once thought to reduce congestion and air pollution, projects that expand highway capacity are now being questioned for their stimulative effect on motor vehicle travel and their support of dispersed metropolitan development patterns, which foster additional automobile dependence and thereby increase emissions.

Legislation similar to the CAAA has not been passed recently in the energy area. However, in the past decade low gasoline prices, growing motor vehicle ownership, and increased motor vehicle travel have raised transportation's share of total petroleum consumption in the United States and increased U.S. energy dependence on foreign oil sources. Although energy efficiency measures are important, they are not viewed as having the same urgency as measures to improve air quality, nor are energy issues likely to be subjects of litigation when highway expansion projects are proposed.

The current concern over the effects of highway building on both the environment and energy use is part of a broader debate over the appropriate direction of metropolitan development and the role of transportation in that process. Many view incremental, evolutionary change as the only realistic and politically feasible course in moving to a less polluting, more energy-efficient transportation system. Others seek major revisions in land use policies and significant increases in the price of motor vehicle travel to promote these goals; they view the CAAA as a strategic instrument for change. The varied approaches reflect different visions of the future; different judgments about the appropriate balance among economic growth, environmental protection, and energy conservation; and different views about the effectiveness of technology versus behavior change for achieving these goals.

This study is cognizant of these larger issues, but it is focused on the more practical questions that policy makers and planners face in complying with the CAAA. Its purpose is to review the current state of knowledge, evaluate the scientific evidence, and narrow the areas of disagreement about the impacts of highway capacity additions on traffic flow characteristics, travel demand, land use, vehicle emissions, air quality, and energy use. Its intended audiences are key policy makers in Congress, the Environmental Protection Agency (EPA), the Federal Highway Administration (FHWA), and the Department of Energy; implementers and overseers of the CAAA, including congressional staff, state and local air quality and transportation agencies, and the courts; and the research community. The study, which was initiated by the Transportation Research Board (TRB) Executive Committee, received broad funding support from FHWA; the American Association of State Highway and Transportation Officials (through the National Cooperative Highway Research Program); EPA; and TRB's Institute for Strategic Transportation Studies, supported by unrestricted grants from the UPS Foundation, the Association of American Railroads, Consolidated Rail Corporation, and Norfolk-Southern Corporation.

TRB formed a study panel of 16 experts under the leadership of Paul E. Peterson, Henry Shattuck Professor of Government at Harvard University. The committee includes specialists in travel behavior and travel demand modeling, traffic engineering, vehicle emissions and air quality modeling, motor vehicle fuel economy, transportation and land use, land use modeling, and transportation and air quality planning. Panel members are drawn from universities, state government, metropolitan planning organizations, environmental organizations, and consulting firms.

With one exception, the committee endorses all of the report findings and recommendations. One committee member, Michael A. Replogle, agreed with many elements of the report but dissented from some of the key findings. His statement is presented in its entirety as Appendix E. In accord with National Research Council policies, this appendix provides the opportunity for the expression of views not shared by the majority of the committee. That a minority view has been offered is not surprising because the study raises complex and difficult questions that have confounded scholars for decades.

The committee wishes to acknowledge the work of many individuals and organizations who contributed to this report. Nancy P. Humphrey managed the study and drafted major portions of the final report under the guidance of the committee and the supervision of Robert E. Skinner, Jr., former Director of Studies and Information Services and current Executive Director of TRB, and Stephen R. Godwin, current Director of Studies and Information Services. Mr. Godwin drafted Chapter 5 and Appendix D. Suzanne Schneider, Assistant Executive Director of TRB, managed the report review process. In accordance with the National Research Council report review procedures, the report was reviewed by an independent group of reviewers.

The committee also wishes to thank many individuals outside TRB whose advice it sought in the course of its deliberations. William Schroeer of EPA's Office of Policy, Planning, and Evaluation and John German of the Certification Division of EPA's Office of Mobile Sources provided useful input to the committee on EPA's regulatory policies and on the Federal Test Procedure Review Project, respectively. Greig Harvey of Deakin, Harvey, Skabardonis, Inc., provided the committee with an overview of the recent court case against the Metropolitan Transportation Commission of the San Francisco Bay Area and its implications for conformity analysis requirements and modeling procedures. Finally, Randy Guensler of the Georgia Institute of Technology prepared special analyses, based on his dissertation results, for the discussion of the uncertainty of emission rate estimates from current models contained in Chapter 3.

The committee also commissioned several papers to inform its deliberations. The papers are appended to the report to make the information available to a broad audience. The interpretations and conclusions reached in the papers are those of the authors; the key findings endorsed by the committee appear in the main body of the report. Harry S. Cohen of Cambridge Systematics, Inc., prepared a literature review of the effects of highway capacity additions on travel demand. The major findings of that report are included in Chapter 4 with supporting detail in Appendix B. Two papers were commissioned on heavy-duty diesel vehicles, because their response to highway capacity additions differs from that of light-duty vehicles. K. G. Duleep of Energy and Environmental Analysis, Inc., reviewed the emission and energy characteristics of heavy-duty diesel vehicles and provided an assessment of how they might be affected by highway capacity additions. His paper is included in its entirety as Appendix A, and its findings are discussed in Chapter 3. Lance R. Grenzeback of Cambridge Systematics, Inc., examined the likely effect of changes in highway capacity on truck travel. His paper is included as Appendix C, and its findings are discussed in Chapter 4. These two papers make a significant contribution to an area about which little has been written.

The final report was edited and prepared for publication under the supervision of Nancy A. Ackerman, Director of Reports and Editorial Services, TRB. Special appreciation is expressed to Luanne Crayton, Norman Solomon, and Lisa Wormser, who edited the report, and to Marguerite Schneider and Frances Holland, who assisted in meetings, logistics, and communications with the committee and provided word processing support for numerous drafts.

Contents

Executive Summary 1

1 Introduction 11
   Regulatory Context   13
   Study Focus   21
   Definition of Terms   22
   Overview of Impacts   24
   Assessment of Impacts   29
   Organization of Report   31

2 Contribution of Motor Vehicle Transportation to
   Air Pollution and Energy Consumption 38
   Transportation and Air Quality   38
   Transportation and Energy Consumption   61
   Modeling Air Quality and Energy Impacts   65
   Summary   75

3 Traffic Flow Characteristics 87
   Overview of Expected Impacts   87
   Review of Effects on Emissions   90
   Summary Assessment of Effects on Emissions and
      Air Quality   122

Review of Effects on Energy Use   124
Summary Assessment and Recommendations for
    Improving the Knowledge Base   127

4   Travel Demand 138
Determinants of Metropolitan Travel Demand and
    Recent Travel Trends in the United States   138
Overview of Expected Impacts and Definition of Terms   143
Theoretical Understanding of Travel Choices and
    Impacts   149
Review of Evidence from Studies   152
Review of Impacts from Travel Demand Models   159
Summary Assessment of the State of Knowledge   162
Review of Impacts on Truck Travel   164
Recommendations for Improving the Knowledge Base   167

5   Land Use and Urban Form 174
Background   176
Theory Linking Transportation and Land Use   183
Empirical Evidence   185
Results from Models   190
Implications of Changes in Population Density for
    Travel and Emissions   194
Summary   201
Recommendations for Improving the Knowledge Base   203

6   Findings and Conclusions 210
Overview   211
Crosscutting Issues   213
Findings for Individual Impact Areas   215
Summary Assessment of Net Effects   224
Recommendations for Research, Modeling Improvements,
    and Data Collection   227
Concluding Observations   230

Appendix A Emission and Energy Characteristics of Heavy-Duty
           Diesel-Powered Trucks and Buses   237
           K. G. Duleep
Appendix B Review of Empirical Studies of Induced Traffic   295
           Harry S. Cohen
Appendix C Impact of Changes in Highway Capacity on Truck
           Travel   310
           Lance R. Grenzeback
Appendix D Review of Studies of Transportation Investments and
           Land Use   345
Appendix E Minority Statement of Michael A. Replogle   354

Study Committee Biographical Information 381

Executive Summary

The Clean Air Act Amendments of 1990 (CAAA) and complementary provisions of the Intermodal Surface Transportation Efficiency Act of 1991 (ISTEA) introduced new constraints on the transportation sector to help ensure that transportation activities do not delay expeditious attainment of national health standards for air quality. As a result highway projects that expand capacity have come under particular scrutiny in many metropolitan areas for their potential to increase motor vehicle traffic and emissions—a primary source of air pollution. The issue is already at the center of legal challenges or threats of litigation in several metropolitan areas, potentially stalling local highway construction programs.

For years transportation agencies have responded to traffic growth by expanding highway capacity to maintain reasonable levels of service. Capacity expansions ranging from small-scale signal-timing improvements to construction of major highways were expected to relieve congestion without substantial negative effects on air quality. In fact, capacity enhancements that raised travel speeds and smoothed traffic flows were believed to reduce vehicle emissions and improve

1

energy efficiency. Further, it was widely accepted that new highway capacity was essential to the continued economic growth and competitiveness of major metropolitan areas.

These views are now being challenged. Some analysts and environmental groups argue that adding highway capacity will result in more traffic, higher emission levels, and greater energy consumption in the long run by stimulating motor vehicle travel and encouraging dispersed, automobile-oriented development. In addition they see continued highway expansion as antithetical to a more environmentally oriented and resource-conscious future that stresses the revitalization of older urban and inner suburban neighborhoods and supports transit and nonmotorized forms of transport.

These issues are part of a larger debate over the appropriate direction of metropolitan growth and the role of transportation in that process. This debate involves value judgments about the relative importance of mobility, economic growth, environmental protection, and energy conservation. It considers a broad range of policies, from investments in transportation supply to demand management and pricing strategies.

This study is focused on a more specific topic: the effects of investment in highway capacity on air quality and energy use in metropolitan areas. Its primary audience is metropolitan planning organizations (MPOs), state officials, legislators, and courts with oversight responsibilities. These agencies and officials are being asked to meet the regulatory requirements of the CAAA by making judgments about the environmental effects of highway capacity expansion on the basis of their interpretation of the best available evidence. Energy issues do not convey the same urgency or require the same regulatory analysis, yet transportation's increasing consumption of the nation's petroleum resources is of concern. To the extent that energy efficiency and energy use are affected by changes in traffic flow characteristics and travel volume from highway capacity expansion, these effects are considered in this study.

The purpose of this study is to review the current state of knowledge, evaluate the scientific evidence, and narrow the areas of disagreement about the impacts of highway capacity additions on traffic flow characteristics, travel demand, land use, vehicle emissions, air quality, and energy use. The state of modeling practice is also examined to assess the reliability of forecasting tools available to planning agencies; research, modeling improvements, and data collection are recommended to help narrow the gap between regulatory requirements and analytic capabilities.

International experience relevant to the study charge was considered, and alternatives to highway capacity expansion, such as "traffic calming," were examined to the extent they shed light on the effect of changes in traffic flow characteristics on vehicle emissions and energy use. In most cases, however, the experience of other countries, particularly European countries, is not directly applicable to the United States because of considerable differences in land availability and cost, population density, mode choice, pricing structures, and institutional governance of regional growth. Wholesale adoption of European transport strategies might produce some reductions in vehicle energy use and emissions and concomitant improvement in metropolitan air quality, but, in the committee's judgment, it would also impose substantial social and economic costs and raise questions about institutional and political feasibility.

REGULATORY CONTEXT

Under the CAAA the U.S. Department of Transportation (DOT) and MPOs are directly accountable for demonstrating the compatibility of transportation investments with timely attainment of national air quality standards. According to the current interpretation in Environmental Protection Agency (EPA) regulations, the act provides a grace period for states to revise their air quality attainment plans, which set emissions limits by source. In the meantime, transportation agencies in metropolitan areas that have not attained national standards must meet strict interim conformity requirements to prevent air quality degradation. Specifically, nonattainment areas are required to prove that (a) projects in regional transportation improvement programs and plans will not lead to motor vehicle emissions higher than in a 1990 baseline year and (b) by building these projects, emissions will be lower in future years than if the projects are not built (the "build–no-build" test).

Once EPA approves new state air quality attainment plans the conformity test changes: the emissions that result from carrying out regional transportation improvement programs and plans in nonattainment areas must not exceed target emissions caps for transportation sources established in the EPA-approved state air quality plans. The conformity test still requires a regional emissions analysis, but the criterion for comparison is less demanding: predicted regional emissions from transportation sources must be within state-determined emissions budget caps. The most analytically demanding comparison—estimating changes in emission levels in future years from marginal expansions of regional transportation networks relative to maintaining the status quo—would no longer be required.

The committee did not limit its examination of the effects of highway capacity additions to a specific time frame. However, particular attention was paid to the 20-year time frame established by the CAAA for attainment of air quality standards, because this represents the planning and forecasting horizon within which local planning agencies are required to make judgments about the air quality effects of highway projects.

ANALYTIC REQUIREMENTS

Providing a precise assessment of the net effects of expansions of highway capacity on air quality and energy use is not straightforward. Addressing the questions raised in this study requires modeling a complex sequence of interrelated events—from initial impacts on traffic flows to longer-term consequences on travel demand, automobile ownership, and residential and business location in a metropolitan area. It also requires modeling the emissions generated by the predicted travel impacts and forecasting their effects on air quality at or near the points of emission and throughout the region. There is significant uncertainty in predicting precise quantitative outcomes at each stage in the analysis. In addition, different levels of analysis are required to distinguish project-level from regional effects.

Determination of initial effects is complicated by the network character of the transportation system. The ability of drivers to change their route, time, and mode of travel means that adding highway capacity and thus reducing travel time at one location in the system will affect other locations as users take advantage of the new capacity. Modifications in traffic flows and volumes on this broader system of facilities, and their effects on emissions and energy use, must be taken into account.

User responses also change over time. The response to large reductions in travel time is likely to be greater in the long run than initially, as highway capacity additions influence decisions about location and automobile ownership. The key uncertainty is at what point, or whether at any point, the emissions increases from the new development and traffic growth stimulated by the capacity addition will offset the initial emission reductions gained from smoothing traffic flows. Assessment of net project effects on emissions and energy use depends on the length of time over which the effects are analyzed and the value placed on long-term versus more immediate effects. The longer the prediction period the more likely other, often unpredictable factors such as changes in demographic or economic conditions are to intervene and diminish forecasting accuracy.

Forecasts of the net effects of adding highway capacity also involve comparisons with alternatives. Not investing in highway capacity or undertaking other investments or demand management strategies has consequences for air quality and energy use. A comparison of outcomes requires estimating how sensitive users are to changes in travel time and cost and to what extent travel by transit or other modes can be substituted for automobile travel. It also requires understanding how growth would be distributed both within and outside the metropolitan area if highway capacity expansions were restricted. Paradoxically, because of past and ongoing efforts to reduce vehicular emissions, it will become more difficult to discern differences in emissions resulting from different transportation and demand management strategies. These alternative strategies all represent small changes to a declining base of emissions from highway sources.

FINDINGS

After examining the considerable literature on the relationships among transportation investment, travel demand, and land use as well as the current state of the art in modeling emissions, travel demand, and land use, the committee finds that the analytical methods in use are inadequate for addressing regulatory requirements. The accuracy implied by the interim conformity regulations issued by EPA, in particular, exceeds current modeling capabilities. The net differences in emission levels between the build and no-build scenarios are typically smaller than the error terms of the models. Modeled estimates are imprecise and limited in their account of changes in traffic flow characteristics, trip making, and land use attributable to transportation investments. The current regulatory requirements demand a level of analytic precision beyond the current state of the art in modeling.

The state of emissions modeling illustrates the problem well. In theory the initial effect of a highway capacity addition on traffic flow characteristics and the resulting changes in vehicle emissions should be measurable for the current fleet. Despite considerable research and vehicle testing, however, no definitive and comprehensive conclusions can be reached. Virtually all motor vehicle testing has been based on a limited set of driving test cycles that inadequately represent current urban driving conditions. In addition, current emission models rely on average trip speed as the sole descriptor of traffic flows. Variability in speed, road grade, and other factors that strongly influence emissions is not explicitly incorporated into the models. Changes in vehicle emission rates thus cannot be predicted reliably for a wide range of changes in average trip speeds, many of which are in the range of average speed changes expected from highway capacity additions.

Current emissions models were developed to estimate motor vehicle emissions at the regional level. They cannot be appropriately applied to estimate the emissions effect of changes in traffic flow patterns at specific highway locations. Even for regional estimates, current models significantly underpredict emissions of some pollutants. Models can be developed that are more sensitive to vehicle operations and traffic conditions; some research and testing have already begun. However, development and incorporation of new models into the regulatory process will take substantial time and investment and require close coordination between the transportation and the regulatory communities.

The initial effects on energy use from highway capacity additions can be predicted more reliably than effects on emissions because fuel economy is not as sensitive as emissions to traffic flow conditions, particularly speed variation. However, energy and emissions estimates must both be linked with reliable data on the likely impacts of highway capacity additions on traffic, travel demand, and location decisions. Here, too, the available travel demand and land use models provide imprecise and limited estimates of likely outcomes. Improvements in modeling capability will also require substantial investment.

More research and improved models can help narrow the gap between regulatory requirements and analytic capabilities. The conformity tests required by current regulations will themselves change as the build–no-build test is phased out once state air quality plans are approved by EPA. However, the complex and indirect relationship between highway capacity additions, air quality, and energy use, which is heavily dependent on local conditions, makes it impossible to generalize about the effects of added highway capacity on air quality and energy use, even with improved models.

On the basis of current knowledge, it cannot be said that highway capacity projects are always effective measures for reducing emissions and energy use. Neither can it be said that they necessarily increase emissions and energy use in all cases and under all conditions. Effects are highly dependent on specific circumstances, such as the type of capacity addition, location of the project in the region, extent and duration of preexisting congestion, prevailing atmospheric and topographic conditions, and development potential of the area.

Nevertheless, some general findings do apply. Within developed areas, traffic flow improvements such as better traffic signal timing and left-turn lanes that alleviate bottlenecks may reduce some emissions and improve energy efficiency by reducing speed variation and smoothing traffic flows without risking large offsetting increases from new development and related traffic growth. However, the cumulative effect of multiple small improvements in traffic flows may attract increased traffic, at least in the vicinity of the improvements. In less-developed portions of growing metropolitan areas—where developable land is available and most growth is occurring—major highway capacity additions such as a freeway bypass or a major interchange reconstruction are likely to attract further development to these locations and increase motor vehicle travel, emissions, and energy use in these areas. Whether these outcomes lead to a net increase in regional emissions and energy use depends on whether the highway expansion redistributes growth that would have occurred elsewhere in the region or whether it stimulates productivity gains that result in net new growth.

CONCLUDING OBSERVATIONS

Despite the considerable uncertainties in predicting the effects of expanding highway capacity on air quality given the current state of knowledge and modeling practice, policy makers and planners must comply with current environmental regulatory requirements and make decisions on the basis of the best available information. Thus, the committee thought it should provide its best judgment on the likely payoffs of pursuing current policies.

In its opinion, the current regulatory focus on curbing growth in motor vehicle travel by limiting highway capacity is at best an indirect approach for achieving emissions reductions from the transportation sector that is likely to have relatively small effects, positive or negative, on metropolitan air quality by current attainment deadlines. Historically, measures to control traffic demand have had limited effects (Apogee Research, Inc. 1994). According to estimates from local studies using current emission models, these traditional transportation control measures (TCMs), which include traffic flow improvements among others, are likely to yield changes of 1 or 2 percentage points individually in regional emissions of key pollutants by attainment deadlines (DOT and EPA 1993, 9). The effects of traffic flow improvements could be positive or negative, depending on offsetting increases in traffic. These are small changes on a declining base, given EPA projections of continuing emission reductions for carbon monoxide and volatile organic compounds (DOT and EPA 1993, 9).

In the committee's opinion, major highway capacity additions are likely to have larger effects on travel and to increase emissions in the affected transportation corridors in the long run unless some mitigating strategy is implemented in conjunction with the capacity addition. However, because of the large investment implicit in current metropolitan spatial patterns, it may be years before changes in land use and related traffic patterns induced by the added capacity make a significant difference in regional emission levels and air quality.

Curtailment of all highway capacity expansion that has any potential for increasing emissions risks pitting environmental against economic concerns. In the past, when environmental goals have conflicted with economic objectives, the response has been to delay or reassess environmental regulations. It is easy to envision these pressures building again. In addition, requiring policy decisions to hinge on uncertain model outputs leaves the entire process vulnerable to error and manipulation.

In the committee's view, a more constructive approach is to look for ways to reconcile air quality with economic goals. The committee believes that technology improvements can yield more significant benefits for air quality relative to the current focus on curbing travel growth. Catalytic converters, electronic fuel injection, and unleaded gasoline have resulted in substantial reductions in vehicle emissions in the past 20 years (Nizich et al. 1994). EPA predicts further emission reductions for major pollutants on the order of one-quarter to one-third from 1990 baseline levels by attainment deadlines simply from continued vehicle fleet turnover and implementation of CAAA-required vehicular and fuel standards and enhanced vehicle inspection and maintenance programs (Nizich et al. 1994, 5-4, 5-6).

Market solutions also have promise, although the feasibility of some approaches is untested. For example, potential increases in traffic from new highway capacity such as added expressway lanes might be reduced by imposing tolls varied by time of day (i.e., congestion pricing) and collected electronically to control travel growth on the expanded facility. A recent National Research Council report on congestion pricing (NRC 1994) has examined in depth the technical and political feasibility of this approach. Applied in a limited setting, it would not require major changes in current highway finance patterns. It would allow highway capacity to be provided where it is needed but could mitigate negative effects on emissions from travel growth.

In the long run, stronger measures, such as pricing motor vehicle travel to better reflect the full social costs of highway travel and the introduction of areawide, time-of-day tolls, may be necessary to provide direct incentives for reducing or shifting travel demand in ways that use highway capacity more efficiently and with less cost to the environment. Local land use and zoning measures that increase building density and support mixed-use development could be introduced more widely. Land use measures may reduce areawide automobile travel and emissions, but the changes are likely to occur gradually and will have more significant effects if they are implemented in conjunction with pricing measures. Finally, radical advances in vehicle technology could produce cleaner transportation, substantially reducing the level of vehicle emissions.

These more radical solutions are neither new nor easy. Major technological improvements require substantial investment and time to produce results. Changes in pricing or land use policies require significant institutional changes—such as more powerful regional institutions to coordinate areawide pricing schemes and land use strategies—and more public acceptance than has been demonstrated in the past. In the judgment of the committee, however, as long-run alternatives to current policy, they offer better prospects for reconciling economic and environmental goals.

REFERENCES

ABBREVIATIONS

DOT   U.S. Department of Transportation
EPA   Environmental Protection Agency
NRC   National Research Council

Apogee Research, Inc. 1994. *Costs and Effectiveness of Transportation Control Measures (TCMs): A Review and Analysis of the Literature.* National Association of Regional Councils, Bethesda, Md.
DOT and EPA. 1993. *Clean Air Through Transportation: Challenges in Meeting National Air Quality Standards.* Aug.
Nizich, S.V., T.C. McMullen, and D.C. Misenheimer. 1994. *National Air Pollutant Emission Trends, 1900–1993.* EPA-454/R-94-027. Office of Air Quality Planning and Standards, Research Triangle Park, N.C., Oct., 314 pp.
NRC. 1994. *Special Report 242: Curbing Gridlock: Peak-Period Fees to Relieve Traffic Congestion, Volumes 1 and 2.* Transportation Research Board and Commission on Behavioral and Social Sciences and Education, National Academy Press, Washington, D.C.

1

Introduction

The Clean Air Act Amendments of 1990 (CAAA) (Public Law 101-549, 42 U.S.C. 7401, et seq.) and complementary provisions of the Intermodal Surface Transportation Efficiency Act of 1991 (ISTEA) (Public Law 102-240, 49 U.S.C. 101 note) tightened controls on the transportation sector to help ensure that transportation activities contribute to timely attainment of national health standards for air quality. As a result traditional transportation projects, such as additions to highway capacity, have come under close scrutiny as potential contributors to air pollution.

For years transportation officials have relied on adding highway capacity—building new expressways and adding lanes to existing freeways—to accommodate travel demand in growing metropolitan areas. Such increases in capacity were thought not only to bring congestion relief but also to improve air quality and fuel efficiency by contributing to freer-flowing traffic conditions.

This conventional wisdom has been challenged by environmental planners and other analysts who take a long-term perspective on the effects of additional highway capacity. They concede that adding highway capacity may initially reduce some vehicle emissions and improve fuel efficiency by smoothing traffic flows and reducing stop-and-go traffic, although the benefits may not be as significant as were once believed. However, these positive effects may be eroded over time by growth in travel stimulated by the new capacity. Improved levels of highway service may encourage shifts from less polluting modes of transportation and induce new or longer trips once discouraged by congested conditions. As traffic volume grows, traffic operations may deteriorate, producing levels of congestion comparable with previous conditions but at higher traffic volumes. In the long run, these analysts maintain, new highway capacity will improve access and may encourage development in low-density areas not amenable to transit. Low-density development requires more frequent and longer trips, increasing emission levels and energy use and further degrading air quality.

The issue of highway capacity and air quality is already at the center of legal challenges brought by environmental groups to many additions to highway capacity in metropolitan areas. This issue is likely to receive more attention as metropolitan areas grapple with the stricter requirements of the CAAA. The act allows citizen suits to be brought for the first time against the U.S. Department of Transportation (DOT) and the Environmental Protection Agency (EPA) for noncompliance with legislative requirements and timetables, which opens the door to increased litigation.

Assessment of the precise consequences for air pollution and energy use of any particular addition to highway capacity is uncertain, given the current state of knowledge and modeling practice. Travel demand forecasting models—the basis for determining the effect of increased highway capacity on travel demand—were originally developed to help determine the appropriate size of new capital facilities. They are not well suited to providing the detailed data, such as speed data and travel data by time of day, needed for modeling and analysis of vehicle emissions and air quality impacts. Nor can most current travel demand models adequately measure the effect of improvements in highway service on the amount of travel or on land use patterns, which in turn could affect future demand for travel and its distribution in a region.

Emissions models, which measure the polluting effects of motor vehicle travel, inadequately represent the emission performance of in-service vehicles. Current data on the relationship between vehicle speeds and emission levels—critical to analyzing highway capacity projects that will change the distribution of traffic speed levels and variability of speeds—are based on averages that mask wide variances across individual vehicle performance, roadway conditions, and driving behavior. Moreover, the models do not adequately capture major suspected sources of emissions from vehicle accelerations and high speeds, although some research is under way to understand these phenomena. Planning agencies often apply current speed-emission relationships as if they were precisely known.

Despite the limitations of the existing knowledge base, engineers and scientists are being pressed to provide reliable estimates of the likely effects of adding highway capacity on emissions and energy use to assist legislators, state officials, metropolitan planning organizations (MPOs), and judges in reaching decisions on these issues. Thus a review of the current state of knowledge has been undertaken to evaluate the scientific evidence concerning these effects and to narrow areas of disagreement. The specific questions at issue are described and, where possible, research or analyses that could be conducted to speed their resolution are recommended. More specifically, the study committee

- Critically reviews existing research of the links among highway capacity, traffic flow characteristics, travel demand, land use, vehicle emissions, air quality, and energy use in metropolitan areas;
- Identifies the conditions most likely to affect emissions and energy use;
- Reviews the reliability of models and analyses that regional and state planning agencies use to forecast travel demand and land use, emission levels, and energy consumption; and
- Recommends research strategies, modeling improvements, and data collection efforts to improve analytic capabilities.

REGULATORY CONTEXT

The enactment of the CAAA has refocused attention on the effects of transportation activity on air quality, but legislation to set standards for alleviating air pollution and improving the fuel efficiency of motor vehicles dates back to the 1970s.

Clean Air Legislation and Regulatory Requirements

The harmful effects of air pollution on public health were formally recognized by the requirements of the Clean Air Act Amendments of 1970 (Public Law 91-604, 84 Stat. 1676), which mandated establishment of national ambient air quality standards (NAAQS) for six pollutants: carbon monoxide (CO), lead (Pb), nitrogen dioxide (NO_2), ozone (O_3), particulates (PM-10), and sulfur dioxide (SO_2) (Curran et al. 1994, 19). There is no standard for carbon dioxide, the principal greenhouse gas, because carbon dioxide is not toxic and therefore has no direct negative health impact.

Historical Trends

Since 1970 substantial gains have been made in reducing pollution from transportation sources, primarily through technological improvements such as catalytic converters and electronic fuel injection, which are now standard equipment on cars,[1] and through the use of lead-free gasoline. Between 1970 and 1993, for example, highway vehicle emissions of CO and volatile organic compounds (VOCs)[2] (which are a precursor of ozone) declined by 32 percent and 53 percent, respectively; highway vehicle emissions of lead were effectively eliminated (Nizich et al. 1994a, 3-11, 3-13, 3-16; Figure 1-1). However, highway vehicle emissions of nitrogen oxides (NO_x)—the other ozone precursor—remained nearly constant (Nizich et al. 1994a, 3-12).[3] Although the emissions models on which these estimates are based typically have underestimated absolute emission levels, the trend has been downward.

Despite more than two decades of progress in improving air quality, EPA estimated that in 1993 about 59 million people lived in counties that violated one or more of the NAAQS (Curran et al. 1994, 14).[4] Thus, the CAAA contain stringent requirements for further reductions in emissions from transportation sources, backed up by strict monitoring and sanctions for nonperformance, to bring nonattainment areas (i.e., those areas not attaining NAAQS) into compliance.

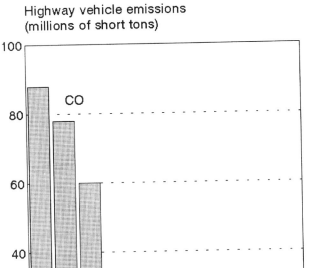

Highway vehicle emissions
(millions of short tons)

FIGURE 1-1 Highway vehicle emissions of selected pollutants: 1970, 1980, and 1993 (Nizich et al. 1994a, E-11–E-13).

Requirements of the 1990 CAAA

The act requires additional technological advances, such as tougher tail pipe standards, enhanced vehicle inspection and maintenance programs, and cleaner fuels programs, which should result in further reductions in emissions as newer, cleaner vehicles replace older ones and as technology-oriented programs are implemented. These measures, however, may not offset growth in emissions from motor vehicle travel. For example, if vehicle miles traveled (VMT) grows at a relatively conservative rate of 2 percent per year[5] and no additional technology advances are made other than those included in the CAAA, EPA estimates that tail pipe emission gains could be offset by 2002 for CO and VOC and by 2004 for NO_x (Figure 1-2).[6] Thus, the CAAA mandate measures to limit automobile trips in the most severely polluted areas and require strict monitoring of VMT growth in less severe nonattainment areas.

Deadlines for reaching attainment vary with the severity of air quality problems.[7] Areas classified as marginal (40 for ozone) have 3 years from the baseline year, 1990, to attain NAAQS; areas classified as moderate (29 areas for ozone, 37 for carbon monoxide) have 6 years. The 12 areas classified as serious for ozone (and 1 for carbon monoxide) have 9 years, whereas the areas classified as severe (9 for ozone) have 15 to 17 years. Los Angeles, the only area classified as extreme (for ozone), has 20 years. Eighty-three areas have been designated as nonattainment for PM-10. Los Angeles is also the only area that does not meet the NO_2 standard.

Levels of effort also vary with the severity of air quality problems. Areas with ozone classifications of moderate or worse must submit revisions to State Implementation Plans (SIPs) (plans that codify a state's CAAA compliance actions) showing that within 6 years the pollutants that create ozone will be reduced by at least 15 percent from 1990 baseline emissions net of any growth in emissions during that period. These areas must achieve an additional 3 percent per year reduction in emissions until attainment is achieved. In addition to the latter requirements, areas classified as severe or extreme must adopt transportation control measures (TCMs) aimed at decreasing automobile travel.[8]

Areas with carbon monoxide designations only, of moderate or worse, must comply with somewhat different requirements. They must forecast VMT annually beginning in 1992, and if actual VMT exceeds forecast, they must be ready to adopt contingency TCMs that must be included in SIPs. TCMs are required for carbon monoxide areas designated as serious.

Finally, the CAAA provide strict sanctions for noncompliance. For example, approval of federally assisted highway projects can be withheld for failure to submit a SIP, EPA disapproval of a SIP, failure to make a required submission, or failure to implement any SIP requirement.[9] Once such sanctions have been imposed—and they must be imposed if EPA determines that the deficiency has not been corrected 18 months after being identified—DOT can only approve highway safety projects or projects that would not increase single-vehicle automobile travel.[10]

Conformity Requirements

The requirements and timetables for meeting CAAA goals and sanctions for noncompliance are stringent, but not unlike mandates of earlier clean air legislation (e.g., in 1970 and 1977). To help ensure attainment of legislative mandates, regulations implementing the 1990 CAAA strengthen existing conformity requirements. Conformity is a determination made by MPOs and DOT that transportation plans, programs, and projects in nonattainment areas are in accord with the compliance standards contained in SIPs (FHWA 1992b, 12). The new conformity rules under the CAAA hold MPOs and DOT directly accountable for demonstrating that transportation activities will not cause or contribute to any new violation of air quality standards, increase the frequency or severity of existing violations, or delay timely attainment of standards (*Federal Register* 1993b, 62,188).

EPA regulations provide a grace period for states to revise their SIPs; revised plans were due November 1994. However, stringent interim conformity guidelines are in effect until EPA has approved these plans to ensure that nonattainment areas do not fall behind in meeting target deadlines for achieving air quality standards. The salient feature of the interim conformity process is project-level review. Specifically, MPOs in nonattainment and maintenance areas must show that (*a*) all federally funded and "regionally significant projects," including nonfederal projects,[11] in regional transportation improvement programs (TIPs) and plans will not lead to emissions higher than in a 1990 baseline year; and (*b*) by building these projects, emissions will be lower than if the projects are not built. Once SIPs are approved by EPA,[12] the conformity test becomes less demanding: MPOs must demonstrate through a regional analysis that the emissions produced by implementation of transportation plans and TIPs will not exceed target levels (known as emission

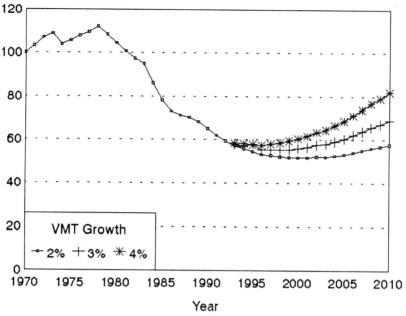

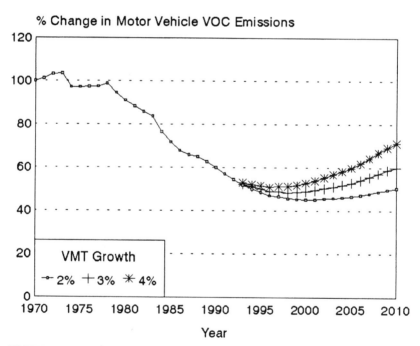

FIGURE 1-2 Relationship between travel growth and motor vehicle emissions (data from EPA Motor Vehicle Emission Laboratory, 1994).

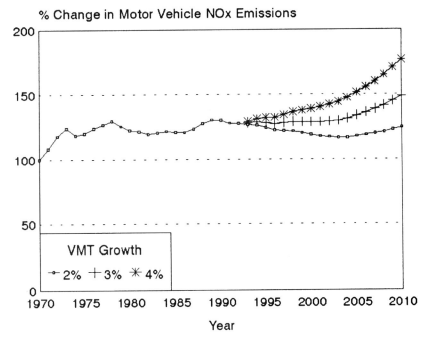

% Change in Motor Vehicle NOx Emissions

VMT Growth

-•- 2% + 3% * 4%

Year

Figure 1-2 (*continued*)

budgets)[13] for motor vehicle emission sources from nonattainment and maintenance areas contained in the SIPs.

The conformity regulations thus provide the teeth to help guarantee compliance with air quality mandates. MPOs must reconcile emission estimates from transportation plans and TIPs with those contained in the motor vehicle emission budgets in SIPs, conduct periodic testing to determine whether actual emissions are in line with estimates, and take remedial action if they are not. Court challenges have already been issued by environmental groups against several state transportation departments to ensure that conformity requirements and attainment deadlines are met.[14]

ISTEA

ISTEA complements the CAAA by reinforcing air quality conformity requirements. The act allows local areas flexibility to shift highway funds to transit and other cleaner modes, enhances the planning responsibilities of MPOs that are responsible for conformity analyses, and creates a new Congestion Mitigation and Air Quality Improvement Program to direct funds to projects and programs in nonattainment areas that will contribute directly to attainment of the NAAQS (FHWA 1992c, 16–17). Metropolitan transportation planning regulations, in particular, were revised in part to ensure greater consistency and coordination between development of transportation and air quality plans (*Federal Register* 1993c).[15]

Energy Regulation

Legislation similar to the CAAA has not been passed recently in the energy area. In response to the oil embargo imposed by the Organization of Petroleum Exporting Countries (OPEC) in 1973 and because the automotive sector is a major consumer of petroleum, Congress passed the Energy Policy and Conservation Act of 1975, which set fuel economy standards requiring that automotive manufacturers increase the corporate average fuel economy (CAFE) of automobiles and light trucks sold in the United States to 11.7 kpl (27.5 mpg) in the 1985 model year and thereafter (NRC 1992, 12).

Between 1970 and 1992, in-use fuel economy for passenger cars rose from an average of 5.7 kpl (13.5 mpg) to 9.2 kpl (21.6 mpg), a 60 percent improvement (Davis 1994, 3–24). The introduction of CAFE standards, technology improvements such as electronic fuel injection and more efficient engines and transmissions, and the reduced weight of passenger vehicles were largely responsible.

Although the standards have been achieved,[16] during the past decade the low price of gasoline, growing motor vehicle ownership, and increased motor vehicle travel have resulted in a steady increase of transportation's share of total petroleum consumption in the United States to 65 percent in 1992 (Davis 1994, 2–7). Also, other sectors have substituted alternative energy sources. Since 1989, U.S. energy dependence on foreign oil sources has reached levels only exceeded in 1979; oil imports accounted for 46 percent of U.S. petroleum consumption in 1992 (Davis 1994, 2–5). Thus, energy officials are seeking ways to improve fuel efficiency and reduce vehicle travel to cut back energy consumption.

STUDY FOCUS

The conformity requirements of the CAAA and, to a lesser extent, concern for energy use will place transportation projects—particularly highway projects in the nation's most polluted areas—under great scrutiny regarding their potential for stimulating automobile travel, raising emission levels, and further increasing dependence on fossil fuels. Local planning agencies, who are responsible for programming highway projects in urban areas and certifying their positive or neutral effects on air quality, are expected to have the analytic and modeling capabilities to forecast project impacts. Such requirements provide the impetus and the focus for this study. The committee did not limit its examination of the effects of highway capacity additions to a specific time frame. However, particular attention was paid to the 20-year time frame established by the CAAA for attainment of air quality standards, because this represents the planning and forecasting horizon within which local planning agencies must make decisions about the air quality effects of highway projects.

The size of the investment in capacity enhancements also warrants close examination of potential impacts. Although construction of new highways has tapered off in recent years, the combination of new construction with capacity additions to existing highways continues to represent a large fraction of the public investment in transportation infrastructure by state and local governments. For example, according to the most recent estimates, capacity improvements to roads and bridges totaled $15.4 billion,[17] accounting for nearly two-fifths (38 percent) of total public capital outlays for highways, bridges, and transit combined (U.S. Congress. House. Committee on Public Works and Transportation. 1993, 4, 76).

Alternative ways of meeting urban transportation needs are not examined in this study, nor are the costs and benefits of alternative approaches to improving air quality and reducing energy use in a metropolitan region analyzed. Instead the study is focused on examining the scientific basis for estimating the impacts of highway capacity enhancement projects, both favorable and unfavorable, on emissions, air quality, and energy consumption.

DEFINITION OF TERMS

Highway capacity projects are defined broadly in this study (see accompanying text box). Additions to highway capacity are often associated with major construction projects, such as building a new highway where none existed before, bypassing an existing route, or adding one or more lanes to an existing highway. Nonetheless, smaller-scale projects, such as traffic signal timing improvements or removal of on-street parking, should also improve traffic flows and thus are included here. Less traditional measures that add capacity but attempt to restrict or manage travel as part of the facility improvement, such as high-occupancy-vehicle (HOV) and express bus lanes or variable tolls by time of day (congestion pricing), are also covered in the definition of highway capacity projects. Finally, many of the new technologies that fall under the category of intelligent transportation systems should also be characterized as capacity enhancement measures because their primary objective is to improve the efficiency of traffic flows on existing facilities.

Highway engineers define capacity of a facility as the maximum hourly rate at which persons or vehicles can reasonably traverse a segment of roadway during a given time under prevailing roadway, traffic, and control conditions (TRB 1992, I-3).[18] The concept of capacity thus involves throughput of people and goods as well as the more traditional notion of vehicle throughput. Both measures are considered in this study, although lack of data on the former (e.g., vehicle occupancies) hampers analysis of emission and energy impacts on a person- or goods-throughput basis. Both freight movement on commercial vehicles and passenger transport are of interest because both types of traffic will be affected by capacity enhancements, although their emissions, energy use, and travel pattern changes will differ. Separate papers to review the likely effects of highway capacity additions on heavy-duty diesel vehicles, particularly heavy-duty trucks, were commissioned for this study.

A concept closely related to capacity is level of service. Although capacity refers to a facility's maximum carrying capacity, highways are rarely designed or planned to operate in this range. Instead, traffic engineers are concerned with estimating the maximum traffic that can be accommodated while maintaining certain operating conditions (TRB 1992, I-3). These conditions, or levels of service, are defined as

ILLUSTRATIVE MEASURES TO ADD HIGHWAY CAPACITY AND IMPROVE TRAFFIC FLOW

New Highways
—New freeways or expressways
—New toll roads
—New arterial streets
—New local streets
—Bypass of an existing route

Reconstruction and Major Widening of Existing Highways
—New lanes on existing freeways
—New lanes on existing arterials
—High-occupancy-vehicle (HOV) or express bus lanes added to freeways or arterials
—New lanes on existing freeways or arterials with variable tolls by time of day (congestion pricing)
—Minor lane additions or widening on arterials
—Addition of auxiliary lanes on freeways or expressways
—Improvement of freeway ramp geometry
—Intersection reconstruction
—Grade separation of major crossings

Other Measures To Improve Traffic Flow
—Advanced vehicle control systems (AVCS)[a]
—Advanced traveler information systems (ATIS)[b]
—Freeway access control measures, such as ramp metering and incident detection
—Synchronization of traffic signals
—Removal of on-street parking
—Addition of exclusive turn lanes

---

[a] One of the Intelligent Transportation System (ITS) technologies that would involve "smart cars," automatic headway and lateral controls, and automatic steering controls to allow vehicle platooning of electronically coupled trains of vehicles on freeways equipped with electronic control instrumentation (TRB 1991, 23).
[b] This ITS technology would provide the traveler with information on location, traffic conditions, route guidance, and parking location (TRB 1991, 22).

ranges in traffic density and are related to qualitative measures, including speed and travel time, freedom to maneuver, traffic interruptions, motorist comfort and convenience, and safety (TRB 1992, I-3). Six levels of service are defined for each type of facility for which analysis procedures are available (see text box). They have letter designations from A to F, with Level-of-Service A representing the best operating conditions and Level-of-Service F the worst (TRB 1992, I-3–I-4). Many capacity enhancements are directed toward improving traffic flow and level of service on a particular facility, and safety is also a consideration in some capacity projects (e.g., left-turn lanes).

The study is focused on additions to highway capacity in metropolitan areas, because the nation's air quality problems are primarily concentrated in its large urban centers. However, the effects of projects may extend beyond current borders. Over time, capacity additions at the urban fringe, which expand development opportunities, may change and expand the geographic boundaries of areas that do not meet air quality standards. Moreover, the decision to add or restrict highway capacity in metropolitan areas could have impacts beyond regional boundaries, affecting the competitive position of one metropolitan area relative to another or of large metropolitan areas generally relative to smaller areas, although systematic evidence of these effects may be difficult to document. For example, businesses could move from congested urban areas that are unable to provide new highway capacity to communities that can; if large metropolitan areas generally cannot provide the additional capacity, growth could be encouraged in medium-size and small cities.

OVERVIEW OF IMPACTS

Estimating the effects of highway capacity additions in metropolitan areas on air quality and energy use involves analyzing a lengthy chain of factors (Figure 1-3). In general, the need or demand for travel arises from the distribution of residences and businesses in a region and their activity requirements. Residential and business location in a region are, in turn, determined by historical development patterns, availability of land, and zoning and land use policies. The amount and frequency of travel are affected by regional economic conditions, area

---

LEVELS OF SERVICE

Level-of-Service A—free flow. Drivers have freedom to select desired speeds, and ability to maneuver within the traffic stream is extremely high.

Level-of-Service B—in the range of stable flow, but the presence of other drivers in the traffic stream begins to be noticeable.

Level-of-Service C—in the range of stable flow, but the operation of individual drivers becomes significantly affected by interactions with others in the traffic stream; the general level of comfort and convenience declines noticeably at this level.

Level-of-Service D—high-density, but stable, flow. Speed and freedom to maneuver are severely restricted.

Level-of-Service E—operating conditions at or near the capacity level. All speeds are reduced to a low, but relatively uniform, value. Freedom to maneuver within the traffic stream is extremely limited. Operations are unstable, because small increases in flow or minor perturbations within the traffic stream will cause breakdowns.

Level-of-Service F—forced or breakdown flow. The amount of traffic approaching a point exceeds the amount that can traverse the point and queues form behind such locations. Operations are characterized by stop-and-go waves and are extremely unstable.

---

demographic and income characteristics, and the cost and availability of local transportation services.

Regional travel is distributed as vehicle and passenger flows on the supply of transportation facilities—the transportation network—which may include more than one mode (e.g., transit and highways) and more than one form of transport (e.g., automobiles, trucks, bicycles, and walking). Motor vehicles operating on specific links of the network emit pollutants and use energy in varying amounts depending on the type of vehicle, its speed and operating condition (i.e., whether it is warmed up), and the length of the trip. In addition, other factors, such as local topography, meteorological conditions, and other

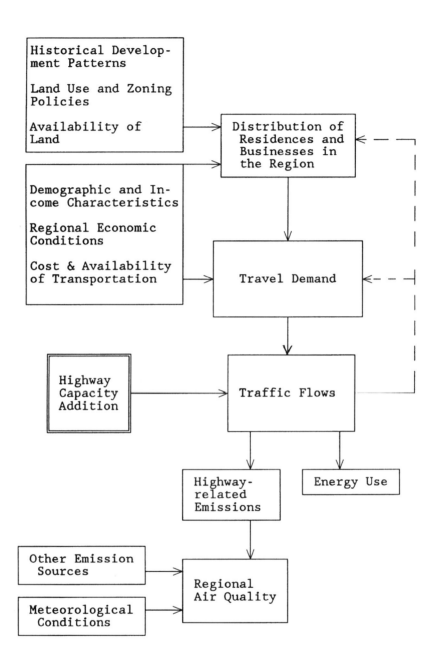

FIGURE 1-3 Overview of initial and longer-term impacts of highway capacity additions and their effects on emissions, air quality, and energy use.

sources of emissions, interact with vehicle emissions to affect regional air quality.

The primary objective of this study is to examine how an increase in the supply of highway facilities affects each of these factors (Figure 1-3). Initial impacts involve a change in traffic flows on the affected links (e.g., changes in the distribution of vehicle speeds, changes in speed variation, and shifts in traffic volumes) and the resulting change in emissions and energy use from the vehicles on those links. Over time the effects could involve a change in the amount of travel and in land use patterns, with corresponding effects on emissions and energy use, as households and businesses react to the network addition. The incremental effects of all these changes on emissions, air quality, and energy use must be estimated to determine the full effects of the capacity increase.

There is both a spatial and a temporal dimension to these analyses. A change in supply may involve adding capacity and improving traffic flow at only one location on the highway system. However, the network character of the system is likely to affect travel patterns at other locations. Traffic may be diverted from alternate routes, or travelers may shift their time of travel to preferred travel times to take advantage of the new capacity or change their mode of travel if they are encouraged to reduce automobile trips by using transit or bicycle or by walking. If the addition to capacity is sufficiently large, it can induce new or longer trips, influence automobile purchasing decisions, and cause residents or businesses to change their location to take advantage of the improved access. Similarly, emissions from these changes are not confined to the location of the project, but depending on local atmospheric conditions (e.g., heat and wind patterns) may have broader effects on the air quality of the region and beyond. Individual highway projects may not have measurable effects on regional air quality, but the cumulative impacts of many projects could. Thus, whereas a highway capacity enhancement project may be localized, its effects are unlikely to be.

Project impacts will change over time. If a highway capacity addition stimulates travel demand or encourages dispersed development patterns, these outcomes will erode initial gains from some capacity projects. However, some of these impacts, such as decisions about changes in the location of residences and businesses and the traffic generated by these changes, are likely to take place over a period of years or even decades. Assessing the net effects of highway capacity projects on emissions and energy use depends on the length of time over which impacts are analyzed and how the flow of future effects is valued (i.e., discounted back to the present). Examination of project effects at a single point in time is misleading.

The size and direction of the effects and the certainty of the predictions depend on several factors. The context in which the capacity enhancement is made is critical: whether existing highways are heavily congested and travel demand is constrained; whether the area is heavily developed and thus the potential for growth is limited; or, conversely, whether the area is relatively undeveloped but conditions for growth are present and thus the rate of growth in development and related traffic is likely to be accelerated. Each of these conditions will result in different project outcomes for travel behavior, land use, and urban form.

The scale of effects also depends on the unit of analysis. Highway capacity additions may have significant effects on travel patterns and development activity in a particular corridor or subregional area. However, the effects may be small at the regional level, at least in the 20-year planning horizon required for metropolitan transportation planning and conformity purposes.[19] Highway capacity additions represent small increments to large existing metropolitan transportation networks and to land use patterns that have evolved over many years.

The type of project also matters. For example, minor capacity improvements on arterials—such as signalization improvements and exclusive turn lanes—may smooth traffic flows, initially reducing emissions and energy use, without major offsetting increases in motor vehicle traffic.[20] However, the size of the benefits will be commensurate with traffic levels on these local routes and may have little measurable impact on regional air quality. A series of relatively minor traffic flow improvements can have a cumulatively larger impact on motor vehicle traffic growth. Major capacity enhancement projects, such as a new freeway or a major new bypass, are likely to have more significant initial effects on emissions and energy use (although effects can be negative as well as positive). They may have adverse effects in the longer term because of increased motor vehicle travel stimulated by the project.

The effects of not adding highway capacity also must be considered in any assessment of net effects on highway emissions and energy use. Is there sufficient capacity in the existing highway network for travelers to change routes and times of travel without significantly adding to highway congestion levels and thereby increasing emissions and energy use? Can other investments in transit facilities or bikeways provide alternative modes of transport with sufficient incentive for travelers to switch from automobile travel to keep highway congestion from growing? If highway congestion increases, will residents and businesses respond by moving to less congested suburban or exurban areas or to smaller, less congested metropolitan areas? Or will congestion simply become worse, making the capacity addition more valuable in the future relative to the no-build option?

Finally, the level of certainty of the predictions will vary. Forecasts of emissions resulting from the initial adjustments in traffic flows and travel patterns because of a highway capacity project should be relatively straightforward, although technical issues involved in modeling vehicle emissions and systems issues (i.e., route shifts and changes in time of travel) must be addressed. Forecasting longer-term effects such as shifts in travel demand and land use changes from capacity additions is more complex and requires predicting behavioral responses that are not fully understood. The longer the time horizon for estimating impacts, the more other, often unpredictable, factors such as changes in demographic or economic conditions are likely to intervene, reducing the ability to forecast accurately.

ASSESSMENT OF IMPACTS

The difficulty of reaching consensus on the direction and size of effects was demonstrated in a recent court case filed in 1989 by the Sierra Club Legal Defense Fund and Citizens for a Better Environment against the Metropolitan Transportation Commission (MTC), the MPO for the San Francisco Bay Area (U.S. District Court 1990a).[21] Environmental groups sued MTC for noncompliance with the obligations contained in the Bay Area's 1982 SIP to meet federal air quality standards by 1987.

A major issue of the court case concerned the extent to which large highway capacity expansions would adversely affect regional air quality and MTC's capacity to model and analyze these impacts. Court testimony by experts provides a good summary of the key arguments put forward by local planners and modelers, environmental groups, theoreticians, and practitioners concerning the effect on air quality of increased highway capacity.

Environmental groups argued that adding highway capacity in a congested system would increase vehicle use by making automobile travel easier and more convenient, thereby offsetting at least some of the initial reduction in emissions from smoothing traffic flows.[22] Specifically, drivers respond to improved levels of highway service by concentrating work trips more in traditional peak periods; shifting from transit and higher vehicle occupancies to automobile and lower, or single, vehicle occupancies; taking more individual trips rather than combining trips (trip chaining); and taking longer trips or trips that might otherwise have been forgone, ultimately producing levels of congestion comparable with previous conditions but at higher traffic volumes.

In the long run, the argument continued, adding highway capacity in a congested system would encourage further decentralization of households and jobs and longer commuting by making travel to out-lying areas easier and faster. Because most major highway capacity investments are being made in suburban areas, these projects would change the distribution of development within the region; low-density, automobile-dependent development at the suburban fringe would be encouraged over redevelopment of core areas that could better sup-port public transit and nonmotorized travel modes. Moreover, if high-way transportation investment stimulates economic growth, as proj-ect proponents frequently claim, then capacity enhancements should increase overall levels of regional growth, drawing new jobs and households to the area and making it even more difficult for the region to meet environmental standards.

Those who supported the MTC argued that capacity additions under most conditions would result in emission reductions and greater fuel efficiencies from freer-flowing traffic.[23] They conceded that adding highway capacity could increase the number and length of trips and that in the long run this could increase levels of automobile ownership and affect the location of population and housing in the region. However, given the scale of most highway projects in the built environment of major metropolitan areas, they argued that adding new highway capacity should not induce new travel at levels that would overwhelm initial emissions and energy benefits. Moreover, they said, there is no empirical support for the proposition that highway capacity additions in regions that are already substantially developed make a measurable difference in overall levels of population or employment growth. Transportation is not the primary determinant of regional development; business and residential location decisions are based on a host of factors (e.g., national and regional economic conditions, local labor force skills, tax levels, and public services) of which transportation is one, but not the major, factor. Thus, providing new capacity would simply accommodate more efficiently the inevitable new development.

After 3 years of litigation, the court found that MTC's adoption of additional TCMs met the "reasonable further progress" requirement toward emission reductions outlined in the Bay Area's 1982 SIP (U.S. District Court 1992). In addition, the court ruled in favor of MTC's proposed modified computer modeling techniques for conformity assessment and lifted a temporary ban on several highway expansion projects (U.S. District Court 1991c). The judge did not require MTC to determine whether the new highway capacity would contribute to regional growth and increase total pollution levels, arguing that EPA has not yet made this a requirement and that the capability to model this relationship does not currently exist (U.S. District Court 1991c).

ORGANIZATION OF REPORT

These issues are explored more systematically in the following chapters. Background information on the effects of motor vehicle transportation on air quality and energy consumption is given in Chapter 2, and the main analytic tools used to model these effects are introduced. The impacts, both initial and long term, of additions to highway capacity on traffic flows, travel demand, and land use and urban form are examined in Chapters 3 through 5, respectively. In each area, what is known from theory, empirical studies, and statistical models is summarized; an assessment of the validity and certainty of the evidence is provided; and recommendations are made for improving the state of knowledge. In Chapter 6, major findings about the relationships between highway capacity additions, emissions, air quality, and energy consumption are summarized, highlighting what is known, what is knowable, and what is not, and conclusions are drawn about the current focus and requirements of the CAAA.

NOTES

1. Catalytic converters, which control for CO, VOC, and NO$_x$ emissions, were introduced in 1978, and carbon canisters, which control hydrocarbon, or VOC, emissions from the fuel system that occur while the car is in operation or while parked by adsorbing the vapors, have been in use since 1975 (NRC 1992, 70).
2. VOCs are also referred to as nonmethane hydrocarbons (NMHC) and as reactive organic gases (ROGs) or total organic gases (TOGs), the terms used in California.
3. Comparative data on emissions from all other sources cannot be provided because the methodologies used to estimate emissions from all sources except highway vehicles changed after 1985. The differences in methodologies result in as much as a 20 percent difference in EPA estimates of CO emission levels in 1985 (Nizich et al. 1994b, 3, 6). Highway vehicle emissions, however, were estimated using a consistent methodology for 1970 through 1993.
4. This population estimate is based on a single year of data and only considers counties with monitoring data for that pollutant (Curran et al. 1994, 14). The data can vary substantially from year to year primarily because of changes in meteorological conditions.
5. VMT has grown at annual rates of 3.5 percent over the past decade (U.S. Congress. House. Committee on Public Works and Transportation. 1993, 37). There is some evidence, however, that future increases in VMT levels may not be as great as in the past because of saturation in vehicle ownership, aging of the driving population, and the like (U.S. Congress. House. Committee on Public Works and Transportation. 1989, 87–91).
6. EPA estimates assume a small increase in the share of diesel vehicles, particularly heavy-duty diesel vehicles, relative to gasoline-powered light-duty vehicles over the 20-year period (personal communication, Natalie Dobie, Technical Support Branch, EPA, Nov. 21, 1994).
7. The following two paragraphs draw heavily from background material on the impact of highway congestion on air quality prepared by Elizabeth Deakin for TRB in March 1991 (Deakin 1991). Data on nonattainment areas were updated using EPA's 1993 *National Air Quality Emissions Trends Report* (Curran et al. 1994).
8. TCMs are activities intended to decrease automotive travel or otherwise reduce vehicle emissions. TCMs are most closely associated with actions

to improve transit, support ridesharing, and encourage employer-based trip reduction programs (FHWA 1992a, 3–4).

9. In a Notice of Proposed Rulemaking (*Federal Register* 1993a), EPA proposed an automatic sanctioning procedure. An EPA finding of noncompliance by a state regarding its SIP would trigger an 18-month clock for the imposition of a two-for-one mandate for industrial emissions, requiring an offset of twice the increased emission from a new or modified point source. If the SIP remains deficient after another 6 months, EPA would then cut off federal highway funds.

10. Such projects include transit, HOV lanes, employee trip reduction programs, emission-reducing traffic flow improvements, fringe parking, pricing programs to restrict vehicle use, and accident management programs.

11. Regionally significant projects include any facility with an arterial or higher functional classification and any other facility that serves regional travel needs and that would normally be included in the modeling for the transportation network (*Federal Register* 1993b, 62,211). Projects that are not regionally significant must also be included in regional emissions analyses, but the effects of these projects, which cannot normally be modeled with a transportation network demand model, may be estimated in accordance with reasonable professional practice (*Federal Register* 1993b, 62,211). Finally, nonfederal regionally significant projects must have been included in a conforming plan or TIP, or included in the original regional emissions analysis supporting the adoption of the plan or TIP, or a new regional emissions analysis must demonstrate that the plan and TIP would still conform if the projects were included and implemented (*Federal Register* 1993b, 62,204).

12. During the period after SIPs have been submitted but have not been approved by EPA, MPOs must demonstrate that TIPs pass the build–no-build test and also that the build scenario does not exceed the emissions budget for motor vehicle emissions contained in the submitted SIP (*Federal Register* 1993b, 62,191).

13. Motor vehicle emission budgets are the motor vehicle-related portions of the projected emission inventory used to demonstrate reasonable further progress milestones, attainment, or maintenance for a particular year specified in a SIP. They establish a cap on emissions that cannot be exceeded by predicted highway and transit vehicle emissions (*Federal Register* 1993b, 62,194).

14. Six environmental groups filed notice of their intention to sue the transportation departments of New York, New Jersey, and Connecticut for approving transportation improvement programs that fail to meet the 1990 CAAA pollution reduction requirements (*AASHTO Journal* 1992, 3–4); suits have been filed against Connecticut and Rhode Island (*AASHTO Journal* 1993, 7–9). The Environmental Defense Fund and other groups

have already brought suit against EPA and DOT to force issuance of various regulations associated with the legislation.

15. For example, among other provisions, metropolitan transportation plans must cover a period of at least 20 years, contain all regionally significant projects, consider the likely effect of transportation policy decisions on land use and development, and, for nonattainment or maintenance areas, contain only conforming projects (*Federal Register* 1993c).

16. The sales-weighted fuel economies of automobiles and light trucks have, on average, met the fuel economy standards set by the federal government. This does not mean, however, that each manufacturer is meeting the standards each year. Some manufacturers still fall short, whereas others exceed the standards (Davis 1994, 3–51).

17. This does not include signalization and other traffic flow improvement projects, which are not broken out separately.

18. The time period used in most capacity analysis is 15 min, the shortest interval during which stable flow exists. Capacity is defined for prevailing roadway conditions (which refer to the geometric characteristics of the facility), traffic conditions (which refer to the characteristics of the traffic stream using the facility), and control conditions (which refer to the types and specific design of control devices and traffic regulations on a given facility); good pavement and weather conditions are assumed.

19. ISTEA requires the metropolitan transportation plan to address a period of at least 20 years (*Federal Register* 1993c, 62,210).

20. To the extent these projects degrade bicycle and pedestrian travel, they may induce some shifts to cars, thus increasing emissions.

21. The lawsuit was filed in the Federal District Court of Northern California. The citation for the consolidated cases is Citizens for a Better Environment et al. v. Peter B. Wilson et al., Civil No. C-89-2044-TEH, and Sierra Club vs. Metropolitan Transportation Commission et al., Civil No. C-89-2064-TEH.

22. The arguments of those who view highway capacity improvements as having a negative effect on air quality are drawn from three sources: (*a*) background material prepared for TRB by Elizabeth Deakin (Deakin 1991), (*b*) testimony by Dr. Peter Stopher, Professor of Civil Engineering, Louisiana State University, and Director of the Louisiana Transportation Research Center, in the MTC case (U.S. District Court 1990b), and (*c*) a paper by Greig Harvey and Elizabeth Deakin (Harvey and Deakin 1991) on regional transportation modeling practice.

23. The arguments of those who view highway capacity improvements as having a positive or neutral effect on air quality are drawn from the background material provided by Deakin (1991), from the Harvey and Deakin 1991 paper, and from the testimony by Elizabeth Deakin, Assistant Professor of City and Regional Planning and member of the research staff of

the Institute of Transportation Studies at the University of California, Berkeley (U.S. District Court 1991a), and Dr. Raymond Brady, Research Director for the Association of Bay Area Governments (U.S. District Court 1991b) in the MTC case.

REFERENCES

ABBREVIATIONS

EPA	Environmental Protection Agency
FHWA	Federal Highway Administration
NRC	National Research Council
TRB	Transportation Research Board

AASHTO Journal. 1992. States May Face Clean Air, ISTEA Suit. Sept. 25, pp.3–6.

AASHTO Journal. 1993. Connecticut, Rhode Island Hit with Environmental Suits. March 26, pp. 7–9.

Curran, T., T. Fitz-Simons, W. Freas, J. Hemby, D. Mintz, S. Nizich, B. Parzygnat, and M. Wayland. 1994. *National Air Quality and Emissions Trends Report, 1993.* 454-R-94-026. U.S. Environmental Protection Agency. Research Triangle Park, N.C., Oct.

Davis, S.C. 1994. *Transportation Energy Data Book: Edition 14.* ORNL-6798. Center for Transportation Analysis, Energy Division, Oak Ridge National Laboratory, Tenn., May.

Deakin, E. 1991. *Scoping Study: Impact of Highway Congestion on Air Quality.* University of California at Berkeley, March, 22 pp.

Federal Register. 1993a. Application Sequence for Clean Air Act Section 179 Sanctions. Vol. 58, No. 189, Oct. 1, pp. 51,270–51,279.

Federal Register. 1993b. Criteria and Procedures for Determining Conformity to State or Federal Implementation Plans of Transportation Plans, Programs, and Projects Funded or Approved Under Title 23 U.S.C. or the Federal Transit Act. Vol. 58, No. 225, Nov. 24, pp. 62,188–62,253.

Federal Register. Part II. 1993c. Statewide Planning. Metropolitan Planning. Vol. 58, No. 207, Oct. 28, pp. 58,040–58,179.

FHWA. 1992a. *Transportation and Air Quality: Searching for Solutions: A Policy Discussion Series.* No. 5, FHWA-PL-92-029. U.S. Department of Transportation, Aug., 30 pp.

FHWA. 1992b. *A Summary: Transportation Programs and Provisions of the Clean Air Act Amendments of 1990.* FHWA-PD-92-023. U.S. Department of Transportation, Oct.

FHWA. 1992c. *A Summary: Air Quality Programs and Provisions of the Intermodal Surface Transportation Efficiency Act of 1991.* FHWA-PD-92-022. U.S. Department of Transportation, Aug.

Harvey, G., and E. Deakin. 1991. *Toward Improved Regional Transportation Modeling Practice.* Deakin Harvey Skabardonis, Inc., Berkeley, Calif., Dec., 68 pp.

Nizich, S.V., T.C. McMullen, and D.C. Misenheimer. 1994a. *National Air Pollutant Emission Trends, 1900–1993.* EPA-454/R-94-027. Office of Air Quality Planning and Standards, Research Triangle Park, N.C., Oct., 314 pp.

Nizich, S.V., W.R. Barnard, and D.Y. Linderman. 1994b. *Preparation of a National Emission Data Base for Trends and Other Analyses.* EPA and E.H. Pechan & Associates, Inc. Presented at the Emission Inventory Specialty Conference, Air and Waste Management Association, Nov. 1–3, Raleigh, N.C., 12 pp.

NRC. 1992. *Automotive Fuel Economy: How Far Should We Go?* National Academy Press, Washington, D.C., 259 pp.

TRB. 1991. *Special Report 232: Advanced Vehicle and Highway Technologies.* National Research Council, Washington, D.C., 90 pp.

TRB. 1992. *Special Report 209: Highway Capacity Manual* (2nd edition revised). National Research Council, Washington, D.C.

U.S. Congress. House. Committee on Public Works and Transportation. 1989. *The Status of the Nation's Highways and Bridges: Conditions and Performance and Highway Bridge Replacement and Rehabilitation Program 1989.* Committee Print 101-2. Government Printing Office, June.

U.S. Congress. House. Committee on Public Works and Transportation. 1993. *The Status of the Nation's Highways, Bridges, and Transit: Conditions and Performance.* Committee Print 103-2. Government Printing Office, March.

U.S. District Court for the District of Northern California. 1990a. *Memorandum of Points and Authorities in Support of Revised Conformity Assessment Procedures.* Civil No. C-89-2044-TEH and C-89-2064-TEH [consolidated], July 3, pp. 9–10.

U.S. District Court for the District of Northern California. 1990b. *Declaration of Dr. Peter R. Stopher in Support of Sierra Club's Objections to MTC's Proposed Conformity Assessment.* Civil No. C-89-2044-TEH and C-89-2064-TEH [consolidated], Aug. 20.

U.S. District Court for the District of Northern California. 1991a. *Declaration of Elizabeth Deakin in Support of MTC's Proposed Revised Conformity Assessment Procedure.* Civil No. C-89-2044-TEH and C-89-2064-TEH [consolidated], Feb. 25.

U.S. District Court for the District of Northern California. 1991b. *Declaration of Raymond J. Brady in Regard to Metropolitan Transportation Commission's Proposed Conformity Assessment Procedures*. Civil No. C-89-2044-TEH and C-89-2064-TEH [consolidated], Feb. 26.

U.S. District Court for the District of Northern California. 1991c. *Henderson Court Order Approving MTC Procedures*. Civil No. C89-2064-TEH (Consolidated Cases), March 11.

U.S. District Court for the District of Northern California. 1992. *Order*. Civil No. C89-2064 TEH (Consolidated Cases), May 11.

2

Contribution of Motor Vehicle Transportation to Air Pollution and Energy Consumption

Motor vehicles run on fossil fuels, emitting pollutants that are a major cause of poor air quality in metropolitan areas and consuming a large fraction of the nation's petroleum resources. In this chapter, the impacts of motor vehicle transportation on air quality and energy consumption are described and the models that are commonly used to analyze these impacts are introduced.

TRANSPORTATION AND AIR QUALITY

The four principal sources of polluting emissions from man-made sources are transportation (primarily highway vehicles), stationary fuel combustion (especially electrical utilities), industrial processes such as chemical refining, and solid waste disposal (Horowitz 1982, 21). Emissions that either directly cause or combine to form pollution (called primary and secondary pollutants, respectively) may also be classified as stationary, area, or mobile, depending on the magnitudes and geographical distributions of their emissions (DOT and EPA

1993, 2).[1] Pollutants from motor vehicle transport, the focus of this study, are commonly referred to as mobile source emissions.

To comply with the requirements of the 1970 Clean Air Act, the Environmental Protection Agency (EPA) developed national ambient air quality standards (NAAQS) that set allowable concentration and exposure limits for six pollutants considered harmful to public health. The NAAQS are expressed as average concentrations of pollutants over some period of time (see box).[2] EPA tracks both the emissions or flows of harmful materials from polluting activities, such as factories and transportation, on the basis of the best available engineering and modeling estimates, and the accumulation of these emissions in the air as concentrations of pollutants, which are directly measured at selected sites throughout the country (Curran et al. 1994, 20; Horowitz 1982, 3–4). Regulatory activities are directed toward attainment of NAAQS (i.e., concentration standards), because health effects are directly related to public exposure to pollutants at specific concentrations.

Transportation-Related Pollutants

According to current estimates, transportation sources account for about 45 percent of nationwide emissions of EPA's six criteria pollutants. The range is considerable for each pollutant source (Table 2-1) and there is a high degree of uncertainty with respect to many of the estimates. Ground-level ozone is the most pervasive of the transportation-related pollutants; in 1993 approximately 51 million persons lived in counties that exceeded the ozone standard. Nearly 12 million persons lived in counties that did not meet the carbon monoxide (CO) standard in the same year (Curran et al. 1994, 15).

Highway vehicles are the largest source of transportation-related emissions for nearly every type of pollutant (Table 2-1). In total, they contribute slightly more than one-third of nationwide emissions of the six criteria pollutants.

Formation of Motor Vehicle Emissions

The primary sources of motor vehicle emissions are exhaust emissions from chemical compounds that leave the engine through the tail pipe system and the crankcase and evaporative emissions from the fueling

National Ambient Air Quality Standards (NAAQS) in Effect in 1991 (Curran et al. 1994, 19)

| POLLUTANT | PRIMARY (HEALTH RELATED) | | SECONDARY (WELFARE RELATED) | |
	TYPE OF AVERAGE	STANDARD LEVEL CONCENTRATION[a]	TYPE OF AVERAGE	STANDARD LEVEL CONCENTRATION
CO	8-hr[b]	9 ppm (10 mg/m^3)	No secondary standard	
	1-hr[b]	35 ppm (40 mg/m^3)	No secondary standard	
Pb	Maximum quarterly average	1.5 μg/m^3	Same as primary standard	
NO$_2$	Annual arithmetic mean	0.053 ppm (100 μg/m^3)	Same as primary standard	
O$_3$	Maximum[c] daily 1-hr average	0.12 ppm (235 μg/m^3)	Same as primary standard	
PM-10	Annual arithmetic mean[d]	50 μg/m^3	Same as primary standard	
	24-hr[d]	150 μg/m^3	Same as primary standard	
SO$_2$	Annual arithmetic mean	80 μg/m^3 (0.03 ppm)	3-hr[b]	1300 μg/m^3 (0.50 ppm)
	24-hr[b]	365 μg/m^3 (0.14 ppm)		

NOTE: CO = carbon monoxide; Pb = lead; NO$_2$ = nitrogen dioxide; O$_3$ = ozone; PM-10 = particulate matter; SO$_2$ = sulfur dioxide; ppm = parts per million; μg/m^3 = micrograms per cubic meter; mg/m^3 = milligrams per cubic meter.
[a] Parenthetical value is an approximately equivalent concentration.
[b] Not to be exceeded more than once a year.
[c] The standard is attained when the expected number of days per calendar year with maximum hourly average concentrations above 0.12 ppm is equal to or less than 1, as determined according to Appendix H of the Ozone NAAQS.
[d] Particulate standards use PM-10 (particles less than 10μ in diameter) as the indicator pollutant. The annual standard is attained when the expected annual arithmetic mean concentration is less than or equal to 50 μg/m^3; the 24-hr standard is attained when the expected number of days per calendar year above 150 μg/m^3 is equal to or less than 1; as determined according to Appendix K of the PM NAAQS.

TABLE 2-1 Transportation Contribution to Emissions of Major Air Pollutants in the United States, 1992 (Millions of Short Tons) (Nizich et al. 1994, 3-11–3-16)

SOURCE CATEGORY	POLLUTANT						
	CO	NO_x	VOC	PM-10	Pb	SO_2	TOTAL
Transportation							
Total	75.3	10.4	8.3	0.6	1.6	0.7	96.9
Highway vehicle share	60.0	7.4	6.1	0.2	1.4	0.4	75.5
Fuel combustion	5.4	11.7	0.6	1.2	0.5	19.3	38.7
Industrial processes	5.2	0.9	3.1	0.6	2.3	1.9	14.0
Solid waste disposal	1.8	0.1	10.4	0.3	0.5	0	13.1
Miscellaneous	9.5	0.3	0.9	42.8	0	0	53.5
Total	97.2	23.4	23.3	45.5	4.9	21.9	216.2
Share of total (percent)							
All transportation	77	44	36	1	33	3	45
Highway vehicles	62	32	26	0.4	29	2	35

NOTE: CO = carbon monoxide; VOC = volatile organic compounds; NO_x = oxides of nitrogen; PM-10 = particulate matter; Pb = lead; SO_2 = sulfur dioxide.

system [mainly volatile organic compounds (VOCs)](NRC 1992, 69). For most motor vehicles (i.e., those powered by gasoline), exhaust emissions are formed in a two-stage process: emissions originate as a result of the combustion of fuel in the engine (engine-out emissions) and are then reduced by passing through a catalytic converter (tail pipe or exhaust emissions). For diesel-powered vehicles, the process of producing exhaust emissions is simpler, because there is presently no aftertreatment (i.e., catalytic converter).

Carbon monoxide and VOCs are the product of incomplete combustion of motor fuels and, in the case of VOCs, of fuel vapors emitted from the engine and fuel system (NRC 1991, 257). Oxides of nitrogen (NO_x) are formed differently; they are the product of high-temperature chemical processes that occur during the combustion process itself (NRC 1991, 261). Particulates, another compound mainly found in diesel exhaust, are formed primarily from incomplete combustion of diesel fuel and lubricating oil (Weaver and Klausmeier 1988, 2–7; Conte 1990, 58).

The air/fuel (A/F) ratio, which is controlled by the carburetor or fuel injection system, is the most important variable affecting the efficiency of catalytic converters and thus the level of exhaust emissions (Johnson 1988, 40). Because concentrations of key emissions are not at a minimum at the same A/F ratio (CO and VOCs are highest under fuel-rich conditions and NO_x is highest under fuel-lean conditions), manufacturers must optimize catalytic converter operation within a narrow A/F ratio range, known as stoichiometry, to achieve the greatest control efficiency for all three pollutants (Figure 2-1).

Major Pollutants by Type

Transportation is the dominant source of U.S. CO emissions, and highway vehicles contribute nearly two-thirds of the total (Table 2-1). Carbon monoxide is an odorless gas that forms from incomplete combustion of motor fuels. The higher the share of fuel in the air-fuel mixture, the more CO is produced (NRC 1992, 69). Fuel-rich operations occur under cold-start conditions, when the vehicle has been turned off for some time and the catalytic converter is cold, or under heavy engine loads (e.g., during rapid accelerations, on steep grades, or at high speeds). CO concentrations tend to be high on and near con-

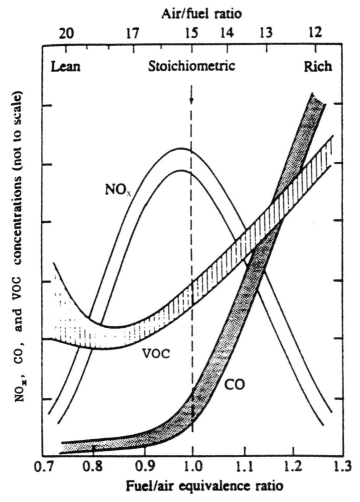

FIGURE 2-1 Variation of CO, VOC, and NO$_x$ concentration in the exhaust of a conventional spark-ignition engine with fuel/air equivalence ratio. Adapted from J. B. Heywood, *Internal Combustion Engine Fundamentals*, McGraw-Hill, 1988, p. 571. Reproduced with permission of McGraw-Hill, Inc.

gested roadways and at other locations where traffic densities are high. These concentrations are often referred to as CO hot spots. However, CO can also be viewed as a regional problem, with frequent reported exceedances of the 8-hr average concentration standards. Finally, CO contributes indirectly to greenhouse gas emissions (Gordon 1991, 60).[3]

Motor vehicles are also a major contributor to smog, the haze that hangs over many large urban areas, which has harmful health effects, contributes to the greenhouse problem, and adversely affects crops and vegetation (MacKenzie and Walsh 1990, 7). Ground-level ozone, an important constituent of smog, is not emitted directly into the atmosphere. Rather it is formed as a secondary pollutant through a chemical reaction between the ozone precursors, VOCs and NO_x, which is stimulated by heat and sunlight (Gordon 1991, 62). Highway vehicles account for about one-quarter of total VOC emissions and about one-third of total NO_x emissions (Table 2-1). EPA's estimates of VOC emissions, in particular, have been challenged in a National Research Council report as understating actual emission levels by a factor of 2 to 4 (NRC 1991, 7).[4]

Because it is a chemically reactive pollutant, ozone behaves quite differently from CO. The relation between ozone concentrations and VOC and NO_x emissions is both nonlinear and synergistic; thus, changes in VOC and NO_x emissions can have impacts on ozone that are difficult to predict. For example, ozone concentrations often are lower near large sources of motor vehicle emissions, because exhaust emissions of nitrogen oxide (NO) break down the ozone molecule.[5] This is referred to as ozone scavenging. Also, spatial variations in ozone concentrations tend to be much more gradual than in CO concentrations (Horowitz 1982, 63).

The role of NO_x in urban ozone pollution has received attention recently from the scientific and regulatory communities. NO_x emissions from motor vehicles consist of a mixture of NO and nitrogen dioxide (NO_2) (NO being the dominant constituent), which is formed by high-temperature chemical processes during the combustion of fossil fuels (Horowitz 1982, 17; NRC 1991, 261). High concentrations of NO_2, which are responsible for the yellowish-brown color of the sky in many smoggy areas, are caused primarily by the oxidation of NO from engine exhaust and other sources to NO_2 through the chemical processes that produce ozone (Horowitz 1982, 77). The NRC report (1991) argued that it is the balance between ambient levels of VOCs and NO_x that determines ozone levels in a particular area, and that efforts to reduce NO_x may be the most effective ozone abatement strategy in many of the nation's most polluted urban areas (NRC 1991, 7).[6] In its final conformity regulations following the Clean Air Act Amendments of 1990 (CAAA), EPA requires that transportation improvement programs proposed by metropolitan planning organizations (MPOs) show reductions in NO_x as well as VOCs from a 1990 baseline scenario (*Federal Register* 1993, 62,226).[7]

Particulates from diesel-fueled vehicles, primarily trucks and buses, contribute to pollution from inhalable particulate matter (PM-10).[8] Overall, tail pipe emissions of highway vehicles account for less than 1 percent of total PM-10 emissions (Table 2-1). The major source of particulates is road dust, which is a function of vehicle traffic, wildfires, and agricultural activity (Curran et al. 1994, 53). Particulate emissions are raising renewed concern because of medical evidence of their contribution to lung cancer (Dockery et al. 1993, 1753).

Transportation no longer accounts for a large share of pollution from lead; use of unleaded gasoline has resulted in a 99 percent reduction in total lead emission levels from highway vehicles since 1970 (Nizich et al. 1994, 3-16).

Finally, transportation is not a major contributor to sulfur dioxide (SO_2) (Table 2-1). Although heavy trucks and buses emit oxides of sulfur because of the high sulfur content of diesel fuel, coal-fired electric utilities are the dominant source of SO_2 emissions (Curran et al. 1994, 12).

Pollutants by Vehicle and Fuel Type

Emissions of specific pollutants vary by vehicle and fuel type. The primary emissions of gasoline-powered, passenger vehicles—the most common vehicle on the road—are CO, followed by much smaller emissions of VOCs and NO_x. Most heavy-duty diesel vehicles—combination trucks and buses—use diesel fuel.[9] Their primary emissions are NO_x, followed by smaller emissions of CO, PM-10, SO_2, and VOCs (Figure 2-2).

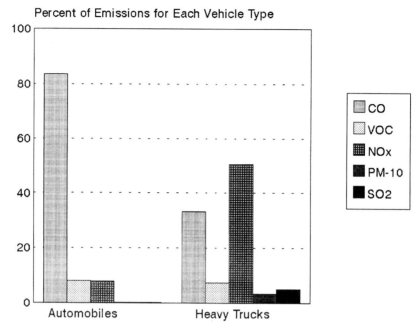

FIGURE 2-2 Comparison of national emission estimates (measured in short tons) for gasoline-powered, light-duty automobiles and diesel-powered heavy-duty vehicles (Nizich et al. 1994, A-4, A-8, A-15, A-19, A-24).

Heavy-duty diesel vehicles produce about 5 percent of total emissions from all highway vehicles, roughly proportional to their share of highway travel but small compared with the emissions of gasoline-powered passenger vehicles, which represent nearly two-thirds of total emissions from highway vehicles.[10] Diesel-powered vehicles, however, contribute a disproportionate share of total highway vehicle emissions of PM-10, SO_2, and NO_x: 72, 47, and 27 percent, respectively (Nizich et al. 1994, A-8, A-19, A-24).

High levels of NO_x emissions from heavy-duty vehicles are caused by the characteristics of diesel engines. Diesel engines typically run at higher combustion chamber pressures and temperatures than gasoline engines (Lilly 1984 in Guensler et al. 1991, Appendix A). Both conditions are conducive to high NO_x emission levels.

PM-10 and SO_2 emissions are also higher for heavy-duty diesel vehicles than for gasoline-powered automobiles. Catalytic converters have not been used with diesel engines because of particulates and concentrated sulfur gases in the exhaust gas, which could clog or deactivate the catalyst (Guensler et al. 1991, Appendix A).

Particulates in diesel exhaust originate mainly from unburned fuel and oil (Weaver and Klausmeier 1988, 2–7; Conte 1990, 59, 61).[11] However, introducing higher combustion temperatures to burn the fuel more completely and reduce particulates leads to higher NO_x emissions. The challenge facing diesel engine manufacturers is to reduce emissions of both pollutants at the same time to meet NO_x and particulate standards.

Emissions of SO_2 are also substantially higher for diesel than for gasoline engines because of the high sulfur content of diesel fuel. However, mandatory use of low sulfur or "clean" diesel fuel, which began in October 1993, should substantially reduce SO_2 emissions as well as PM-10 emissions[12] from heavy-duty, diesel-powered vehicles.

Factors Affecting In-Use Emission Levels

Actual emission levels from transportation sources are a function of several variables that can be grouped under four main categories: travel-related factors, driver behavior, highway network characteristics, and vehicle characteristics. Highway projects that add capacity and smooth traffic flows should affect emissions related to travel, driving patterns, and physical characteristics of the highway itself.

Travel-Related Factors

Trips and Vehicle Use

Emissions are a function of trip taking as well as distance traveled. Trips matter because emissions vary depending on the share of the trip associated with different vehicle operating modes. Exhaust emissions, one of the major sources of emissions from motor vehicle operation, include vehicle start-up emissions (start-ups are classified as cold or hot starts depending on how long the vehicle has been turned off[13]) and running emissions, which occur when the vehicle is warmed up and operating in a hot stabilized mode (Sierra Research 1993, 18, 19). Evaporative emissions, the other major source, consist entirely of

VOCs. They include running losses, which occur when the vehicle is operating in a hot stabilized mode; hot soak emissions, which result from fuel evaporation from the still-hot engine at the end of a trip; and diurnal emissions, which result from evaporation of fuel from the gasoline tank whether the vehicle is driven or not (Sierra Research 1993, 19, 20).[14]

Vehicle technology improvements have been focused primarily on reducing running emissions, which are a function of vehicle miles traveled (VMT). However, vehicle emissions from a cold start when the catalytic converter is not functioning at optimal temperatures, which are a function of trip making rather than VMT, can account for more than half of total CO and VOC emissions (FHWA 1992, 6).[15]

The importance of trips relative to VMT is most evident for VOC emissions as illustrated by the following example of a prototypical 32-km (20-mi) trip (Figure 2-3). In this example, vehicle start-up contributes approximately one-third of total VOC emissions and trip end contributes one-sixth. Neither of these emissions is a function of VMT, but together they account for about half of the total VOCs emitted.[16] Thus, the impact of highway capacity additions on trips as well as VMT is of interest in assessing the effect on emissions.

Speed, Acceleration, and Load

Emission levels depend not only on the number of trips taken and VMT but also on the speed and acceleration of the vehicle and the load on the engine over the distance of the trip.[17] In current emission models, vehicle speed and acceleration are combined into a single average speed for various trip types (i.e., drive test cycles) so that emission levels vary with average trip speed. The severe limitations of this approach are discussed in Chapter 3. Engine loads are generally not varied to reflect different vehicle operating or highway conditions (e.g., road grade) in modeling emission estimates.[18]

Figures 2-4 through 2-6 show current model estimates of emission factors for key pollutants expressed in grams per mile for light-duty, gasoline-powered automobiles representing the 1990 fleet mix, for a range of average trip speeds.[19] The data are based on the most recent emission models—MOBILE5a developed by EPA and EMFAC7F developed by the California Air Resources Board (CARB) and approved

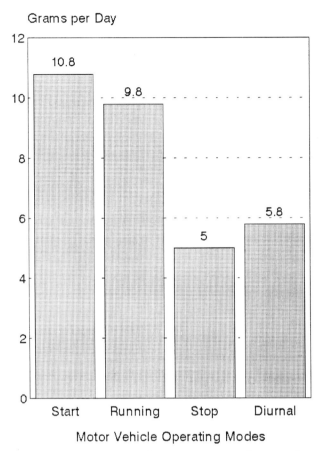

FIGURE 2-3 Sources of VOC emissions by type for a prototypical trip (Outwater and Loudon 1994, 17). Based on a 32-km (20-mi) round-trip in 1990 for a light-duty automobile traveling in the Bay Area of California at an average speed of 64 kph (40 mph).

by EPA for use in that state. A more detailed discussion of the test procedures and models used to estimate emissions is included in the final section of this chapter and in Chapter 3.

According to the estimates, emissions are generally highest in low-speed, congested driving conditions. In intermediate-speed, freer-flowing traffic conditions, emissions fall. They rise again at high

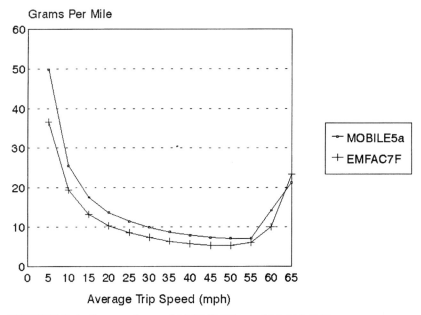

FIGURE 2-4 Comparison of MOBILE5a and EMFAC7F emission factors for carbon monoxide as a function of average trip speed, 1990 fleet average for light-duty gasoline vehicles (data from Sierra Research, June 1994). Note: confidence intervals around point estimates may be large and encompass positive and negative values. See discussion of uncertainty about emission estimates from EMFAC by Guensler (1994, Chapter 13) and in Chapter 3. 1 mi = 1.6 km.

speeds, but not to initial levels. NO_x emissions are the exception; they rise at relatively low speeds and are highest at high speeds. Confidence in current speed-emission relationships, however, is severely limited by test data that poorly represent urban driving conditions and large variances in emission rates for a wide range of changes in average trip speeds. These topics are discussed further in Chapter 3.

Emission factors for heavy-duty diesel vehicles (also representing the 1990 fleet mix) as a function of average trip speed are shown in Figures 2-7 through 2-9. The data show emissions of CO and VOC falling as speeds rise, but at high speeds they remain relatively constant (Figures 2-7 and 2-8). Emissions of NO_x have the same characteristic U-shaped curve as for automobiles (Figure 2-9). Esti-

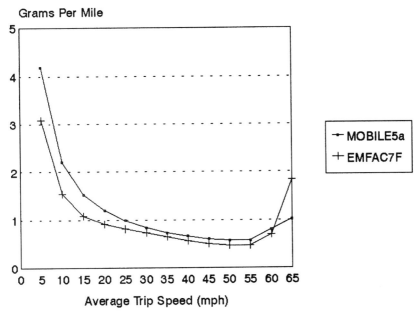

Grams Per Mile

Average Trip Speed (mph)

FIGURE 2-5 Comparison of MOBILEa and EMFAC7F emission factors for volatile organic compounds as a function of average trip speed, 1990 fleet average for light-duty gasoline vehicles (data from Sierra Research, June 1994). Note: confidence intervals around point estimates may be large and encompass positive and negative values. See discussion of uncertainty about emission estimates from EMFAC by Guensler (1994, Chapter 13) and in Chapter 3. 1 mi = 1.6 km.

mates for particulate emissions as a function of speed are not available. Particulate emissions are believed to follow the same trend as VOC emissions because both result from incomplete combustion of motor fuels (see Appendix A). However, the behavior of diesel particulates at high speeds is not well understood (see Appendix A). The final section on modeling describes the test procedures for estimating diesel emissions; the certainty of these estimates is discussed in Chapter 3.

Because highway capacity additions will increase average vehicle operating speeds, at least initially, they will have a direct effect on emission levels. However, the applicability of current average speed-emission relationships to assessing the emission effects of specific

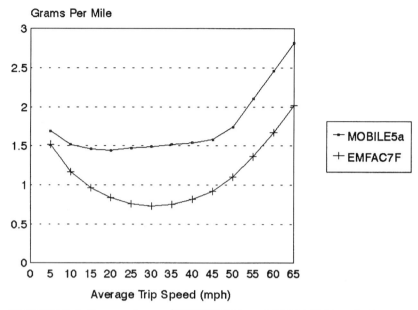

FIGURE 2-6 Comparison of MOBILE5A and EMFAC7F emission factors for oxides of nitrogen as a function of average trip speed, 1990 fleet average for light-duty gasoline vehicles (data from Sierra Research, June 1994). Note: confidence intervals around point estimates may be large and encompass positive and negative values. See discussion of uncertainty about emission estimates from EMFAC by Guensler (1994, Chapter 13) and in Chapter 3. 1 mi = 1.6 km.

capacity-enhancing projects is problematic. The emission factors relate to average trip speed, not to the portion of the trip on which the speed improvement is being made. Furthermore, by focusing on average speed, many of the variables of interest, such as the emission effects of traffic flow smoothing from a capacity project, cannot be analyzed directly. These limitations will be addressed more fully in the following chapter.

Driver Behavior

Recent research suggests that emissions are also affected by smoothness and consistency of vehicle speed, which are heavily affected by

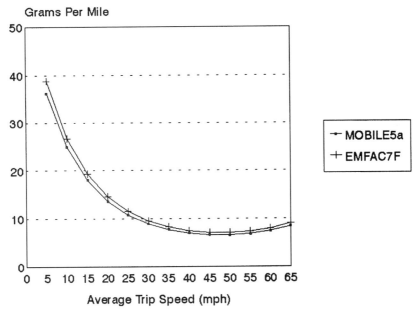

FIGURE 2-7 Comparison of MOBILE5a and EMFAC7F emission factors for carbon monoxide as a function of average trip speed, 1990 fleet average for heavy-duty diesel vehicles (data from Sierra Research, June 1994). Note: confidence intervals around point estimates may be large and encompass positive and negative values. See discussion of uncertainty about emission estimates from EMFAC by Guensler (1994, Chapter 13) and in Chapter 3. 1 mi = 1.6 km.

driving behavior and traffic conditions. Sharp accelerations from passing or changing lanes, merging onto a freeway from a ramp, or leaving a signalized intersection impose heavy loads on the engine that result in high emission levels.

Vehicle accelerations produce emissions because of an engine operating strategy called power enrichment. When heavy loads are placed on the engine by acceleration, vehicles are designed to operate with a richer fuel-to-air mixture (more fuel than air) to prevent engine knock and damage to the catalytic converter (EPA 1993, 19). This provides good driving performance but causes the catalytic converter to be overridden (there is insufficient oxygen for efficient performance of the catalyst), thereby producing high levels of emissions (EPA 1993,

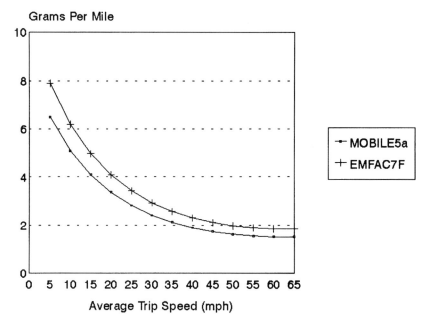

FIGURE 2-8 Comparison of MOBILE5a and EMFAC7F emission factors for volatile organic compounds as a function of average trip speed, 1990 fleet average for heavy-duty diesel vehicles (data from Sierra Research, June 1994). Note: confidence intervals around point estimates may be large and encompass positive and negative values. See discussion of uncertainty about emission estimates from EMFAC by Guensler (1994, Chapter 13) and in Chapter 3. 1 mi = 1.6 km.

19). Carbon monoxide emissions are most affected, followed by VOCs; there is little effect on NO_x emissions.[20]

Research is under way to measure the effects of accelerations on emission levels. Although widespread testing of a range of vehicle types and model years has not been completed, testing of individual vehicles suggests that the effects can be large. The staff of CARB, for example, have reported that for some vehicles, one heavy acceleration may produce more VOC emissions than the remainder of a 16-km (10-mi) trip (FHWA 1992, 29). Sierra Research has reported that aggressive driving (with many accelerations) results in CO emission levels 15 times higher, and VOC levels 14 times higher, than those resulting from "average" driving. These results were obtained by

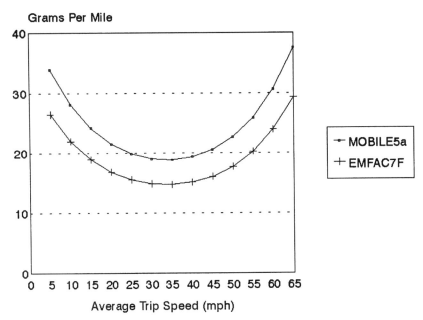

FIGURE 2-9 Comparison of MOBILE5a and EMFAC7F emission factors for oxides of nitrogen as a function of average trip speed, 1990 fleet average for heavy-duty diesel vehicles (data from Sierra Research, June 1994). Note: confidence intervals around point estimates may be large and encompass positive and negative values. See discussion of uncertainty about emission estimates from EMFAC by Guensler (1994, Chapter 13) and in Chapter 3. 1 mi = 1.6 km.

comparing time-speed-emission traces for the same 11-km (7-mi) trip from downtown to an outlying area (Figures 2-10 and 2-11).

Highway capacity additions should initially smooth traffic flows; researchers have found reductions in heavy accelerations and greater frequency of cruise-type driving at higher speeds (Effa and Larsen 1993, 3). Capacity additions should thus reduce emissions from accelerations. In the long run, it is likely that extreme impacts from power enrichment will gradually be ameliorated as new emission standards are established. Both EPA and CARB are presently working on certification test cycles for new vehicles that will include heavy accelerations. However, these new standards are not expected to be in place until the late 1990s.

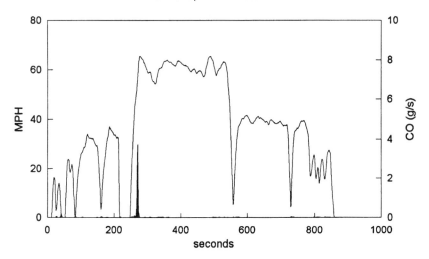

Driver B, from downtown

Overall CO emissions 2.36 g/mi
Line plot represents speed (left axis); area plot represents emissions (right axis)

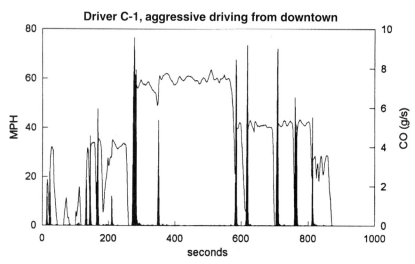

Driver C-1, aggressive driving from downtown

Overall CO emissions 35.72 g/mi
Line plot represents speed (left axis); area plot represents emissions (right axis)

FIGURE 2-10 Time-speed emission traces for carbon monoxide for an "average" and aggressive driver in an 11-km (7-mi) trip from downtown (data from Sierra Research, September 1993). Note: 1 mi = 1.6 km.

Driver B, from downtown, drive no. 07206.prn

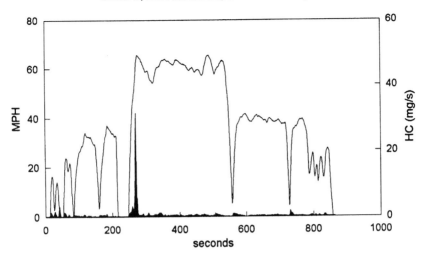

Overall VOC emissions 0.06 g/mi
Line plot represents speed (left axis); area plot represents emissions (right axis)

Driver C-1, aggressive driving from downtown, drive no. 072012.prn

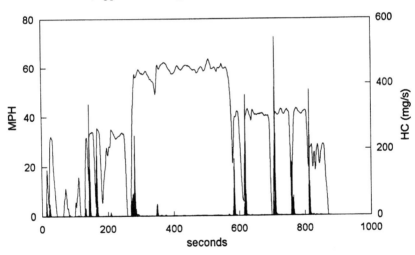

Overall VOC emissions 0.85 g/mi
Line plot represents speed (left axis); area plot represents emissions (right axis)

FIGURE 2-11 Time-speed-emission traces for volatile organic
compounds for an "average" and aggressive driver in an 11-km (7-mi)
trip from downtown (data from Sierra Research, September 1993).
Note: 1 mi = 1.6 km.

Highway-Related Factors

The physical characteristics of the highway network itself can affect emission levels. The presence of highways with long grades, freeway ramps, signalized intersections, major arterials with numerous driveways and significant volumes of traffic entering the traffic flow, and rough pavement are all network conditions that can increase emission levels primarily because of engine enrichment from accelerations as described above (Meyer et al. 1993, 227). Certain highway capacity additions—including improvements to freeway ramp geometry, intersection reconstruction, grade separation of major crossings, synchronization of traffic signals, and other measures to improve traffic flow such as the application of intelligent transportation system technologies—should reduce these emission-creating situations.

Vehicle-Related and Other Factors

Although not directly affected by highway capacity additions, other factors such as vehicle characteristics, fuels, and temperature can interact with changes in highway capacity and alter their effect on emissions. Future changes in vehicle technologies, fuels, and inspection and maintenance programs to reduce emissions will also reduce the emissions impact of traffic flow pattern changes due to highway capacity additions.

Emissions vary with vehicle age. Older carbureted vehicles have less precise fuel control than newer fuel-injected vehicles, resulting in higher average emissions during normal operation and vehicle starts and a greater incidence of malfunctions (Enns et al. 1993, 7–8). In addition, older vehicles have not met the more stringent emissions standards for the newer vehicle fleet. For example, 1990-model vehicles emit VOCs and CO at only one-third the rate of 1975-model vehicles (DOT and EPA 1993, 33).

Vehicle condition—whether the vehicle is well maintained, whether the catalytic converter has been tampered with or is malfunctioning—is even more critical than vehicle age in determining total emission levels. In conducting surveys of vehicle condition, researchers have documented the extent of tampering, particularly in areas without inspection and maintenance programs, and its effect on

Driver B, from downtown, O2 sensor disconnected, drive no. 07233.prn

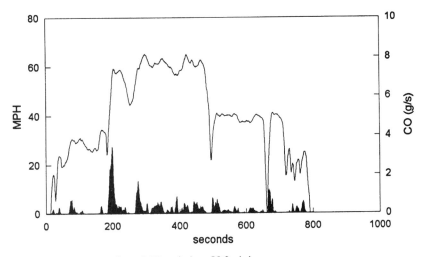

Overall CO emissions 20.8 g/mi
Line plot represents speed (left axis); area plot represents emissions (right axis)

Driver B, from downtown, O2 sensor disconnected, drive no. 07233.prn

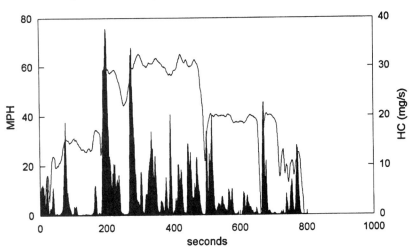

Overall VOC emissions 0.41 g/mi
Line plot represents speed (left axis); area plot represents emissions (right axis)

FIGURE 2-12 Time-speed-emission traces for carbon monoxide (*top*) and volatile organic compounds (*bottom*) for an 11-km (7-mi) trip from downtown with the catalytic converter disconnected (data from Sierra Research, September 1993). Note: 1 mi = 1.6 km.

emission levels (Greco 1985 in Johnson 1988, 50–51). More recently, using a roadside measuring device, researchers have been able to test the emissions of vehicles in operation, confirming that a few vehicles, commonly known as superemitters, account for a large share of emissions of CO and VOCs (Stedman 1991; Naghavi and Stopher 1993, 9–10).[21] Two additional speed-time-emission traces from Sierra Research (Figure 2-12), which can be compared with Driver B in Figures 2-10 and 2-11, show the effect on CO and VOC emissions of driving with the catalytic converter disconnected; emissions are approximately 7 to 10 times larger, respectively. The CAAA requirements for enhanced vehicle inspection and maintenance programs in areas that do not meet air quality standards—annual or biennial high-technology emission testing supplemented with on-the-road testing—should help reduce the number of vehicles that are out of compliance with emission standards.[22] Because emissions of superemitters are always high, however, their emission levels are generally less sensitive to changes in speed and sharp accelerations than are those of other vehicles.

As discussed earlier, the mix of vehicles, particularly the amount of heavy truck traffic, affects the types of pollutants emitted. Substantial truck traffic can affect the behavior of other vehicles and their emission levels. For example, slower-moving trucks, particularly in locations with grades, can contribute to more frequent accelerations and decelerations by passenger vehicles as they attempt to navigate around the trucks.

The type of fuel used also has important ramifications for emission levels. The nearly universal use of lead-free gasoline has effectively eliminated lead as a pollutant from transportation sources. The use of reformulated and oxygenated fuels as well as low-sulfur diesel fuel, and the introduction of clean fuels programs for vehicle fleets required by the CAAA in the nation's most polluted areas, will also help reduce emission levels.

Finally, ambient temperature affects both exhaust and evaporative emissions. Exhaust emissions increase below 24°C (75°F); at colder temperatures the engine and emission control system take longer to warm up, increasing cold start emissions (Sierra Research 1993, 122). Evaporative emissions increase above about 24°C, with higher emission rates the higher the maximum temperature (Sierra Research 1993, 125).[23]

Translating Emissions into Air Quality

Examining the changes in vehicle emissions that will result from highway capacity additions is only the first step in understanding how these emissions are likely to be dispersed in the atmosphere and affect the air quality of a metropolitan area.

Meteorological conditions (e.g., wind and temperature) have a major effect on the transport and dispersion of emissions and hence their concentration in a region, which is the primary criterion of concern from a public health perspective (Horowitz 1982, 39). For example, the highest concentrations of CO generally occur in the winter, when atmospheric conditions tend to be more stable and wind speeds are lower, causing reduced dispersion and increased concentrations of CO (Horowitz 1982, 45). Because the chemical reaction that creates ozone is stimulated by heat and sunlight, ozone concentrations tend to be higher from midspring to midfall than during the rest of the year (Horowitz 1982, 74). The atmospheric mixing and transport of ozone concentrations long distances from the sources of the precursors is a well-known phenomenon (Horowitz 1982, 74).

Local topography—both man-made (e.g., tall buildings near a highway) and natural (e.g., mountains)—can also affect the rate of dispersion of emissions from their source.

TRANSPORTATION AND ENERGY CONSUMPTION

The dominant energy source for the transportation sector is petroleum (96.6 percent), and nearly two-thirds of the petroleum consumed in the United States is in this sector (Davis 1994, 2-7, 2-10). The highway mode accounts for nearly three-fourths of total transportation energy use with about 80 percent from automobiles, light trucks, and motorcycles and about 20 percent from heavy trucks and buses (Davis 1994, 2-16). Petroleum energy users are heavily dependent on imported oil; nearly half of all petroleum consumed in the United States comes from foreign sources (Davis 1994, 2-5).

Energy and the Environment

In addition to energy dependence, concerns about global warming have stimulated interest in improving motor vehicle fuel efficiency. Global warming occurs from the emission of carbon dioxide (CO_2) and other gases into the upper atmosphere, which trap heat and warm the earth; hence the term greenhouse effect (Gordon 1991, 55; Greene et al. 1988, 215). Although there is great uncertainty about the likely climatic changes from the greenhouse effect and the timing of these changes, transportation's contribution to the problem is well understood. Carbon dioxide, the principal greenhouse gas, is a by-product of any engine that burns carbon-based, fossil fuels. The U.S. fleet of gasoline-powered automobiles and light trucks contributes about one-fifth of total U.S. CO_2 emissions (NRC 1990 in NRC 1992, 71). Improvements in fuel economy will result in reduced CO_2 emissions. For example, a 10 percent reduction in the fuel consumption of the vehicle fleet will result in an estimated 2 percent reduction in total U.S. emissions of CO_2 (NRC 1992, 71).

Improved fuel economy could also reduce other automotive emissions, such as VOC emissions, which affect ground-level pollution. Improvements in fuel economy may or may not reduce tail pipe VOC exhaust emission levels, depending on corresponding manufacturer changes to emission control systems (DeLuchi et al. 1993, 8).[24] If demand for gasoline is reduced, total VOC emissions are likely to be lower because of reduced motor vehicle evaporative emissions and reduced emissions from fuel extraction, refining, processing, distribution, and vehicle refueling (DeLuchi et al. 1993, 3).

Factors Affecting In-Use Fuel Economy

The primary factors affecting fuel economy fall into the same categories as those affecting emissions. Highway projects that add capacity, increasing average vehicle speeds and smoothing traffic flows, will have the greatest effect on those fuel economy factors related to travel conditions, driver behavior, and the physical characteristics of the highway.

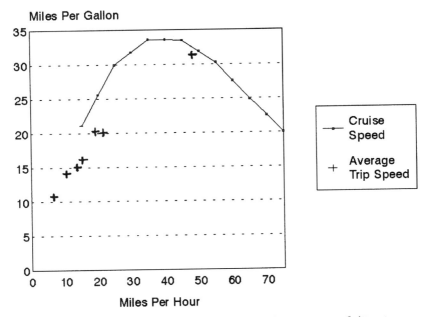

FIGURE 2-13 Fuel economy as a function of cruise speed (Davis 1994, 3-56) and average trip speed (An and Ross 1993b, 76). Note: 1 mi = 1.6 km; 1 gal = 3.8 liters.

Travel-Related Factors

Fuel consumption is a function of different traffic characteristics. Fuel efficiency under steady state, cruise-type driving conditions, measured in miles per gallon for a sample of automobiles and light trucks, peaks at speeds of 56 to 72 kph (35 to 45 mph) and then rapidly declines at higher speeds (Figure 2-13). At lower speeds, engine friction, tires, and accessories (e.g., power steering and air conditioning) reduce fuel efficiency; at high speeds the effect of aerodynamic drag on fuel efficiency, which increases exponentially as a function of speed, dominates (An and Ross 1993a, Figure 2).

Fuel efficiency under start-and-stop traffic conditions shows somewhat different patterns. The data points in Figure 2-13 show modeled estimates of fuel economy as a function of the average trip speed of various drive-test cycles, which are based on different trip types, locations, and traffic conditions (An and Ross 1993b, 76). Fuel economy is somewhat poorer at lower average trip speeds, reflecting greater amounts of acceleration and stopping. At higher average trip speeds, the modeled estimates tend to converge with the cruise speed results, reflecting more cruise-type driving and less acceleration and stopping at these speeds. The results confirm earlier research findings that of all the travel-related factors affecting fuel economy, average vehicle speed explains most of the variability in fuel consumption and is a good predictor of fuel economy for most urban trips (Evans et al. 1974, 16; Murrell 1980, 132). The effect on fuel economy of highway capacity additions, which initially raise average vehicle speeds, depends on average traffic speeds before and after the project.

The modal operation of the vehicle also affects fuel consumption. Vehicles get lower fuel efficiency when started cold than when fully warmed up (Murrell 1980, 142).

Driver Behavior

Fuel economy is sensitive to driving behavior, including accelerations (Murrell 1980, 156), braking, and gear shifting. Aggressive braking and accelerations are both associated with reduced fuel economy. Energy is lost from braking as it is dispersed into heat. Repeated braking can account for as much as 15 percent of fuel use in an urban driving trip (An et al. 1993, 5). Aggressive accelerations result in higher engine speeds and greater fuel consumption than constant "cruise" driving.[25] Researchers have estimated that, in a congested urban setting, aggressive driving with rapid accelerations will result in a 10 percent increase in fuel use (An et al. 1993, 4). This is a considerably smaller impact, however, than the impact on emissions (Figures 2-10 and 2-11).

Thus, highway capacity additions that smooth traffic flows, reducing the incidence of sharp accelerations and rapid braking, should improve fuel economy initially.

Highway-Related Factors

The characteristics of the highway itself can affect fuel economy. For example, steep grades and rough roads reduce fuel efficiency, the former from increased fuel use as a function of heavy loads on the engine and the latter from increased rolling resistance and aerodynamic drag (Murrell 1980, 119, 121). To the extent that highway capacity additions improve these conditions, fuel efficiency can be gained.

Vehicle-Related and Other Factors

The primary vehicle-related factors affecting fuel economy are vehicle weight and technology. In general, larger and heavier passenger vehicles, vehicles with automatic transmissions, and vehicles with more power accessories (e.g., power seats and windows, power brakes and steering, and air conditioning) all consume more fuel on the average (Murrell 1980, 126, 199, 202).

Vehicle maintenance is also a factor. For example, wheels that are out of alignment and tires that are underinflated increase rolling resistance and hence degrade fuel economy (Murrell 1980, 176, 179). Out-of-tune engines as well as inadequate lubrication to reduce engine friction also take their toll on fuel economy (Murrell 1980, 84, 180).

The mix of vehicles, particularly the amount of heavy truck traffic, affects total fuel consumption. The fuel economy for the U.S. fleet of heavy combination trucks currently averages about 2.4 kpl (5.6 mpg), whereas the fuel economy for the population of passenger vehicles averages about 9.2 kpl (21.6 mpg) (Davis 1994, 3-24, 3-39). However, relative to their weight, heavy-duty diesel-powered trucks are very fuel efficient (O'Rourke and Lawrence 1993, 11).[26]

Finally, climate is a factor. Fuel economy is poorer at low temperatures (Murrell 1980, 107) and with high winds, which result in aerodynamic losses (Murrell 1980, 114).

MODELING AIR QUALITY AND ENERGY IMPACTS

A range of models are available to estimate the effects of motor vehicle transportation on air quality and energy use. However, many of them are not well suited to the more specific task of estimating the effects of facility-specific highway capacity enhancement projects.

An introduction to the key models of interest, an overview of the state of the practice, and a brief discussion of the key limitations of current modeling practice are provided in this section. More detailed discussions of the problems with individual modeling approaches as well as recommendations for improvements in practice, including research, are included in each of the following three chapters.

Introduction to Modeling Requirements and Approaches

Modeling the effects of additions to highway capacity on air quality and energy use requires a chain of different models—from land use and travel demand models used to generate trip and traffic volume data to emission, dispersion, and energy models used to estimate the impacts of changes in travel activity on emission levels, regional air quality, and energy use, respectively (Figure 2-14).

Many of these models were not developed to provide the type of analysis required of them today. For example, travel demand models were originally developed to help size and locate highway and transit facilities in a region. Travel volume forecasts could be approximate for estimating capacity requirements, but such forecasts are inadequate for providing the facility- and time-specific travel volume and speed data necessary to estimate the emission impacts of specific projects (Harvey and Deakin 1993, 3–6; DeCorla-Souza 1993b, 6). Similarly, mobile emission models were designed to predict macro-level emissions for input into emissions inventories,[27] not to provide precise estimates of emission rates for vehicles traveling on individual highway links (Guensler 1993, 12).

Land Use and Travel Demand Models

Land use and travel demand models are critical to forecasting changes in travel demand from capacity additions to the highway network in a regional area. Only a few MPOs have developed fully integrated, state-of-the-art, land use–transportation models that would enable them to model the impacts of highway supply changes on travel demand and land use. More MPOs are expressing interest in developing this capability as a result of the CAAA and ISTEA (Putman 1994, 2).

Land Use Models

A growing number of metropolitan areas have formal land use modeling capabilities; however, their use is still restricted to a minority of

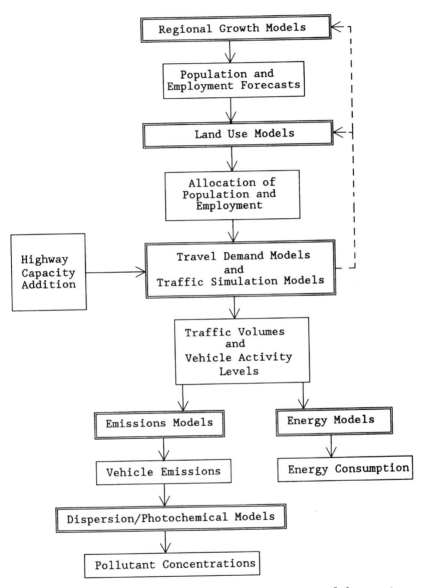

FIGURE 2-14 Modeling chain for estimating impacts of changes in travel activity on emissions and pollutant concentrations and energy use (adapted from DeCorla-Souza 1993a, 1).

regions in the United States (Harvey and Deakin 1993, 3-14–3-15). The available models generally use time series data on population, employment, household income, land availability,[28] and accessibility to allocate regional population and employment forecasts to geographic subareas of a region (Harvey and Deakin 1993, 3-15).

The main allocation modeling approach in use in the United States[29] is the DRAM-EMPAL (Disaggregated Residential Allocation Model–Employment Allocation Model) components of the Integrated Transportation and Land Use Package (ITLUP) (Putman 1991).[30] The DRAM-EMPAL models allocate projected employment and households in a region on the basis of the current distribution of jobs and population, travel times, and multivariate measures of the attractiveness of various locations (Putman 1993). For example, the attractiveness of specific household locations depends on such factors as the amount of vacant developable land and the characteristics (e.g., income range) of households already living in specific areas (Putman 1993). The DRAM-EMPAL models can be used alone or linked to a travel demand model. A variety of other land use models have been developed and used overseas, many of which are complex and data intensive, but none are currently in use in the United States (Cambridge Systematics, Inc. 1991, 9; Wegener 1994).

One criticism of DRAM-EMPAL is that it does not describe all of the major factors (e.g., housing and land values, tax rates, and crime rates)[31] that determine the location decisions of firms or households (Harvey and Deakin 1993, 3-15). This limits the precision of its predictions. However, sensitivity tests of the DRAM-EMPAL models demonstrate the models' ability to reproduce large regional patterns (Putman 1993). Thus, the models should be able to provide a sense of the direction and magnitude of locational changes from major additions to regional highway capacity.

Travel Demand Models

Many MPOs have a travel demand modeling capability.[32] Figure 2-15 provides an overview of the typical four-step sequential approach used to forecast regional travel demand; each step is a model representing a different aspect of the traveler's decision (Shunk 1992, 109). The first step in the process, trip generation, is a function of exogenously

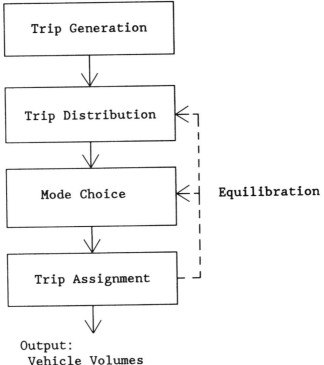

FIGURE 2-15 Four-step travel demand process
(DeCorla-Souza 1993b, 1).

determined demographic patterns and economic activity in a region
(DeCorla-Souza 1993b, 3). The remaining three steps, which are followed sequentially, simply allocate the trips among alternative destinations in trip distribution, alternative modes of travel in mode
choice, and alternative highway (and transit if appropriate) routes in
trip assignment (DeCorla-Souza 1993b, 2). Trip assignment is based
primarily on minimizing travel time through an iterative process that
feeds back to mode choice, and sometimes to trip distribution, in an
effort to equate initial with final travel time estimates (Harvey and
Deakin 1991, 10-11). The outputs of the process are vehicle and passenger volumes on highway and transit routes, respectively (DeCorla-
Souza 1993b, 2) (Figure 2-15).

A primary limitation of current travel demand modeling practice is the lack of integration with land use models. With few exceptions[33] the models do not provide feedback loops so that analysts can examine the long-term impact of changes in the transportation network and network performance on travel demand and land use patterns and the trips generated by these effects. Because trip generation is exogenously determined in most conventional travel demand models, few MPOs can examine how highway additions might affect the regional distribution of population and economic activity, or regional growth in general (Deakin 1991, 11). In fact, there are no operational models that formally analyze the impact of transportation improvements on aggregate regional growth, in part because of lack of a theoretical basis for determining the relationship between transportation improvements and population and economic growth (Deakin 1991, 11).

In addition, conventional travel demand models do not provide the level of accuracy or detail on vehicle or travel activity by time of day that is needed for accurate emission and air quality modeling of the impacts of additions to highway capacity. The reliability of data on speed and traffic volume forecasts is poor,[34] and other detailed data needed for emission and air quality analyses—such as temporal distribution of travel volumes and trips, vehicle type, and vehicle operating mode—are not direct outputs of the models.[35]

Traffic Simulation Models

Traffic models, as mathematical representations of real-world phenomena, comprise the tools used by traffic engineers to assess the relationships between capacity, levels of service, speed, and delay. Simulation models, as computer implementations of traffic models, provide a more detailed representation of traffic flow, including information on speed, acceleration, and deceleration of individual vehicles.[36] Several of the traffic and simulation models in current use have been adapted to provide estimates of emissions and fuel use.

Why are these models then not used more widely to address the questions raised in this study? One reason is that many of the models are extremely data intensive and are thus beyond the data capabilities of many MPOs (Harvey and Deakin 1993, 3-77). Another reason is that, although traffic simulation models provide sophisticated analyses of the impacts of traffic flow improvements on roadway and vehicle performance, they are not well equipped to make similarly sophisticated assessments of changes in traffic volumes that will accompany these measures (Horowitz 1982, 212). Thus, they fall short in their ability to analyze the longer-term impacts of traffic flow improvements of interest in this study.

Under the auspices of the jointly funded federal Travel Model Improvement Program,[37] a multimodal traffic simulation model is being developed at the Los Alamos National Laboratory. The model as planned will provide detailed estimates of household trips and travel and vehicle movements in a metropolitan area, which can then be linked with emissions, airshed, and energy use models (presentation by G. Shunk, fourth study committee meeting, July 11, 1994). Although more detailed estimates of the physical effects of transportation activities on emissions, air quality, and energy use will be available, the model will not have any forecasting capacities to examine behavioral effects; forecasts of land use and trip generation patterns must be prepared separately and input into the model (Shunk, July 11, 1994).

Emission and Atmospheric Dispersion Models

Emission and atmospheric dispersion models are critical to assessing the impacts of motor vehicle travel on pollutant emissions and concentrations.

Emission Models

Two main emission models are currently in use in the United States: (a) the EPA MOBILE model, which is the most widely used emission model, and (b) the CARB EMFAC model, which is used in California. The structure of the models is the same: activity-specific emission rates estimated by the models are multiplied by emission-producing vehicle activities to provide emission outputs by pollutant (i.e., grams per vehicle-mile for MOBILE and, in addition, grams per vehicle-hour and per vehicle trip for EMFAC) (Guensler 1993, 3) (Figure 2-16). In both models, emission rates are a function of vehicle type and age, vehicle speed, ambient temperature, and vehicle operating mode (DeCorla-Souza 1993a, 2).

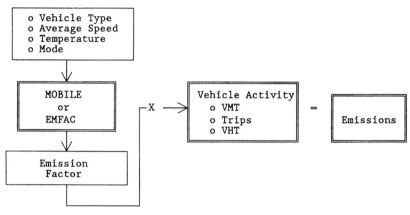

FIGURE 2-16 Emission modeling process (DeCorla-Souza 1993a, 1).

Baseline emission rates are derived from a laboratory test procedure known as the Federal Test Procedure (FTP), which has been used to determine compliance of light-duty vehicles and light-duty trucks with federal emission standards since the 1972 model year (EPA 1993, 11). The FTP driving cycle consists of a sequence of accelerations, decelerations, cruise speeds, and idles based on actual home-to-work commute trips in the 1960s on Los Angeles freeways and surface arterials. A review of the FTP required by the CAAA has found that it underrepresents the high-speed driving and high acceleration rates that are common features of today's driving patterns and are key causes of high emissions (EPA 1993, 3).[38] Several of the 11 other driving cycles used to develop speed correction factors, which adjust emissions rates for vehicles traveling at average speeds other than the FTP baseline speed, are also not considered to be adequately representative of today's urban driving conditions.

Procedures for determining heavy-duty vehicle emissions differ significantly from those for determining light-duty vehicle emissions. Heavy-duty vehicle testing is generally performed on an engine dynamometer[39] rather than the full chassis dynamometer, which is used for light-duty vehicles, with the result that conversion factors must be used to produce emission rate data on a grams per vehicle-mile basis equivalent to light-duty vehicles. However, the speed correction factors for emissions of heavy-duty diesel vehicles, which are embodied in the MOBILE model, are based on chassis dynamometer testing of 22 1979-vintage heavy-duty diesel trucks conducted in the early 1980s (see Appendix A).

Emission models have several shortcomings as analytic tools for assessing the impacts that are of interest in this study. Among these are reliance on a limited number of drive cycles that do not adequately represent current driving on urban highways and understate key sources of high emissions; limited testing of passenger vehicles at high speeds and of heavy-duty vehicles at all speeds; and emission rates that reflect average trip speeds rather than average link speeds. These shortcomings are critical because emission estimates from current models are sensitive to assumptions about average vehicle speeds and the underlying drive cycles on which they are based.

Atmospheric Dispersion Models

Atmospheric dispersion or diffusion models translate emission levels into atmospheric concentrations of pollutants. Regional models take input data on grid-based rates and locations of emissions in a region and on the region's topography and meteorology (i.e., wind speeds and directions) to determine the atmospheric transport, diffusion, and chemical reactions of pollutants. Data on concentrations of pollutants at particular locations and times are the result (Horowitz 1982, 311; NRC 1991, 303).

Under the CAAA, ozone nonattainment areas designated as extreme, severe, serious, or multistate-moderate are to use photochemical, grid-based air quality models, such as the Urban Airshed Model, to demonstrate attainment of NAAQS (NRC 1991, 81). These models require detailed travel activity data that are spatially and temporally allocated (e.g., by link by grid; by season, month, and weekday or weekend day) to reflect the episode being modeled[40] (DeCorla-Souza 1993a, 1).

Dispersion models are also used to estimate concentrations of pollutants near particular facilities, such as intersections. For example, air quality intersection models estimate CO concentrations using data on traffic, intersection geometry, vehicle characteristics, emission factors generated from emission models, and meteorological conditions (O'Connor et al. 1993, 1). The CAL3QHC model, which is recommended by EPA guidance for intersection modeling, is used in most states except California, where use of the CALINE 4 model is recommended (O'Connor et al. 1993, 1).

Model uncertainties about chemical mechanisms, wind-field modeling, and removal processes as well as problems with input data—difficulties in obtaining accurate measures of VOC emissions and detailed spatial and temporal data on travel activity from conventional travel demand models—limit the effectiveness of dispersion modeling for ozone (NRC 1991, 10-11). Similar data gaps as well as placement and location of receptors are problems for CO modeling. For example, a recent survey on current practices in intersection air quality modeling (O'Connor et al. 1993, 29) found that critical determinants of predicted concentrations of CO, such as data on queuing, vehicle operating modes, fleet age and composition, speeds in highly congested flows, accelerations, and turning movements, are not commonly available for specific intersections.

Energy Models

A major source of highway vehicle fuel economy estimates is the simulation model developed by the Oak Ridge National Laboratory for the Federal Highway Administration in the mid-1980s. The model, which is based on on-road vehicle tests (12 gasoline-powered and 3 diesel-powered light-duty vehicles) and laboratory (dynamometer) testing, estimates fuel consumption as a function of vehicle speed and acceleration (McGill 1985, 3). The simulation model provides a good approximation of actual fuel use. The variance in individual vehicle performance, particularly the effect of speed variation at lower speeds, is less for fuel economy than for emissions. At high speeds, the test results converge, reflecting more steady-state, cruise driving (McGill 1985, 49). More recently, simplified analytic models have been developed that can estimate fuel economy within a 5 percent error range on the basis of vehicle parameters that specify the make and model of vehicle and driving patterns that reflect the level of traffic congestion (An and Ross 1993a, 1).

Limitations of Current Modeling Practice

The key limitations of current models can be summarized under three broad categories. More in-depth discussion, particularly of the uncertainties of the models, can be found in the following chapters.

- *Appropriateness of the models*: The models are being used to solve problems for which they were not originally designed. Many are ill suited to provide the detailed analyses of the impacts of link-specific highway capacity additions on travel behavior and vehicle performance that are the focus of this study.
- *Validity of the models*: There are large uncertainties in the models themselves, which are manifested in wide variances around some model estimates. These reflect the limited state of the knowledge of the underlying phenomena the models are attempting to capture. A better understanding is needed of travel and driving behavior, which are critical to accurate travel demand and emission modeling, respectively. Models are validated, that is, a comparison of estimated with actual measured data is made, when sufficient survey data are available.[41] Too often the information is dated or limited.
- *Links between the models*: There is a mismatch of detail between the outputs generated and the inputs required by several of the models in the modeling chain. Lack of adequately detailed data from travel demand models for input into emission and atmospheric dispersion models is a particular problem for accurate estimation of the impacts on air quality of highway capacity additions.

SUMMARY

Motor vehicles are a major source of air pollution in the nation's metropolitan areas, and they are major users of petroleum. According to currently available estimates, transportation sources account for about 45 percent, and highway vehicles slightly more than one-third, of nationwide emissions of EPA's six criteria pollutants. However, the range is considerable for each pollutant source and for different vehicle and fuel types. Moreover, there is a high degree of uncertainty with respect to many of the estimates.

Gasoline-powered passenger vehicles—the most common vehicle on the road—are the primary source of CO highway vehicle emissions and contributors to the ozone precursor emissions from highway vehicles (VOCs and NO_x). Heavy-duty diesel vehicles contribute a disproportionate share of total highway vehicle emissions of PM-10, SO_2, and NO_x.

The transportation sector accounts for nearly two-thirds of the petroleum consumed in the United States. The highway mode accounts for about three-quarters of the transportation total. The gasoline-powered motor vehicle fleet also contributes about 20 percent of total U.S. CO_2 emissions, the principal greenhouse gas.

Vehicle emission levels are a function of trip taking as well as distance traveled, because emissions vary depending on whether the vehicle is warmed up. Emission levels are sensitive to average vehicle speed over the distance of the trip and vary as a nonlinear function of average trip speed. In addition, emissions are affected by smoothness and consistency of vehicle speeds, which vary by trip type. Sharp accelerations, in particular, are an important source of CO and VOC emissions, which are not well reflected in current emissions models. Thus, average trip speed alone is not a good predictor of emission levels.

Fuel economy is also sensitive to average vehicle speed but somewhat less so to aggressive accelerations and braking. Thus, average trip speed is a good predictor of fuel economy for most urban trips. Highway capacity additions, which will increase average trip speeds and smooth traffic flows, should directly affect emission levels and fuel economy.

A range of models are available to estimate the effects of motor vehicle transportation on emissions, air quality, and energy use. However, many were developed to predict macro-level, regional effects; they are not well suited to assessing the impacts of link-specific highway capacity enhancement projects at the level of precision that is being required of them today. Nor were the different types of models (e.g., land use models, travel demand models, emission models) designed to be easily integrated in their operations. Data requirements— both the currency of the data and the detail needed for impact analyses—are also problems. Finally, the models are based on a limited understanding of the underlying relationships. Greater knowledge of travel and driving behavior, in particular, is critical to improved modeling of the travel demand and emission effects of highway capacity enhancement projects.

NOTES

1. A stationary or point source is a large, geographically concentrated emitter, such as a coal-fired electrical power plant, whose emissions rates are large enough to be significant by themselves even if no other emission sources are present (Horowitz 1982, 7). An area source is a collection of small, geographically dispersed emitters that are not significant individually but that are important collectively, such as dry cleaning establishments (Horowitz 1982, 7). A mobile source, such as an automobile, is characterized as not emitting from a fixed location.
2. Short-term (24-hr or less) averaging times were designated for some pollutants, such as CO and O_3, to protect against acute, or short-term, health effects; long-term averaging times (annual average) were established for other pollutants to protect against chronic health effects (Curran et al. 1994, 20).
3. CO contributes to the buildup of tropospheric (ground-level) ozone (the principal ingredient of smog) and methane, both major greenhouse gases. First, CO helps convert nitric oxide to nitrogen dioxide, a crucial step in ozone formation. Second, CO reacts with the hydroxyl radical (OH), which eventually removes CO from the atmosphere; however, OH is also the principal chemical that destroys ozone and methane. Thus, if carbon monoxide levels increase, OH concentrations will fall, and regional concentrations of ozone and methane will rise (MacKenzie and Walsh 1990, 8).
4. After the report was completed, EPA recomputed emissions from highway vehicles using the most recent version of its emission factor model, MOBILE5a (Curran et al. 1994, 22), but EPA estimates are still thought to be low by many in the scientific community.
5. Nitrogen oxide (NO), the dominant constituent of vehicle exhaust emissions of NO_x, combines with ozone (O_3) to form NO_2 and O_2. However, ozone is subsequently regenerated by further chemical reactions stimulated by the presence of sunlight (see NRC 1991, 168 for a more detailed discussion).
6. The problem is the consistent underestimate of VOC emissions, which leads to estimates of relatively low VOC to NO_x ratios. The nation's ozone reduction strategy has been based largely on the premise that VOC/NO_x ratios in the most polluted areas, where VOC control is more effective, are low (i.e., in the less-than-10 range). An upward correction in VOC emission inventories could indicate the need for a fundamental change

in ozone abatement strategies to greater use of NO_x controls in many geographic areas (NRC 1991, 7).

7. This regulation, however, is an interim requirement, that is, it applies to all projects contained in new or revised transportation improvement programs until EPA approves state implementation plans. In the latter, a state could choose to accommodate NO_x emissions generated by new transportation projects by reducing emissions from other sectors (*AASHTO Journal* 1994, 10–11.)

8. In 1987 EPA replaced earlier standards for particulate matter with the more stringent PM-10 standard, which focuses on the smaller particles likely to be responsible for adverse health effects because of their ability to reach the lower regions of the respiratory tract (Curran et al. 1994, 10).

9. The 1987 Truck Inventory and Use Survey reported that 67 percent of combination vehicles used diesel fuel, but most trucks operating only in local areas (96 percent) are fueled by gasoline (Bureau of the Census 1990, 37, 48).

10. In 1993 emissions from all highway vehicles, gasoline and diesel powered, for CO, NO_x, PM-10, SO_2, and VOC were 74,155 thousand short tons. Emissions from diesel-powered, heavy-duty vehicles for the same pollutants were 3,986 thousand short tons, or 5.4 percent of the total; emissions from light-duty passenger vehicles were 46,941 thousand short tons, or 63 percent of the total (Nizich et al. 1994, A-4, A-8, A-15, A-19, A-24). In the most recent year for which data are available (1992), all motor vehicles accounted for 2,239,828 million vehicle miles of travel; combination trucks and buses accounted for 104,771 million vehicle miles of travel, or nearly 5 percent of the total, and passenger vehicles accounted for 1,595,438 million vehicle miles of travel, or 71 percent of the total (FHWA 1993, 207).

11. The primary components of diesel particulates are soot formed during combustion (40 to 80 percent of the total); particulate sulfates, which depend on operating conditions and the fuel's sulfur content (5 to 10 percent of the total); and heavy hydrocarbons condensed or adsorbed on the soot from the fuel and lubricating oil and also formed during combustion (the remainder) (Weaver and Klausmeier 1988, 2-7–2-8).

12. Even if all fuel were burned in the combustion process, thereby eliminating particulates from incomplete combustion, impurities in the fuel would burn and appear in the exhaust as particulates; the primary offender is sulfur (Conte 1990, 61). With lower sulfur levels in fuel, this source of particulates should also be reduced.

13. EPA considers a cold start for a catalyst-equipped vehicle to occur after the engine has been turned off for 1 hr. For noncatalyst vehicles, a cold start occurs after the engine has been turned off for 4 hr (Sierra Research 1993, 18).

14. Refueling losses and crankcase emissions are also generally considered in the evaporative emissions category as is a new category, resting losses. The latter was previously included under the hot soak and diurnal categories (Sierra Research 1993, 20).

15. VOC and CO emissions are higher when a cold engine is first started, because a fuel-rich mixture must be provided to achieve adequate combustion during warm-up and the excess fuel is only partially burned. In addition, the catalytic converter does not provide full control until the vehicle is warmed up (Sierra Research 1993, 18). It takes between 1 and 3 min for modern, properly operating vehicles to warm up. Catalysts also cool off faster than engines and are completely cold in 45 to 60 min (EPA 1993, 115; Enns et al. 1993, 3). Preheated catalytic converters may ameliorate the problem. The California Air Resources Board estimates that they would decrease cold-start emissions by half or more but would not eliminate the problem (FHWA 1992, 28).

16. The number would be even larger if running loss evaporative emissions, which are included under running emissions, were separated out.

17. Loads are a function of vehicle operating conditions (e.g., number of passengers, whether a trailer is being towed, whether the air conditioning is on), highway conditions (e.g., road grade), and driver behavior (e.g., aggressive driving with sharp accelerations). The latter two conditions are described in subsequent sections.

18. The exceptions are air conditioning and towing corrections, which can be input by the user in running the emissions models.

19. Emissions were calculated under hot stabilized operating conditions.

20. CO emissions, which are a product of incomplete combustion of motor fuels, are most affected. Engine-out CO emissions increase because of incomplete fuel combustion under fuel-rich conditions and exhaust emissions increase because the catalyst is overridden (personal communication, John German, EPA, Feb. 4, 1994). VOCs are affected but to a lesser extent. They result from unburned fuel in the engine. As fuel is increased with the richer air-fuel mixture, the level of engine-out VOC emissions goes up proportionately; these emissions are not handled by the catalyst, which is overridden under fuel-rich conditions, thereby increasing exhaust emissions (personal communication, John German, EPA, Feb. 4, 1994). NO_x engine-out emissions decrease under rich operation, but NO_x reduction efficiencies in the catalyst also drop (EPA 1993, 19). Overall, there may be a slight increase in exhaust NO_x emissions under rich operation, but the effect is relatively minor and varies from vehicle to vehicle (EPA 1993, 19).

21. From a sample of 24,000 emissions measurements made over a 4-day period, Naghavi and Stopher (1993) found that more than half of the CO was emitted by 6.9 percent of the vehicles and that about half of the VOC was emitted by 20 percent of the vehicles (p. 1).

22. These programs are required in areas designated "serious" or above for ozone and "high moderate" or above for CO. EPA estimates that innovative inspection and maintenance programs could yield a 28 percent reduction in emissions (DOT and EPA 1993, 33).

23. Exhaust emissions of CO and VOC also increase at temperatures above 24°C (75°F), but not as sharply as at lower temperatures. The increase is primarily the result of an increase in vapors purged from the evaporative emission control system, leading to rich operation (Sierra Research 1993, 122).

24. For example, if VOC emission formation in the engine (engine-out emissions) is reduced because less fuel is being delivered to the engine chamber per engine cycle, these gains will show up as lower tail pipe exhaust emissions only if manufacturers do not cut back on catalyst emission-control systems (tail pipe emissions) and do not take advantage of some of the savings (DeLuchi et al. 1993, 7-8).

25. The problem is not the quick acceleration, but the delay in gear shifting. Drivers with manual transmissions shift later (at higher engine speeds); with automatic transmissions, the system delays shifting up, both with the same result—high engine speeds and high fuel consumption (An et al. 1993, 4).

26. A fully loaded diesel truck realizes 3 to 3.4 kpl (7 to 8 mpg) on the highway, or approximately 108.9 to 123.4 metric ton-km per liter (280 to 320 ton-mi per gal). A car weighing 2268 kg (5,000 lb) can realize 11 to 12.7 kpl (26 to 30 mpg), or 25 to 28.8 metric ton-km per liter (60 to 75 ton-mi per gal) (Duleep 1992 in O'Rourke and Lawrence 1993, 11).

27. Emission inventories contain the relative contributions, current and projected, of emissions and pollution levels from mobile and stationary sources, drawing upon regional models and data (Harvey and Deakin 1993, 2-1–2-2).

28. Population and employment forecasts for a region may be provided by econometric models or derived from federal or state sources (Harvey and Deakin 1993, 3-11). Land use data are obtained from local land use plans. Local development policies are important to understanding potential constraints on land availability and development intensity (Shunk 1992, 107).

29. Putman reports, for example, that there are 14 MPOs in various stages of implementing DRAM-EMPAL for regional forecasting and policy evaluation efforts (Putman 1994, 1). Eleven have completed preliminary calibrations of both models using their own region's data and four are working on developing direct linkages between their transportation and land use models (Putman 1994, 2). Other land use models in use in the United States include POLIS in the San Francisco Bay Area, EMPIRIC in Atlanta, and PLUM in Washington, D.C. (Shunk 1992, 107).

30. In the early 1980s the entire ITLUP was distributed as a supplement to the Urban Transportation Planning System (UTPS) package, a travel demand modeling system package developed by the Federal Highway Administration (Harvey and Deakin 1993, 3-16).

31. The DRAM model, however, includes the income distribution of residential households, which is a proxy for several of these factors.

32. Many MPOs use the UTPS software package (Harvey and Deakin 1993, 3-5).

33. The MTC of the San Francisco Bay Area and the Puget Sound Council of Governments in the Seattle area have formal land use models, which are integrated into their regional travel demand models in a manner that allows for feedback between transportation and land use over time (Cambridge Systematics, Inc. 1991, 42). Cambridge Systematics, Inc., has been working with the Portland, Oregon, metropolitan area through the Land Use Transportation Air Quality Connection project to develop this capacity. Finally, the Southern California Association of Governments has recently completed a full test run of an integrated land use (DRAM-EMPAL)–transportation model (Putman 1994, 3).

34. Direct estimates of travel speed are not an output of travel demand models. Instead, link speeds are adjusted through an iterative process of assigning trips to the shortest network path to arrive at travel volume estimates (Meyer and Ross 1992, 6). Traffic volumes are often calibrated with actual traffic counts, but no attempt is made to check travel speeds or travel time against observed speeds (DeCorla-Souza 1993b, 5-6), with the result that model-derived speeds tend to overestimate actual link speeds, particularly under congested conditions (Meyer and Ross 1992, 6; Harvey and Deakin 1993, 3-63). Estimated traffic volumes on specific links may be in error by as much as 15 to 50 percent, depending on the total traffic volume on the link (DeCorla-Souza 1993b, 2).

35. Travel demand models provide no information on cold starts, because trips are not chained and travel is not tracked by time of day (Ducca 1993, 3). Travel demand models typically provide data on average weekday traffic levels by traffic zone. Hourly data on episode days by grid square, however, are needed for photochemical modeling (DeCorla-Souza 1993a, 3; Ducca 1993, 3). Information on vehicle type and age and vehicle operating mode cannot be directly obtained from travel demand model output (DeCorla-Souza 1993a, 4-5).

36. Some of the most common models for simulating traffic flows on freeways and estimating the effects of bottlenecks and ramp metering are FREQ, TRAFLO, and INTRAS. NETSIM was designed to simulate traffic changes from traffic signalization and intersection design improvements. TRANSYT and PASSER simulate traffic flows on arterials and changes in performance, such as travel times and delays that result from traffic flow improvement measures (Harvey and Deakin 1993, 3-77).

37. The U.S. Department of Transportation and the Environmental Protection Agency have already authorized $3 million; Department of Energy support is also being sought for a long-term program total of $25 million.
38. An analysis of instrumented vehicles driven in the Baltimore area for the FTP review found that about 18 percent of total Baltimore driving time was composed of higher speeds and sharper accelerations than those represented on the FTP [i.e., maximum speeds of 90.7 kph (56.7 mph) and maximum acceleration rates of 5.3 kph/sec (3.3 mph/sec)] (EPA 1993, 3-4).
39. An engine-based test procedure was adopted because engine manufacturers are distinct from truck manufacturers and because the same engine can be used with a wide variety of trucks with different transmissions and axles (see Appendix A).
40. The models are validated for predictive purposes on the basis of their ability to simulate adequately a base-year episode day of high concentrations of ozone (NRC 1991, 308).
41. Validation of emissions data is further complicated, as is discussed in the following chapter, by identifying what actual data (e.g., what drive cycle) to measure.

REFERENCES

ABBREVIATIONS

DOT	U.S. Department of Transportation
FHWA	Federal Highway Administration
EPA	Environmental Protection Agency
NRC	National Research Council
TRB	Transportation Research Board

AASHTO Journal. 1994. Browner Responds on NO_x Issue. Feb. 18, pp. 10–11.
An, F., and M. Ross. 1993a. Model of Fuel Economy and Driving Patterns. Presented at 72nd Annual Meeting of the Transportation Research Board, Washington, D.C., 22 pp.
An, F., and M. Ross. 1993b. A Model of Fuel Economy and Driving Patterns. No. 930328. Society of Automotive Engineers, International Congress and Exposition, Detroit, Mich., March 1–5, pp. 63–79.
An, F., M. Ross, and A. Bando. 1993. *How To Drive To Save Energy and Reduce Emissions in Your Daily Trip*. RCG/Hagler, Bailly, Inc., Arlington, Va., and The University of Michigan, Ann Arbor, 10 pp.
Bureau of the Census. 1990. *Truck Inventory and Use Survey*. 1987 Census of Transportation, TC87-T-52. U.S. Department of Commerce, Aug., 166 pp.

Cambridge Systematics, Inc. with Hague Consulting Group. 1991. *Making the Land Use Transportation Air Quality Connection: Vol. I: Modeling Practices.* Oct., 84 pp.

Conte, F. 1990. Trucking in the '90s: Emissions. *Owner Operator.* Sept., pp. 58–65.

Curran, T., T. Fitz-Simons, W. Freas, J. Hemby, D. Mintz, S. Nizich, B. Parzygnat, and M. Wayland. 1994. *National Air Quality and Emissions Trends Report, 1993.* 454-R-94-026. U.S. Environmental Protection Agency. Research Triangle Park, N.C., Oct., 157 pp.

Davis, S.C. 1994. *Transportation Energy Data Book: Edition 14.* ORNL-6798. Center for Transportation Analysis, Energy Division, Oak Ridge National Laboratory, Tenn., May.

Deakin, E. 1991. *Scoping Study: Impact of Highway Congestion on Air Quality.* University of California at Berkeley, March, 22 pp.

DeCorla-Souza, P. 1993a. Travel and Emissions Model Interactions. Presented at Transportation-Air Quality Conference, Washington, D.C., Feb. 23–26.

DeCorla-Souza, P. 1993b. Travel Forecasting Process. Presented at Transportation-Air Quality Conference, Washington, D.C., Feb. 23–26.

DeLuchi, M., D.L. Greene, and Q. Wang. 1993. *Motor-Vehicle Fuel-Economy: The Forgotten Hydrocarbon Control Strategy?* UCD-ITS-RR-93-3. Institute of Transportation Studies, University of California, Davis, Jan., 25 pp.

Dockery, D.W., A. Pope, X. Xu, J.D. Spengler, J.H. Ware, M.E. Fay, B.G. Ferris, and F.E. Speizer. 1993. An Association Between Air Pollution and Mortality in Six U.S. Cities. *New England Journal of Medicine*, Vol. 329, No. 24, Dec. 9, pp. 1754–1808.

DOT and EPA. 1993. *Clean Air Through Transportation: Challenges in Meeting National Air Quality Standards.* Aug.

Ducca, F.W. 1993. *Future Directions in Travel Forecasting.* Federal Highway Administration, U.S. Department of Transportation, 9 pp.

Duleep, K.G. 1992. Analysis of Heavy Duty Fuel Efficiency to 2001. Presented at 71st Annual Meeting of the Transportation Research Board, Washington, D.C.

Effa, R.C., and L.C. Larsen. 1993. Development of Real-World Driving Cycles for Estimating Facility-Specific Emissions from Light-Duty Vehicles. Presented at the Air and Waste Management Association Specialty Conference on The Emission Inventory: Perception and Reality, Pasadena, Calif., Oct. 18–20, 20 pp.

Enns, P., J. German, and J. Markey. 1993. *EPA's Survey of In-Use Driving Patterns: Implications for Mobile Source Emission Inventories.* Office of Mobile Sources, U.S. Environmental Protection Agency.

EPA. 1993. *Federal Test Procedure Review Project: Preliminary Technical Report.* Office of Mobile Sources, May, 161 pp.

Evans, L., R. Herman, and T. Lam. 1974. *Multivariate Analysis of Traffic Factors Related to Fuel Consumption in Urban Driving*. GMR-1710. Research Laboratories, General Motors Corporation, Warren, Mich., Oct.

Federal Register. 1993. Criteria and Procedures for Determining Conformity to State or Federal Implementation Plans of Transportation Plans, Programs, and Projects Funded or Approved Under Title 23 U.S.C. or the Federal Transit Act. Vol. 58, No. 225, Nov. 24, 62,188–62,253.

FHWA. 1992. *Transportation and Air Quality: Searching for Solutions: A Policy Discussion Series*. No. 5, FHWA-PL-92-029. U.S. Department of Transportation, Aug., 30 pp.

FHWA. 1993. *Highway Statistics 1992*. FHWA-PL-93-023. U.S. Department of Transportation, 235 pp.

Gordon, D. 1991. *Steering a New Course: Transportation, Energy, and the Environment*. Island Press, Washington, D.C., 244 pp.

Greco, R. 1985. *Motor Vehicle Tampering Survey—1984*. Office of Air and Radiation, U.S. Environmental Protection Agency, July.

Greene, D.L., D. Sperling, and B. McNutt. 1988. Transportation Energy to the Year 2020. In *Special Report 220: A Look Ahead: Year 2020*. Transportation Research Board, National Research Council, Washington, D.C., pp. 207–231.

Guensler, R., D. Sperling, and P. Jovanis. 1991. *Uncertainty in the Emission Inventory for Heavy-Duty Diesel-Powered Trucks*. UCD-ITS-RR-91-02. Institute of Transportation Studies, University of California, Davis, June, 146 pp.

Guensler, R. 1993. *Transportation Data Needs for Evolving Emission Inventory Models*. Institute of Transportation Studies, University of California, Davis, 27 pp.

Guensler, R. 1994. *Vehicle Emission Rates and Average Operating Speeds*. Ph.D. dissertation. University of California, Davis.

Harvey, G., and E. Deakin. 1991. *Toward Improved Regional Transportation Modeling Practice*. Deakin Harvey Skabardonis, Inc., Berkeley, Calif., Dec., 68 pp.

Harvey, G., and E. Deakin. 1993. *A Manual of Regional Transportation Modeling Practice for Air Quality Analysis*. Deakin Harvey Skabardonis, Inc., Berkeley, Calif., with Cambridge Systematics, COMSIS, Dowling Associates, Gary Hawthorne Associates, Parsons Brinckerhoff Quade & Douglas, and Ann Stevens Associates, July.

Heywood, J.B. 1988. *Internal Combustion Engine Fundamentals*. McGraw-Hill Book Company.

Horowitz, J.L. 1982. *Air Quality Analysis for Urban Transportation Planning*. MIT Press, Cambridge, Mass., 387 pp.

Johnson, J.H. 1988. Automotive Emissions. *Air Pollution, the Automobile, and Public Health*. Health Effects Institute. National Academy Press, Washington, D.C.

Lilly, L.R.C. (ed.). 1984. *Diesel Reference Book.* Butterworths, Boston, Mass.

MacKenzie, J.J., and M.P. Walsh. 1990. *Driving Forces: Motor Vehicle Trends and Their Implications for Global Warming, Energy Strategies, and Transportation Planning.* World Resources Institute, Washington, D.C., Dec., 49 pp.

McGill, R. 1985. *Fuel Consumption and Emission Values for Traffic Models.* FHWA/RD-85/053. Oak Ridge National Laboratory, Tenn., May, 90 pp.

Meyer, M., and C. Ross. 1992. *Transportation and Air Quality Modeling: Fitting a Square Block into a Round Hole.* Georgia Institute of Technology, Atlanta, 11 pp.

Meyer, M.D., M. Rodgers, C. Ross, F.M. Saunders, and C.T Ripberger. 1993. *A Study of Enrichment Activities in the Atlanta Road Network,* pp. 225–233.

Murrell, D. 1980. *Passenger Car Fuel Economy: EPA and Road.* U.S. Environmental Protection Agency, Jan., 305 pp.

Naghavi, B., and P. Stopher. 1993. Remote Sensing, Means, Medians, and Extreme Values: Some Implications for Reducing Automobile Emissions. Presented at 72nd Annual Meeting of the Transportation Research Board, Washington, D.C., 28 pp.

Nizich, S.V., T.C. McMullen, and D.C. Misenheimer. 1994. *National Air Pollutant Emissions Trends, 1900–1993.* EPA-454/R-94-027. Office of Air Quality Planning and Standards, Research Triangle Park, N.C., Oct., 314 pp.

NRC. 1990. *Confronting Climate Change: Strategies for Energy Research and Development.* National Academy Press, Washington, D.C.

NRC. 1991. *Rethinking the Ozone Problem in Urban and Regional Air Pollution.* National Academy Press, Washington, D.C., 489 pp.

NRC. 1992. *Automotive Fuel Economy: How Far Should We Go?* National Academy Press, Washington, D.C., 259 pp.

O'Connor, K., L.L. Duvall, and R.G. Ireson. 1993. *Intersection Air Quality Modeling: Review of Ambient Data and Current Modeling Practices: Vol. 2: Survey on Current Practices in Air Quality Modeling.* Systems Applications International, San Rafael, Calif., 49 pp.

O'Rourke, L., and M.F. Lawrence. 1993. Strategies for Goods Movement in a Sustainable Transportation System. Presented at Transportation and Energy Strategies for a Sustainable Transportation System, Asilomar Conference System, Pacific Grove, Calif., Aug. 23, 35 pp.

Outwater, M.L., and W.R. Loudon. 1994. Travel Forecasting Guidelines for the Federal and California Clean Air Act. Presented at 73rd Annual Meeting of the Transportation Research Board, Washington, D.C., 24 pp.

Putman, S. 1991. *DRAM/EMPAL ITLUP: Integrated Transportation Land-Use Activity Allocation Models: General Description.* S.H. Putman Associates, Philadelphia, Pa., Jan.

Putman, S. 1993. Sensitivity Tests with Employment and Household Location Modes. Presented at Third International Conference on Computers in Urban Planning and Urban Management, Georgia Institute of Technology, Atlanta, July 23–25.

Putman, S. 1994. Integrated Transportation and Land Use Models: An Overview of Progress with DRAM and EMPAL with Suggestions for Further Research. Presented at 73rd Annual Meeting of the Transportation Research Board, Washington, D.C., 28 pp.

Shunk, G.A. 1992. Urban Transportation Systems. In *Transportation Planning Handbook* (J.D. Edwards, Jr., ed.), Institute of Transportation Engineers, Prentice Hall, N.J., pp. 88–122.

Sierra Research, Inc. 1993. *Evaluation of "MOBILE" Vehicle Emission Model.* Report SR93-12-02. Sacramento, Calif., Dec. 7.

Stedman, D. 1991. Presentation at The Transportation-Land Use-Air Quality Connection: A Policy and Research Symposium. Public Policy Program, University of California Extension at Los Angeles, Lake Arrowhead, Calif., Nov. 6–8.

Weaver, C.S., and R.F. Klausmeier. 1988. *Heavy-Duty Diesel Vehicle Inspection and Maintenance Study. Final Report, Volume II: Quantifying the Problem.* Radian Corporation, Sacramento, Calif., May 16.

Wegener, M. 1994. Operational Urban Models: State of the Art. *Journal of the American Planning Association*, Vol. 60, No. 1, Winter, pp. 17–29.

3
Traffic Flow Characteristics

Highway capacity enhancement projects have long been viewed as providing emission reductions and energy efficiencies by contributing to freer-flowing traffic conditions. In this chapter, the current knowledge about the initial effects of highway capacity additions on emissions and energy use is presented. Gaps and uncertainties in current understanding are identified. Finally, a summary appraisal of the factors most likely to affect outcomes is given, and recommendations for improving the state of knowledge are made.

OVERVIEW OF EXPECTED IMPACTS

The shaded box in Figure 3-1 illustrates the fundamental relationships involved in analyzing the initial impacts of a highway capacity addition. The primary impacts are changes in traffic flow patterns on the facilities affected by the improvement. Expansion of highway capacity should reduce the probability of stop-and-start traffic, raise average ve-

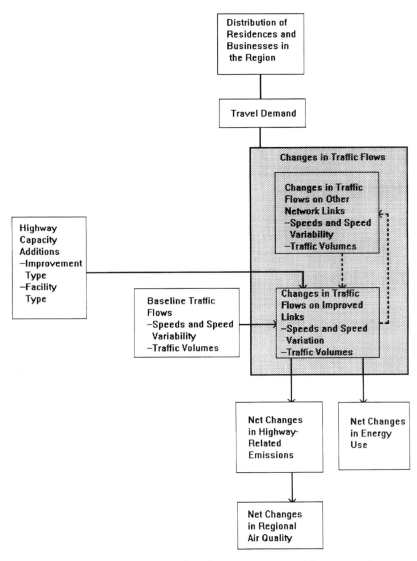

FIGURE 3-1 Initial impacts of highway capacity additions and effects on air quality and energy use.

hicle speeds, and reduce speed variability (i.e., smooth the traffic flow). All else being equal, stop-and-start traffic, low speeds, and highly variable speeds are all associated with high emission levels and poor fuel economy. Expansion of highway capacity should also reduce traffic density[1] and improve levels of service (LOS) on the affected facilities.

As capacity is added and congestion is eased on one link in the system, the effects will spill over onto other routes. Travelers who divert from other routes or shift their time of travel to take advantage of the new capacity will affect traffic flow patterns and traffic volumes on the broader network of highways (Figure 3-1), making the task of assessing the net effects on emissions and energy use more complex.

Highway capacity additions can also affect other modes of travel. New capacity that reduces highway congestion and commuting time may encourage mass transit riders to switch back to their cars. Bicycle and pedestrian travel may be discouraged if the capacity addition (e.g., intersection widening) improves traffic flow patterns for automobiles and trucks to the detriment of slower-moving modes.

The effects on travel demand of all these network changes—route shifts, shifts in time of travel, and mode shifts—are considered in Chapter 4; this chapter is focused primarily on the effects of these changes on the physical traffic flow. For the purpose of analyzing the initial impacts of highway capacity additions, travel demand is assumed to remain constant. Any additional traffic volume on expanded highway links is presumed to be a reallocation of existing traffic.

Determining the net energy and emissions effects of changes in traffic flow patterns from a highway capacity addition also requires taking into account the construction phase of the project. Construction of certain capacity projects may cause traffic delays and create stop-and-start traffic conditions conducive to high emission levels.

Finally, determining net effects depends on the consequences if the project is not undertaken: whether congestion will worsen if the new capacity is not added, whether there is adequate capacity in the system to avert congestion if travelers shift their travel routes and times of travel, or whether investments in other modes (e.g., transit and bicycle facilities) can accommodate travel needs. These outcomes must be compared with those of the "build" option to determine net effects.

REVIEW OF EFFECTS ON EMISSIONS

Effects of Changes in Traffic Flow Patterns

Drive Cycles and Average Speed

A motor vehicle trip consists of a beginning and an end connected by a series of accelerations, decelerations, constant speed cruising, and idling. To measure emissions and fuel consumption, trips are simulated on laboratory dynamometers and motor vehicles are tested using standardized drive cycles. Each drive cycle is composed of a unique profile of stops, starts, constant speed cruises, accelerations, and decelerations and is characterized by an overall average speed (Guensler 1994, 24). All vehicle trips at the same average speed are assumed to have the same underlying drive cycle regardless of facility type, roadway conditions (e.g., grade), or driver behavior.

Different drive cycles are used to represent driving under different traffic conditions (Guensler and Geraghty 1991, 5–6). For example, the New York City cycle with an average trip speed of 11.4 kph (7.1 mph) reflects city driving at very heavy levels of congestion; vehicle speeds are low and vehicle movements consist primarily of stops, starts, and accelerations (Figure 3-2). The Highway Fuel Economy Test cycle with an average speed of 77.3 kph (48.3 mph) was originally created to reflect rural highway driving. Vehicle speeds are higher and there is more cruise-speed driving, although accelerations are still evident (Figure 3-2). As discussed in the following sections, however, current drive cycles do not adequately represent real-world driving conditions.

Estimates from Current Emission Models

Current estimates of emission rates embodied in the Environmental Protection Agency's (EPA's) MOBILE model and the California Air Resources Board's (CARB's) EMFAC model are expressed as functions of average speeds and are based on vehicle testing on a limited number of drive cycles.

Baseline emission rates for light-duty motor vehicles are derived from the Federal Test Procedure (FTP) cycle. Emission rates at other average speeds are calculated by testing automobiles on 11 other drive

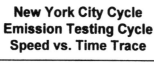

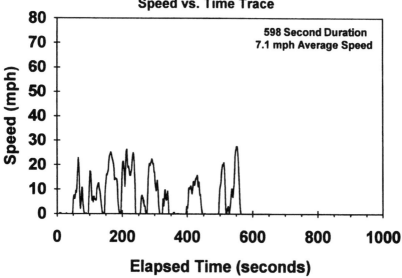

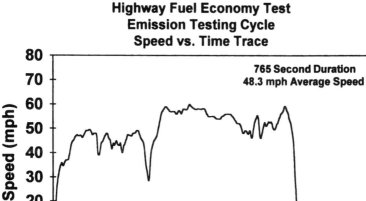

FIGURE 3-2 Drive cycles illustrating low-speed and high-speed driving profiles (Guensler 1994, Appendix A). Note: 1 mph = 1.6 kph.

cycles and heavy-duty trucks on 4 drive cycles, including a baseline composite cycle (Table 3-1); adjusting baseline rates with the appropriate speed correction factors; and applying them to the appropriate vehicle class (see accompanying text box).[2]

The resulting average trip speed–emission curves (Figures 2-4 to 2-9) can be used to give a preliminary estimate of a highway capacity addition's effect on emissions by comparing the distribution of traffic speeds on the affected highway links before and after the project (Figure 3-1). These curves can also be used to estimate predicted emission levels for the affected highway links both with and without the project. The comparisons are not exact, however, because average trip speeds are not equivalent to link-specific speeds for portions of vehicle trips.

According to current models, if traffic is heavily congested and contributes to low average trip speeds [i.e., below 32 kph (20 mph)], capacity enhancements should initially reduce emissions of carbon monoxide (CO) and volatile organic compounds (VOCs) for automobiles and emissions of CO, VOC, and oxides of nitrogen (NO_x) for heavy-duty diesel vehicles (HDDVs). Reductions in NO_x emissions are likely to be small for automobiles; these emissions increase with speed at low average trip speeds [i.e., above 32 kph (20 mph) according to the MOBILE model and above 56 kph (35 mph) according to the EMFAC model]. If traffic is moderately to lightly congested and average trip speeds following a capacity addition exceed about 80 kph (50 mph), emissions initially should increase for all pollutants for automobiles and for NO_x for HDDVs. Emissions of CO and VOCs should remain relatively flat at high speeds for HDDVs.

If congestion is moderate and initial and final average trip speeds are in the intermediate range where the curves flatten out [i.e., between 32 and 80 kph (20 and 50 mph)], then capacity enhancement projects should only result in small emissions changes for both automobiles and HDDVs; emissions of CO and VOCs should be slightly reduced but partially offset by rising emissions of NO_x.

Modeled emissions estimates for particulates as a function of speed are unavailable, but industry data suggest that diesel particulate exhaust emissions follow the same trend as VOC emissions (i.e., they decline) up to about 80 kph (50 mph). Particulate exhaust emission levels at higher speeds are not well understood (Appendix A).

TABLE 3-1 Speed Correction Factor Emission Testing Cycles
(Guensler 1994, 24, 25, 31; Appendix A; Guensler et al. 1991, 40)

| CYCLE | AVERAGE SPEED | | NO. OF VEHICLES TESTED |
	MPH	KPH	
Light-Duty Vehicles[a]			
Low Speed 1	2.5	4.0	236
Low Speed 2	3.6	5.8	236
Low Speed 3	4.0	6.4	236
New York City Cycle	7.1	11.4	464
Speed Cycle 12	12.1	19.4	464
Federal Test Procedure			
MOBILE	19.6	31.4	533
EMFAC	16.0	25.6	533
Speed Cycle 36	35.9	57.4	489
Highway Fuel Economy Test	48.3	77.3	533
High Speed 1	45.1	72.2	25
High Speed 2	51.0	81.6	25
High Speed 3	57.8	92.5	69
High Speed 4	64.4	103.0	69
Heavy-Duty Diesel Trucks			
New York Nonfreeway	7.3	11.7	22[c]
Los Angeles Nonfreeway	16.8	26.9	22
Composite[b]	18.8	30.1	22
Los Angeles Freeway	46.9	75.0	22

[a]All of the testing cycles are conducted with vehicles in the hot stabilized mode with the exception of the FTP for the MOBILE model, which includes the weighted emission contributions from hot and cold start operations.

[b]The composite, baseline cycle is composed of the Los Angeles Freeway cycle and three nonfreeway cycles—the Los Angeles Nonfreeway and the New York Nonfreeway repeated twice.

[c]Thirty diesel engines were tested, but results from only 22 were used (9 medium heavy-duty trucks and 13 heavy heavy-duty trucks) to develop emission rate estimates.

CALCULATION OF VEHICLE EMISSION RATES AND DERIVATION OF SPEED CORRECTION FACTORS

Baseline emission rates were derived by driving thousands of new and in-use light-duty motor vehicles through the Federal Test Procedure (FTP), an emission test composed of a defined cycle of starts, stops, accelerations, and constant-speed cruises conducted on laboratory dynamometers (computerized treadmills). Emissions are collected in bags (part in the start mode, both cold and hot—Bags 1 and 3, respectively—and part in the hot stabilized mode—Bag 2). For the EPA MOBILE model, the emissions from vehicles operating in all three phases are used to calculate baseline emissions. The baseline emission rate (calculated in grams per mile) for a vehicle class is the averaged result from the three phases of the FTP for that vehicle class operating at an average speed of 31.6 kph (19.6 mph), the average test speed of the entire FTP. For the California EMFAC model, the baseline emission rate is the average emission result for the vehicle class operating under Bag 2 of the FTP, the hot stabilized cycle with an average operating speed of 25.6 kph (16 mph) (Guensler et al. 1993, 3–4).

To estimate the emission rate for any vehicle at an average operating speed other than that of the FTP, the baseline emission rate is multiplied by the appropriate speed correction factor (SCF) associated with the applicable vehicle class and the operating speed to be modeled. SCFs are derived statistically. Emission data are again gathered from vehicles operating in the hot stabilized mode (Bag 2) on a number of different drive cycles with different profiles of stops, starts, constant speed cruises, and accelerations; each cycle has a different overall average speed. The SCFs are derived by regressing the average cycle speed on the average emission rate for the cycle (grams per mile from the aggregate bag sample of emissions and cycle distance). Thus, speed-corrected emission rates used in emission models are related to the average cycle speed and not to constant cruise speeds (Guensler and Geraghty 1991, 5–6).

MOBILE5 baseline emission rates and SCFs for heavy-duty diesel trucks are based on tests using chassis dynamometers of 30 in-use heavy-duty diesel trucks (tests from 22 diesel engines were usable) on three drive cycles and a composite baseline cycle with the vehicles operating in the hot stabilized (Bag 2) mode (Appendix A). CARB has used the same SCFs in its EMFAC model, although new factors are under development (Appendix A).

Certainty of Emission Estimates from Current Models

Unfortunately, estimates of the emission effects of changes in traffic flow patterns from a highway capacity addition are not nearly as precise as implied by the complex functions used to derive the speed-corrected emission rates. First, current model estimates are based on a limited set of drive cycles (Table 3-1) that inadequately represent specific traffic flow conditions. Many of the drive cycles on which emission estimates are based were developed decades ago (the FTP is more than 20 years old), when laboratory testing equipment capabilities were more limited.[3] They are not believed to be representative of current real-world driving conditions (Effa and Larsen 1993, 1).[4] For example, a comparison of three cycles with approximately the same average speed—the baseline FTP cycle and two cycles recently developed from driving on arterial roads and freeways in the Los Angeles area—shows the extent to which the baseline FTP drive cycle underestimates driving at higher speeds and accelerations, both of which are believed to be sources of high emissions (Figures 3-3 and 3-4).[5]

Another problem is that little effort has been devoted to the development of driving cycles that represent high-speed operation. The only cycle developed from actual data on in-use operation is the Highway Fuel Economy Test, with an average speed of 77.3 kph (48.3 mph) (Figure 3-2, bottom). Because vehicles routinely travel at substantially higher average speeds on freeways, CARB developed a series of higher-speed cycles (Figure 3-5). Each uses the same portion of the Highway Fuel Economy Test cycle except that more time is allowed at the beginning and end for vehicles to accelerate to a higher initial cruising speed and to decelerate to a stop. The vehicles are required to perform the same accelerations at successively higher speeds, increasing engine power demands and the likelihood of higher emissions. The problem with this approach is that the cycles have not been validated with actual on-road data from customer service, and thus the resulting emissions estimates may be biased and may not represent real-world operation.

A second issue related to the certainty of emission estimates is that current models predict the effects of changes in traffic flow characteristics on emissions solely on the basis of changes in average speed. This one-dimensional approach cannot adequately describe the un-

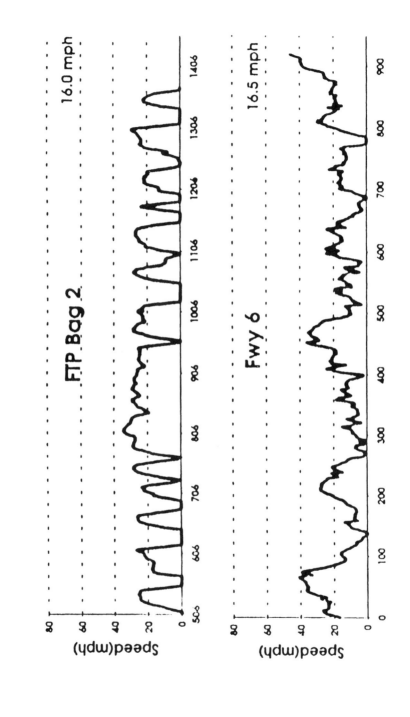

FTP Bag 2

16.0 mph

Fwy 6

16.5 mph

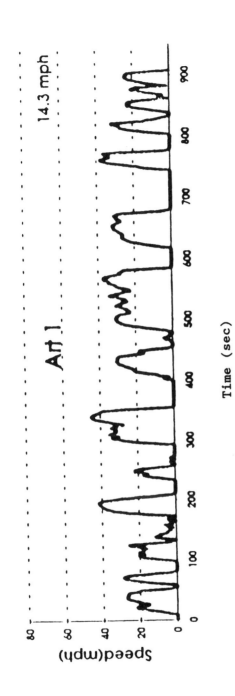

FIGURE 3-3 Speed-time traces of driving cycles with similar mean speeds (Effa and Larsen 1993, 18).
Note: 1 mph = 1.6 kph.

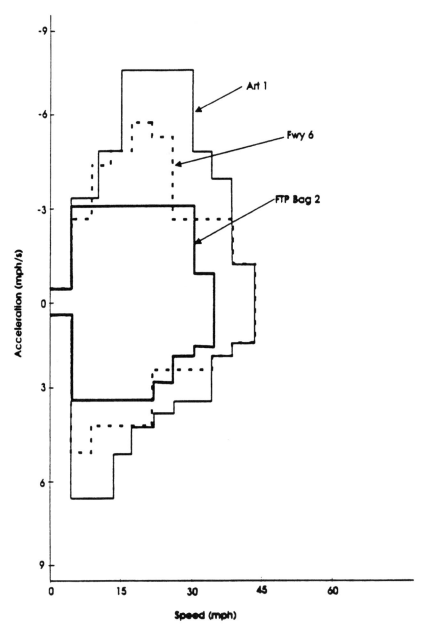

FIGURE 3-4 Envelope of speeds and accelerations for three cycles with similar mean speeds (Effa and Larsen 1993, 20). Note: 1 mph = 1.6 kph.

derlying distribution of speeds and accelerations, which vary by type of facility and level of congestion and produce potentially large variations in emission levels. For example, existing emission models do not distinguish between driving on arterial highways and driving on freeways (Figure 3-6), although each has quite distinct frequency distributions for speed and acceleration, likely to result in different emission levels (Effa and Larsen 1993, 19).

Finally, current models cannot accurately predict emission rate changes for light-duty vehicles for a wide range of changes in average trip speeds. As will be shown, many of these speed changes are within the range of average speed changes expected from highway capacity additions. Guensler (1994) examined the confidence intervals[6] for changes in predicted emission rates of CO, VOC, and NO_x for late-model-year, fuel-injected, light-duty vehicles as a function of changes in average trip speeds using the EMFAC model.[7] Figure 3-7a shows the results for speed changes in 8-kph (5-mph) increments for CO, VOC, and NO_x; the initial average trip speed is shown on the x axis. Speed changes in 16-kph (10-mph) and 32-kph (20-mph) increments are shown in Figures 3-7b and 3-7c.

With the exception of NO_x, variances are large relative to predicted changes in emissions. In many cases the lower bound of the confidence interval is negative and the upper bound is positive, so that it is impossible to determine the direction, much less the magnitude, of the expected change (Guensler 1994, 167). For example, the 95 percent confidence interval for the reduction in CO emissions associated with an increase in average trip speeds from 64 kph (40 mph) to 72 kph (45 mph) encompasses a 40 percent reduction and a 19 percent increase in emission rates (Figure 3-7a). Even for NO_x emission changes, which have small variances, the questionable representativeness of the drive cycles on which the estimates are based leaves the validity of the results uncertain.

The committee did not conduct an in-depth review of the statistical approaches used to generate the confidence intervals, but it believes that the analysis illustrates the uncertainty of emission rate estimates based on current models. The analysis also suggests that current models do not reflect important explanatory variables that can significantly affect emission levels, such as the incidence of sharp accelerations at lower and moderate speeds.

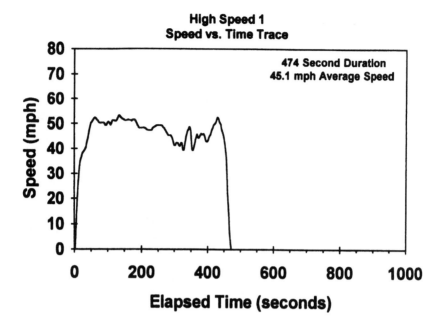

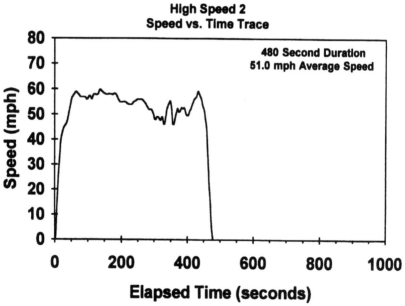

FIGURE 3-5 High-speed drive test cycles (Guensler 1994, Appendix A). Note: 1 mph = 1.6 kph.

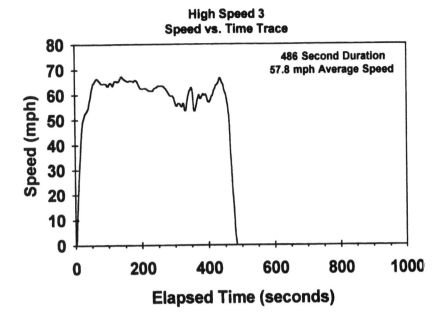

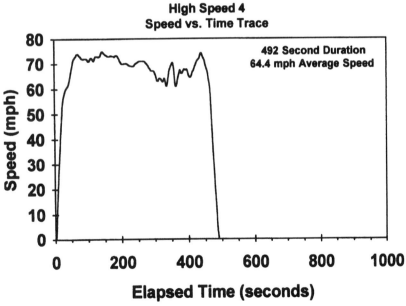

FIGURE 3-5 (*continued*)

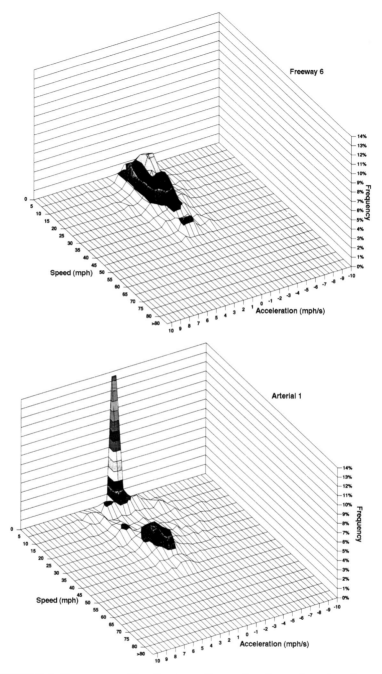

FIGURE 3-6 Frequency distribution of speed and acceleration for freeway and arterial driving cycles with similar mean speeds (Effa and Larsen 1993, 19). Note: 1 mph = 1.6 kph.

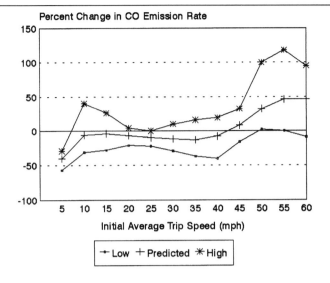

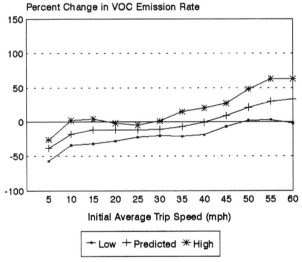

FIGURE 3-7a Predicted percent changes in emission rates, measured in grams per mile, by pollutant for an 8-kph (5-mph) increase in average trip speed with 95 percent confidence intervals (Guensler 1994). Note: Assumes 1986 and later model year fuel-injected vehicles; base emission rates represent Bag 2 emissions estimates at 26 kph (16 mph) for vehicles tested in the CARB speed correction factor data base. 1 mph = 1.6 kph. (*continued on next page*)

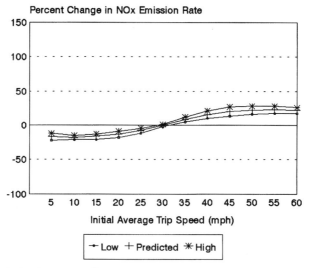

FIGURE 3-7a (*continued*)

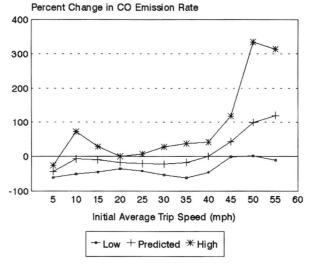

FIGURE 3-7b Predicted percent changes in emission rates, measured in grams per mile, by pollutant for a 16-kph (10-mph) increase in average trip speed with 95 percent confidence intervals (Guensler 1994). Note: Assumes 1986 and later model year fuel-injected vehicles; base emission rates represent Bag 2 emissions estimates at 26 kph (16 mph) for vehicles tested in the CARB speed correction factor data base. 1 mph = 1.6 kph. (*continued on next page*)

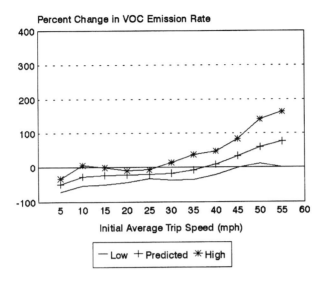

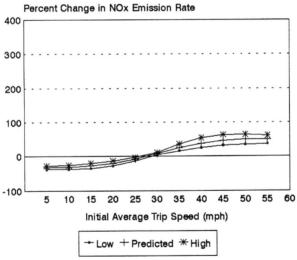

FIGURE 3-7b (*continued*)

Diesel emissions have not received the same scrutiny as emissions from gasoline-powered light-duty vehicles. Although emission estimates for HDDVs are based on a very limited number of drive cycles, the variance in their emission performance is believed to be considerably less than that of light-duty vehicles (a complete discussion of the emissions and energy characteristics of heavy-duty, diesel-

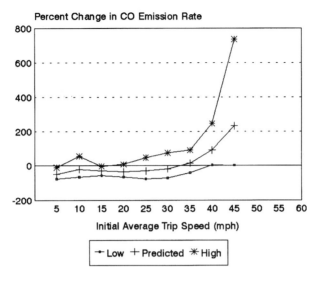

Percent Change in CO Emission Rate

Initial Average Trip Speed (mph)

— Low + Predicted * High

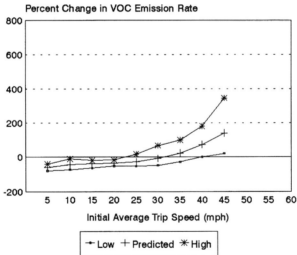

Percent Change in VOC Emission Rate

Initial Average Trip Speed (mph)

— Low + Predicted * High

FIGURE 3-7c Predicted percent changes in emission rates, measured in grams per mile, by pollutant for a 32-kph (20-mph) increase in average trip speed with 95 percent confidence intervals (Guensler 1994). Note: Assumes 1986 and later model year fuel-injected vehicles; base emission rates represent Bag 2 emissions estimates at 26 kph (16 mph) for vehicles tested in the CARB speed correction factor data base. 1 mph = 1.6 kph. (*continued on next page*)

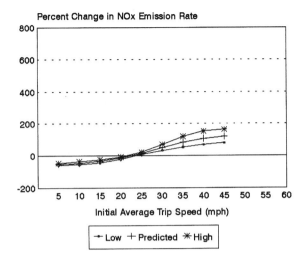

FIGURE 3-7c (*continued*)

powered trucks and buses is presented in Appendix A). Diesel engine emissions can be predicted with greater certainty because the process of generating and controlling them is less complex than is the process for cars (i.e., HDDVs do not yet have exhaust aftertreatment; modeling their emissions thus does not require predicting catalyst efficiency). Diesel engines also require little cold start or acceleration enrichment, which significantly increases the variation in emission levels for light-duty vehicles (Appendix A).[8]

Important exceptions to these generalizations exist. The absence of data on particulate matter exhaust emissions as a function of speed is troublesome. HDDVs are the primary highway vehicle source of these emissions, and particulate concentrations are a risk factor for lung cancer. In addition, particulates are the most sensitive of all regulated diesel emissions to deterioration and malperformance of vehicle components from poor maintenance or tampering (Appendix A). Engineering analysis suggests that estimates of other diesel exhaust emissions may be incorrect at high speeds. In particular, diesel emissions of NO_x at very high speeds [e.g., 112 kph (70 mph)] are probably overstated, whereas diesel emissions of VOCs at similar speeds are probably understated by current model estimates (Appendix A).

In summary, although considerable research and vehicle testing have been performed, no definitive conclusions can be reached about how highway capacity additions and their effects on traffic flow characteristics change vehicle emission levels. The analysis requires examination of relatively small changes in average trip speeds using emissions data with large variances. In addition, the data are based on a small number of test cycles that do not adequately represent real-world driving conditions. Finally, the application of models based on average trip speeds to facility-specific speeds reflecting portions of trips is inappropriate. Emission models were not developed to provide microscale detail on vehicles traveling on particular highway links; their original purpose was to provide macroscale data on transportation emissions for input into emission inventories.

Linking Emissions Estimates with Data on Traffic Flow Characteristics

Analyzing the effects of highway capacity additions on emissions also requires accurate baseline data on traffic flow patterns to which emission rates can be applied. Traffic engineers have developed speed-flow-density relationships for different types of highway facilities on the basis of field surveys and have linked these critical traffic flow variables to operational levels of service. The speed-flow curve for freeways (Figure 3-8) shows that average travel speeds are relatively high and stable for a wide range of service conditions, averaging between 88 and 112 kph (55 and 70 mph) for LOS A through C.[9] Average travel speeds fall only under more heavily congested conditions (i.e., LOS D and E) and then only by a modest amount—to between 80 and 96 kph (50 and 60 mph) until breakdown levels (LOS F) occur. Less extensive data for urban arterials, which link average speeds with LOS, indicate much lower average travel speeds in general and a wider divergence between free-flow speeds (LOS A) and speeds under more heavily congested conditions (LOS D and E). Table 3-2 displays these differences.

These speed-capacity relationships by type of facility can be used to predict the likely distribution of traffic speeds and speed variation before and after different types of capacity projects, and the likely ef-

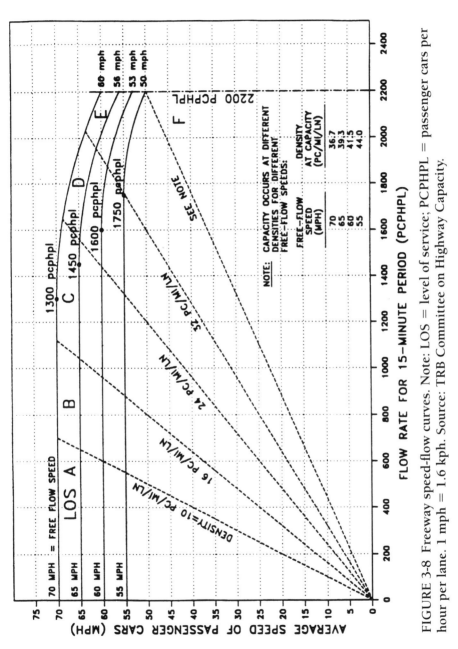

FIGURE 3-8 Freeway speed-flow curves. Note: LOS = level of service; PCPHPL = passenger cars per hour per lane. 1 mph = 1.6 kph. Source: TRB Committee on Highway Capacity.

TABLE 3-2 Urban Arterial Speed–Level of Service Relationships and Arterial Class Characteristics

	ARTERIAL CLASS		
	I (SUBURBAN DESIGN)	II (INTERMEDIATE)	III (URBAN DESIGN)
Range of free-flow speeds			
Miles per hour	45 to 35	35 to 30	35 to 25
Kilometers per hour	72 to 56	56 to 48	56 to 40
Typical free-flow speeds			
Miles per hour	40	33	27
Kilometers per hour	64	53	43
Average travel speed (mph)			
Level of Service A	35	30	25
Level of Service B	28	24	19
Level of Service C	22	18	13
Level of Service D	17	14	9
Level of Service E	13	10	7
Level of Service F	13	10	7
Average travel speed (kph)			
Level of Service A	56	48	40
Level of Service B	45	38	30
Level of Service C	35	29	21
Level of Service D	27	22	14
Level of Service E	21	16	11
Level of Service F	21	16	11

Design category			
Control of access	Partial to almost full	Partial	Little or no control
Arterial type	Multilane divided; two-lane with shoulders	Multilane divided or undivided; one-way; two-lane	Undivided one-way; two-way, two or more lanes
Parking	No parking	Some parking	Parking permitted
Separate left-turn lanes	Yes	Some	No
Signals per mile	1 to 4	4 to 8	8 to 12
Speed Limits			
Miles per hour	40 to 45	30 to 40	25 to 35
Kilometers per hour	64 to 72	48 to 64	40 to 56
Pedestrian interference	None	None	Some
Roadside development	Low density	Moderate	High density

SOURCE: TRB Committee on Highway Capacity, 1993.

fect of these changes on emissions. The accompanying text box shows typical before and after speeds for a range of capacity projects on freeways and arterial roads, which range from about an increase of 8 kph (5 mph) for capacity-enhancing, traffic engineering improvements to an increase of 32 to 48 kph (20 to 30 mph) for new freeway lanes. Many speed changes are small although the variance in emission changes is large (Figure 3-7a).

Traffic simulation models are generally used to estimate traffic flow changes on affected facility links as the result of highway capacity expansions. As with emission models, however, most currently available traffic simulation models provide data only on average vehicle speeds. For several of the microscale models—which involve tracking individual vehicles—vehicle flow profiles showing the distribution of vehicle accelerations, decelerations, cruise speed operations, and idling could be made available with modest revisions to the programs (Table 3-3). Traffic flow data also could be made available by vehicle type (Table 3-3). However, modeled estimates of vehicle velocities and accelerations should be validated with actual on-road vehicle operation data if they are to be used to provide inputs to emission models. Because variance in vehicle operation has a significant effect on emissions, the accuracy of these inputs is critical.

Some traffic simulation models (e.g., NETSIM and FRESIM) already provide data on emissions and fuel use for light-duty vehicles. However, the emissions estimates are based on a limited and dated sample of vehicles (15 light-duty, 1981 to 1984 model-year vehicles) and reflect steady-state operating conditions.[10]

Status of Current Research and Modeling Efforts

Research on In-Use Vehicle Emissions and Emission Modeling Improvements

Research that should improve understanding of the emission characteristics of motor vehicles under real-world driving conditions has begun. A significant investment is required to expand and accelerate this effort so that a better emission rate model can be developed and incorporated into the regulatory process.

**TYPICAL BEFORE AND AFTER AVERAGE SPEEDS FOR
SELECTED HIGHWAY CAPACITY PROJECTS**

Freeway Capacity Additions
New freeway lanes
   40–56 kph (25–35 mph) to 88 kph (55 mph)
HOV lanes
   56 kph (35 mph) to 96 kph (60 mph) in the HOV lane
   56 kph (35 mph) to 67 kph (42 mph) in non-HOV lanes
Freeway ramp metering
   72 kph (45 mph) to 48 kph (30 mph) on the ramp
   88 kph (55 mph) to 91 kph (57 mph) on the freeway

Arterial Capacity Additions
New arterial lanes
   48 kph (30 mph) to 56 kph (35 mph) in mid-block only
Intersection grade separation
   40 kph (25 mph) to 56 kph (35 mph)
Major intersection improvement
   40 kph (25 mph) to 48 kph (30 mph)
Other traffic engineering improvements
   48 kph (30 mph) to 56 kph (35 mph)
   64 kph (40 mph) to 72 kph (45 mph)

NOTE: Changes in average speeds are estimated only for the
improved link. HOV = high occupancy vehicle.
SOURCE: W.R. Reilly, Catalina Engineering, Inc., March 10, 1994

The research to date has focused on the effects of such driving patterns on emissions as sharp accelerations and high speeds. Neither is well represented by current drive cycles, and they are suspected of being major reasons for current underestimation of emission levels (LeBlanc et al. 1994, 2). The research was initiated in response to a requirement of the Clean Air Act Amendments of 1990 (CAAA) that EPA review current vehicle testing procedures to ensure that they re-

TABLE 3-3 Data Available on Traffic Flow Patterns and Vehicle Characteristics from a Sample of Traffic Simulation Models

Model Name	Application	Type	Data Output	Individual Vehicles Followed	Acceleration/ Deceleration Cycles Noted	Individual Vehicle Flow Profiles Produced	Individual Vehicle Class Noted	Flow Characteristics by Vehicle Class
TRANSYT7F	Urban arterials and small networks with signals	Macro	Optimize signal timing. Estimates of emissions and fuel use	No	No	No	No	No
TRAF-NETSIM	Urban arterial networks with signals	Micro	Flow parameters (average speed, etc.) Estimates of emissions and fuel use	Yes	Yes	No[a]	Yes	b
FRESIM	Freeway sections	Micro	Flow parameters (average speed, etc.)	Yes	Yes	No[a]	Yes	b
CORFLO	Freeways and arterial networks (combines FREFLOW and NETFLO)	Macro	Flow parameters (average speed, etc.)	No	No	No	No	No
FREQ	Freeway sections	Macro	Flow parameters (average speed, etc.)	No	No	No	No	No
EVIPAS	Isolated signalized intersections	Micro	Actuated signal timing	Yes	Yes	No[a]	Yes	No

[a] Federal Highway Administration indicates that individual vehicle flow profiles could be produced if a modest revision were made to the current program.
[b] NETSIM provides traffic operations information by vehicle type (automobile, bus, and truck). FRESIM provides traffic operations information by seven different vehicle types.
SOURCE: W.R. Reilly, Catalina Engineering, Inc., July 1994.

flect actual driving conditions. EPA has conducted surveys of driving behavior in selected cities, and CARB has sponsored similar research in the Los Angeles area (EPA 1993, 1–2).[11]

The research sponsored by EPA has confirmed that sharp accelerations and high speeds are not well represented in the baseline FTP drive cycle. The current maximum acceleration rate of 5.3 kph/sec (3.3 mph/sec) is frequently exceeded in on-the-road driving (EPA 1993, 3). Similarly, the current maximum FTP speed of 90.7 kph (56.7 mph) is routinely exceeded (EPA 1993, 3).

Research on Emissions Effects of Sharp Accelerations and Fuel Enrichment

Preliminary results suggest that sharp accelerations,[12] which cause a vehicle to operate in a fuel-rich mode, contribute significantly to high emission levels for CO and VOCs (Sierra Research 1993; Kelly and Groblicki 1993; LeBlanc et al. 1994). For example, Sierra Research found CO emission levels 15 times higher, and VOC levels 14 times higher, from aggressive driving (with sharp accelerations) on the same trip (Figures 2-10 and 2-11). Using instrumented vehicles in Atlanta, researchers found that most vehicles spend less than 2 percent of total driving time in this mode, but this small fraction of the trip can account for up to 40 percent of total CO emissions (LeBlanc et al. 1994, 11).

Sharp accelerations that command fuel enrichment have little effect on NO_x emissions. Engine-out NO_x emissions decrease under fuel-rich operation, but reduction in catalyst efficiency can produce offsetting effects (EPA 1993, 19). Tail pipe emissions of NO_x may increase slightly overall under fuel enrichment conditions, but the effect is relatively minor and varies from vehicle to vehicle (EPA 1993, 19). In contrast, limited testing of 28 new-technology vehicles by EPA suggests that mild accelerations, which do not cause fuel enrichment, increase NO_x emissions because of the higher loads placed on the engine. NO_x emissions under conditions of mild accelerations can be 2 to 3 times higher than under cruise-type driving (personal communication, John German, EPA, Jan. 11, 1995). Thus, traffic-smoothing projects, which keep speeds constant, should initially reduce emissions of all three pollutants.

Sharp accelerations appear to be most common at lower and moderate speeds, where speed variability is greatest (LeBlanc et al. 1994, Figure 3a). Mild accelerations occur at all speed ranges. A related finding from drive cycle research in Los Angeles suggests much greater frequencies of sharp accelerations and much lower frequencies of cruise-type conditions on arterial roads than on freeways (Effa and Larsen 1993, 3).[13] Sharp accelerations at high speeds, although less frequent, can also cause emission increases.[14] The situations most conducive to sharp accelerations at high speeds include entering expressways from metered ramps, maneuvering within merging lanes, and passing slower vehicles in freeway-like conditions (Cicero-Fernández and Long 1993, 7).

Evaluations of traffic-calming projects—projects designed to slow cars and make streets more accessible to bicycles and pedestrians in downtown commercial areas and residential neighborhoods[15]— suggest the emission benefits from reducing accelerations and speed variation. In Buxtehude, Germany, for example, traffic calming in the 2.5-km^2 historic core of the city resulted in reduced emissions for all of the major pollutants.[16] The primary reason for the improvement was the encouragement of steady driving speeds—reducing accelerations, decelerations, and idle time—and the areawide implementation of the scheme, which prevented traffic diversions to other routes (Pharoah and Russell 1989, 16, 48).[17]

Research on Emissions Effects of High-Speed Driving

CARB is testing 125 light-duty vehicles on newly developed drive cycles—seven freeway cycles and three arterial cycles—that were constructed from actual highway driving (Effa and Larsen 1993, 9). Preliminary results from testing 86 vehicles on the freeway cycles, which do not include the artificially sharp accelerations of the old high-speed drive cycles (Figure 3-5), show no increase in CO and VOC emissions up to 96 kph (60 mph) (personal communication, Bob Dulla, Sierra

Research, Oct. 14, 1994). These results have called into question existing model estimates, which show CO and VOC emissions of light-duty vehicles increasing above approximately 80 kph (50 mph) (Figures 2-4 and 2-5). CO and VOC emissions will increase with higher loads on the engine from aerodynamic drag, but additional research is required to understand at what speed this occurs and by how much emissions are increased.

Preliminary results for NO_x show a steady but slow increase in emissions as a function of increasing speed (personal communication, Bob Dulla, Sierra Research, Oct. 1994). However, as illustrated by changes in the speed correction factors for NO_x for each of the last three versions of the MOBILE model (Figure 3-9), there is still considerable disagreement about the speed at which NO_x emissions begin to increase and the magnitude of the increase. Specifically, it is unclear to what extent increasing NO_x emissions under cruise-type conditions are offset by decreasing NO_x emissions from reduced accelerations and smoother traffic flow conditions. Further research and testing are required to resolve these uncertainties.

The preliminary results confirmed previous results indicating that emissions of all pollutants are highest at very low average trip speeds.

Implications of Research for Emissions Modeling

Current research to develop new drive cycles that better represent contemporary driving conditions should provide much of the empirical data needed for more valid estimates of emission rates.[18] Considerable data have been collected on individual vehicles for a range of different driving conditions. It is too early to determine how vehicle emissions will be affected in the aggregate (i.e., for the current vehicle fleet) and thus how current emission models should be modified.

EPA's efforts are focused on using the results of the drive cycle research to develop an alternative to or modify the FTP drive cycle for certification purposes. The agency has conducted a limited test program on current technology vehicles (Enns et al. 1993, 4), but further testing has not been planned and major modifications to the MOBILE model are unlikely.[19] EPA's Office of Research and Development, which

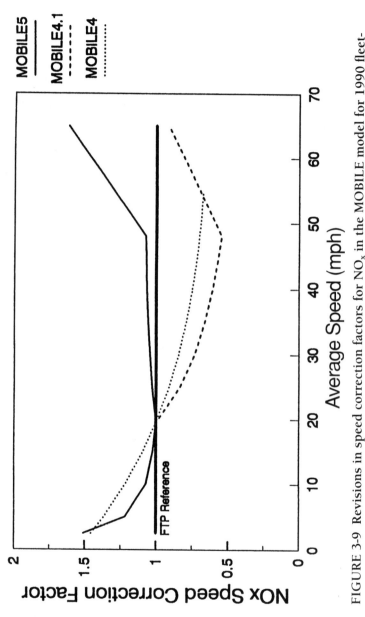

FIGURE 3-9 Revisions in speed correction factors for NO_x in the MOBILE model for 1990 fleet-year light-duty gasoline vehicles (Sierra Research, Inc. 1993, 56). Note: MOBILE4.1 and MOBILE5 speed correction factors are equivalent below 31.5 kph (19.6 mph). 1 mph = 1.6 kph.

is responsible for the agency's long-term research program, is pursuing research on drive cycles toward development of a modal emissions model.[20] However, implementation of a fully operational model is several years away (personal communication, Carl T. Ripberger, EPA, Aug. 19, 1994).

CARB, by comparison, is using the drive cycle research results not only to certify new vehicles but also to test a representative sample of vehicles to quantify differences in emissions from alternative drive cycles. The results will then be used to modify the speed correction curves contained in the EMFAC model.

Perhaps the most comprehensive effort to date is the state-initiated research project to develop and verify a modal emissions model within 3 years (NCHRP 1994, 1). The states have pooled funds through the National Cooperative Highway Research Program (NCHRP) to develop a model that accurately reflects the impacts of speed, engine load, and start conditions on emissions under a comprehensive variety of driving characteristics and vehicle technologies (NCHRP 1994, 1). A primary purpose of the model is to reliably estimate emission impacts from changes in driving characteristics associated with traffic operations and transportation system improvements. The model will also be responsive to the regulatory compliance needs of transportation and air quality agencies (NCHRP 1994, 1).

Controlling the variability of emission results so that modal models more accurately and reliably predict emission levels for different speeds and acceleration rates is a significant challenge. Modal emissions are affected by vehicle condition and state of repair. More to the point, the new models must reflect transient vehicle operations that are representative of on-road driving.[21] The inherent variability of vehicle emissions is one of the difficulties in developing predictive models that can estimate with precision the emission impacts of highway capacity additions.

Traffic Simulation Modeling Improvements

The multimodal traffic simulation model being developed at the Los Alamos National Laboratory will be able to provide second-by-second data on vehicle movements in traffic combined with detailed modeled estimates of emissions and pollutant concentrations. This system of integrated models is several years from being fully operational, much less widely available to metropolitan planning organizations.[22] Moreover, a complementary emission factor model must still be developed to drive the emissions element of this program.

The Federal Highway Administration has contracted with the Oak Ridge National Laboratory (ORNL) to improve the accuracy of emissions and fuel consumption estimates used in traffic simulation models. ORNL will collect modal emissions and fuel consumption data for a limited sample of vehicles and develop a model to estimate emissions and fuel use for alternative traffic patterns.[23]

Effects on Travel Volumes

The aggregate emissions impact of highway capacity additions depends on the traffic volume on the affected link as well as the changes introduced in traffic flow patterns. The magnitude of effects on traffic volume in turn relates to the type of capacity improvement and facility. The emissions effect of many traffic flow improvement measures (e.g., intersection improvements, improved signalization, or reduced on-street parking) is apt to be modest because such relatively small-scale improvements affect a relatively small amount of traffic volume for a relatively short distance. For example, an intersection improvement typically affects traffic for only $\frac{1}{4}$ mi on either side of the intersection. In contrast, large capacity additions (e.g., new freeway links or lanes added to existing freeways) are likely to have major aggregate effects on emissions, affecting traffic for a substantial distance. Depending on initial and post-improvement distributions of speeds and accelerations, these more significant effects could be either positive or negative.

The traffic volume on the link affected by the capacity expansion is also likely to change during the course of the day. The effects will be greatest for facilities that are congested for most of the day.[24] For facilities that experience only peak-period congestion—a more common occurrence—the amount of traffic volume affected by the capacity addition will decline during off-peak periods. Whether the overall effect on emissions will be positive or negative depends on the initial and post-improvement distributions of speeds and accelerations during peak and off-peak travel times.

Network Effects

Impacts of highway capacity additions may spill over onto neighboring routes, with mixed effects on emissions. Traffic may be diverted to the newly enhanced link, easing traffic congestion on other routes but increasing the traffic volume (and reducing speeds and increasing speed variability again) on the improved link. Route shifts can result in large emission reductions if traffic is diverted from heavily congested facilities. New freeway capacity, for example, may relieve very slow, heavily polluting, stop-and-start traffic on parallel arterials.

Travel times may also be affected. Commuters may take advantage of the new capacity to schedule their trips at more desired peak travel times, again reducing some of the freer-flow traffic conditions generated by the capacity addition at certain times of day.

Finally, highway capacity expansion may encourage mode shifts. Mass transit riders may find it desirable to drive to work if peak-period traffic congestion is alleviated by the capacity addition. If highway capacity expansions, particularly intersection and signalization projects, are designed to improve automobile and truck traffic flow without adequate attention to pedestrian and bicycle traffic, these other modes may be discouraged. These mode shifts will increase automobile traffic, reducing levels of service on the facilities affected by the capacity addition.

The magnitude of these network effects depends on the type of capacity improvement and, to a lesser extent, on its design. Minor traffic flow improvements are likely to have limited spillover effects on other routes, but mode of travel may be affected if the project design does not accommodate system users other than motorists, such as bicyclists and pedestrians. Major capacity additions are likely to have spillover effects on other roads that may be as important as the change in traffic flow patterns on the improved facility itself.

SUMMARY ASSESSMENT OF EFFECTS ON EMISSIONS AND AIR QUALITY

Net Effects on Emissions

The effects of highway capacity additions on emissions are much less certain than generally believed.

To the extent that capacity enhancement projects smooth traffic flows, reducing speed variability and the incidence of sharp accelerations, they should initially reduce emissions of CO, VOCs, and NO_x. The effect is most pronounced for CO and VOC emissions from light-duty vehicles, particularly if traffic smoothing reduces the incidence of sharp accelerations. Exhaust emissions of CO and VOCs from HDDVs will be less affected because diesel engines do not require acceleration enrichment. Emission reductions from traffic smoothing should occur when capacity is added to heavily congested facilities, such as urban arterials or congested freeway segments. The effects are greater for projects enhancing capacity on roads that experience heavy congestion for a large part of the day, that affect large travel volumes for significant distances, and that divert significant traffic from other heavily congested facilities. Of course, the potentially negative emissions effects of traffic delays and stop-and-start traffic during the construction phase of the project must also be considered.

The initial effect on emissions of highway capacity additions that result in free-flow traffic operations at freeway speeds [i.e., above 80 kph (50 mph)] is less certain. The effect on light-duty vehicle emissions of CO and VOCs is not well understood. At high speeds, increased power demands on the engine cause CO and VOC emissions to increase, but it is unclear at what speed this occurs and by how much emissions are increased. NO_x emissions also increase, although there is considerable uncertainty about the speeds at which this increase begins and the rate of the increase. NO_x emissions are thought to increase gradually at speeds well below free-flow freeway speeds. Exhaust emissions of VOC and NO_x from HDDVs also rise at high speeds. The increase in NO_x emissions from automobiles and HDDVs could pose a serious problem for those ozone nonattainment areas where NO_x emissions are already high because of the stringent requirements for NO_x reduction in conformity regulations.

For a broad range of intermediate conditions, highway capacity additions are likely to have modest effects on smoothing traffic flows and result in small upward shifts in the distribution of traffic speeds. The effects on emission levels are unknown; the changes are too small, and the variances around emission rates too large, to determine effects with any degree of confidence. Each of these conditions must be evaluated with reference to predicted changes in traffic flow characteristics and emission levels if the project is not undertaken, to determine net effects.

Changes in vehicle technology and new regulations for vehicle testing over the next decade may reduce the traffic-related effects of highway capacity additions, both positive and negative, on emission levels. For example, electronically controlled, multipoint fuel injection technology, which has largely replaced the older carbureted fuel delivery systems,[25] can be programmed to reduce emissions of CO and VOCs during sharp accelerations as easily as they now are programmed for power enrichment. Several automobile manufacturers (e.g., Ford Motor Company and Mercedes Benz) have developed vehicles that rarely go into the power enrichment mode. If EPA changes the FTP certification cycle to capture high-speed, high-acceleration driving that is currently outside the FTP envelope, automobile manufacturers will be required to take these factors into account in optimizing vehicle performance (personal communication, John German, EPA, Dec. 13, 1993). These changes will only reflect certification of new vehicles; it will take 10 to 15 years of vehicle turnover for them to work their way through the vehicle fleet. However, in the long run, they will weaken the emission-reduction potential of many highway capacity enhancement projects.

Effects on Regional Air Quality

Understanding the effects of highway capacity additions on regional air quality requires looking beyond changes in motor vehicle emissions to determine how concentrations of pollutants in the atmosphere will be affected. Highway capacity additions should help relieve localized concentrations of CO, or hot spots, by eliminating bottlenecks where congestion builds and traffic speeds are highly variable.

Effects on ozone concentrations are less clear. Many highway capacity additions are likely to have a neutral or negative effect on NO_x, one of the major ozone precursors, unless congestion is near breakdown levels before the capacity expansion. VOCs, the other ozone precursor, are likely to be reduced by traffic flow–smoothing projects, but such projects will affect only running emissions. Because most vehicles are fully warmed by the time they reach an arterial street or freeway—the location of most highway capacity projects—the projects will not affect cold start or evaporative emissions, which account for more than half of total VOC emissions on automobile trips.[26] Finally, regional concentrations of ozone are as much a function of local meteorological conditions and topography as of local travel patterns (Horowitz 1982, 76–77).

REVIEW OF EFFECTS ON ENERGY USE

Estimates from Current Models

A simulation model developed by ORNL in the mid-1980s (described in Chapter 2), which used data from on-road and laboratory testing of light-duty motor vehicles (McGill 1985, 50), provides the basis for estimating the initial impacts of highway capacity projects on energy use of automobiles. Model estimates suggest that measures that increase vehicle speeds from about 32 kph (20 mph) to 56 to 72 kph (35 to 45 mph) should improve fuel economy (Figure 2-13). At higher speeds, fuel economy degrades rapidly.

Improvements in fuel economy are largest in the intermediate speed ranges—from about 32 kph (20 mph) to about 72 kph (45 mph)—suggesting that the greatest benefits for fuel economy will come from highway capacity projects that raise the distribution of traffic speeds within this range. Traffic flow improvements on urban arterials, where average vehicle speeds fall within this range, are most likely to meet these conditions.

Automotive fuel economy is also affected by speed variation, but not as dramatically as are emission levels. Aggressive driving with sharp accelerations increases fuel consumption by about 10 percent (An et al. 1993, 4). Fuel use is minimized in cruise-speed driving conditions and worsens as speeds slow and stop-and-start driving conditions become prevalent. Of course, all improvements in fuel economy will be accompanied by reductions in CO_2 emissions (NRC 1992).

The fuel economy of heavy-duty diesel trucks varies with truck design and load. Heavy-duty trucks with gross vehicle weights (GVW) in the range of 6350 to 14 969 kg (14,000 to 33,000 lb) are less sensitive to speed changes than over-the-road heavy trucks in the GVW range of 14 969 to 36 287 kg (33,000 to 80,000 lb), which are more highly optimized for highway use (Appendix A).

Few data on how fuel economy varies with speed are publicly available from tests of HDDVs conducted under controlled conditions on a chassis dynamometer (Appendix A). However, selected data from simulation models developed by truck manufacturers[27] and on-road data collected by DOT in 1974 indicate that fuel economy for HDDVs improves as speeds increase up to about 80 kph (50 mph) but declines sharply at higher speeds largely because of the rapid rise of aerodynamic drag (Appendix A).

Certainty of Fuel Economy Estimates

How reliable are fuel economy predictions? Automotive fuel use is believed to be relatively well approximated by current models, in part because fuel economy is not as sensitive as emissions to changes in traffic flow conditions, particularly speed variation. The largest source of variance in estimating fuel economy is differences in vehicle design and technology. An analysis of the relationship between fuel consumption and speed, using data on 350 automobiles manufactured between model years 1967 and 1977, found that fuel economy decreased with increasing speed and engine size (Greene 1981, 441). The estimates from the ORNL simulation model corroborated these results. Fuel economy for the 12 light-duty test vehicles varied by a factor of nearly 3 at intermediate speeds, but the direction is the same: an improvement in fuel economy. At higher speeds [i.e., above 88 kph (55 mph)], fuel economy estimates begin to converge in a negative direction; that is, fuel economy declines sharply (Davis and Hu 1991, 3-68).[28] The same pattern is evident for heavy-duty diesel trucks (Appendix A).

Given the importance of differences in vehicle type on speed-fuel economy estimates, prediction ability could be strengthened considerably by a sample that better reflects the current mix of vehicles in the fleet.

Fuel economy estimates as a function of average speed are based on many of the same drive cycles commonly used in modeling motor vehicle emissions (An et al. 1993, 3), thus raising similar questions concerning the validity of the simulations. However, testing on a broader range of drive cycles has not been a research priority and is unlikely to become one, because of the relatively minor effects of accelerations on fuel use (An and Ross 1993, 12)[29] and the fact that fuel economy estimates converge at higher speeds.

Net Effects on Energy Use

Highway capacity additions that raise vehicle speeds and reduce speed variation should improve fuel economy as long as speeds do not exceed approximately 72 kph (45 mph) for automobiles and 80 kph (50 mph) for HDDVs on the affected facilities. The greatest improvements in fuel economy for automobiles should be realized by highway capacity additions that raise vehicle speeds from about 32 kph (20 mph) to about 56 to 72 kph (35 to 45 mph). The magnitude of the improvements depends on the traffic volume affected by the project and the extent of adjustments on other routes. Net effects also depend on predicted changes in fuel economy had the project not been undertaken.

SUMMARY ASSESSMENT AND RECOMMENDATIONS FOR IMPROVING THE KNOWLEDGE BASE

Adding highway capacity will not necessarily produce across-the-board reductions in emissions and fuel consumption, as generally has been believed. Although the current state of knowledge does not allow for precise estimates of the emissions and energy effects of traffic flow changes from capacity enhancement projects, a basic understanding of the major factors contributing to high emission levels and poor fuel economy for the current vehicle fleet suggests where benefits are most and least likely.

Currently available information indicates that the highest levels of emissions and fuel consumption are associated with heavily congested traffic conditions, in which traffic is moving at low and highly variable speeds with frequent stops, idling, and accelerations. These conditions are prevalent on urban arterials with very low speeds and stop-and-start traffic. High levels of congestion are also found on some freeways, particularly at freeway-to-freeway interchanges. Capacity enhancement measures that result in significant smoothing of traffic flows and reductions in speed variability on these facilities, ideally at off-peak as well as peak-period travel times, should initially reduce emissions of all pollutants and conserve energy. The effects will be greater for emissions than for energy use, for CO and VOCs than for NO_x, and for light-duty vehicles than for HDDVs. All else being equal, the more traffic volume affected by the improvement, including traffic on routes parallel to the improved facility, the greater the impact.

Highway capacity additions under moderate or lightly congested conditions at which traffic speeds are less variable will have limited effects on smoothing traffic flows and may result in free-flowing traffic at freeway speeds that will increase energy use and emissions of some pollutants. Fuel use is known to increase rapidly at speeds above 56 to 72 kph (35 to 45 mph) for automobiles and above 80 kph (50 mph) for HDDVs. NO_x emissions for automobiles, and NO_x and VOC emissions for HDDVs, will increase although there is considerable uncertainty about the speed at which these increases begin and the magnitude of the increase for light-duty vehicles. Knowledge about the behavior of CO and VOC emissions at free-flow freeway speeds is uncertain.

For a broad range of intermediate traffic conditions, highway capacity additions are likely to have modest effects on traffic smoothing and to result in small upward shifts in the distribution of traffic speeds. The effects of such relatively small changes on traffic flow characteristics and related emissions and energy use cannot be predicted with confidence by current models.

Evaluating the net effects of highway capacity expansion projects also requires taking into account any negative effects on emissions and energy use from traffic disruptions during project construction. Finally, it requires predicting changes in traffic flow characteristics and related effects on emissions and energy use had the project not been undertaken.

Understanding how highway capacity additions are likely to change emission levels is only one step in determining how the projects ultimately will affect air quality. CO concentrations, which tend to be localized in a region and exacerbated by congested traffic conditions, are likely to be reduced by capacity enhancement projects that eliminate bottlenecks and smooth traffic flows on major highway links. The effects on ozone are likely to be more problematic. Emissions of NO_x, an ozone precursor, will increase as a result of highway capacity projects that produce free-flow traffic conditions, particularly at freeway speeds. This could pose serious problems in ozone non-attainment areas where conformity requirements mandate reductions in NO_x emissions. Although VOCs, the other major ozone precursor, would be reduced by traffic flow smoothing, other major sources of VOC emissions (i.e., cold starts and evaporative emissions) would remain largely unaffected by capacity enhancement projects.

The ability to predict effects, particularly emission reductions for light-duty, gasoline-powered automobiles, is severely limited. Current emission models rely on average trip speed as the sole descriptor of traffic flow. Variability in speed, road grade, and other factors that strongly influence emissions are not explicitly dealt with. In addition, virtually all emissions testing has been based on a limited set of test cycles with questionable representativeness for specific traffic flow conditions. Finally, model estimates of predicted changes in emission levels tend to have large variances for a wide range of changes in average trip speeds that are typical of many highway capacity additions.

Diesel emissions can be predicted with greater certainty. They can be measured more directly (no aftertreatment is involved yet), and diesel engines require very little cold start or acceleration enrichment, which are large sources of variance for light-duty vehicle emissions. However, detailed data on diesel particulate emissions as a function of speed are not available. This is a troubling omission, because HDDVs are the primary source of highway vehicle particulate exhaust emissions, and particulate concentrations pose a significant health risk.

Fuel economy estimates from simulation models are relatively reliable and valid indicators of actual in-use vehicle fuel consumption. In part, this reflects the fact that fuel economy is not as sensitive as emissions to changes in traffic flow conditions, particularly speed variation.

Research has begun that could significantly improve understanding of the emissions characteristics of motor vehicles under real-world driving conditions. In response to a requirement of the CAAA, EPA has collected data on driving behavior in selected cities to develop new drive cycles more representative of current driving conditions. CARB has conducted parallel surveys in Los Angeles, has developed new drive cycles, and is testing them on a representative sample of 125 light-duty vehicles. The states have pooled resources to develop and verify a modal emissions model. However, federal leadership and funding are required to expand and accelerate these efforts. The most pressing needs are for the development of an emission rate model sensitive to a wider variety of driving patterns than current models and truly representative of the range of vehicles on the road today and for the collection of vehicle activity data to use as inputs to this model. EPA should become an active participant in developing these models and incorporating them into the regulatory process.

Because the greatest source of variance in estimates of fuel economy is differences in vehicle design and technology, estimates of the in-use fuel economy of the vehicle fleet should be periodically updated. Data and models for representing the effects of speed and acceleration on motor vehicle fuel economy should also be updated from time to time to be representative of the current vehicle fleet. This could be accomplished as part of the vehicle testing described above.

Traffic simulation models should be modified to provide baseline data on travel speed and speed variation for individual vehicles, in addition to the more traditional average speed data for all vehicles that are currently reported. Differentiation should be made between automobiles and trucks. Such disaggregated data are needed to provide better estimates of emission levels. Current modeled estimates of vehicle velocity and acceleration rates should be validated if they are used to provide inputs to emission models. Traffic simulation models should also be integrated with regional forecasting models so that the long-term impacts of highway capacity additions on travel demand and emissions can be estimated.

Finally, as is typical of many interdisciplinary efforts, lack of a common terminology hampers development of appropriate models. The terminology and definitions used by traffic engineers for key traffic flow parameters (e.g., delay) are not always consistent with terms used by air quality analysts. A strong effort is needed to remove such inconsistencies from research projects and bring traffic and air quality into consistent reference frames.

Additional research and vehicle testing should help reduce the uncertainties associated with modeling emissions and energy use. However, it will take substantial time and investment for the results of this knowledge to be implemented in practical models. Although the models can be improved, they still cannot predict outcomes with absolute certainty. Good policy should allow for some variance in modeled results.

In this chapter the current knowledge of the initial effects of highway capacity additions on emissions and energy use has been identified. If capacity enhancement projects stimulate new travel over time or encourage relocation of residences or businesses at more dispersed, automobile-dependent locations, the initial gains from some projects will be eroded. The potential for these outcomes is explored in the following chapters.

NOTES

1. Density is defined as the number of vehicles occupying a given length of a lane or roadway, averaged over time. It is generally expressed as vehicles per mile (TRB 1992, 1–6). See discussion of level of service in Chapter 1 of this report.

2. EPA has not developed separate emission factors or speed correction factors for diesel buses. Available data suggest that bus emissions are significantly higher than truck emissions (Appendix A).

3. The old belt-driven chassis dynamometers could not handle acceleration or deceleration rates that exceeded 5.3 kph/sec (3.3 mph/sec) (EPA 1993, 13).

4. Another flaw of the drive cycle tests is that not all vehicles were tested at all speeds.

5. CARB is in process of testing 125 vehicles representative of the current fleet (reduced from an initial testing program of 250 vehicles because of budgetary constraints), to determine emission levels for these and several other cycles (personal communication, L. Larsen, CARB, April 14, 1995).

6. Confidence intervals measure the likelihood, frequently at a 95 percent level of confidence, that the predicted mean for a random sample will lie within the confidence interval bounds. A large confidence interval indicates a wide range of variability around the mean.

7. Guensler uses the same vehicle test data base that CARB used in developing the speed correction factors in the EMFAC model. He reran the regressions and developed confidence intervals using disaggregated test results. By contrast, the data aggregation techniques used by CARB did not retain the data variability necessary to establish confidence intervals. Guensler is undertaking the same kind of analysis for the MOBILE model, but the results are not yet available.

8. Transient and cold start effects account for 10 percent or less of VOC and NO_x emissions for heavy-duty diesel trucks (Duleep 1994, 16). Thus, it is possible to develop emission estimates for almost any arbitrary driving cycle with reasonable accuracy from a steady state emissions map of the engine (Appendix A).

9. The actual level of the average speed depends on the free-flow speed of the facility, that is, the speed of a passenger car traveling at low traffic volume conditions (LOS A).

10. The emissions and fuel consumption data were developed by the Oak Ridge National Laboratory for the Federal Highway Administration in the mid-1980s (see discussion in Chapter 2). These data are currently being updated.

11. Two methodological approaches were used. The first used instrumented vehicles recruited from inspection and maintenance stations to collect second-by-second data on driving behavior. This approach allows for collecting data on the full vehicle trip but may be biased because of the driver's knowledge of the instrumentation. The second approach involved chase cars, which followed randomly selected target vehicles. The approach is nonintrusive but does not allow data to be collected for complete trips (EPA 1993, 36, 43).

12. Decelerations, another characteristic of stop-and-start driving, were not found by EPA to increase emissions significantly. However, testing was performed on current technology (multipoint fuel injection) vehicles. With older carbureted technology, some increase in VOC emissions could occur (personal communication, John German, EPA, Feb. 23, 1994).

13. On arterial roads, 18.7 percent of the driving was at acceleration rates greater than 4.8 kph (3 mph) per second, versus 2.3 percent on freeways. Twenty-eight percent of the driving was at cruise-type conditions on arterials versus 53 percent on freeways. The freeway driving, however, did not include driving on ramps to enter the freeway (Effa and Larsen 1993, 3).

14. Although these events are less common, sharp accelerations at high speeds [i.e., above 80 kph (50 mph)] contribute a disproportionate share of total CO emissions (LeBlanc et al. 1994, Figure 3b). Duration of accelerations also appears to matter; CO emissions increase rapidly as the duration of a severe acceleration event increases (LeBlanc et al. 1994, 10).

15. Traffic-calming techniques fall into two general categories: traffic management strategies (e.g., signalization system improvements, transportation system and parking management, truck restrictions, and speed limits and enforcement) and physical design (e.g., narrowing and curving roadways, speed bumps, and pavement design) (Project for Public Spaces 1993, 15).

16. Emissions were estimated by driving instrumented cars both aggressively and calmly through the traffic-calmed area. These estimates are subject to the same limitations as is instrumented vehicle drive cycle research in the United States: potential bias because the driver is aware of the instrumentation and representativeness of individual driving patterns of

the entire traffic stream (personal communication, Carmen Hass-Klau, consultant, June 3, 1994. Hass-Klau believes that if traffic calming is introduced in a widespread way, driving behavior will be affected).

17. Schemes designed to encourage steady driving speeds are believed to be more effective in reducing emissions than those designed to encourage slow speeds per se. A comprehensive evaluation of traffic-calming projects (Pharoah and Russell 1989, 48–49) found that schemes that have resulted in very low speeds increase emissions of CO and VOCs because they caused more acceleration and deceleration and greater use of second gear. However, there was generally no net increase in air pollution because of the overall reduction in traffic volume.

18. Driving cycles more representative of current driving patterns are being developed. Sierra Research, for example, under contract to EPA, has developed three cycles in addition to the FTP to represent the range of in-use vehicle operation: (*a*) a start cycle that represents driving that occurs during the first 4 min after the start of the vehicle, (*b*) a non-FTP cycle that represents the distribution of speeds and accelerations outside the boundary of the FTP, and (*c*) a remnant cycle that represents everything else (Enns et al. 1993, 3, 4). CARB has developed seven freeway cycles and three arterial cycles, which are discussed in the text.

19. EPA may add an option to account for some "off-cycle" events (e.g., high speeds and high accelerations) in its next revision of the MOBILE model (person communication, Dave Brzezinski, EPA, Aug. 17, 1994). In fact, the agency has introduced a proposed rulemaking to add a supplementary cycle to the FTP, which would capture some of these off-cycle events (*Federal Register* 1995).

20. The work is being performed under contract to the Georgia Institute of Technology. No extensive vehicle testing is planned, however (personal communication, Carl T. Ripberger, EPA, Aug. 19, 1994).

21. Modal models predict second-by-second emissions for a wide range of engine speeds and loads under steady-state operations. The problem in predicting emissions at a particular engine speed and load is that the results are affected by vehicle operation in the period preceding the desired predicted value. For example, a modal model could predict emissions for a vehicle operating at a speed of 40 kph (25 mph) and an acceleration rate of 4.8 kph/sec (3 mph/sec). However, predicted emissions at 40 kph (25 mph) would differ depending on whether the vehicle has accelerated from 32 to 40 kph (20 to 25 mph), whether it is operating at a steady-state speed of 40 kph (25 mph), or whether it has decelerated from

48 to 40 kph (30 to 25 mph). The challenge is to capture these transient operations. An alternative approach—an "event-based" modal model—could partially address these concerns. In an event-based model, modal emissions are predicted for a complete driving event representative of actual driving conditions, such as a 15-sec acceleration from 0 to 80 kph (0 to 50 mph). This approach captures the variability in emissions introduced by prior operations.

22. The Volpe National Transportation Systems Center has developed a PC-based model framework to estimate the relative impacts on emissions (and fuel economy) of intelligent transportation system user services. The models include a regional planning model (SYSTEM II), two traffic simulation models (FREQ, a freeway/ramp model, and TRANSYT-7F, an arterial model), and VEHSIME, a modal model that produces second-by-second estimates of emissions and fuel consumption under hot stabilized vehicle operation (Sierra Research 1994).

23. Researchers at the University of California, Riverside, are also developing a modal emissions model that can be integrated with traffic simulation models to more accurately portray the emissions effects of dynamic vehicle activities (e.g., accelerations and decelerations) on traffic networks. Although the researchers are using data from their own instrumented vehicle, they are depending primarily on outside sources for vehicle modal emissions data (CE-CERT 1993, 12).

24. However, morning congestion may be more important for the ozone precursors, because the pollutants have more time to be exposed to sunlight, which drives the chemical reactions that form ozone (Horowitz 1982, 70).

25. In 1993, approximately 90 percent of the fleet was equipped with the newer multipoint injection technology (personal communication, John German, EPA, Dec. 13, 1993). The technology enables each engine cylinder to operate with a more consistent air-fuel ratio.

26. Cold starts are not a large problem for diesel-powered heavy-duty trucks. VOC and particulate emissions are about 10 percent higher in the cold start mode (Duleep 1994, 12).

27. The Navistar model is well documented; its representatives claim that the model has been validated to within ±5 percent in real-world tests. The model has three built-in cycles to represent city, suburban, and highway driving conditions with average real-world tests. The model has three built-in cycles to represent city, suburban, and highway driving conditions with average speeds of 32, 64, and 88 kph (20, 40, and 55 mph), respectively (Appendix A).

28. The range between the highest and lowest estimates of fuel economy for the 12 light-duty, gasoline-powered test vehicles is as follows: 40 kph, 15.0 kpl; 56 kph, 12.8 kpl; 72 kph, 5.6 kpl; 88 kph, 6.1 kpl; 104 kph, 5.1 kpl; and 120 kph, 4.4 kpl (25 mph, 35.4 mpg; 35 mph, 30.1 mpg; 45 mph, 13.1 mpg; 55 mph, 14.4 mpg; 65 mph, 12.1 mpg; and 75 mph, 10.4 mpg).

29. An et al. (1993) found that three variables—average speed, free-flow speed or maximum attempted speed when there is no congestion, and the percentage of total trip time the vehicle is stopped—explained more than 90 percent of the variations from using different drive cycles (p. 3). Diesel engines do not require acceleration enrichment, and the air-fuel ratio during a transient acceleration/deceleration is more carefully controlled than in a gasoline engine (Appendix A).

REFERENCES

ABBREVIATIONS

CARB	California Air Resources Board
CE-CERT	College of Engineering–Center for Environmental Research and Technology
EPA	Environmental Protection Agency
NCHRP	National Cooperative Highway Research Program
NRC	National Research Council
TRB	Transportation Research Board

An, F., and M. Ross. 1993. Model of Fuel Economy and Driving Patterns. Presented at the 72nd Annual Meeting of the Transportation Research Board, Washington, D.C.

An, F., M. Ross, and A. Bando. 1993. *How To Drive To Save Energy and Reduce Emissions in Your Daily Trip*. RCG/Hagler, Bailly, Inc., Arlington, Va., and the University of Michigan, Ann Arbor, 10 pp.

CE-CERT. 1993. *The Development of an Integrated Transportation/Emissions Model to Predict Mobile Source Emission*. South Coast Air Quality Management District Contract AB2766/C0004. University of California, Riverside, May.

Cicero-Fernández, P., and J.R. Long. 1993. Modal Acceleration Testing on Current Technology Vehicles. Presented at Conference on the Emission Inventory: Perception and Reality, Pasadena, Calif., Oct. 18–20.

Davis, S.C., and P.S. Hu. 1991. *Transportation Energy Data Book: Edition 11*. ORNL-6649. Center for Transportation Analysis, Energy Division, Oak Ridge National Laboratory, Tenn., Jan.

Duleep, K.G. 1994. *Briefing on Heavy Duty Diesel Vehicle Emissions.* Energy and Environmental Analysis, Inc., Arlington, Va.

Effa, R.C., and L.C. Larsen. 1993. Development of Real-World Driving Cycles for Estimating Facility-Specific Emissions from Light-Duty Vehicles. Presented at Conference on the Emission Inventory: Perception and Reality, Pasadena, Calif., Oct. 18–20, 20 pp.

Enns, P., J. German, and J. Markey. 1993. *EPA's Survey of In-Use Driving Patterns: Implications for Mobile Source Emission Inventories.* Office of Mobile Sources, Certification Division, U.S. Environmental Protection Agency, Ann Arbor, Mich.

EPA. 1993. *Federal Test Procedure Review Project: Preliminary Technical Report.* Office of Air and Radiation, May, 161 pp.

Federal Register. 1995. Proposed Regulations for Revisions to the Federal Test Procedure for Emissions from Motor Vehicles. Vol. 60, No. 25, Feb. 7, pp. 7404–7424.

Greene, D.L. 1981. Estimated Speed-Fuel Consumption Relationships for a Large Sample of Cars. *Energy,* Vol. 6, pp. 441–446.

Guensler, R., and A.B. Geraghty. 1991. A Transportation/Air Quality Research Agenda for the 1990s. Presented at the 84th Annual Meeting and Exhibition, Air and Waste Management Association, Vancouver, British Columbia, Canada, June 16–21, 32 pp.

Guensler, R., D. Sperling, and P. Jovanis. 1991. *Uncertainty in the Emission Inventory for Heavy-Duty Diesel-Powered Trucks.* UCD-ITS-RR-91-02. Institute of Transportation Studies, University of California, Davis, June, 146 pp.

Guensler, R., S. Washington, and D. Sperling. 1993. A Weighted Disaggregate Approach To Modeling Speed Correction Factors. Presented at the 72nd Annual Meeting of the Transportation Research Board, Washington, D.C., 44 pp.

Guensler, R. 1994. *Vehicle Emission Rates and Average Operating Speeds.* Ph.D. dissertation. University of California, Davis.

Horowitz, J.L. 1982. *Air Quality Analysis for Urban Transportation Planning.* The MIT Press, Cambridge, Mass., 387 pp.

Kelly, N.A., and P.J. Groblicki. 1993. Real-World Emissions from a Modern Production Vehicle Driven in Los Angeles. *Air and Waste,* Vol. 43, Oct., pp. 1351–1357.

LeBlanc, D., M.D. Meyer, F.M. Saunders, and J.A. Mulholland. 1994. Carbon Monoxide Emissions from Road Driving: Evidence of Emissions due to Power Enrichment. Presented at the 73rd Annual Meeting of the Transportation Research Board, Washington, D.C., 23 pp.

McGill, R. 1985. *Fuel Consumption and Emission Values for Traffic Models.* FHWA/RD-85/053. Oak Ridge National Laboratory, Tenn., May, 90 pp.

NCHRP. 1994. *Research Problem Statement: Development of a Modal-Emissions Model*. NCHRP Project 25-11. Transportation Research Board, Oct. 6, 4 pp.

NRC. 1992. *Automotive Fuel Economy: How Far Should We Go?* National Academy Press, Washington, D.C., 259 pp.

Pharoah, T., and J. Russell. 1989. *Traffic Calming: Policy and Evaluations in Three European Countries*. Occasional Paper 2/89. Department of Planning Housing and Development, South Bank Polytechnic, London, United Kingdom, 67 pp.

Project for Public Spaces. 1993. *The Effects of Environmental Design on the Amount and Type of Bicycling and Walking*. National Bicycle and Walking Study. FHWA Case Study 20. FHWA-PD-93-037. Federal Highway Administration, U.S. Department of Transportation, April, 40 pp.

Sierra Research, Inc. 1993. *Evaluation of "MOBILE" Vehicle Emission Model*. Report SR93-12-02. Sacramento, Calif., Dec. 7.

Sierra Research, Inc. 1994. *Development of an Emissions, Fuel Economy, and Drive Cycle Estimation Model for IVHS Benefits Assessment Framework*. SR94-07-01. Sacramento, Calif., July 9.

TRB. 1992. *Special Report 209: Highway Capacity Manual*. 2nd edition revised. National Research Council, Washington, D.C.

4

Travel Demand

An argument against adding highway capacity is that the roads will simply fill up again with traffic as service levels improve. Traffic conditions, the argument continues, will become congested again but with larger traffic volumes, thus increasing total emissions and energy consumption. In this chapter the current knowledge about the stimulative effects of highway capacity projects on motor vehicle trips and travel is reviewed (Figure 4-1). An introductory section on the primary determinants of travel demand and recent travel trends is provided.

DETERMINANTS OF METROPOLITAN TRAVEL DEMAND AND RECENT TRAVEL TRENDS IN THE UNITED STATES

Travel is a derived demand; that is, it is derived from the activities of households and businesses that locate in a metropolitan area. Travel activities can be classified as commercial, involving goods movement and distribution, and personal. Personal travel is typically categorized as work travel and other personal travel (e.g., for shopping or recreation).

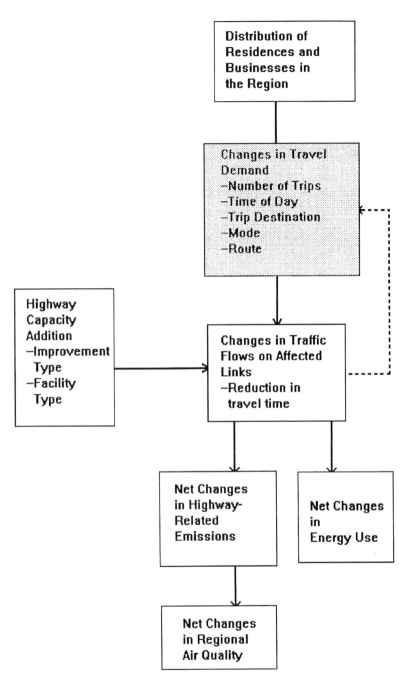

FIGURE 4-1 Impacts of highway capacity additions on travel demand.

The primary factors affecting metropolitan travel growth are demographic and economic. Metropolitan areas have grown tremendously in population. In 1990, nearly half the population (124 million people) lived in metropolitan areas with populations of more than 1 million, a 60 percent increase since 1960 (Rossetti and Eversole 1993, ES-2). Growth has been particularly rapid in the South and West, fueled in part by high rates of immigration (Pisarski 1992a, 4). During the same period household size has dropped sharply, from 3.24 to 2.65 persons per household (Rossetti and Eversole 1993, 2-1). To the extent that there are economies of scale in household trip making, persons organized in smaller households make more trips on the average than if they were part of larger households.

Metropolitan area economic growth has accompanied population increases. Job growth in metropolitan areas outpaced the national average between 1960 and 1990, reflecting in part the entrance of the baby boomers into the work force (Rossetti and Eversole 1993, 2-1). The number of workers per household also grew. Women in the work force increased from one-third to nearly one-half of the metropolitan area work force, becoming an important factor affecting travel demand (Rossetti and Eversole 1993, 2-1). During the same period, growth in personal income resulted in increased household automobile ownership and travel.

These growth trends have led to substantial increases in both trips and travel in urban areas.[1] According to the Nationwide Personal Transportation Survey,[2] between 1983 and 1990 household vehicle trips increased by 22 percent and household vehicle miles traveled (VMT) by 34 percent[3] (Vincent et al. 1994, 10). Although travel for commuting purposes still represents the largest share of urban VMT (36 percent), travel for family and other personal business other than shopping was the fastest-growing element of household VMT. Trips for this purpose exceeded work trips for the first time in 1990 (Vincent et al. 1994, 1-1, 2-1). The implications of this shift for travel demand are important because a larger portion of nonwork trips are likely to be discretionary and thus more responsive to changes in the cost of travel.

The location of population growth and economic activity in metropolitan areas has also affected the amount and type of travel. Most population and job growth has taken place in the suburban portions of metropolitan areas (Mieszkowski and Mills 1993; Chinitz 1993). The trend toward decentralization has increased average trip lengths for all travel purposes between 1983 and 1990, with commute trips increasing the most (Vincent et al. 1994, 3-3). However, commuting trip speeds have remained relatively stable,[4] reflecting more travel on higher-speed, suburban roads and a shift from slower to faster commuting modes (i.e., a decrease in transit use and carpooling and an increase in driving alone).

Low density suburban growth is correlated with more automobile travel and higher automobile trip rates than occurs in core central cities where alternative modes of travel are available (Dunphey and Fisher 1993). For all urban areas in the United States, the share of urban trips made by automobile is 87 percent. The corresponding figure for urban areas with rail transit systems and populations greater than 1 million is only 78 percent (Vincent et al. 1994, 4-4, 6-11). These locations provide a variety of transportation services and have residential and employment densities that promote less reliance on the private vehicle for trip making (Vincent et al. 1994, 2, 4-2).

Most personal travel in urban areas is by automobile, reflecting both low-density development that does not support alternatives to driving for most travel activities and the travel speed advantages of private vehicles.[5] In 1990, 87 percent of all urban person-trips were made by private vehicle, 2 percent by public transportation, and the remainder by all other modes[6] (Vincent et al. 1994, 4-4). Commercial travel in major metropolitan areas is primarily by truck, although some rail shipments are brought to key distribution centers in urban areas.

The cost of transportation to the individual and to businesses also affects the demand for travel. Although the provision of highway capacity in urban areas has tapered off in recent years,[7] it has resulted in high levels of accessibility and substantial reductions in the time-related cost of motor vehicle travel. Out-of-pocket costs of motor vehicle travel have also declined as a share of household budgets with the rise in personal income and the drop in oil prices over the past decade. Consumer surveys suggest that about 9 percent of typical household budgets is spent on gas and oil and other vehicle expenses (BTS 1994, 2).[8] In the manufacturing and retail sectors, transportation costs typically account for between 1 and 4 percent of total production costs (Appendix C). All else being equal, the lower the cost of highway travel, the greater the propensity to travel and the less priority residents and businesses will give to transportation relative to other preferences and costs of doing business.

The link between the low cost of and increased demand for travel suggests that raising the price of travel should reduce demand. Empirical evidence suggests that motorists respond to increases in bridge and turnpike tolls, transit fares, and parking fees (Harvey 1994). The decline in demand depends on the size of the price increase, the current costs of travel, and the capacity of alternative roads and transit systems (Bhatt 1994).

Are current travel trends likely to continue? There is evidence that the rate of travel growth may be slowing. Historical trends indicate some reduction in the rate of growth of urban VMT (Figure 4-2). In addition, automobile ownership patterns may be reaching a saturation point. In 1989 there were 0.95 vehicles per person of driving age (Lave 1992, 5-7). As the proportion of household members who are eligible to drive and have access to a car approaches 100 percent, trip making per household and VMT per vehicle increase, but at a less rapid rate, with the purchase of additional vehicles (Hu and Young 1992, 30; Vincent et al. 1994, 1-16). Moreover, although the number of households with more than one vehicle has grown, households with three or more vehicles are mostly located in rural states (Pisarski 1992b, 19–20).[9] Finally, some researchers argue that the potential for substantial additions to the driver pool is limited by the aging of the driving population and a reduction in the rate of growth of women in the work force.

Offsetting these trends are the rise in young immigrant populations and the potential for increased travel by older drivers. For example, individuals 65 years old or older took 6 percent more trips and traveled 25 percent more on the average in 1990 than in 1983. However, travel in this age group in 1990 was still 30 percent below the average annual number of trips and 42 percent below the average annual miles traveled of all other age groups (Hu and Young 1992, 42).

In summary, regional and metropolitan differences in immigration levels, work force participation levels, and overall rates of population and economic growth are likely to determine travel and trip demand levels in specific metropolitan areas.

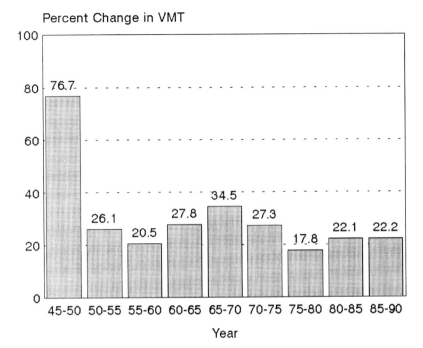

FIGURE 4-2 Changes in the rate of growth of urban VMT,
1945–1990 (FHWA 1987, 225-228; FHWA 1992, 193).

OVERVIEW OF EXPECTED IMPACTS AND DEFINITION OF TERMS[10]

By reducing the onerousness of travel as perceived by individuals, expansion of highway capacity can affect decisions about where, when, and how to travel. The primary impact of adding highway capacity is to reduce travel times in the corridor in which the improvement is located.

Highway capacity additions can also improve the reliability of travel by diminishing the day-to-day variability in the time required to make a trip. Vehicles using congested facilities experience daily delays and unanticipated delays that can occur because of disabled vehicles and crashes. Adding capacity to these facilities reduces the likelihood[11] and severity of delays from both recurring congestion and nonrecurring incidents.

Finally, highway capacity additions can also affect the out-of-pocket cost of highway travel to the extent that fuel consumption and other vehicle operating costs vary with speed and level of congestion. These effects are generally much smaller than travel time effects and are not perceived by most drivers.

Description of Effects

Potential direct effects of highway capacity improvements on travel patterns include the following:

- *Changes in the route used to make a given trip*: Construction of a new highway or the addition of capacity to an existing highway will allow some automobile users to reduce their travel times by shifting their route to the new or improved facility. Route shifts can increase or decrease total highway system use as measured in VMT by increasing or decreasing the circuity of trips. In most cases these effects are minor. Of more importance from an environmental perspective, route diversion can result in traffic shifts toward or away from areas that are more sensitive to local air quality and noise impacts.
- *Changes in the time of day a given trip is made*: Travelers may alter the time of day during which a trip is made in response to congestion levels. For example, individuals may deliberately avoid periods of congestion in scheduling shopping or other nonwork trips. Also, to the extent that their work requirements permit, individuals may schedule journeys to and from work outside of the period of most severe congestion. Adding capacity to a highway can reduce the severity and duration of congestion experienced on that facility. When peak-period congestion decreases, some of the trips that were shifted in time to avoid congestion in peak periods may be shifted back to the peak period.
- *Changes in the mode used to make a given trip*: Capacity additions can increase speeds and reduce automobile travel times, enhancing the attractiveness of highway use relative to other modes that do not benefit from the capacity improvement. The importance of mode shifts as a source of additional highway use depends heavily on the presence, type,[12] and use of alternative modes such as transit[13] in the corridor where capacity additions are made. Bicycle and pedestrian travel may also be discouraged if capacity

additions improve traffic flow for motor vehicles to the detriment of slower-moving modes.

- *Changes in trip destinations*: Capacity additions can increase the relative attractiveness of some trip destinations by reducing travel times to those destinations. Capacity additions can thus cause individuals to shift the destinations of their trips. This effect is more important for shopping and recreational travel (for which individuals have some flexibility in choosing destinations) and less important for work-related travel (for which individuals have little or no flexibility in choosing destinations in the short term). The substitution of one trip destination for another can increase or decrease total highway system use measured in VMT, depending on which destination is closer. The net effect of changes in trip destinations because of highway improvements is usually to increase VMT (i.e., new destinations are typically further away than the destinations they replace).

- *Increases in the number of trips made*: Because travel is a derived demand that reflects the need to carry out other activities, highway capacity additions are unlikely to significantly affect the number of home-to-work trips made. However, capacity additions could influence travel associated with more discretionary activities, for which the cost of travel might be an appreciable part of the total cost of the activity. In addition, improved travel times may reduce driver incentives to link trips (e.g., stopping for gas on the way home from the grocery store).

The time periods over which these changes occur will likely vary. Most route diversion (which merely involves a shift from one route to another with no change in destination or time of day) may occur soon after a new or expanded facility opens, as drivers learn about the new route and the time savings it offers. Changes in the time of day for shopping trips may also occur soon after the new or expanded facility opens. Changes in the mode used for work travel, shifts in trip destinations, and new trips could occur more gradually because they involve more significant changes in travelers' activity patterns.

In addition to the direct effects on traffic noted above, highway capacity additions can influence traffic levels by affecting other types of decisions, as illustrated by the following:

- *Automobile ownership*: A traveler's shift from transit to automobile use for the journey to work might contribute to a household's decision to acquire an additional automobile. The availability of an additional automobile may lead to more of the household's non-work trips being made by automobile. Interrelationships among mode choice, destination choice, and automobile ownership are poorly understood and, as discussed later in this chapter, are seldom taken into account in conventional travel forecasting procedures.
- *Land use and related travel*: Highway capacity additions can improve access to developable land in outlying areas of a metropolitan area. The improved access makes these areas more attractive for future development and influences the location decisions of residents, employers, and shopping facilities. Shifts in the location of residences, jobs, and shopping opportunities affect trip distances and the potential for trips to be made by modes other than the automobile. The impacts of highway capacity additions on land use and related effects on travel are discussed in Chapter 5.

Definition of Induced Travel

The primary focus of this chapter is induced traffic, which is defined here as the increase in highway system use caused by an addition to highway capacity. Induced traffic thus includes new and longer motor vehicle trips that are made because the highway capacity addition has reduced the cost (primarily the time cost) of travel. Induced traffic does not include shifts in the route used to make a trip or shifts in the time of day a trip is made, because such changes generally do not result in a net increase in highway system use. Induced traffic does not include increases in traffic that occur for other reasons such as population and income growth.

Changes in travel patterns because of capacity expansion should be distinguished from changes caused by other factors. Highway system use has grown because of increases in population, automobile ownership, and income, as well as expansion of the highway system itself. In the shorter term, highway system use can increase or decrease in response to such factors as fuel prices and economic conditions. In practice it is difficult to separate these effects because changes in highway use attributable to such factors as population and income growth often occur in parallel with additions to highway capacity and may either influence or be influenced by them.

Figure 4-3 shows how highway capacity additions and other factors, such as population growth, can affect travel costs (user costs per mile of travel) and the amount of travel (vehicle miles). The demand for travel, Curve D, illustrates the relationship between the amount of travel and travel cost at a given time. The curve indicates that as the cost of travel decreases, the amount of travel increases. The corresponding supply relationship, Curve S, illustrates the congestion-induced effect of highway system use on travel cost. As use increases, travel cost (primarily time) also increases. The intersection of these two curves at Point a represents the short-term equilibrium between supply and demand. The travel volume and costs of travel represented by this point are the values observed in the transportation system.

The effect of an addition to highway capacity is represented by a new supply curve, S', which lies below Curve S except at very low traffic volumes, at which there will be little or no reduction in travel time from an expansion of highway capacity. In the absence of any increase in travel because of external factors (population and income growth), the additional highway capacity would result in a new equilibrium at Point c with increased travel volume and decreased travel cost. In this case the increased travel is induced by the reduction in travel cost.

The demand for travel will generally increase over time because of such factors as population and income growth. This results in a rightward shift of the demand curve (i.e., population and income growth will result in increased travel for each level of travel cost). This growth in demand is represented by Curve D'. Its intersection with Curve S at Point b represents the changes in travel—higher volume and higher cost—that will occur in the absence of changes in the transportation system. However, when there is also an expansion of highway capacity, the combined effect of the capacity addition and external growth is represented by Point d. Travel volume will be higher than the original travel volume. Whether the cost of travel is higher or lower than the original cost depends on the magnitude of the supply increase compared with the growth in travel due to external factors. In this example the travel cost is slightly higher.

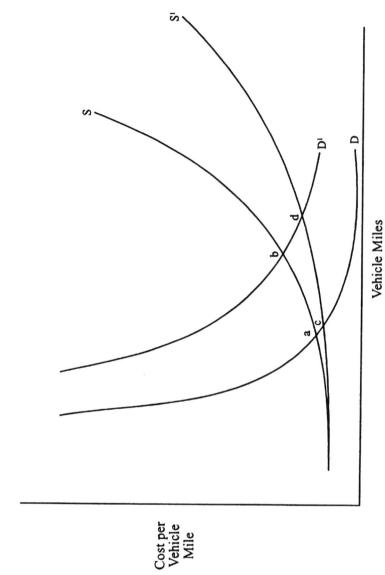

FIGURE 4-3 Combined effects of highway capacity additions and travel growth from other factors on highway use.

Only part of the combined effect is attributable to the highway capacity addition. The net effect of the addition can be determined by comparing Point *b* (which shows the effect of a change in demand from external factors without a change in highway capacity) with Point *d* (which shows the effect of a change in demand both from external factors and from increased highway capacity). The net effect of the capacity addition is to decrease the cost of travel and increase the amount of travel compared with what would occur without a capacity increase (Point *b*).

This simplified presentation neglects the possibility that the highway capacity addition itself may induce regional growth that will cause additional demand for travel. The likelihood of this outcome is discussed in Chapter 5.

THEORETICAL UNDERSTANDING OF TRAVEL CHOICES AND IMPACTS

Within the supply and demand framework, the potential for a highway capacity addition to affect travel decisions depends on the size of travel cost reductions resulting from the expansion project. Capacity additions that provide larger time savings are expected to have a greater effect on travel decisions. Transportation system management actions such as traffic signal retiming, channelization, and other intersection improvements generally have modest effects on travel times and are therefore expected to have modest induced traffic effects. Adding lanes to a congested freeway can result in large time savings during peak periods. Larger induced traffic effects along with some shifting of traffic from other time periods might be expected during these periods. During off-peak periods, when the facility operates at close to free-flow speeds without the added capacity, little induced traffic would be expected. The largest induced traffic effects are expected for the construction of a new freeway in a congested corridor that currently does not have a freeway, because the new facility would provide significant travel time savings during both peak and off-peak periods.

Some analysts have contended that new or expanded highways fill up as a result of induced traffic, so that travel times after the capacity has been added are no better than they would have been without the expansion. Highway improvements can increase the number of motor vehicle trips and vehicle miles by making travel less onerous. However, the absence of a difference in travel time with and without the expansion is inconsistent with the idea that the onerousness of travel is reduced by the expansion. Hence, highway capacity additions can cause induced traffic only to the extent that travel times after an expansion is completed are lower than they would have been without the capacity addition.

The time savings provided by highway capacity additions should be considered relative to the total cost of a trip. A 10-min time savings on a trip that previously took 20 min is thus expected to have a greater effect than a 10-min time savings on a trip that took 60 min. Other elements of travel cost may also be important in determining the potential effects of time savings. A given time savings will provide a smaller percentage reduction in the total cost of making a trip if that trip involves large costs for parking or tolls.

Potential increases in traffic from highway capacity additions might be reduced by imposing or raising tolls on the improved facilities. For example, consider a highway that currently carries 6,000 vehicles per hour in the peak period under stop-and-go conditions. Adding a lane might increase the volume to 8,000 vehicles per hour. If tolls were imposed on the improved highway using electronic toll collection technologies, the tolls could be set so that the volume is again 6,000 vehicles per hour, now moving at higher speeds and lower travel times because of the added lane. The combined effect of the highway capacity addition and tolls would be to reduce energy use and emissions of some pollutants by eliminating heavy congestion on the facility while VMT is kept constant.[14] The general public would benefit from toll revenues, which could more than offset the cost of the highway capacity addition. The effect on users of the facility would be mixed. Some users, generally those with higher incomes, would be better off because they perceive the benefits of reduced travel times as exceeding the added tolls. Other users, generally those with lower incomes, would be worse off because they perceive the tolls as more than offsetting the travel time improvements. Decisions about equity effects and the use of toll revenues, which are both critical to the success of time-of-day tolls, are discussed in depth in a recent report on congestion pricing (NRC 1994).

Economists use elasticities to measure the responsiveness of the demand for a good to changes in its price. The elasticity of demand is the percentage change in demand for a good divided by the percentage change in its price.[15] Travel demand researchers have adopted this concept to estimate the percentage change in highway system use (e.g., as measured in VMT) resulting from percentage changes in the cost of highway travel. The magnitude and direction of demand elasticities depend on the measure of travel cost used. The elasticity of demand with respect to travel time is negative since longer travel times result in less demand for travel. The elasticity of demand with respect to capacity (e.g., lane miles) is positive since more capacity results in shorter travel times and more demand for travel.

Elasticities provide a convenient way to summarize the results of empirical studies about how highway capacity additions affect highway use. However, caution should be exercised in applying elasticities from one highway capacity project to other types of highway capacity projects in other locations. Important considerations include the following:

- Where was highway use measured? Was volume on the expanded facility itself measured, was volume on a screenline (i.e., on the expanded facility and other parallel facilities) measured, or were the total VMT calculated in the affected area?
- For what time period was highway use measured? Was the measure peak-period travel, average weekday travel, or annual average travel?
- What effects are included in the change in highway use? Does the change include shifts in travel among time periods or routes, or does it represent a net increase in highway system use?
- What are the measures used to describe the improvement in travel conditions (e.g., lane miles, vehicle miles of capacity, speeds, or travel times), and how stable are the relationships between these measures and the costs of travel as perceived by highway users?
- How long after the capacity addition was highway use measured? Does the elasticity include both short- and long-run effects?

Estimates of elasticities produced by researchers and their transferability will be discussed in the next section of this chapter.

REVIEW OF EVIDENCE FROM STUDIES

Several recent reports (Hansen et al. 1993; Dowling et al. 1994; SACTRA 1994) have provided literature reviews of studies in which the effects of increased highway capacity on travel behavior are investigated. In this section the methodological difficulties in studying induced traffic are discussed, the results of key studies are summarized, and generalizations are drawn from a review of individual studies. The detailed review of individual studies itself is presented in Appendix B.

Facility-Specific Studies

The travel forecasting literature includes a number of facility-specific studies of the traffic-generating effects of projects that expand highway capacity (Jorgensen 1947; Lynch 1955; Frye 1964a; Frye 1964b; Holder and Stover 1972; Ruiter et al. 1979; Pells 1989; Bovy et al. 1992; Hansen et al. 1993).

Methodological Problems

Facility-specific studies generally involve measurements of traffic levels before and after the project, together with estimates of how traffic would have grown in the absence of the capacity addition. The possible causes of traffic levels higher than those expected from normal growth include diversion from other routes, diversion from other modes, shifts in trip destinations, and entirely new trips. Sorting out these causes can be difficult and has proven to be an obstacle in interpreting the results of several of the early studies (Frye 1964a; Frye 1964b; Holder and Stover 1972).

In attempting to separate the effects of diverted from induced traffic, researchers usually identify parallel facilities from which traffic might be diverted to the improved facility. If too few parallel facilities are considered, route diversion will be misidentified as induced traffic. The possibility of induced and diverted traffic on parallel facilities themselves should also be considered if diversion from these facilities (due to a capacity addition elsewhere) results in significantly higher speeds on them. Considering a very large set of parallel facilities reduces the chance that important diversion effects will be missed. However, it increases the cost of data collection and the possibility that unrelated factors (such as traffic changes due to economic conditions) will result in an overstatement or understatement of induced traffic.

A second set of methodological problems in studying induced traffic for specific facilities has to do with the development of this phenomenon over time. As noted earlier in this chapter, not all induced traffic effects appear immediately after a new highway facility is opened or an expanded facility is completed. It is desirable to collect data for at least several years after a highway capacity project is completed to capture the effect of induced traffic. However, increasing the time period over which traffic volumes are to be measured and compared makes it more difficult to separate the effects of factors not directly related to the highway capacity addition.

Properly accounting for the effects of destination shifts can be difficult in studying induced traffic on specific facilities. Consider an individual who formerly traveled from A to B and who now travels from A to C as a result of a highway improvement. The net effect on highway system use should be calculated by subtracting vehicle miles for the A-to-B trip from vehicle miles for the A-to-C trip. However, this adjustment is generally not done in studies of induced traffic for specific facilities.

Study Results

A recent investigation of the traffic effects of adding highway capacity was performed by Berkeley researchers (Hansen et al. 1993) using data on changes in traffic volume from 1970 to 1990 for 18 major highway links on which capacity was expanded in the outer suburbs of urban California counties. The analysis showed that (a) capacity expansion (measured in lane miles) did increase traffic (measured as VMT) on the improved facility, (b) the effect occurred over an extended period and grew over time, but (c) the growth in traffic remained less than the capacity added, thus improving the level of service, for nearly the analysis period of 20 years (Hansen et al. 1993, 3-29). Elasticities were 0.3 to 0.4 during the first 10 years after the capacity increase and rose to between 0.4 and 0.6 after 16 years. This means that a 10 percent increase in lane miles resulted in a 3 to 4 percent increase in VMT in

10 years and in a 4 to 6 percent increase after 16 years (Hansen et al. 1993, 3-27, 3-28). The authors note, however, that the VMT estimates refer only to the improved segment itself and do not take into account how other segments were affected. They conclude that diversions from these links may account for a substantial share of the additional traffic on the improved link, particularly if the traffic effect on the improved link is substantial (Hansen et al. 1993, 3-4).

Another recent study (Bovy et al. 1992) examined the effects on travel and traffic patterns of completion of the Zeeburger tunnel, the final portion of a major, heavily congested beltway—the Amsterdam Orbital Motorway. The extensive before-and-after study involved traffic counts, household interviews, and a roadside origin-destination survey to determine the impacts from the opening of the tunnel in March 1990 until September 1991. The analysis indicated that the primary effects of the tunnel opening were to shift travel routes and change travel times into the peak periods (Bovy et al. 1992, 5). Only small increases were found from modal diversions (from transit), destination changes, and greater frequency of trips (Bovy et al. 1992, 5). The study may understate the latter effects because of the short duration of the study period. Modal diversions and changes in trip destination and frequency of trips are likely to occur gradually because they can represent significant changes in traveler activity patterns.

Ruiter et al. (1979) used transportation forecasting models to estimate the impacts on VMT of two highway projects in California: a new 8-km (5-mi) freeway and a 19-km (12-mi) freeway widening. Compared with most conventional models, trip generation in the Ruiter model is sensitive to changes in travel time (although changes in VMT associated with longer-term changes in land use patterns are not incorporated in the model). The results suggested a relationship between urban highway supply and VMT, but the direction of the change can vary (Ruiter et al. 1979, 4-1, 4-2). The study found that the freeway project, which provided substantial time savings to users in both the peak and off-peak periods, resulted in an increase in the study area VMT (Ruiter et al. 1979, 4-4). The elasticity of VMT to the capacity increase was 0.4. In contrast, the widening project, which provided substantial time savings in the peak period only, resulted in a slight decline in VMT; the primary effect was to shift VMT from off-peak to peak periods (Ruiter et al. 1979, 4-4). The reduced circuity of existing trips resulted in the slight decrease in VMT.

After the study committee's final meeting, the Standing Advisory Committee on Truck Road Assessment (SACTRA) issued a report (SACTRA 1994), the purpose of which was to review for the Department of Transport of the United Kingdom the evidence on whether new or improved roads induce traffic. The assessment is based on a review of theory, empirical studies, and transportation models. The studies, which included only European studies, focused on the Department of Transport's own monitoring efforts comparing forecasts with observed traffic flows for major trunk road improvements (urban and rural). In addition, numerous before-and-after studies of traffic flows on major improved roads and alternative routes were examined. After reviewing the evidence, SACTRA concluded that "induced traffic can and does occur, though its size and significance is likely to vary widely in different circumstances" (SACTRA 1994, 168). It noted, however, that the studies are inappropriate for assessing the relative importance of the components of induced traffic. For example, they cannot distinguish among shifts in the time of travel toward the peak period, new travel generated by general economic growth, and new travel attributable to the road improvement itself (SACTRA 1994, 80, 85). SACTRA concluded that induced traffic is likely to be greatest (*a*) when the network is operating close to capacity, (*b*) when the elasticity of demand with respect to travel cost is high, and (*c*) when a highway capacity addition causes large changes in travel costs (SACTRA 1994, 170). SACTRA also noted that travelers' responses to changes in travel time and cost are likely to be greater in the long run than in the short run (SACTRA 1994, 47). The results confirm that a reduction in travel cost (mainly in travel time) from a highway capacity addition will increase the amount of travel. However, the results also confirm all of the methodological problems noted previously—the difficulty of segregating the specific causes of traffic growth, identifying appropriate control groups in before-and-after studies, and tracking effects over time.

Areawide Studies

Researchers have attempted to overcome some of the shortcomings of the facility-specific studies by examining the relationship between highway capacity and traffic on an areawide basis. They have used data for entire metropolitan areas (or large districts within them) to obtain models that predict VMT within these areas as a function of transportation system supply (usually measured by lane miles or highway miles). Since they examine large areas instead of individual facilities or corridors, these studies capture the effects of diversion and shifts in destinations better than do facility-specific studies. However, they can be subject to other difficulties.

Methodological Problems

First there is a question about the direction of causality in relating highway capacity increases and VMT. Highway planners attempt to predict growth in traffic (from growth in population, employment, and perhaps other factors) when they develop plans for highway capacity additions. Other things being equal, areas that are expected to have more traffic growth will have more highway improvements. The assumption that the additional highway capacity caused the additional traffic may be confusing the cause with the effect.

Second, year-to-year changes in lane miles in large metropolitan areas are small in percentage terms. Separating the effects on traffic of changes in lane miles from the effects of other factors, most notably short-term changes in employment and economic conditions, can be very difficult in practice.

Study Results

In addition to the link-specific analyses previously discussed, Hansen et al. (1993) conducted an areawide analysis to separate traffic shifts from net growth in traffic stimulated by highway capacity additions. Using pooled time series and cross-sectional data for 32 urban counties in California from 1973 to 1990, they examined the effect of lane-mile additions on VMT, holding constant such other variables as population, population density, personal income, and gasoline prices (Hansen et al. 1993, E-4). They found travel elasticities on the order of 0.5 to 0.6, implying that a 10 percent increase in lane miles would result in a 5 to 6 percent increase in VMT (Hansen et al. 1993, E-6).[16] The analysis showed, however, that population growth and other variables captured in a time-adjustment factor, such as the price of gasoline, had a far greater effect on VMT growth than increases in highway supply (Hansen et al. 1993, 6-31).

Both the areawide and the facility-specific analyses raise similar questions about cause and effect in relating highway capacity increases and VMT. They leave unanswered the question of whether expansion of road capacity causes VMT growth or highway capacity additions are a response to VMT growth.

The Hansen elasticity estimates are higher than many earlier areawide studies (summarized in Ruiter et al. 1979) that have attempted to predict VMT as a function of changes in transportation supply. This difference may reflect the fact that many of these studies are crosssectional comparisons (comparing VMT and highway supply across cities at a single time). By contrast, the time-series approach of Hansen et al. examines how VMT and highway supply change over time. Together, however, the elasticities of most of these studies are small (i.e., less than 1.0), indicating that a change in supply is expected to produce a small change in areawide VMT.

Travel Time Elasticities

Several researchers have estimated highway travel time elasticities (defined as the percentage change in travel between two areas divided by the percentage change in travel time). From a theoretical perspective, the use of travel time savings in estimating induced traffic is preferable to the use of measures such as lane miles or vehicle miles of capacity. Travel time savings are the more direct cause of induced traffic (i.e., capacity additions cause additional traffic only to the extent that they reduce the total cost of travel by providing time savings).

Methodological Problems

The estimation and application of travel time elasticities are subject to many practical problems. The time savings provided by highway capacity additions vary considerably by time of day. Widening an existing four-lane freeway to six lanes might provide very large time savings during peak periods but very little time savings during off-peak periods. Hence, application of travel time elasticities requires detailed information on travel volumes and travel times by time of day. Highway capacity additions may also cause shifts in the time of day when trips are made. Accounting for these shifts greatly complicates the problem of estimating and applying travel time elasticities.

Study Results

Estimates by Domencich et al. (1968) of the elasticities of passenger travel demand as a function of travel time and cost support the finding that highway supply changes are likely to affect discretionary travel more significantly than work travel. The researchers found elasticities of −0.82 for automobile work trips and −1.02 for automobile shopping trips (Domencich et al. 1968, 71). Although the methodology results in some overstatement of the magnitude of total travel effects from a reduction in travel time, the relative effects by trip purpose are valid.

Another study found much lower estimated elasticities of vehicle miles as a function of travel time: −0.27 (Burright 1984, 187). When travel from changes in land use and household density is factored in, however, higher elasticities of −0.51 are estimated (Burright 1984, 196), providing some confirmation that the travel effects of a change in supply increase over time.

A recent survey of travel behavior in the San Francisco and San Diego urban areas (Dowling et al. 1994) reinforces the notion that the size of the travel effect depends on the magnitude of the time savings. When offered a hypothetical 5- to 15-min travel time savings for each trip, the respondents indicated little or no change in travel behavior; for 90 to 95 percent of trips there would be no change or only scheduling changes (Dowling et al. 1994, ix). Trip times, on average, were short (the median trip was about 15 min), so the time savings were not perceived as meaningful (Dowling et al. 1994, 25). The survey results should be interpreted cautiously because they are based on responses to a hypothetical situation;[17] they do not distinguish work trips, which may be longer in duration, from errands and other short shopping trips; and they reflect patterns that may not be typical of other urban areas.

The SACTRA report (1994) also reviewed studies on travel time elasticities and concluded that elasticities of −0.5 in the short term and −1.0 in the long term were reasonable for estimating the effects of travel time savings on traffic volumes (SACTRA 1994, 46). These figures imply that a 10 percent reduction in travel time will result in about half of the time saved being spent on additional travel in the short run and nearly all of the time saved being spent on additional travel in the long run (SACTRA 1994, 47). The long-term elasticity estimates are higher than those of studies reviewed for this report, which suggest that only part of the travel time savings will be spent in additional travel.

Summary of Findings from Studies

The studies reviewed for this report support the following generalizations:

- Most of the increase in peak-period traffic observed when the capacity of a congested highway is increased is the result of shifts in traffic from other routes or time periods rather than net increases in highway system use.
- Highway capacity additions for which researchers found significant induced traffic generally involved large time savings during off-peak as well as peak periods.
- The elasticity of highway use (measured as VMT) with respect to travel time lies between 0.0 and -1.0, implying that only part of the time savings from highway capacity additions will be spent in additional travel.
- Elasticities appear to increase over time as travelers gradually modify their activity schedules to take advantage of time savings.
- The greater the travel time savings, the greater the travel effects are likely to be.

REVIEW OF IMPACTS FROM TRAVEL DEMAND MODELS

In this section the procedures currently used to forecast travel are briefly described, and their ability to predict the effects of highway capacity additions on travel demand is assessed.

The traditional procedure for producing travel forecasts includes the following four steps:

- *Trip generation* involves estimating the future number of trips beginning and ending in each analysis zone. Trip generation is usually performed separately for different trip types (e.g., home-based work trips, home-based shopping trips, and non-home-based trips) and is usually based on projections of population, employment, automobile ownership, income, and other socioeconomic data.
- *Trip distribution* involves estimating the amount of travel between all pairs of zones. Trip distribution models usually estimate the volume of travel between two zones on the basis of the number of trips beginning and ending in each zone and the travel time or some other measure of the cost of travel between the zones. Adjustment factors may be used to represent historical relationships between zones.
- *Modal splits* are estimates of the proportion of travel by different modes. Modal splits typically are estimated on the basis of travel times and costs for each of the competing modes and traveler characteristics such as income and automobile ownership.
- *Trip assignment* allocates trips to individual transportation facilities. In the case of highway assignments, vehicles are assigned to routes on the basis of travel times and costs for toll facilities. A key element in traffic assignment is modeling the effects of congestion on speeds for individual highway links.

Three of the four steps—trip distribution, modal split, and trip assignment—require information about travel times on the highway network. However, highway travel times themselves depend on traffic volumes and highway system characteristics. The process by which final estimates of travel times on the highway network are brought acceptably close to the travel time estimates used in trip distribution, modal split, and trip assignment is referred to as equilibration.

Considerable differences exist among the methods and criteria used to equilibrate traffic forecasts. Some analysts may repeat the trip distribution, mode split, and trip assignment several times to achieve equilibrium, whereas others equilibrate only through mode split and assignment. Harvey and Deakin (1993, 3-5) note that the latter approach often has its basis in resource constraints and outmoded software rather than in any compelling theoretical justification. Some analysts argue that current trip distribution models are so approximate in their representation of spatial relationships that they can hardly support an analysis of marginal travel time effects.

Time of day for trips is usually estimated through the application of historical temporal distribution percentages. These percentages may be applied before or after the trip assignment step. In the former case, separate assignments are then made for different time periods (e.g., morning peak, evening peak, and off-peak). In the latter case, traffic assignments produce 24-hr volumes that are distributed by time period.

Historically, the primary objective of the four-step travel forecasting procedure was to forecast highway volumes as a basis for determining the appropriate size (i.e., number of lanes) for new or reconstructed facilities. The accuracy of these procedures was evaluated by their ability to match observed traffic volumes on individual highway segments, not by their ability to measure changes in the amount of travel due to highway capacity additions or other public policy actions. As a result, the procedure has some important limitations as a basis for determining the effects of highway capacity additions on travel demand:

- Trip generation is usually not sensitive to changes in travel times and other travel conditions. Hence, possible effects on the number of trips from travel time savings are not reflected in forecasts.
- Forecasts of the distribution of travel by time of day are usually based on historical percentages. Decisions by travelers to shift the time of certain trips (such as might result from a capacity addition) are not reflected in forecasts.
- Interdependencies among trips are generally not considered in travel forecasting. In some cases this shortcoming may result in an overestimate of highway use due to capacity additions. For example, if a former transit user now drives to work, fewer automobile trips may be taken by other family members since her car is no longer available for their use. However, the availability of an automobile at work may result in additional driving during the day or after work.

To remedy current model deficiencies, the Federal Highway Administration, the Federal Transit Administration, and the Office of the Secretary of the U.S. Department of Transportation; the U.S. Environmental Protection Agency; and the U.S. Department of Energy have initiated a major program to enhance current models and develop new procedures. The objectives of the Travel Model Improvement Program (DOT et al. 1994, 2) are as follows:

- To increase the policy sensitivity of existing travel forecasting procedures and their ability to respond to emerging issues including environmental concerns, growth management, and changes in personal and household activity patterns, along with traditional transportation issues;
- To redesign the travel forecasting process to reflect contemporary traveler behavior, to respond to greater information requirements placed on the forecasting process, and to take advantage of changes in data collection technology; and
- To make travel forecasting model results more useful for decision makers.

Activity-based approaches have been proposed to overcome the shortcomings of the four-step approach. These approaches are used to predict an activity participation plan (describing the number and types of activities in which households or individuals will participate) and travel patterns and trip combinations necessary to satisfy the plan. The effects of travel time and other components of travel cost would be explicitly accounted for in modeling travel decisions.

Activity-based models hold considerable promise; however, they are still in the early stages of development. The feasibility of specifying, calibrating, and applying these models to predict induced traffic has not yet been demonstrated.

SUMMARY ASSESSMENT OF THE STATE OF KNOWLEDGE

The evidence from the studies reviewed here supports the view that highway capacity additions can induce new trips, longer trips, and diversions from transit. However, the increase in highway system use will be significantly less than that required to offset the travel time reductions attributable to the highway capacity additions.

These findings are consistent with the supply-demand framework diagrammed in Figure 4-3. That framework is useful for distinguishing between increases in highway use attributable to an increase in capacity and those attributable to external factors, such as population and income growth. In this framework, an increase in highway capacity (a supply-side shift) causes additional highway use by reducing the cost (primarily time) of motor vehicle travel. Over time, population and income growth may also result in increased highway use (a demand-side shift). The combined effect can eliminate the travel-time advantage of the added highway capacity, as occurs when the new highway capacity fills up with traffic again within a few years of construction. However, only part of the increased highway use can be attributed to the highway capacity addition. If the travel time reduction afforded by the new capacity is eliminated, the reason for new travel induced by the supply increase is also eliminated.

The evidence also supports the view that projects involving the construction of new freeways have much more potential to cause additional highway system use than projects that involve widening of existing freeways or other major roads. New freeways in urban areas can provide significant increases in speeds and travel times during peak periods (by reducing congestion) and during off-peak periods (because freeways have higher speed limits than other arterials). The speed and travel time effects of projects involving widening of existing freeways and other highways occur primarily during peak periods. Much of the additional highway system use during peak periods resulting from a capacity addition appears to come from route diversions or shifts of trips from the off-peak to the peak period.

Because travel is a derived demand it is unlikely that highway capacity additions will significantly affect the number of home-to-work trips. However, capacity additions could significantly affect travel associated with more discretionary activities for which the cost of travel might be an appreciable part of the total cost of the activity. This intuitive result is supported by the finding of some researchers that travel time elasticities are higher for nonwork trips.

The potential for induced travel depends on the total cost of travel. Other things being equal, less induced traffic would be expected in corridors with high tolls or parking charges.

The existing four-step travel forecasting process was developed primarily to assist in determining the size of capital facilities (e.g., number of lanes), not to estimate the amount of travel new facilities might induce. The four-step process, as it is conventionally applied, will generally understate the amount of induced travel because the models used to predict the number of trips are not sensitive to travel times.

Separating cause and effect is an extremely difficult problem in predicting induced travel. Highway capacity additions in a corridor can cause an increase in demand, but they might also be implemented because future growth in corridor demand is expected.

Elasticities provide a useful means of making simple quantitative statements about the responsiveness of highway use to highway capacity additions in a specific context. However, caution should be exercised in applying elasticities developed in one context to other types of highway capacity projects in other locations.

REVIEW OF IMPACTS ON TRUCK TRAVEL

Highway capacity additions should affect freight travel in metropolitan areas in substantially different ways than they affect personal travel. Because of these differences, a separate analysis has been prepared to examine the impacts of highway capacity additions on travel by truck—the dominant carrier of freight within metropolitan areas. The results are summarized in this section and presented in their entirety in Appendix C.

Effects on Truck Traffic

The effects of adding highway capacity are the same for truck drivers as for other highway travelers. Capacity additions reduce travel times, make trip times more predictable, and improve accessibility to new areas and new markets. The response to these changes, however, is likely to differ because of the characteristics of the freight transportation sector.

In the short term, highway capacity additions are unlikely to result in significant changes in truck travel. The demand for truck travel is determined mainly by the level of economic activity in a metropolitan area and the area's role in the national and global economy. Moreover, deregulation of the transportation industry and technological innovations in other freight sectors have decreased the cost of transportation relative to labor and materials, making the cost savings from highway capacity additions less important to the shippers and receivers. Finally, the business cycle of the shippers and receivers of goods insulates many trucks from the morning and evening peak traffic periods, resulting in truck travel that is spread more evenly across the day than automobile travel.

Continuing structural changes in the economy, freight logistics, and the trucking industry may make truck travel more sensitive to highway capacity changes in the future. The dispersion of business and housing across metropolitan areas will expand the service area that trucking firms must cover. High land and labor costs, encroaching residential development, and noise regulations are likely to push warehouses and truck terminals toward the periphery of metropolitan areas, leading to an increase in truck miles of travel. Finally, the adoption of just-in-time manufacturing and retailing practices and the globalization of trade will produce longer and more time-sensitive supply and distribution networks that leave trucks more exposed to the effects of congestion.

However, internal competitive pressures will force the deregulated trucking industry to carry more freight with fewer trucks and fewer truck miles of travel. These productivity improvements are being achieved by automated fleet management technologies and automated urban traffic management systems [intelligent transportation system (ITS) programs]. To date, the former have been adopted by long-haul national truckload carriers, urban courier and parcel services, and large less-than-truckload carriers such as Federal Express and United Parcel Service, but not by smaller urban trucking fleets. ITS programs generally, and ITS programs for trucks specifically, are not yet widespread in urban areas.

A recent report entitled *Transport and the Environment* noted the difficulty of altering highway freight transport patterns in the United Kingdom even with a considerable increase in fuel prices; more regulation and restriction of heavy goods vehicles in certain locations would be required (Royal Commission on Environmental Pollution

1994, 166). The potential for mode shifts is considerably less in metropolitan areas than for long-distance travel because of the greater flexibility and considerable cost advantages trucking offers for short-haul distribution (Appendix C).

Modeling Truck Travel

Regional travel demand models are generally not well equipped to forecast the separate effects of changes in metropolitan highway capacity on truck travel versus automobile travel. Truck travel represents a small share of total traffic, well within the margin of error of the models, so only modest efforts have been made to forecast it separately.

The typical regional model apportions forecast vehicle trips that have been assigned to highways on the metropolitan network among trucks and automobiles. The apportionment is based on traffic counts by functional class of roadway (for the more sophisticated systems) or on a single estimated percentage of truck travel for major roads only. To account for the size difference among trucks and cars, trucks are converted into passenger car equivalents.[18] A few metropolitan areas have developed separate trip tables for trucks on the basis of extensive surveys of shippers and motor carriers in their regions, but these are the exception to the rule. The primary hurdles to developing more sophisticated regional truck travel models are the general lack of data on freight and truck movements in metropolitan areas and the complexity of freight demand estimation and truck trip modeling.

In sum, regional travel models are not well equipped to forecast separately changes in truck travel and changes in automobile travel within metropolitan areas due to an addition to highway capacity. The models cannot examine the effects of reduced travel times on truck behavior or tie the effects to specific carriers, industries, or commodities, because the models do not take into account shipper demand or motor carrier behavior. If the highway capacity addition is modest in scale and limited to a single corridor, the shortcomings of the models can be overcome by using direct interviews with industries and motor carriers to adjust model forecasts. For larger projects in complex metropolitan areas, planners must develop truck trip tables and truck networks and incorporate them into the regional forecasting process.

RECOMMENDATIONS FOR IMPROVING THE KNOWLEDGE BASE

A better understanding of how individual travelers and freight carriers and shippers make travel choices is necessary to forecast more accurately the likely effects on travel demand of changes in highway cost, highway service, and other policy options. For many metropolitan areas, the household travel surveys that provided the origin-destination and mode choice data for regional travel forecasting models are out of date. Changes in demographic characteristics (family size, structure, and income) and in travel conditions and options offer choices that were unavailable when many of the surveys were conducted (Harvey and Deakin 1993, 3-101). Most metropolitan planning organizations (MPOs) have never collected data on the determinants of truck travel in their area.

To remedy this situation, more current household travel survey data should be collected.[19] This activity could be supported by the planning funds given to MPOs to develop the management systems required by the Intermodal Surface Transportation Efficiency Act (ISTEA) if these data were viewed as critical to assessing and monitoring the achievement of air quality goals in metropolitan areas.[20] Although the planning funds are already committed to supporting ISTEA requirements, there may be potential for collecting travel data that support both model improvements and certain of the management systems required by the act.

ISTEA also requires more attention to freight transportation and more private-sector involvement in the planning and programming of highway and other transportation improvements, which could lead to a more sophisticated understanding of freight movement and truck travel. Basic data are needed on freight generation rates by industry and commodity that can be tied to specific land uses and industrial facilities in metropolitan areas, on trip patterns by industry and commodity by different types of carrier, and on the factors that affect truck routing and dispatching decisions and terminal location choices.

Carefully planned longitudinal studies (panel surveys) of a diverse and representative population of travelers, firms, and metropolitan areas to determine the effects of policy actions—such as major transportation investments or pricing changes—on travel behavior should help shed light on how these policy actions affect travel choices over time. A major methodological challenge is to control for the effects of other variables, such as regional population and economic growth, on long-term growth in travel.

The results of these data collection and research efforts should be used to update existing travel forecasting models. In particular, the models should be modified to more adequately represent the effect of changes in the cost of transportation on automobile ownership, the number of trips made, the time of day of travel, the interdependencies among trips (i.e., the opportunities for combining trips), and bicycle and pedestrian travel. Where good historical data are available on changes in transportation facilities and travel demand, they could be used to calibrate regional travel models and "predict" current travel patterns to evaluate their forecasting capabilities.

Development of more sophisticated models of freight transportation in metropolitan areas requires a more substantial effort because of the current state of freight modeling practice. Because of the complexity of freight demand estimation and truck trip modeling, efforts should be focused on corridor-scale models, which can accommodate multiple truck trip tables and truck networks, rather than comprehensive regional freight models.

A new travel forecasting paradigm should be developed in the long run to address the policy questions currently being asked. Activity-based models hold considerable promise for providing more detailed modeling of household activities and travel options. Such models would allow more precise forecasts of likely traveler responses to a range of policy options.

These models, however, are still in the early stages of development. Advancing their development requires collection of substantially enhanced data about the travel behavior of households and individuals; estimation of enhanced models that incorporate more of the behavioral links that affect household travel decisions and take into consideration the importance of trip linkages and time of day in travel choices; and test applications in one or more regions, including the development of implementation software. Model calibration and validation continue to be major challenges. Finally, model results will have to be merged with the results of enhanced emission and energy models to improve prediction of the air quality and energy consequences of traveler responses to highway capacity additions.

Better models more relevant for policy analysis can be developed. Although the limitations of models in the policy process—particularly in the precision of their estimates—should be recognized, they are useful in analyzing complex phenomena.

NOTES

1. Urban area, as defined in the Nationwide Personal Transportation Survey, refers to the urbanized portion of the larger metropolitan area. Urbanized area is a U.S. Bureau of the Census term defined by the presence of a central city, a total population of 50,000 or more, and a population density exceeding 386 persons per square kilometer (1,000 persons per square mile) (Vincent et al. 1994, 2). Data are not available for metropolitan areas.
2. The magnitude of the changes should be interpreted with caution because of changes in sample size and survey methods between the 1983 and 1990 surveys. For example, the sample size was 22,000 in 1990 and only 6,500 in 1983. Telephone surveys were used in 1990 and in-person home interviews in the earlier survey. Finally, some metropolitan area and central city boundaries changed between the survey years (Vincent et al. 1994, 4, 5).
3. These numbers are based on urban trips of less than 121 km (75 mi) (Vincent et al. 1994, 10).
4. The average national travel time to work increased from about 21.7 min in 1980 to about 22.4 min in 1990. The most common trip duration was between 15 and 29 min (Rossetti and Eversole 1993, 4-36). Several large metropolitan areas, however, such as Los Angeles, San Diego, Orlando, and Sacramento, had commuter travel time increases of more than 10 percent (Rossetti and Eversole 1993, 4-38).
5. For example, the average commuting trips by bus transit and private vehicle are similar in distance, but the bus trip takes nearly twice as long (Vincent et al. 1994, 3-1).
6. Other modes include bicycle, walking, taxi, and other. Trips greater than 121 km (75 mi) are excluded (Vincent et al. 1994, 4-4).
7. The Federal Highway Administration's *Highway Statistics* reports the following figures for surfaced road and street mileage in the United States: 1960, 4.1 million km (2.56 million mi); 1970, 4.72 million km (2.95 million mi); 1980, 5.38 million km (3.36 million mi); and 1990, 5.63 million km (3.52 million mi) (in Rossetti and Eversole 1993, 2-4).
8. These figures do not include vehicle purchases, which represent about 7.1 percent of total spending, or purchased transportation, which represents about 1.0 percent of the total (BTS 1994, 2).

9. An exception is California. In the San Francisco area, for example, 20 percent of the households have three or more vehicles. In Los Angeles, 28 percent of homeowner households and less than 10 percent of renter households have three or more vehicles (Pisarski 1992b, 19).

10. The following five sections were written by Harry Cohen of Cambridge Systematics, Inc., as part of a special *Literature Review on Travel Impacts of Highway Capacity Improvements* prepared for the study committee.

11. See Appendix C for a review of the literature on how congestion levels affect crash severity. The literature suggests that accident rates will not be reduced under all conditions. Studies of the relationship between accident rates and congestion levels have found that accident rates are highest at night when traffic volumes are lowest. As traffic volumes increase, accident rates drop, but they begin to climb again as traffic volumes approach 60 to 70 percent of highway capacity, typically during congested daytime traffic.

12. Highway capacity additions that reduce travel times may make bus travel faster and thus more attractive. However, automobile travel times will also be reduced. Diversions from car to bus are likely to depend on bus reliability and comfort as well as travel times.

13. In areas with large transit systems, highway capacity additions that result in large diversions from existing transit services might affect subsidy requirements and the financial viability of these services, which in turn are likely to result in service cutbacks and additional ridership loss.

14. The magnitude of the reductions would depend on traffic speeds realized after the capacity addition (see discussion in Chapter 3). If the capacity addition results in a net increase in free flow freeway speeds during peak and off-peak periods, some of the emission reductions and fuel use savings from peak-period congestion relief will be offset.

15. More specifically, elasticity of demand is the percent change in demand relative to a 1 percent change in price or other measurable attributes of service quality.

16. As discussed in Appendix B, because of data limitations the analysis was focused on estimating how changes in lane miles affect VMT on state highways.

17. Revealed preference surveys, while capturing actual responses to real changes, raise several survey design issues, including identifying the appropriate population to sample (how large an area to cover) and selecting a control location to compare changes with and without the improvement. The revealed preference approach also requires multiple surveys to capture the before-and-after effects (Dowling et al. 1994, 18). The stated preference approach, which was used in this study, overcomes these limitations and costs less, but has the obvious disadvantage that it does not measure actual decisions.

18. Small or medium trucks are represented as equivalent to two passenger cars and large trucks to three passenger cars.
19. A recent report (Hartgen et al. 1994, 18) found that a considerable number of metropolitan regions have begun to conduct travel surveys (19 had done home interviews) or have plans to do so.
20. Both ISTEA and the Clean Air Act Amendments require collection of data on many aspects of the transportation system, such as VMT tracking and monitoring. There is no comparable requirement for travel survey data collection (Harvey and Deakin 1993, 3-101). However, travel data could be collected to support the congestion management systems and, to a lesser extent, the transit and intermodal management systems required by ISTEA.

REFERENCES

ABBREVIATIONS

BTS	Bureau of Transportation Statistics
DOT	U.S. Department of Transportation
DOE	U.S. Department of Energy
EPA	Environmental Protection Agency
FHWA	Federal Highway Administration
NCHRP	National Cooperative Highway Research Program
NRC	National Research Council
SACTRA	The Standing Advisory Committee on Trunk Road Assessment

Bhatt, K. 1994. Potential of Congestion Pricing in the Metropolitan Washington Region. In *Special Report 242: Curbing Gridlock, Vol. 2*, National Research Council, Washington, D.C., pp. 62–88.

Bovy, P.H.L., A.L. Loos, and G.C. De Jong. 1992. *Effects of the Opening of the Amsterdam Orbital Motorway. Final Report Phase I*. Ministry of Transport and Public Works, Transportation and Traffic Research Division, Rotterdam, Netherlands, 83 pp.

Burright, B.K. 1984. *Cities and Travel*. Garland Publishing, New York.

BTS. 1994. *Transportation Statistics: Annual Report, 1994*. U.S. Department of Transportation, 205 pp.

Chinitz, B. 1993. Urban Growth Patterns. Presented at Conference on Metropolitan America in Transition: Implications for Land Use and Transportation Planning, Washington, D.C., Sept. 9–10.

Domencich, T.A., G. Kraft, and J.P. Vallette. 1968. Estimation of Urban Passenger Travel Behavior: An Economic Demand Model. In *Highway Research Record 238*, Highway Research Board, National Research Council, Washington, D.C., pp. 64–78.

Dowling, R.G., S.B. Colman, and A. Chen. 1994. *Effects of Increased Highway Capacity on Travel Behavior*. California Air Resources Board, Dowling Associates, Oakland, Calif., Oct.

DOT, EPA, and DOE. 1994. *Travel Model Improvement Program*. Texas Transportation Institute, College Station, 11 pp.

Dunphey, R., and K. Fisher. 1994. Transportation, Congestion, and Density: New Insights. Presented at the 73rd Annual Meeting of the Transportation Research Board, Washington, D.C.

FHWA. 1987. *Highway Statistics: Summary to 1985*. HPM-10/4-87. U.S. Department of Transportation.

FHWA. 1992. *Highway Statistics, 1991*. HPM-40/10-92. U.S. Department of Transportation.

Frye, F.F. 1964a. Redistribution of Traffic in the Dan Ryan Expressway Corridor. *CATS Research News*, Vol. 6, No. 3, pp. 6–14.

Frye, F.F. 1964b. Eisenhower Expressway Study Area—1964. *CATS Research News*, Vol. 6, No. 4, pp. 7–13.

Hansen, M., D. Gillen, A. Dobbins, U. Huang, and M. Puvathingal. 1993. *The Air Quality Impacts of Urban Highway Capacity Expansion: Traffic Generation and Land Use Change*. UCB-ITS-RR-93-5. Institute of Transportation Studies, University of California, Berkeley, April.

Hartgen, D.T., A.J. Reser, and W.E. Martin. 1994. *State of the Practice: Transportation Data and Modeling Procedures for Air Quality Emissions Estimates*. Center for Interdisciplinary Transportation Studies, The University of North Carolina at Charlotte, July.

Harvey, G.W. 1994. Transportation Pricing and Travel Behavior. In *Special Report 242: Curbing Gridlock, Vol. 2*, National Research Council, Washington, D.C., pp. 89–114.

Harvey, G., and E. Deakin. 1993. *A Manual of Regional Transportation Modeling Practice for Air Quality Analysis*. National Association of Regional Councils, Washington, D.C., July.

Holder, R.W., and V.G. Stover. 1972. *An Evaluation of Induced Traffic on New Highway Facilities*. Texas A&M University, College Station, March.

Hu, P.S., and J. Young. 1992. *Summary of Travel Trends: 1990 Nationwide Personal Transportation Survey*. FHWA-PL-92-027. Oak Ridge National Laboratory, Oak Ridge, Tenn., March, 43 pp.

Jorgensen, R.E. 1947. Influence of Expressways in Diverting Traffic from Alternate Routes and in Generating New Traffic. *HRB Proc.*, Vol. 27, pp. 322–329.

Lave, C. 1992. Cars and Demographics. *Access,* No. 1, Fall, pp. 4–11.

Lynch, J.T. 1955. Traffic Diversion to Toll Roads. *Proc.,* American Society of Civil Engineers, No. 702, June, pp. 1–27.

Mieszkowski, P., and E. Mills. 1993. The Causes of Metropolitan Suburbanization. *Journal of Economic Perspectives,* Vol. 7, No. 3, pp. 135–147.

NRC. 1994. *Special Report 242: Curbing Gridlock: Peak-Period Fees to Relieve Traffic Congestion, Volumes 1 and 2.* Transportation Research Board and Commission on Behavioral and Social Sciences and Education, National Academy Press, Washington, D.C.

Pells, S.R. 1989. *User Response to New Road Capacity: A Review of Published Evidence.* Working Paper 283. Institute for Transport Studies, The University of Leeds, United Kingdom, Nov.

Pisarski, A.E. 1992a. *Travel Behavior Issues in the 90s.* FHWA-PL-93-012. Federal Highway Administration, U.S. Department of Transportation, July, 82 pp.

Pisarski, A.E. 1992b. *New Perspectives in Commuting.* FHWA-PL-92-026. Federal Highway Administration, U.S. Department of Transportation, July, 37 pp.

Rossetti, M.A., and B.S. Eversole. 1993. *Journey to Work Trends in the United States and Its Major Metropolitan Areas, 1960–1990.* FHWA-PL-94-012. Volpe National Transportation Systems Center, U.S. Department of Transportation, Cambridge, Mass., Nov., 245 pp.

Royal Commission on Environmental Pollution. 1994. *Transport and the Environment.* Eighteenth Report, London, Oct.

Ruiter, E.R., W.R. Loudon, C.R. Kern, D.A. Bell, M.J. Rothenberg, and T.W. Austin. 1979. *The Relationship of Changes in Urban Highway Supply to Vehicle Miles of Travel.* Final report (preliminary draft). Cambridge Systematics, Inc., Cambridge, Mass. and JHK & Associates, Alexandria, Va., March.

SACTRA. 1994. *Trunk Roads and the Generation of Traffic.* Department of Transport, London, Dec.

Vincent, M.J., M.A. Keyes, and M. Reed. 1994. *NPTS Urban Travel Patterns, 1990 Nationwide Personal Transportation Survey (NPTS).* FHWA-PL-94-018. Federal Highway Administration, U.S. Department of Transportation, June, 152 pp.

5

Land Use and Urban Form

As described in the previous chapter, a highway expansion can induce traffic increases by releasing suppressed demand or attracting travelers away from other modes. The concern of this chapter is whether, over the long term, increased highway capacity results in development that fosters additional motor vehicle travel and hence degrades air quality and increases energy consumption (Figure 5-1). In the first section of this chapter the debate is framed against the backdrop of the influences on metropolitan decentralization. In the next three sections an overview is given of the current knowledge—from theory, empirical research, and modeling—about transportation's effect on land use. In the fifth section the efforts to change population densities through land use and transportation policies are discussed, and the possible effect of these changes on regional air quality and energy consumption is examined. In the final two sections the chapter is summarized and recommendations are made for research to improve the ability to estimate the land use, air quality, and energy consumption consequences of expanded highway capacity.

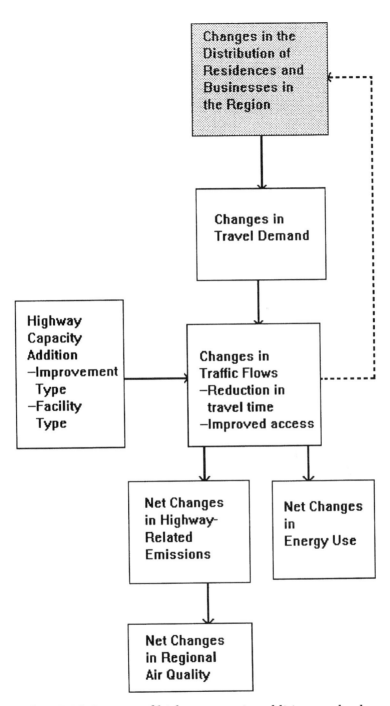

FIGURE 5-1 Impacts of highway capacity additions on land use and urban form.

BACKGROUND

Arguments Against Capacity Additions

Arguments about the adverse air quality and energy effects of shifts in land use patterns related to expanded highway capacity can be distinguished at two levels of impact. The initial impact is at the project level, at which the capacity expansion on an individual link improves the access between points at either end. Over time, the improved access may facilitate more economic activity and more development, which will result in more traffic.

At the general level, it can be argued that increased roadway capacity, especially projects serving the periphery of urban areas, supports continued low-density land development. Such development further encourages automobile use and ultimately increases air pollution and energy consumption (Figure 5-2).

Between these two extremes the potential for a network effect also exists. New capacity on a link serving two points will improve access to those points from other locations that are connected by the road system [although in some cases improvements in the flow between two points in a complex network can actually worsen system performance because of Braess's paradox (Bass 1992)]. As access is improved between any two points in a network, economic growth may follow, which would ultimately result in more traffic on adjoining segments of the network because of the improved link.

As noted earlier in this report, the scale of capacity enhancements ranges from modest (such as improved signalization) to major (such as new links or new beltways). The potential land use consequences of these varied levels of expansion increase with scale.

Research Questions

The air-quality arguments against expanding capacity must be framed as research questions in which the net traffic, air quality, and energy impacts are considered. The questions that arise can be grouped into the following categories:

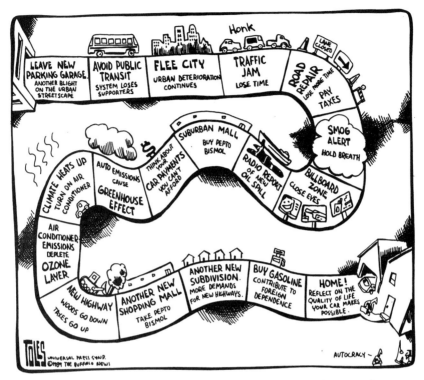

FIGURE 5-2 Highway capacity effect on land use and air quality?
(Toles © 1989 *The Buffalo News*. Reprinted with permission of
Universal Press Syndicate. All rights reserved.)

- *Direct effect*: Will the increased traffic and emissions between
  Points A and B as a result of new development negate the air-
  quality benefits of improved traffic flow? Will the period of net
  benefits outweigh the period of net costs? If so, over what period
  (e.g., 5 years, 10 years, 20 years)?
- *General effect*: Do capacity expansions result in or contribute to
  low-density land use developments that spawn automobile-
  oriented life-styles, increased traffic, higher energy consumption,
  and additional air pollution?
- *The counter-factual case*: Will congestion worsen in the absence
  of an expanded link or new facility because of growth (indepen-

dent land use changes) at both A and B that increases traffic between A and B? Is this scenario better or worse for air quality and energy use than building the facility?

• *Direction of causality*: Does the improved link between A and B cause the growth between them or is the pressure to improve the link caused by expectations of or demand for growth?

As will be described in the following sections, few of these questions can be fully answered using available theory and research. The main reason is that the research must address a very complex and indirect process. Answering the question raised in this study—what are the long-term effects of adding highway capacity on air quality and energy use—requires first an examination of the impacts of capacity additions on land use and development patterns; then identification of the related impacts on travel patterns; and finally an assessment of the effects of changes in travel patterns on vehicle emissions, air quality, and energy use. There are extensive literatures on many of these individual topics (e.g., the linkage between highway improvements and land use patterns and between transportation investments and regional growth) and numerous models developed to estimate these relationships (e.g., location theory). However, only a limited number of studies are available that examine directly the link between expansion of highway capacity, land use, and air quality.

In addition, many methodological problems arise in trying to address these questions. For example, as described later, although the provision of transportation is a requirement for suburbanization, the trend toward suburban development is influenced by far more than transportation capacity itself; the pressures for suburbanization themselves may create the demand for highway capacity. In addition, development spawns new and often unanticipated demands for transportation. Thus transportation and land use are interconnected. Moreover, land use changes take many years, if not decades, to unfold.

Before turning to the theories, studies, and models that have been used in an attempt to answer some of these questions, the context of land use changes in metropolitan areas is reviewed to better appreciate the complexity of the process and transportation's role in development and economic growth.

Context of Transportation–Land Use Relationship

The questions listed earlier assume a direct and discernable relationship between transportation investments and land use. This assumption appears well founded in light of the history of urban development and changes in transportation technologies. When walking and horse-drawn vehicles were the principal modes of transportation, cities supported high population densities with a dense network of narrow streets (Garrison and Deakin 1992). With the advent of technological innovations such as the streetcar, residential development began to shift away from the congested inner core. This was particularly evident in Philadelphia between 1840 and 1880 (Putman 1977). The early electrified rail transit systems of the era between 1870 and 1910 further expanded the process of decentralization. Finally, the advent of the automobile permitted the dispersed low-density suburban development characterizing contemporary metropolitan areas. Throughout this period, land use policies were limited to serving the interests of developers and landowners. Where zoning was practiced its scope was limited to minimizing conflicts between incompatible uses (Garrison and Deakin 1992). Both transit systems and road building served suburbanization. Many analysts have argued that this process was accelerated after World War II by federal policies such as mortgage underwriting standards and support for road construction. These policies are believed by some to have facilitated the development of the detached, single-family homes so typical of suburbia. The evidence regarding decentralizing land uses around cities, however, suggests a more complicated set of forces.

Metropolitan areas in the United States and abroad have been decentralizing, as measured by population density, since at least the middle of the 19th century (Mills and Tan 1980; Meyer and Gomez-Ibanez 1981; Mieszkowski and Mills 1993). Cities became increasingly dense during the early stages of the Industrial Revolution but then began decentralizing, particularly as resident incomes and transportation facilities improved.

The decentralization of cities can be measured using a density gradient. Density is measured by the number of people per unit of land and the gradient is a measure of the declining density away from the center. Cities are typically denser at the middle than at the periphery. At least since records have been kept, population densities at the urban center have declined, as have densities on the periphery. With some notable exceptions such as Tokyo, which does not have inexpensive land for expansion, this change has occurred independently of changes in transportation technology or degree of automobile use (Meyer and Gomez-Ibanez 1981).[1] There is no clear evidence that the federal and state housing and transportation policies of the postwar period accelerated this trend. The period of most rapid decentralization occurred between 1920 and 1950 (Mieszkowski and Mills 1993).

In addition to the transportation-related explanations, various causes have been advanced to explain this process in the United States. Various urban fiscal and social stresses have been cited as having encouraged substantial proportions of the urban population to leave for suburbs that are racially and ethnically homogeneous, have lower taxes, and offer better schools (Mieszkowski and Mills 1993).[2] Rising incomes in the urban population also play a major role in suburbanization. As incomes rise, individuals seek larger residences, which are typically less expensive at the periphery because of lower land costs (Gomez-Ibanez 1985). Mieszkowski and Mills (1993) point out that rising incomes are influential in both the transportation-related and fiscal and social stress-related classes of explanations for decentralization.

Suburbanization is unquestionably facilitated by state and federal support of road building and by local land use policies encouraging low-density development. However, density gradients in the United States and abroad suggest that much decentralization would have occurred in any event. Moreover, many argue that the policies of road building and support for detached single-family housing are strongly favored by the population at large (Downs 1993). Thus it is open to question whether the policies have shaped the preferences or vice versa. Before turning to the research itself, it is important to acknowledge the difficulty of disentangling transportation's role in land use from this mix of fiscal and social stresses, rising incomes, and public preferences.

Net Growth and Redistributed Growth

The effects of transportation in facilitating physical development are not necessarily the same as its effects on economic growth. Part of the argument made against expanded highway capacity is that by facilitating increased economic activity in a region, the expanded capacity will encourage more traffic and more air pollution. If a region is growing economically, development will occur somewhere within or near it. Combined with the effects of land use and zoning policies, transportation investments influence the location of growth, but they alone do not cause the growth. A number of highway and transit projects that were built to facilitate development, which did not subsequently occur, could be cited as evidence. Although transportation capacity is necessary for growth, it is not sufficient. Other conditions must be present—such as better access to labor, agglomeration economies (in which similar industries cluster together), or previously inaccessible natural resources—for a transportation project to contribute to net economic growth.

Transportation investments may affect growth, when other conditions hold, but it is important to distinguish between net new growth and redistributed growth. A highway project providing access to undeveloped land may encourage a shift of future development from a developed to an outlying area, but this may merely be a redistribution of growth that would have occurred elsewhere in the region. Redistributed growth at low densities raises concerns about increased traffic, but this is not the same as the traffic that might be generated by net new growth. Transportation investment, however, may result in productivity advantages associated with a location change, which could lead to net new growth. For example, a new factory located on the periphery of an urban area may be able to reorganize its work flows in more productive ways, or the employer may be able to hire labor at lower costs. If the owner of the factory is able to sell more of its product, the factory may be expanded. Thus transportation investments can influence private productivity, which in turn can stimulate new growth.

A debate has emerged over the stimulative effects of public infrastructure investments, of which transportation is a major component. In a series of articles Aschauer (1989a, 1989b, 1991) has argued that national public infrastructure investments (highways, transit, airports, and water and sewer supply) have a major stimulative effect on private productivity and output. Aschauer's application of a production function model at the national level implies that a $1 increase in public infrastructure investment will increase private output by roughly 40 cents. Munnell (1990, 1991) obtains similar results. The national effects of public investments, as estimated by these approaches, are much larger than the multistate, state-level, or metropolitan estimates developed by Munnell and others (Hulten and Schwab 1991). For example, Eberts's (1988) study of metropolitan areas found that a $1 increase in public investment increased private output by 7.5 cents. Munnell (1991) argued that one should not make too much of the size of these estimates; the pertinent fact is that they are all positive and statistically significant. Hulten and Schwab (1993), however, show that plausible corrections to the statistical procedures used by Aschauer, Munnell, Eberts, and others can alter both the sign and the statistical significance of the relationships they report. Whereas all of these authors would agree that individual projects can influence private output if other conditions hold, there is little agreement about their effects in general. Thus the highway capacity expansions of interest in this report cannot be assumed to stimulate growth, although they do when other conditions, such as the presence of agglomeration economies or improved access to labor or materials, hold.

Demographic Influences on Growth

Metropolitan decentralization has created a demand for transportation capacity not merely because of redistributed growth but also because many regions, particularly those in the South and West, are growing even as they decentralize. Population growth in the United States increased by approximately 10 percent between 1980 and 1990, but almost all of this increase occurred in metropolitan areas (Bureau of the Census 1994, Table 41). During that period population increased by 11.8 percent in metropolitan areas but by only 2.7 percent in nonmetropolitan areas (Table 5-1). The growth in metropolitan population is unevenly distributed around the nation, with metropolitan areas in the South and West growing much faster than those in the Northeast and Midwest (Table 5-1).

Changes in the location preferences of firms and individuals across regions appear to create much of the demand for new transportation capacity. The transportation capacity is not itself attracting population

TABLE 5-1 Percentage Change in U.S. Population, 1980–1990 (Bureau of the Census 1994, Table 41)

	METROPOLITAN AREAS	NON-METROPOLITAN AREAS
United States	11.8	2.7
Northeast	3.2	5.2
Midwest	2.7	−2.0
South	17.7	3.0
West	24.1	12.0

and employment to the South and West, nor is it attracting growth to metropolitan areas. As described in later sections, however, transportation capacity affects the location and shape of development.

THEORY LINKING TRANSPORTATION AND LAND USE

In the early 1900s Von Thunen and Ricardo recognized that agricultural land values depended in large measure on the accessibility of the land. Farmers valued land located closer to markets or linked by superior road access more highly than land located farther away. These insights were applied to residential land values in urban areas by Alonso (1964), who advanced the theory that residential land values closer to the center would be valued more highly than those on the periphery. Residents would balance housing costs against travel costs, and when travel costs (principally in the form of time) were high, residents would pay a premium for housing near the center. Alternatively, transportation improvements serving the periphery would reduce transportation costs and increase the value of land there while reducing the value of land in the central area. Reductions in commuting costs therefore would tend to cause cities to spread out.

The shape of cities, of course, is also heavily influenced by the location preferences of commercial entities. Giuliano (1989a) groups commercial location theories into three categories: (a) retail and service, (b) industrial, and (c) business location. Retail and service enterprise location is based on central place theory, which predicts location on the basis of population characteristics and the willingness of residents to travel for different kinds of goods (Christaller 1966; Giuliano 1989a).

> According to this theory, a reduction in transport cost would result in larger, more dispersed centers, because consumers would be willing to travel farther to shop and consume services. Conversely, an increase in travel cost would result in smaller, more concentrated centers, all things being equal. (Giuliano 1989a)

Industrial location theory traces to Weber's early work during the 1920s, which is focused on the location advantages of regions. Firms are postulated to locate where the costs of transporting inputs to production and serving markets are minimized.

Business location theory is an extension of residential location theory; it holds that expanding transportation capacity to the periphery will increase the value of land at the periphery because of shifts in residential demand. The shifts will reduce the relative value of land at the center, which businesses can then use to their advantage, but the attractiveness will depend on whether the business is labor- or land-intensive. Thus, this theory predicts that reductions in transportation cost will have a decentralizing effect for residents, a centralizing effect for businesses seeking agglomeration economies or access to labor with specialized skills, and a decentralizing effect for businesses seeking access to land or lower-cost labor (Giuliano 1989a).

Several insightful reviewers have pointed out the limitations and weaknesses of location theory (Meyer and Gomez-Ibanez 1981; Gomez-Ibanez 1985; Giuliano 1989a; Giuliano 1989b; Garrison and Deakin 1992; Moore and Thorsnes 1994). Their conclusions are summarized in this section. It is acknowledged at the outset that all theories tend to oversimplify, for example by treating only a single mode or type of trip; assuming a homogeneous housing stock; or dealing with residential location while holding business location constant or vice versa, although the two are logically related. Perhaps most significant, most theories assume a monocentric city whereas current metropolitan areas—at least those that are growing—are polycentric.[3] Industrial location theory has been criticized for focusing on cost minimization rather than consumer demand and for ignoring other conceptually important location factors such as agglomeration economies, labor force availability, and economies of scale. Location theories in general ignore the durability of location decisions and their impact on urban form over long periods of time. Theories do not capture key elements that influence location and growth, such as the physical attractiveness of one location over that of another within a region. Setting aside the problems of oversimplification and the partially offsetting tendencies toward centralization for some kinds of businesses, location theories taken together point toward net decentralization whenever transportation costs decline.

EMPIRICAL EVIDENCE

Many different studies have been conducted to trace the impact of specific transportation investments on the physical development of metropolitan areas. All such studies face substantial methodological problems. Various case studies have been conducted, but whether any can be generalized is questionable. One class of studies compares metropolitan areas on the basis of type of investment, such as the presence or absence of beltways. A problem with this approach is the difficulty of finding appropriate comparisons. Another class of studies compares urban form before and after a specific investment is made. One problem with this approach is that land use changes occur over very long periods of time; it is difficult to control for other influences on development that are independent of the transportation investment. Another problem is the difficulty of isolating the extent to which public and private investment decisions anticipate one another (Meyer and Gomez-Ibanez 1981, 116).

The earliest statistical studies examining the impact of streetcar systems on urban form and the impacts of the earliest freeways found a significant relationship between transportation and land use (Giuliano 1989a). Many early studies indicated a positive effect on land values near major new highway projects, representative examples of which are cited in Table 5-2. Subsequent analyses of the impact of major investments such as beltways and rail transit systems in the 1970s and 1980s, however, have found mixed results.

TABLE 5-2 Effects of Highway Projects on Land Use and Land Values (Adapted from M. Meyer and E. Miller, *Urban Transportation Planning*, McGraw-Hill, 1984, Table 2-19. Reproduced with Permission of McGraw-Hill)

AUTHOR	DATE	TYPE OF FACILITY	CONCLUSIONS
Adkins	1959	Expressway	Value of land closest to the expressway increased 300 to 600 percent. Land farther from the expressway experienced smaller increases in value
Ashley and Bernard	1965	Highway	Major development at interchanges was caused by many factors including market conditions and financing arrangements
Mohring	1961	Highway	Increase of land value near highway was balanced by relative decreases elsewhere
Payne-Maxie and Blayney-Dyett	1980	Beltway	No strong evidence exists to suggest that beltways improve a metropolitan region's competitive advantage. Differences in housing development patterns between beltway and nonbeltway cities were not statistically significant

An extensive statistical analysis of the difference between metropolitan areas with and without beltways found little difference in terms of changes in population, job location and type, or overall economic activity (Payne-Maxie and Blayney-Dyett 1980). (See Appendix D for a summary of the studies discussed in this section.) It proved difficult, however, to establish a group of cities without beltways that would provide a meaningful comparison group for cities with beltways. Even cities without beltways were likely expanding their road networks in ways that would improve the accessibility and attractiveness of land on the suburban periphery. In addition, cross-sectional analyses attempting to control for the confounding effects of other influences on land use suffer from interdependence among the explanatory variables.

Detailed analysis of several expansions of major highways in California indicates that such investments in capacity accelerated residential development in areas served by the corridors. Whether the capacity expansion shifted development from other parts of the region was not determined (Hansen et al. 1993). Even the more limited finding of accelerated development was not corroborated by the opinions of developers or planners. The consensus among these groups was that the residential development was unrelated to the capacity expansions. Whereas opinion surveys of this type are not conclusive, they highlight the difficulty of establishing the direction of cause and effect. The road capacity expansions in these examples occurred before the residential development, but the road capacity expansions would have been planned for many years. Developers' decisions about where and when to expand residential capacity may have been influenced by the plans for road building or by the expectation that road capacity would be adequate to allow the developers to sell the units. Alternatively, the plans for road building may have been influenced by the public sector's expectations concerning growth in residential development. The extent to which developer and public investment decisions anticipate one another raises a complex methodological problem for studies that attempt to relate the timing of private investment decisions to the provision of public infrastructure.

Major rail investments are thought to encourage higher-density development. Analyses of their impact on urban development in the United States suggest that their effects have been small (Knight and Trygg 1977). Some transit stations have stimulated surrounding development and—when accompanied by changes in land use policies—

have resulted in more clustered, dense development. These successes are limited, however. Jurisdictions have found it difficult to change land use policies in favor of higher densities because of residents' fears about the effects on low-density neighborhoods. Lack of coordination in regional land use planning has stymied some of the effects on urban form that might have occurred from rail transit investments. The analyses of the land use consequences of major rail investments, however, along with the more recent studies of the consequences of major highway investments, have usually examined relatively short-term effects. (An exception is the study of highway capacity additions in California, which examined the effects of some projects over a period of 15 to 20 years.)

Cross-National Comparisons

The evidence regarding the impact of transportation investments on land use in the United States in recent decades implies small-scale consequences, at least in the short term. Yet cross-national comparisons of urban form and transportation investment policies have led some to argue that they can have major effects (Newman and Kenworthy 1989). In comparing 32 cities from around the world, Newman and Kenworthy (1989) showed that per capita gasoline consumption—a proxy for automobile use—is far higher in U.S. cities than abroad, which they attribute to lower metropolitan densities in the United States.

Although the data that Newman and Kenworthy present on per capita gasoline consumption in cities with different urban forms and transportation policies are disputed, most criticism has been aimed at their methodology. Gomez-Ibanez (1991) points out that the correlation they draw between gasoline consumption and urban form does not control simultaneously for gasoline prices, incomes, the durability and value of the existing built environment, and other variables. Among the other variables that could be added is the mere availability of relatively inexpensive, undeveloped land on the periphery of urban areas.

In addition, cross-national comparisons do not allow an accurate prediction of what might happen in any particular country because of the great differences in law, policy, institutions, and fuel prices. For example, the former West Germany has almost as many automobiles per capita as the United States, but the ability to exercise regional land use policies and to link land use and transportation plans has made it possible to ensure that new development on the edge of existing cities occurs at fairly high densities (Pucher and Clorer 1992). Similarly, the impact of rail transit investments in Toronto on land use goals is made possible "by the local government's coordination of the subway system's development with zoning and other land-use policies *in a way unique to North American experience*" (Meyer and Gomez-Ibanez 1981, 117) (emphasis added). Pucher's (1994) more recent comparison between transit use in the United States and Canada also emphasizes the differences between zoning, land use, and transportation planning policies in the two nations. In Canada, regional transportation planning is made more successful by less fragmented local government and by the inability of local governments to pursue land use and zoning policies at variance with those of provincial regulatory boards (Pucher 1994). Although regional land use plans can be developed in the United States (with some difficulty), the conflicting interests of individual jurisdictions within regions have long impeded the exercise of any real control over land use in accordance with these plans. Even if more coordinated land use policies were adopted, the magnitude of likely effects on automobile use and emission levels would have to be examined—a topic that is discussed later in this chapter.

Studies of Housing and Residential Location

As indicated in the section on location theory, residents are assumed to choose housing that minimizes commuting. Research on commuting patterns within the current distribution pattern of jobs and residences in the Los Angeles metropolitan area, however, indicates that commuting trips are two-thirds greater than would be required if workers were located in neighborhoods that minimized their commutes (Small and Song 1992). This indicates that a key assumption of location theory does not hold in practice. The excess commuting that occurs may be explained by preferences for neighborhoods with low crime rates or amenities such as schools; the difficulty of minimizing commutes for both workers in dual worker households; and other influences, such as racial discrimination (Giuliano and Small 1993; Mills 1994). Location theory does not capture these qualitative factors, which appear to affect location preferences.

RESULTS FROM MODELS

Models provide an alternative means of testing theoretical relationships between highway capacity expansion and land use. Models make it possible to hold constant the complex set of external influences on land use, aside from transportation, to isolate transportation's effects on residential and business location. A great deal of complexity is still required to adequately represent the potential effects of transportation capacity expansion on urban form. Models approaching this complexity make such large data and computational demands that the models have never been estimated. Some approaches simplify the models to make them more workable, but in doing so they sacrifice theoretical purity for practicality.

Many models that deal with land use and transportation have been developed over the last three decades. The literature on such models is voluminous. The following discussion draws heavily on reviews of the modeling systems by Berechman and Small (1988), Meyer and Gomez-Ibanez (1981), Giuliano (1989a), and Wegener (1994). The intent is not to catalog the full array of models or to fully discuss their strengths and weaknesses. Rather, basic approaches and their potential contribution to addressing the policy question at hand are examined in this section. For simplicity, two classes of models are described: (*a*) optimization models, based on microeconomic theory, and (*b*) spatial interaction models, whose origins are traced to geographically based land use models. In the next section, only those models developed for metropolitan areas in the United States that can analyze both land use and transportation policies are discussed. Other models have been developed for metropolitan areas abroad but have not been applied in the United States (Wegener 1994).

Optimization Models

To estimate how changes in the capacity of the transportation system affect land use, economic optimization models incorporate the theoretical influences of capacity changes on residential and business location within a metropolitan area. As indicated in the section on theory, reductions in travel costs can have both centralizing and decentralizing consequences depending on how these reductions induce firms or employees to change location. The models required to capture these potential changes are complex. To estimate the consequences for residential location, optimization models represent a regional housing market along with the utility-maximizing behavior of individuals. To estimate the consequences for commercial enterprises of changing location, the models must calculate their profit-maximizing behavior. Various models have been developed that include at least some of the most desirable features.

The Herbert-Stevens model was the first to incorporate economic principles of behavior as they would apply in a metropolitan area (Berechman and Small 1988). The model incorporates a housing market and the utility-maximizing behavior of individuals. The model also makes some simplifying but unrealistic assumptions. For example, it assumes homogeneous preferences for housing. The original model treated the transportation system as given, a limitation that has been overcome in subsequent extensions. The model takes the locations of employment and the supply as given, which weakens its application to the question at hand.

The Mills model, which has been extended by several modelers, is based on the microeconomic approach developed by Mills during the 1970s (Berechman and Small 1988). In its extensions, particularly the Mills-Kim version, the model incorporates residential location and a transportation system. The model, however, is based on a monocentric city and is not intended to represent any given city (it also assumes a fully priced transportation system). The Mills-Kim model assumes that residential location is based solely on the minimization of travel costs, but as indicated previously cost minimization is only one of many determinants of residential location. The model estimates an efficient, long-run equilibrium result, rather than capturing any of the dynamics of short-term location change in response to short-term changes in the transportation system. The Mills-Kim model also takes employment location as given, but the basic disadvantage of this approach is its computational complexity, which has prevented it from being applied in its full form (Giuliano 1989a).

According to Berechman and Small (1988), the most fully specified model has been developed by Anas (1984). It is a general equilibrium model that incorporates land use, employment and residential location, and a highway network in which the effects of congestion can be simulated. The Anas model, like the Mills model, has never been applied in practice. Because so many features of interest are incorporated into the model, it includes an enormous number of variables and equations. The complexity creates demands for extensive data. A more practical model based on Chicago (the CATLAS model) was developed by Anas, but it is also extremely complicated and has only been estimated in a simplified form.

Other models of urban systems in the United States have been developed, but they do not represent one or more of the key features of interest in this study. David Boyce of the University of Illinois at Chicago, for example, has developed a unified model of a metropolitan area that can analyze alternative transportation policies, but it does not model land use policies (Wegener 1994).

Spatial Interaction Models

Perhaps the most widely known and used models were originally based on the gravity model developed by Lowry in the mid-1960s, which was later reformulated and extended by Garin (Berechman and Small 1988). In the early formulations, gravity models predicted residential location (assuming a fixed location for employment) based on the ways that activities in one area are estimated to attract work, shopping, social, or recreational trips from other areas.

The basic disadvantage of early versions of gravity models was their lack of a theoretical basis. They did not incorporate individual utility maximization. Moreover, in modeling land use, they ignored land and housing prices as determinants of urban form (the lack of both current and trend data on housing prices in almost all U.S. metropolitan areas poses a practical constraint on all models incorporating housing markets). The criticism that gravity-type models lack a theoretical basis has been muted by the recognition that (a) the mathematical form of spatial interaction models is quite similar to that of modeling procedures used in optimization models and (b) the model, recast in logit form, can be derived from the same theories of consumer behavior that underlie optimization models (Evans 1973; Wilson et al. 1981; Anas 1983).

This aggregate mutlinomial logit model approach to land use has been integrated with travel forecast models by Putman—ITLUP, the Integrated Transportation Land-Use Package (Putman 1991)—and by Harvey (Harvey and Deakin 1991). These approaches explicitly reflect the transportation system and can estimate the land use consequences of changes in highway capacity. They offer another advantage over optimization models in that they can be (and are being) estimated and applied to policy questions being asked at the metropolitan level.

Integrated models have drawbacks. Because the influences on residential and business location in most of these models are driven by transportation costs and access to jobs, the models tend to overestimate the land use effects of changes in transportation costs by leaving out the qualitative features that influence location choice. Most models do not explicitly incorporate housing and land markets, although Putman's ITLUP model has incorporated surrogate measures of housing and land availability. Surrogate measures of housing such as the income distribution of households do not capture all of the qualitative features of housing and neighborhoods that lead to the excess-commuting phenomenon discussed earlier, but they temper the tendency to overestimate the land use effects of changes in transportation costs. (Such models incorporate the effect of transportation on the distribution and location of development but do not include any of the net growth-inducing effects of transportation on the demand for land.) Large-scale integrated models can be useful in comparing scenarios but are inappropriate for analyzing specific effects, such as comparing the land use consequences of a bus investment with those of a rail investment in a specific corridor (Giuliano 1994, 25).

Despite their weaknesses, spatial interaction models produce plausible results and can be used to compare policy options at the regional level. Sensitivity analyses of ITLUP for the Southern California region, for example, indicate that over a 20-year forecast period a 20 percent change in travel time results in changes in residential densities of between 1.5 and 5 percent, depending on household income (Putman 1993). Model analyses of the possible effects of highway capacity expansions on land use provide a sense of both the direction and magnitude of change. For example, the Association of Bay Area Governments (ABAG) used the region's POLIS model to estimate the consequences for land use of the highway capacity expansions in the

Metropolitan Transportation Commission's 1989 transportation improvement program (ABAG 1991). A comparison of the build and no-build scenarios for 2010 suggested changes in the locations of jobs and housing in the region of less than 1 percent—a difference that was not statistically or practically significant. Some of the projects increased population density, others decreased it. (As discussed later in this chapter, these predictions did not consider changes to existing land use and zoning regulation, which would alter the potential effects.) The changes are small in part because the built environment in the Bay Area is so large that incremental changes in highway capacity have little regional consequence.

IMPLICATIONS OF CHANGES IN POPULATION DENSITY FOR TRAVEL AND EMISSIONS

The decentralization process that characterizes metropolitan growth has been occurring for many reasons other than increases in transportation capacity. Nonetheless, transportation capacity decisions combine with land use policies to influence the form of the decentralization process. They have long-term consequences for regional automotive emissions and energy consumption. In U.S. metropolitan areas, most road capacity expansion is taking place at the urban fringe; the suburban and exurban development being served is typically low density and automobile oriented. Moreover, the spatial separation of housing, jobs, and shopping caused by zoning practices leads to more travel and trips than would mixed-use developments at moderate to higher densities (Harvey and Deakin 1991; Cervero 1991). Thus the more that development occurs in low-density areas, the more it appears that automobile use will be encouraged, and the worse will be the consequences for emissions and energy consumption.[4] The severity of the impact is mitigated in part because jobs appear to be decentralizing along with residences (Gordon and Richardson 1989). In principle this could lead to shorter work trips. To date work trips from suburb to suburb tend to be longer in distance (although not necessarily in time) than trips from suburbs to city centers.[5]

Data indicate that automobile mileage increases as population density decreases (Table 5-3). The data in Table 5-3 are taken from the

TABLE 5-3 Average Vehicle Miles Traveled at Different Levels of Density (Dunphey and Fisher 1994, Table 4)

Density (Persons per Square Mile)	Percent Change in Density	Vehicle Miles Traveled	Percent Change in Vehicle Miles Traveled
1,280	—	6,500	—
2,688	208	6,500	0
6,400	238	5,500	−15
14,700	230	4,500	−18
33,280	220	2,500	−45

NOTE: 1 mi = 1.6 km; 1 mi^2 = 2.6 km^2.

1990 Nationwide Personal Transportation Survey (NPTS) and are based on (a) the respondents' estimates of annual motor vehicle use and (b) the density of the zip code in which the respondents reside (Dunphey and Fisher 1994). Although these data indicate that vehicle travel decreases with density, there are several caveats to consider.

First, major demographic differences exist in the resident populations at different densities, and these differences affect automobile use (Dunphey and Fisher 1994). Low-income residents without automobiles and high-income single adults and couples without children tend to predominate in dense urban environments, whereas families with children tend to predominate in suburbs. These groups have different travel characteristics. For example, families with young children have the highest levels of personal travel, and inner-city residents with the lowest income have the lowest levels of mobility. Thus the changes in travel with density shown in Table 5-3 partially reflect the differing travel demands of different types of households.

From an air-quality perspective, the distance of automobile travel is not the only important criterion; the number of trips is almost as important as the vehicle miles of travel. Roughly half of automotive volatile organic compounds (VOCs) emitted from a trip are caused by engine starts. Cold starts account for most of these emissions, but some result from evaporative emissions (hot soak) after the automobile has stopped. [The number of trips, as opposed to distance traveled, is of importance for both VOC and carbon monoxide (CO) emissions, but less so for emissions of oxides of nitrogen.] The number of automobile trips declines with population density, but only in the densest parts of the largest metropolitan areas (Figure 5-3).[6] The cold start/hot soak problem may diminish in time with the introduction of heated catalytic converters, but until this technology is introduced engine starts will remain an important contributor to air quality problems.

Very few areas have the high densities at which trip-making is likely to decline. These densities are only reached in the most heavily populated central cities. Metropolitan area growth, however, is occurring on the periphery, as is most of the demand for highway capacity. Cer-

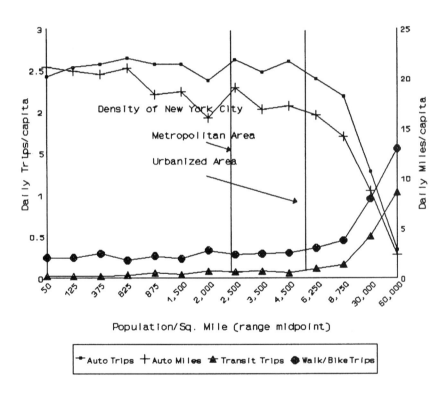

FIGURE 5-3 Average trips by mode and population density (Dunphey and Fisher 1994, Table 5). Note: 1 mi = 1.6 km; 1 mi^2 = 2.6 km^2.

tainly no urbanized area within a metropolitan area in the United States has an overall density sufficient to cause the major shifts in per capita travel shown in Table 5-3 and Figure 5-3 (Table 5-4).[7] Of the 50 largest metropolitan areas in the United States, the average density within the urbanized area is 965 persons per square kilometer (2,500 persons per square mile) (Schrank et al. 1993). For entire metropolitan areas, which usually include less intensely developed land on the periphery, the average densities are much lower. For the 39 metropolitan areas with more than 1 million population, the average density is 256 persons per square kilometer (664 persons per square mile) (Rossetti and Eversole 1993). These low densities are likely to persist for some time. Existing homes and commercial buildings in suburban areas have lifetimes of 50 to 100 years, and current homeowners resist efforts to increase the density of development (Downs 1993).

There is interest in some jurisdictions in combining land use policies, investment in transit, and the physical design of residential and

TABLE 5-4 Population Density in 1990 in the 10 Metropolitan Areas with the Densest Urbanized Areas (Schrank et al. 1993, Table 35; Rossetti and Eversole 1993)

| | DENSITY (PERSONS PER SQUARE MILE) | |
NAME	URBANIZED AREA[a]	METROPOLITAN AREA[b]
New York City	5,270	2,446
Los Angeles	5,225	428
Honolulu	4,890	N.A.
San Francisco–Oakland	4,350	849
Miami	3,855	1,012
Chicago	3,775	1,435
Philadelphia	3,735	1,104
Washington, D.C.	3,690	989
Baltimore	3,620	913
San Diego	3,230	594

NOTE: 1 mi^2 = 2.6 km^2. N.A. = not applicable.
[a]Schrank et al. 1993, Table 35.
[b]Rossetti and Eversole 1993.

suburban commercial developments to reduce automobile use in newly developing or redeveloping areas (Cervero 1991; Cambridge Systematics et al. 1992; Atash 1993). For example, Cervero (1991) points to major suburban commercial developments in Washington State and Texas, where 20 percent of trips are made by ridesharing or bus transit as a result of land use restrictions requiring dense, mixed development.

The largest such effort has been undertaken by 1,000 Friends of Oregon, a public interest group that is sponsoring a project entitled "Making the Land Use, Transportation, and Air Quality Connection" (LUTRAQ). Instead of building a highway bypass around the western part of Portland (Washington County) to accommodate expected growth in population, employment, and automobile travel, the LUTRAQ project proposes requiring future commercial and residential development in Washington County to use transit- and pedestrian-oriented designs. The new areas would be served by a light rail system accompanied by expanded bus service (a plan referred to as LUTRAQ I). Employment centers and shopping areas would be located along the rail system and would be near enough to the residential areas to encourage transit, walking, and bicycling for work trips. In an expanded version (LUTRAQ II), automobile use would be discouraged with parking fees one-third as high as those of downtown Portland, and transit use for commuting would be encouraged with free transit passes.

The project researchers are applying transportation and land use models to compare the consequences of the LUTRAQ approach with building the Western Bypass. Although the emissions and air quality effects of the alternative investment strategies have not yet been analyzed, interim analyses have been conducted of the travel-related effects of the different scenarios, including the effects on trip making and mode choice. Interim modeling results of the effects of land use controls and physical designs in LUTRAQ I suggest modest increases in transit, walking, and carpooling shares of trips in the study area (Table 5-5). More substantial changes appear possible when parking charges and free transit passes are added in LUTRAQ II; the travel demand measures increase both transit use and carpooling more than the land use and design measures. The shifts in mode shares for work trips result in a substantial decrease in peak-period travel; LUTRAQ

TABLE 5-5 Mode Shares: LUTRAQ Western Bypass Study Area (Cambridge Systematics et al. 1992 and Parsons-Brinckerhoff in Giuliano 1994)

	MODE SHARE (PERCENT)		
ITEM	BYPASS	LUTRAQ I	LUTRAQ II
Home-based work trips			
Walk	2.5	3.5	3.5
Solo drive	75.1	72.7	63.9
Carpool	13.6	13.8	19.7
Transit	8.8	10.0	12.8
All Trips			
Walk	3.7	4.5	4.5
Automobile	89.0	87.6	87.0
Transit	7.3	8.0	8.6

II would reduce total automobile travel in the afternoon peak by 13.6 percent (Giuliano 1994, 30).

It is difficult to predict how much pedestrian- and transit-oriented residential designs in newly developing or redeveloping locations in a metropolitan area might affect automobile travel and how these changes, in turn, would affect regional air quality. Density benefits in terms of reduced automobile travel are partially offset by increased emissions due to traffic congestion. Modeling results from the Denver metropolitan area, for example, suggest that restricting almost all future development to transit corridors would substantially increase population density and transit use in these corridors by 2010, but no net improvement in regional air quality would result (May and Scheuernstuhl 1991). According to these estimates, carbon monoxide emissions would increase because of increased congestion, whereas other emissions would be largely unchanged. This study, however, assumed that pedestrian trips would not replace automobile trips within the transit corridors, which could bias the results. Nor did the study model the possible effects of complementary travel demand policies such as pricing parking. More important to understanding the implications for regional emissions is the low density of the existing metropolitan area. As with most western and southern metropolitan areas where population is growing, Denver's urbanized area has a relatively low population density [687 persons per square kilometer (1,780 persons per square mile)]. Even for the forecast year of 2010, 70 percent of Denver's population and 60 percent of employment locations are already in place. Thus substantially increased density, which at current growth rates would not be reached until well after 2010, would be required for these shifts in transportation and land use policies to substantially affect mode choice and trips at the regional level.

The regional consequences of added highway capacity and its effects on transportation, land use, and air quality are being estimated in many metropolitan areas because of the requirements in the Clean Air Act Amendments of 1990 (CAAA) and the Intermodal Surface Transportation Efficiency Act of 1991 that state air quality plans and transportation capital investment plans conform with one another. The San Francisco Bay Area's transportation investment plan has been extensively analyzed for its potential effects on air quality. These analyses were generated in part by litigation to stop the expansion of highway capacity in the region (Harvey and Deakin 1991). The new traffic that could be generated by the plan was estimated, and its effects on land use and regional air quality were forecast. The forecasts indicated that capacity increases internal to the region resulted in net reductions in emissions, whereas capacity increases in the fringe areas resulted in net increases in emissions. The overall effects of the build scenario were small, however; the transportation investment plan was estimated to reduce regionwide CO and VOCs by about 1 percent by 2010. These results are well within the forecast error of the models. The results could become negative if plausible changes in assumptions, such as more or faster automobile travel, are made (Harvey and Deakin 1991).[8] Current zoning and development restrictions also affect the results. When these restrictions are relaxed, specific communities can experience significant increases or decreases in density because of shifts in development and employment within the region (ABAG 1991), but the overall regional effects, positive or negative, remain small. Similar results have been obtained in the conformity analyses conducted by other metropolitan planning organizations (Hartgen et al. 1993; Hartgen et al. 1994). The modeling procedures used to calculate these effects, although state of the art in some regions, are fairly crude in others. Concerted research on such topics as travel behavior and modeling improvements is required to enhance the ability to estimate the consequences of highway capacity expansion on land use and air quality.

SUMMARY

Highway capacity expansions are criticized because they are thought to lead to suburban sprawl, greater automobile use, and increased energy consumption and air pollution. The factors causing the decentralization of urban areas, however, are far more complex than just the expansion of highway capacity. Highway access to outlying areas is certainly necessary to support decentralization, but rising incomes, home buyers' desire for larger homes and more land, and flight from problems in central cities have also influenced decentralization. It remains an open question whether the provision of road capacity helped cause the decentralization of urban areas or whether the demands for decentralization caused the roads to be built or expanded.

Highway expansions, combined with prevailing land use and automobile pricing policies, have influenced the form of metropolitan development. Most metropolitan areas have grown in population and spread that population over a larger land area. This has been particularly true in the south and west over the last decade. Highway expansions have helped redistribute this growth. Capacity expansions tend to redistribute growth that would have occurred anyway, but they can result in net new growth if they stimulate productivity gains in the private sector. This can happen if an expansion allows firms to improve access to labor, capital, or markets.

Theory predicts that a reduction in transportation costs due to an expanded highway will have a decentralizing effect on residential development and both centralizing and decentralizing effects on businesses. Businesses that serve individuals tend to follow them. Businesses exporting goods and services out of the urbanized area may or may not decentralize depending on the importance of agglomeration economies and the extent to which they are labor or land intensive. The net effect of reduced transportation costs, however, will be toward decentralization.

Early case studies indicated that highway investments had powerful effects on land values and suburban development. More recent studies of major highway and transit investments do not indicate large effects. Analysts have advanced a number of reasons why transportation investments in recent decades have small effects on land use. Part of the problem is methodological. The cause-and-effect relationships are difficult to distinguish, even with sophisticated statistical techniques. Moreover, the impacts affect subsequent development for many decades, but most studies examine short-term consequences.

There are practical reasons why highway capacity expansions have relatively minor effects, at least over a 5- to 10-year period. The out-of-pocket cost of transportation is low (and falling), which reduces the importance of location relative to other preferences. It could be that once a basic level of accessibility is established, other preferences—for housing, neighborhood, or schools—take precedence (Giuliano 1989b). In addition, the transportation infrastructure in large urbanized areas is extensive and affords a high degree of personal mobility. Even substantial new investments in capacity will make only incremental changes in the infrastructure and will therefore have small effects on regional land use. (The effects within specific corridors, however, can be substantial.)

By contrast, past changes in transportation technology that influenced urban form were dramatic (Meyer and Gomez-Ibanez 1981, 105). Shifting from walking to horse-and-buggy to streetcar to automobile produced sharp changes in travel speed, which facilitated a dispersal of residential development around metropolitan areas. These changes helped shape land use when they were introduced, but no similar changes have occurred in recent decades (Gomez-Ibanez 1985; Meyer and Gomez-Ibanez 1981, 105) or are anticipated in the near term.

Given the extensive highway network and the low-density built environment around it, even large expansions of highway and transit capacity are unlikely to have more than marginal consequences on land use in a 5- to 10-year time frame. It follows that small changes in capacity, such as improved traffic flow from signalization, will have negligible effects on land use.

Integrated models have been developed to examine the transportation-land use relationship. These models are far from perfect, but they provide a sense of the direction and magnitude of change. They confirm that highway capacity expansions on the periphery of an urban area lead to decentralization as the theory predicts, but they also indicate that the effects on density, and hence air quality, are small over a 20-year forecast period. Conformity analyses of metropolitan areas to meet the requirements of the CAAA, for example, indicate that the differences between the build and no-build scenarios are typically within the forecast errors of state-of-the-art models. Because highway expansions and low-density development patterns determine land uses over many decades, the effects of even marginal increases in highway capacity in any given year are likely to compound beyond the 20-year forecast used in most analyses.

Policies that encourage higher residential densities are being pursued in some metropolitan areas to reduce automobile use. Given the prevailing use of automobiles—and the subsidies that encourage their use (e.g., subsidized parking)—it would take large increases in density for trip making to shift from automobiles to other modes. Modest increases in density can reduce the amount of automobile travel, but the density of the average urbanized area would have to more than double to significantly affect mode choice. Moreover, most development is occurring on the periphery of urbanized areas, where the existing densities are far lower than within the urbanized area. Current policies and practices in most metropolitan areas make changes in density sufficient to affect mode choice and regional air quality difficult to achieve. Neighborhoods resist measures to increase density or to provide mixed uses, and close-in suburbs impose growth restrictions or use zoning practices that force development farther out. Efforts to reduce automobile use and improve regional air quality will have more potential if society is willing to make major changes in land use planning at the regional level and to fully price the use of the highway system.

RECOMMENDATIONS FOR IMPROVING THE KNOWLEDGE BASE

Behavioral Research

An improved understanding of behavioral responses to transportation capacity expansions, among other influences shaping location preferences, is fundamental to efforts to better predict the land use and environmental effects of increased highway capacity. Because land uses change very slowly, behavioral responses to changes in highway capacity must be measured over forecast periods of 20 to 40 years to fully appreciate the implications of the capacity change. Longitudinal studies are required to address these issues. The main methodological problem to be solved is how to control for and isolate the effects of other influences shaping location preferences so that the effects of transportation investment can be studied. Methodological problems are compounded by the lack of adequate historical data on the many components to be measured. Finally, the cost and lack of funding for ongoing longitudinal studies make it difficult to mount a research program that might provide additional insights into the issues. The committee recognizes the significant methodological and empirical problems in addition to the costs of performing such analyses. Nevertheless, longitudinal studies are necessary to understand how the effects of changes such as highway capacity additions accumulate and unfold over decades. Research is needed on appropriate methodologies and data collection strategies.

Cross-sectional domestic and international comparisons of trip making as a function of land use patterns (e.g., density, land use mix, and urban design)—with controls for life-style, demographic, and household characteristics—should also be pursued to better understand how travel behavior can be affected through land development policies.

Modeling

Suggestions for improving both the theoretical framework and the application of land use models have recently been made by other scholars (Wegener 1994; Deakin 1991) and are not repeated here. One of the key deficiencies is the lack of practical models that can be applied in metropolitan planning practice for policy analysis. Existing land use models could be improved by validating their ability to forecast. This could be done by first calibrating the models on existing historical data and then testing their ability to "predict" the present. In a few metropolitan areas the data exist to make such analyses possible.

The linkages between land use and transportation forecast models should be improved so that the long-term effects of transportation policies, such as adding highway capacity, on land use and related travel behavior can be examined comprehensively and with greater accuracy.

NOTES

1. See especially the arguments advanced by Meyer and Gomez-Ibanez in Chapter 2 and Appendix A of their book, which builds upon the paper by Mills and Tan (1980).
2. Mieszkowski and Mills (1993) provide a critical review of the different explanations of suburbanization. Whereas crime, educational attainment, and taxes were not found to influence the decentralization of U.S. cities, race was found to be influential. Comparisons between Canadian and U.S. cities, which were found to be decentralizing at the same rate between 1950 and 1970, were unable to distinguish the influence of the more centralized land use planning and transit-dependent policies on the higher densities of Canadian cities from social stresses such as crime and schooling.
3. Moore and Thorsnes (1994) point out that the monocentric model provides important and useful insights that inform the development of a polycentric model, but the polycentric model is much more complicated because it is multidimensional.
4. For simplicity of exposition, this discussion assumes that increased regional automobile travel will have similar emissions consequences across regions. Because of the variability in meteorological conditions, the effects of increased travel on ozone formation will vary considerably across regions (NRC 1991).
5. The effects on air quality of jobs following residents in a decentralized pattern are complex. They include the consequence of less transit use but, as discussed in Chapter 3, are also greatly influenced by the automobile speed of the trips they replace. Depending on speed, speed variability, traffic volume, and local climatic conditions, this could be better or worse for air quality.
6. Ewing et al. (1994) obtain similar results for the effects of density on travel and trips in a microlevel analysis of travel in six South Florida communities of widely varying densities.
7. Urbanized area is a Bureau of the Census term defined by total population, presence of a central city, and population density. There must be a total population of 50,000 or more, and population density must exceed 386 people per square kilometer (1,000 people per square mile). An urbanized area can be parts of counties, unlike metropolitan areas, which are defined by county boundaries.

8. The effects of capacity expansions on total traffic and emissions were also influenced by existing constraints on development. Growth controls in inner suburbs, for example, restrict the ability to increase density (and thereby reduce automobile use) as a result of expanded capacity in the urban core. By removing these restrictions on development, "the [modeling] results would have been somewhat different . . . specifically, highway investment in the core would lead to some densification . . ." (Harvey and Deakin 1991).

REFERENCES

ABBREVIATIONS

ABAG   Association of Bay Area Governments
NRC   National Research Council

ABAG. 1991. *Assessing the Future: A Sensitivity Analysis of Highway and Road Improvements on Growth in the San Francisco Bay Area.* Working Paper 91-4. Oakland, Calif.

Alonso, W. 1964. *Location and Land Use: Toward a General Theory of Land Rents.* Joint Center for Urban Studies Publication Series. Harvard University Press, Cambridge, Mass.

Anas, A. 1983. Discrete Choice Theory, Information Theory, and the Multinomial Logit and Gravity Models. *Transportation Research B*, Vol. 17, pp. 13–23.

Anas, A. 1984. Discrete Choice Theory and the General Equilibrium of Employment, Housing and Travel Networks in a Lowry-Type Model of the Urban Economy. *Environment and Planning A*, Vol. 16, pp. 1489–1502.

Aschauer, D. 1989a. Is Public Expenditure Productive? *Journal of Monetary Economics*, Vol. 23, No. 2, March, pp. 177–200.

Aschauer, D. 1989b. Does Public Capital Crowd Out Private Capital? *Journal of Monetary Economics*, Vol. 24, No. 2, Sept., pp. 171–188.

Aschauer, D. 1991. *Public Investment and Private Sector Growth: The Economic Benefits of Reducing America's "Third Deficit."* Economic Policy Institute, Washington, D.C.

Atash, F. 1993. Mitigating Traffic Congestion in Suburbs: An Evaluation of Land-Use Strategies. *Transportation Quarterly*, Vol. 47, No. 10, pp. 507–524.

Bass, T. 1992. Road to Ruin. *Discover*, May, pp. 56–61.

Berechman, J., and K. Small. 1988. Modeling Land Use and Transportation: An Interpretive Review for Growth Areas. *Environment and Planning A*, Vol. 20, pp. 1285–1309.

Bureau of the Census. 1994. *Statistical Abstract of the United States, 1993*. U.S. Department of Commerce.

Cambridge Systematics et al. 1992. *The LUTRAQ Alternative/Analysis of Alternatives: An Interim Report*. Parsons Brinckerhoff, Portland, Oreg.

Cervero, R. 1991. Congestion Relief: The Land Use Alternative. *Journal of Planning Education and Research*, Vol. 10, No. 2. pp. 119–129.

Christaller, W. 1966. *Central Places in Southern Germany* (C.W. Baskin, translator). Prentice Hall, Englewood Cliffs, N.J.

Deakin, E.A. 1991. Jobs, Housing, and Transportation: Theory and Evidence on Interactions Between Land Use and Transportation. In *Special Report 231: Transportation, Urban Form, and the Environment*, Transportation Research Board, National Research Council, Washington, D.C., pp. 25–42.

Downs, A. 1993. *Stuck in Traffic: Coping with Peak-Hour Traffic Congestion*. Brookings Institution.

Dunphey, R., and K. Fisher. 1994. Transportation, Congestion, and Density: New Insights. Presented at 73rd Annual Meeting of the Transportation Research Board, Washington, D.C.

Eberts, R. 1988. *Estimating the Contribution of Public Capital Stock to Metropolitan Manufacturing Production*. Working Paper 8610 (revised). Federal Reserve Bank of Cleveland, Cleveland, Ohio.

Evans, S. 1973. A Relationship Between Gravity Models for Trip Distribution. *Transportation Research*, Vol. 7, pp. 39–61.

Ewing, R., P. Haliyur, and G.W. Page. 1994. Getting Around a Traditional City, a Suburban PUD, and Everything In Between. Presented at the 73rd Annual Meeting of the Transportation Research Board, Washington, D.C.

Garrison, W., and E. Deakin. 1992. Land Use. In *Public Transportation*, 2nd edition (G. Gray and L. Hoel, eds.), pp. 527–550.

Giuliano, G. 1989a. *Literature Synthesis: Transportation and Urban Form, Report 1*. Contract DTFH61-89-P-00531. Federal Highway Administration, U.S. Department of Transportation.

Giuliano, G. 1989b. New Directions for Understanding Transportation and Land Use. *Environment and Planning A*, Vol. 21, pp. 145–159.

Giuliano. G. 1994. Land Use Impacts of Transportation Investments: Highway and Transit. In *The Geography of Urban Transportation*, 2nd edition (S. Hanson, ed.), in press. Guilford Press, New York.

Giuliano, G., and K. Small. 1993. Is the Journey to Work Explained by Urban Structure? *Urban Studies*, Vol. 30, No. 9, pp. 1,485–1,500.

Gomez-Ibanez, J. 1985. Transportation Policy as a Tool for Shaping Metropolitan Development. *Research in Transportation Economics*, Vol. 2, pp. 55–81.

Gomez-Ibanez, J. 1991. A Global View of Automobile Dependence. *Journal of the American Planning Association*, Vol. 55, No. 3, pp. 376–391.

Gordon, P., and H. Richardson. 1989. Gasoline Consumption and Cities: A Reply. *Journal of the American Planning Association*, Vol. 55, No. 3, pp. 342–346.

Hansen, M., D. Gillen., A. Dobbins, Y. Huang, and M. Puvathingal. 1993. *The Air Quality Impacts of Urban Highway Capacity Expansion: Traffic Generation and Land Use Change*. UCB-ITS-RR-93-5. Institute of Transportation Studies, University of California at Berkeley, April.

Hartgen, D., et al. 1993. *Non-Attainment Areas Speak: Present and Planned MPO Responses to the Transportation Requirements of the Clean Air Act of 1990*. Federal Highway Administration, U.S. Department of Transportation.

Hartgen, D.T., A.J. Reser, and W.E. Martin. 1994. *State of the Practice: Transportation Data and Modeling Procedures for Air Quality Emissions Estimates*. National Cooperative Highway Research Program Project 25-7.

Harvey, G., and E. Deakin. 1991. *Toward Improved Regional Transportation Modeling Practice*. National Association of Regional Councils, Washington, D.C.

Hulten, C., and R. Schwab. 1991. Is America Really on the Road to Ruin? *The Public's Capital*, Spring, pp. 6–7.

Hulten, C., and R. Schwab. 1993. Infrastructure Spending: Where Do We Go from Here? *National Tax Journal*, Vol. 46, No. 3., Sept., pp. 261–273.

Knight, R., and L. Trygg. 1977. *Land Use Impacts of Rapid Transit: Implications of Recent Experience*. U.S. Department of Transportation.

May, J., and G. Scheuernstuhl. 1991. Sensitivity Analysis for Land Use, Transportation, and Air Quality. In *Transportation Research Record 1312*, Transportation Research Board, National Research Council, Washington, D.C.

Meyer, J., and J. Gomez-Ibanez. 1981. *Autos, Transit, and Cities*. Harvard University Press, Cambridge, Mass.

Meyer, M., and E. Miller. 1984. *Urban Transportation Planning: A Decision-Oriented Approach*. McGraw-Hill, New York.

Mieszkowski, P., and E. Mills. 1993. The Causes of Metropolitan Suburbanization. *Journal of Economic Perspectives*, Vol. 7, No. 3, pp. 135–147.

Mills, E., and J. Tan. 1980. A Comparison of Urban Population Density Functions in Developed and Developing Countries. *Urban Studies*, Vol. 17, No. 3, pp. 313–321.

Mills, E. 1994. *Excess Commuting in U.S. Metropolitan Areas*. Presented at Conference on Network Infrastructure and the Urban Environment: Recent Advances in Land Use-Transportation Modeling, Aug. 18–20, Stockholm, Sweden, 18 pp.

Moore, T., and P. Thorsnes. 1994. *The Transportation/Land Use Connection*. Planning Advisory Service Report 448/449. American Planning Association, Chicago, Ill.

Munnell, A. 1990. How Does Public Infrastructure Investment Affect Regional Economic Performance? In *Is There a Shortfall in Public Capital Investment?* (A. Munnel, ed.), Federal Reserve Bank of Boston, Conference Series No. 34, Boston, Mass., pp. 69–103.

Munnell, A. 1991. Is There Too Little Public Capital? *The Public's Capital*, Spring.

NRC. 1991. *Rethinking the Ozone Problem in Urban and Regional Air Pollution.* National Academy Press, Washington, D.C., 489 pp.

Newman, P., and J. Kenworthy. 1989. Gasoline Consumption and Cities: A Comparison of U.S. Cities with a Global Survey. *Journal of the American Planning Association*, Vol. 55, No. 1, pp. 24–37.

Payne-Maxie and Blayney-Dyett. 1980. *The Land Use and Urban Development Impact of Beltways.* Final report. DOT-OS-90079. U.S. Department of Transportation and U.S. Department of Housing and Urban Development, Oct.

Pucher, J., and S. Clorer. 1992. Taming the Automobile in Germany. *Transportation Quarterly*, Vol. 46, No. 3, July, pp. 383–395.

Pucher, J. 1994. Public Transport Developments: Canada vs. the United States. *Transportation Quarterly*, Vol. 48, No. 1, Winter, pp. 65–78.

Putman, S. 1977. Calibrating a Residential Location Model for 19th-Century Philadelphia. *Environment and Planning A*, pp. 449–460.

Putman, S. 1991. *Integrated Urban Models 2: Policy Analysis of Transportation and Land Use.* Pion Limited, London, 355 pp.

Putman, S. 1993. Sensitivity Tests with Employment and Household Location Models. Presented at the 3rd International Conference on Computers in Urban Planning and Urban Management, Georgia Institute of Technology, July.

Rossetti, M., and B. Eversole. 1993. Journey to Work Trends in the United States and Its Major Metropolitan Areas. FHWA-PL-94-012. Federal Highway Administration, U.S. Department of Transportation.

Schrank, D., S. Turner, and T. Lomax. 1993. *Estimates of Urban Roadway Congestion, 1990.* Research Report 1131-5. Texas Transportation Institute, College Station, March.

Small, K., and S. Song. 1992. "Wasteful" Commuting: A Resolution. *Journal of Political Economy*, Vol. 100, No. 4, pp. 888–898.

Wegener, M. 1994. Operational Urban Models: State of the Art. *Journal of the American Planning Association*, Vol. 60, No. 1, Winter, pp. 17–29.

Wilson, A., et al. 1981. *Optimization in Locational and Transport Analysis.* John Wiley and Sons, New York.

6
Findings and Conclusions

Despite more than two decades of clean air legislation and considerable progress in reducing pollution from transportation sources, many major metropolitan areas continue to be out of compliance with national air quality standards. The Clean Air Act Amendments of 1990 (CAAA) introduced more stringent controls to help ensure further reductions in motor vehicle emissions coupled with new milestones and deadlines for attaining compliance, strict monitoring procedures, and automatic sanctions for noncompliance that include loss of federal highway funds.

Legislation similar to the CAAA has not been passed recently in the energy area. However, transportation's share of petroleum consumption in the United States has steadily increased during the past decade, and dependence on foreign oil sources has reached levels exceeded only in 1979. Thus energy officials are seeking ways to improve fuel efficiency and reduce vehicle travel to cut back energy consumption.

OVERVIEW

The CAAA require close scrutiny of metropolitan area transportation improvement programs (TIPs), particularly projects, such as highway capacity additions, that could stimulate new motor vehicle travel and thus increase vehicle emission levels. The conformity process required by regulation is the primary instrument by which transportation agencies in nonattainment areas and maintenance areas[1] must demonstrate the compatibility of TIPs with state implementation plans (SIPs) for meeting air quality standards by attainment deadlines.

The conformity process as it is currently interpreted in Environmental Protection Agency (EPA) regulations places heavy demands on the modeling and analytic capabilities of metropolitan planning organizations (MPOs). Until SIPs are revised and approved by EPA,[2] areas that have not attained national standards must demonstrate that (*a*) projects in regional plans and TIPs[3] will not result in motor vehicle emission levels higher than those in a 1990 baseline year and (*b*) by building these projects, emissions will be lower in future years[4] than if the projects are not built (i.e., the build–no-build test). Once new SIPs are approved, with new budgets established for motor vehicle emissions, the conformity test changes.[5] The build–no-build test is no longer required, but nonattainment areas must demonstrate through regional emissions analyses using network-based transportation demand models that the TIP will not produce aggregate emission levels in excess of the motor vehicle emissions budget in the approved SIP (*Federal Register* 1993, 62,193–62,194, 62,249).[6]

The tests required by the conformity regulations, particularly the build–no-build analysis mandated by the interim conformity process, require a precise assessment of whether specific investments in highway capacity at specific locations in metropolitan areas will result in a net gain or a net loss in regional air quality. This assessment would be difficult to make under the best of circumstances. Not only does it involve estimating initial changes in vehicle emissions from changes in traffic flow characteristics as a result of the new capacity, it also requires the long-term responses by transportation system users to be forecast. Travel time savings and the improved access provided by new capacity will influence travel demand.

MPOs, states, federal agencies, and courts that must exercise oversight responsibility are being asked to make judgments on the basis of their interpretations of the available scientific evidence. This study was motivated in large part by the practical needs of policy makers and decision makers in meeting regulatory requirements.

The study task was complicated by the recognition that the concern for the environmental effects of highway building is part of a larger debate over the appropriate direction of metropolitan development and the role of transportation investments in shaping such development. There is an emerging consensus that a less polluting, more energy efficient transportation system is desirable (Deen and Skinner 1994, 11). Yet there are strongly held differences of opinion concerning the speed with which this goal should be pursued, the emphasis that should be placed on mobility and economic growth vis-à-vis environmental protection, and the extent of government regulation and intervention that is appropriate (Deen and Skinner 1994, 11).

The benefits of the nation's highway system are well documented. Highways are a major component of the infrastructure base that has supported the growth and development of the nation's metropolitan areas. An extensive highway network affords a high degree of mobility for people and freight at low out-of-pocket costs.

These benefits are not without costs. Highway vehicles, the dominant form of passenger and freight transport, are a major source of pollutants and a major user of fossil fuels. Highways have supported the decentralization of U.S. metropolitan areas, increasing reliance on motor vehicle travel with the associated emissions and energy use, although many other factors have influenced dispersed urban settlement patterns. The private cost of motor vehicle transport does not adequately capture the full social costs of congestion, air pollution, and energy use.

Public policies could change travel patterns and location preferences in ways that reduce trips and encourage travel by less polluting modes. Such policies include pricing motor vehicle travel to more fully recover its social costs from users and encouraging more coordinated land use to cluster development. The current debate turns on how large these changes should be, how feasible they are to introduce, and how quickly they will bring about substantial changes in travel behavior.

Although massive investments in new highway infrastructure are unlikely in the post-Interstate era, pressure for expanding highway capacity will continue in the growing suburban and exurban portions of large metropolitan areas. These locations are where most new road construction or expansion is expected and where the potential for increasing emission levels and energy use is greatest. Thus, this study has reviewed what is known and what is not known about the likely size and direction of these effects.

In the following sections the crosscutting issues are reviewed, committee findings are presented for each impact area, and the net effects of highway capability expansion on air quality and energy use are assessed. Recommendations for research and data collection that could advance the state of knowledge are then provided. Concluding observations address the current focus of the CAAA.

CROSSCUTTING ISSUES

At the conclusion of its review, the study committee identified several issues that had complicated the study task:

- **Changes in highway capacity affect the urban transportation system in complex ways that are not always obvious. The primary effect of adding highway capacity is to reduce travel time on the specific facility with increased capacity, but because of the network character of the transportation system, a reduction in travel time from expanding a particular highway facility affects travel on other routes and modes.** The spatial extent of these changes varies from case to case but is related to the magnitude of the highway capacity addition and traffic flow conditions on the larger network. These complex network adjustments must be considered in assessing the overall impact of highway capacity additions.

  Users of the transportation system will respond to improvements in the system by changing their travel behavior when it is to their advantage to do so. These responses will change not only the travel volumes on different facilities but also total travel on the highway network because of mode shifts and changes in the number and length of trips. In addition, users may change the time of day they travel to more preferred travel times. These adjustments must be taken into account in an overall assessment of the impact of highway capacity additions.

- **Changes in highway capacity must be assessed with reference to conditions on the rest of the urban transportation system.** The impacts will differ depending on local factors–congestion levels, automobile ownership levels, and land use densities. The effects of not adding highway capacity or of making alternative investments must also be compared with the build option to determine net effects. This involves an assessment of whether congestion will worsen if the new capacity is not added, whether there is adequate capacity in the system so that congestion can be averted if travelers shift their routes and times of travel, or whether investments in other modes (e.g., transit or bicycle facilities) can accommodate travel needs. Estimating these effects is also difficult.

- **The effects of major highway capacity additions vary over time.** User responses to travel service changes are likely to be more significant in the long run than initially as highway capacity additions influence long-term decisions about the location of development in a metropolitan area and automobile ownership. A key uncertainty is at what point, or whether at any point, the emission increases from the development and traffic stimulated by the capacity addition will offset initial emission reductions from smoothing traffic flows. Estimates of overall net effects on emissions and energy use depend on the length of time over which the effects are analyzed and the value placed on long-term versus more immediate effects.

- **Forecasting the long-term impacts as well as the initial impacts of highway capacity additions requires modeling a complex sequence of interrelated changes in land use, travel behavior, traffic patterns, vehicle emissions, and energy use. There is considerable uncertainty about the quantitative outcome of many of these components.** The predicted impacts for each component in the modeling system typically are small and have relatively large variances. These uncertainties are likely to be compounded through the entire sequence of models and for longer forecast horizons.

• **The effects of highway capacity additions on emissions are highly dependent on the state of vehicle design, automotive and motor fuel technology, and emission controls.** Major changes in any of these factors that reduce the overall level of vehicle emissions or the emissions response to traffic flow variables will proportionally reduce the positive or negative effects of highway capacity additions on vehicle emission levels. Changes in emission levels from major alterations in vehicle design, motor vehicle technology, and emissions regulations will occur gradually (over 10 to 15 years) because of the slow pace of vehicle turnover. Other changes, such as the introduction of less polluting motor vehicle fuels (e.g., reformulated gasoline and low-sulfur diesel fuels) will have more immediate effects.

FINDINGS FOR INDIVIDUAL IMPACT AREAS

After reviewing what is known from theory, empirical research, and modeling about the relationships among highway capacity additions, emissions, air quality, and energy use, the study committee summarized its findings for each of the three impact areas.

Initial Impacts on Traffic Flow Characteristics

The committee focused its attention first on the initial effects of highway capacity additions. It attempted to isolate the effects of changes in traffic flow patterns on emission levels and energy use from longer-term effects on travel demand and location decisions.

The primary impacts of interest are changes in traffic flow patterns, particularly speed levels and speed variability. The effects of these changes on vehicle emissions and energy use, both positive and negative, depend on changes in the level and daily pattern of congestion experienced before and after the project, the traffic volume affected by the capacity addition, and the amount of traffic diverted from other heavily congested facilities. To determine net effects on emissions and energy use, these changes must also be compared with changes in traffic flow patterns that would have occurred had the highway capacity addition not been made.

To clarify what is known about the initial impacts of highway capacity additions, net increases in highway use attributable to capacity expansions are assumed to be negligible. (This assumption is relaxed in the following section.) This is a reasonable assumption for initial conditions, because initial increases in traffic volume on expanded highway links typically reflect diversions from other routes or from travel at other times of day.

Finding 1: Although considerable research and vehicle testing have been performed, few definitive and comprehensive conclusions can be reached about how highway capacity additions and their effects on traffic flow characteristics change vehicle emission levels. Virtually all vehicle emissions testing has been based on a limited set of driving test cycles whose representativeness for specific traffic flow conditions is doubtful.

Finding 2: Current emission models rely on average trip speed as the sole descriptor of traffic flow. Variability in speed, roadway grade, and other factors that strongly influence emissions are not explicitly dealt with. This one-dimensional approach cannot adequately describe the variety of traffic flow conditions that occur for different facility types and levels of congestion. People do not drive at average speeds. Under heavily congested traffic conditions, vehicle speeds are not only low but also highly variable; many stops, starts, accelerations, and decelerations occur. Under moderate to light levels of congestion, vehicle speeds are higher and less variable; there is more opportunity for cruise-type driving. These differences, particularly speed variations that produce large variations in emission levels, are not adequately reflected in current emission models.

Finding 3: Current emission models cannot predict with confidence net changes in emission rates for a wide range of changes in average trip speed that can be expected from many highway capacity additions. The predicted changes are not significantly different from zero.

Finding 4: Smoothing traffic flows reduces travel speed variation and the incidence of vehicle accelerations, which place heavy loads on the engine, thereby initially reducing emissions of carbon monoxide (CO), volatile organic compounds (VOCs), and oxides of nitrogen (NOx). The effect is most pronounced for emissions of CO and VOCs, which increase dramatically when the vehicle operates in a fuel-rich mode in response to sharp accelerations.

Finding 5: Highway capacity additions that provide relief from heavily congested traffic by smoothing traffic flows should initially reduce emissions of all three pollutants from vehicles traveling on the improved facility. Congested conditions are most common on urban arterial roads, but high levels of congestion are also found on some freeways, particularly at freeway-to-freeway interchanges.

Finding 6: The emissions reductions produced by capacity additions that smooth traffic flows (i.e., reduce acceleration variance but do not raise average speeds) will be diminished if the additions lead to average speed increases. There is considerable uncertainty, however, about the exact average speeds at which the initial reductions are lost. NOx emissions will increase gradually as speeds increase and the acceleration variance is reduced. At higher speeds (i.e., free-flow, freeway speeds), the increased power demands on the engine will cause CO and VOC emissions to increase.

Finding 7: Highway capacity additions that result in increased speeds and cruise-type driving will initially increase NOx emissions from vehicles traveling on the improved facility. However, the magnitude of the increase cannot be predicted reliably at present. The effect of such capacity increases on CO and VOC emissions is currently not well understood. High-speed, cruise-type conditions are most likely to occur when capacity is added to freeways, which operate at relatively high average speeds for a broad range of service conditions.

Finding 8: The overall initial effect of highway capacity additions on emission levels depends on changes in the distribution and daily flow of traffic on all affected network facilities, which in

turn depend on the magnitude of the highway capacity addition and on local traffic conditions. All else being equal, the emissions effects are greater the more traffic is diverted from other congested roads, the greater the level and duration of congestion experienced before the capacity addition, and the greater the total volume of affected traffic.

Finding 9: Diesel emissions from heavy-duty vehicles have not received the same scrutiny as emissions from gasoline-powered, light-duty vehicles, but it is likely that, with the exception of particulate exhaust emissions, the former can be predicted with greater certainty than emissions from gasoline-powered automobiles. The reasons are as follows: (*a*) diesel engines do not yet use any exhaust aftertreatment, so modeling their emissions does not require predicting catalyst efficiency; and (*b*) diesel engines require little cold start or acceleration enrichment, which significantly increases the variation in emission levels for gasoline-powered vehicles.

Finding 10: Current emission models predict that highway capacity additions will initially reduce all diesel emissions from heavy-duty trucks with speeds up to about 56 to 64 kph (35 to 40 mph). At higher speeds NOx and VOC emissions increase, with VOC emissions increasing more sharply. The certainty of these results must be qualified because they are based on test data from a small sample of 1979 model year, in-use diesel heavy-duty trucks.

Finding 11: Detailed data on diesel particulate exhaust emissions as a function of speed are unavailable. Trends in particulate exhaust emissions may follow those for VOC emissions because both result from incomplete combustion of motor fuels. The lack of data on particulates is troublesome because exhaust emissions from diesel-powered, heavy-duty vehicles are the primary highway vehicle source of particulate exhaust emissions and are the most sensitive of all regulated diesel emissions to deterioration and poor performance of vehicle components from inadequate maintenance or tampering. High concentrations of particulates over extended periods are a risk factor for lung cancer.

Finding 12: The initial effects on air quality of improved levels of service from highway capacity additions vary by pollutant. Localized CO hot spots will be relieved by capacity additions that eliminate bottlenecks where congestion occurs. Ozone nonattainment areas sensitive to NOx precursor emissions could be adversely affected if capacity expansions result in high-speed, cruise-type traffic operations.

Finding 13: The initial effects on energy use from highway capacity additions can be predicted more reliably than effects on emissions because fuel economy is not as sensitive to traffic flow conditions, particularly speed variation, as are emissions.

Finding 14: Current fuel economy models suggest that highway capacity additions that increase vehicle speeds from low speeds [32 kph (20 mph)] to about 56 to 72 kph (35 to 45 mph) for automobiles and about 80 kph (50 mph) for heavy-duty trucks should improve fuel economy. [Of course, all improvements in fuel economy will be accompanied by corresponding reductions in emissions of carbon dioxide (CO_2), the principal greenhouse gas.] At higher speeds, fuel economy degrades rapidly. The certainty of these results must be qualified because they are based on a sample of vehicles that is not representative of the current fleet mix.

Impacts on Travel Demand

Over time, by reducing travel time and improving the reliability of travel, highway capacity additions can induce increased highway use by encouraging more frequent trips, longer trips, and shifts from other modes. Because net increases in regional trips and travel mean increased aggregate emission levels and higher total energy use, the central concerns are to determine the conditions most conducive to stimulating new highway use and the likely magnitude of the increase.

It is important to distinguish shifts in travel, such as changes in travel routes or the time of day of travel, from new travel because the former generally do not result in a net increase in highway system use.[7] It is also important to distinguish increases in highway use that occur because of population or regional economic growth from increases attributable to the supply addition, the primary focus of this study.

Finding 1: Highway capacity additions that reduce travel time and the day-to-day variability in travel time will induce increased highway use as long as travel times are shorter and the reliability of motor vehicle travel is improved, all else being equal.

Finding 2: Highway use also increases in response to population growth, rising personal income, increased automobile ownership, regional economic growth, effective reductions in fuel prices, and land use policies that favor dispersed development patterns. Expansion of highway capacity interacts with these factors to expedite the growth in highway use and channel the location of growth within the metropolitan area. It is difficult to separate these effects because changes in development and other factors contributing to highway use often occur together with, and may either influence or be influenced by, additions to highway capacity.

Finding 3: The greatest effect on travel demand from added highway capacity is to shift traffic from other routes and other times of day to the newly expanded facility at peak travel periods. Some shifts in travel destination and mode of travel may also occur. New trips and increased automobile ownership induced by the capacity expansion are likely to be modest initially; over the long run both may increase. The greatest net increase in highway use occurs when there are large time savings from the new capacity during both peak and off-peak travel times. When capacity additions reduce only peak-period travel times, most of the perceived increase in highway use is the result of shifts in traffic from other times of day or other routes rather than a net increase in highway system use. The potential for mode shifts from transit to automobile is greatest in large metropolitan areas with extensive rail transit systems serving commuter travel in the same corridor as the expanded highway facility. Shifts from other travel modes such as walking and bicycling will occur to the extent that the highway capacity addition makes motor vehicle travel more attractive relative to those other modes. This effect is minor compared with the others discussed in this finding.

Finding 4: Highway capacity additions will not greatly increase the amount of truck travel in metropolitan areas. Truck travel responds to shippers' scheduling demands and already tends to seek the most cost-effective travel times and routes. However, highway capacity additions that serve a major port or industrial area or rail intermodal facilities could have a major stimulative effect on truck traffic. Depending on the location of these facilities, the effect on air quality would be to shift emissions either away from or toward areas of pollutant concentrations.

Finding 5: The size of the travel effect depends in part on the amount of the travel time savings relative to the total cost of the trip. The smaller the travel time savings relative to total trip time, the smaller the effect. In addition, the smaller the travel time savings relative to total trip costs (time-related and out-of-pocket), the smaller the effect, particularly for trips that require large tolls or parking charges. The latter suggests that induced traffic from highway capacity additions might be reduced by introducing or raising tolls on the improved facilities.

Finding 6: Existing travel demand forecasting models do not adequately reflect the effects of reductions in travel time or increased travel time reliability that result from an expansion of highway capacity. Of particular concern is the inability of current models to represent the effects of increased highway capacity on automobile ownership, the number of trips made, the time of day of travel, interdependencies among trips (i.e., trip chaining), and nonmotorized travel. Other travel model components—trip destination, mode choice, and route choice—are sensitive to travel time, but the effects on these choices of a reduction in travel time from a highway capacity addition must be explicitly reflected at each appropriate point in the modeling process. **With few exceptions, regional travel demand models cannot adequately forecast truck travel or the likely effects of travel time reductions from highway capacity additions on carrier and shipper behavior.**

Impacts on Land Use and Urban Form

Highway capacity additions that improve access to developable land in outlying areas of metropolitan regions can also induce increased highway use by encouraging decentralized development that increases trip distances and travel by automobile. The evidence for these impacts and their likely effects on regional emission levels, air quality, and energy use are discussed in the following findings.

Finding 1: Additions to highway capacity that reduce the cost of travel have a decentralizing effect on urban development. This effect is most pronounced when the added capacity provides improved access to developable land in outlying areas. Households and the businesses that serve them will tend to move to the suburbs or exurbs, where land costs are low. Firms exporting goods and services out of the urbanized area may or may not decentralize, depending on the importance of agglomeration economies and the extent to which they are labor or land intensive.

Finding 2: Provision of highways, combined with transportation and land use policies that have fostered motor vehicle travel and low-density development, has supported the decentralization of metropolitan areas in the United States. Many other factors have influenced the process as well: rising incomes, preferences for single-family homes, more land, suburban amenities, and flight from the social problems in central cities. The combination of influences affecting decentralization makes it difficult to isolate the role of any single factor.

Finding 3: Highway investments contribute to metropolitan economic growth, but their effect on economic growth is highly dependent on other factors. Highway investments made in concert with economic growth are likely to influence land use patterns and the distribution of economic activities. Where land is available and zoning policies are conducive to development, highway projects can direct the location of economic activity by altering the relative attractiveness of corridors within a region and accelerating the rate of corridor development.

Finding 4: Early major highway capacity expansions had major impacts on land use and urban form in metropolitan areas because of the dramatic reduction in travel costs they afforded,

which in turn increased access to undeveloped land. **In general, currently planned expansions of existing highway networks in built-up metropolitan areas are not as likely to result in major structural changes in metropolitan development patterns** for the following reasons: (*a*) metropolitan areas are not expected to grow as fast as they have in the past; (*b*) there exists a durable built environment structured around highway travel; and (*c*) an extensive highway network is already in place, and the general level of accessibility it provides is unlikely to change without major new technological advances.

Finding 5: Planned major highway capacity expansions in relatively undeveloped areas, such as outer beltways at the urban fringe, that significantly reduce travel times and improve accessibility to developable land will influence development patterns in these corridors. The expansions may extend metropolitan area boundaries if other conditions necessary for development are present.

Finding 6: State-of-the-art operational land use models, assuming current land use policies and controls, predict small changes (i.e., plus or minus only a few percentage points) in regionwide locations of employment and households in built-up metropolitan areas over a 20-year forecast period, even from systemwide changes in travel times of as much as 20 percent. The results reflect the stability and massive investment implicit in current metropolitan spatial patterns in developed areas. The use of such forecasts in air quality calculations will yield changes in calculated air quality so small as to be well within the error range of model predictions. The models corroborate empirical evidence that the effects of highway capacity expansions take years to accumulate and significantly affect regional land use patterns and air quality.

Finding 7: State-of-the-art operational land use models can provide a sense of the likely magnitude of locational changes resulting from expansions in highway system supply. However, these models cannot accurately estimate the effects of relatively small changes to highway networks. Model formulations were developed in the absence of reliable time-series data regarding metropolitan spatial patterns. As a result, their forecasts are strongly influenced by cur-

rent spatial distributions of households and employment in metropolitan areas. In addition, the near-term effects being modeled are
themselves usually small, although the cumulative effects of these
small network changes over long periods may be considerably greater.

SUMMARY ASSESSMENT OF NET EFFECTS

On the basis of its review and findings, the committee finds that the
state of knowledge and modeling practice are not adequate for predicting with certainty the impacts of highway capacity additions. In
particular, the models are not well suited to the types of analyses and
levels of precision called for by the conformity regulations. They were
developed to address different questions and cannot be readily adapted
to the task at hand.

In addition, the current regulatory requirements demand a level of
analytic precision beyond the current state of the art in modeling. For
example, a recent review of modeling procedures and data used by
MPOs to analyze the effects of transportation activities on air quality
for conformity and other regulatory purposes found that MPO comparisons of build–no-build scenarios for forecast years typically indicated very small differences between the two alternatives. Current
forecasting models cannot reliably estimate differences to that degree
of accuracy (Hartgen et al. 1994, 31).

Generalizing about the effects of highway capacity additions on air
quality and energy use is likely to remain difficult because metropolitan areas differ in key dimensions that determine likely outcomes:
location of population and economic activity, extent and performance
of local transportation systems, climate and meteorological conditions,
and prospects for population and economic growth. Moreover, the impacts are not static; over time, they contribute to and are shaped by
other factors that influence net effects on air pollution and energy use.

Nevertheless, some generalizations about net effects are possible.
On the basis of current knowledge, it cannot be said that highway capacity projects are always effective measures for reducing emissions
and energy use. Neither can it be said that they necessarily increase
emissions and energy use under all conditions. Effects are highly dependent on specific circumstances. Among the factors most likely to
affect impacts are the following:

- **Location of project in the region:** Because of the high costs of acquiring right-of-way to construct or expand highways in central cities and the concentration of new population and job growth in suburban areas, most major highway capacity additions will be built at the urban fringe. Conversely, most minor traffic flow improvements will be undertaken to reduce congestion in developed areas, either in central cities or congested suburban locations; undeveloped areas typically do not have enough congestion to require minor capacity enhancements.

- **Extent of congestion:** The extent of congestion affects highway capacity projects in two ways. Initially, adding highway capacity under heavily congested traffic conditions tends to reduce emissions and energy use by smoothing traffic flows, all else being equal. However, the travel time savings from congestion relief can stimulate travel demand and, over the long term, set the stage for development and travel growth if other conditions are present. In central cities and other built-up areas these longer-term impacts are likely to be small because the potential for development is limited. The greatest probability of large development and travel impacts occurs where major highway capacity additions provide access to developable land in outlying suburban areas.

- **Conditions present for regional growth:** In areas experiencing rapid population and economic growth, where land is available and land use policies are conducive to development, major highway capacity additions can contribute to economic growth.[8] Major highway investments made in concert with population and economic growth are likely to influence the location of growth by altering the relative attractiveness of locations within a region. The presence of new highway capacity also can accelerate the rate of development and associated travel in the area served by the highway project. Whether the development and travel lead to a net increase in regional emission levels and energy use depends on whether the development represents net new growth or a redistribution of growth that would have occurred elsewhere in the region.

- **Existing metropolitan air quality and meteorology:** The unique pollution problems and meteorology of individual metropolitan areas will influence the likely impacts of highway capacity additions on air quality. For example, in nonattainment areas where ozone formation is NO_x limited, speed-enhancing highway capacity additions that increase NO_x emissions will exacerbate the conditions leading to ozone formation. On the other hand, in areas with localized pollution problems, such as high concentrations of CO on particular corridors, highway capacity additions are likely to relieve the hot spots, at least initially, by eliminating bottlenecks where congestion is heavy and traffic speeds are highly variable.

- **Consequences of alternative scenarios:** The effect of highway capacity additions also depends on the likely outcomes of alternative futures. For example, not adding highway capacity has consequences. If congestion is predicted to grow in the absence of the project, the effects of the capacity addition could become more valuable over time in comparison with the no-build scenario. Alternatively, highway funding could be used to support other investments such as improvements in transit service. In this case, a comparison of the relative effects of the two alternatives would entail making judgments about such issues as the substitutability of and elasticity of demand for automobile and transit trips. Assumptions about the future growth of the region also affect predicted outcomes. Would growth occur without the new highway? Would that growth take place in central locations in the region or in more distant exurban areas, or would the growth occur in other, less congested metropolitan areas?

Certain combinations of conditions suggest where highway capacity additions are more or less likely to reduce emissions and energy use. For example, traffic flow improvements that alleviate bottlenecks in developed areas may reduce some emissions and energy use by smoothing traffic flows with limited risk of offsetting increases from major new development and traffic growth. The cumulative effect of multiple small improvements in traffic flows, however, may attract increased traffic even in developed areas, at least in the vicinity of the improvements.

Major highway capacity additions in less developed parts of metropolitan areas, where most growth is occurring, pose a greater risk of increasing emission levels and energy use in those areas. If developable land is available and other growth conditions are present, new capacity is likely to attract more development and related traffic to the location of the improvement. Corresponding increases in emission levels and energy use in these areas are likely. Because of the durability of current metropolitan spatial patterns, however, it may be years before these changes make a significant difference in regional emission levels and air quality.

RECOMMENDATIONS FOR RESEARCH, MODELING IMPROVEMENTS, AND DATA COLLECTION

Better models and data supported by research can help increase the certainty with which the impacts of highway capacity additions can be predicted and can narrow the gap between regulatory requirements and analytic capabilities.

Two key areas are identified where further work could significantly improve the current level of knowledge.

Emissions Modeling

Regulatory requirements of the CAAA have placed great importance on emissions modeling to demonstrate conformity, yet as discussed in the previous sections, current models are not up to this task. The most pressing needs are for the development of an emission rate model that is sensitive to a wider range of typical driving patterns than current models and is truly representative of the range of vehicles on the road today, and for the collection of vehicle activity data to use as input to this model.

Several efforts are under way to achieve this end, but with the possible exception of a state-funded effort, a sense of urgency is not apparent. Funding levels are not adequate to produce results in a timely manner to meet regulatory requirements. Perhaps the most comprehensive effort is the state-initiated research project to develop and verify a modal emissions model within 3 years, supported by state-pooled funds through the National Cooperative Highway Research Program (NCHRP 1994).[9] EPA, through its Office of Research and

Development, and the California Air Resources Board are also conducting research on drive cycles leading to development of modal emissions models, although fully operational models may be more than 3 years from completion. The Federal Highway Administration (FHWA) has funded the Oak Ridge National Laboratory to improve the accuracy of emissions (and fuel consumption) estimates used in traffic models.[10] Finally, a multimodal traffic simulation model, sponsored by FHWA, is being developed at the Los Alamos National Laboratory. The model is expected to be capable of providing second-by-second data on individual vehicle movements that can be combined with correspondingly detailed emission rates to determine emission levels. However, this system of integrated models is also several years from being fully operational.

Federal leadership and funding are required to accelerate and better coordinate these efforts. Model development requires extensive and expensive vehicle testing to develop emission rates representative of the current vehicle fleet and typical vehicle operations. The cost of the testing could be substantially reduced if the research is coordinated and well focused. Incorporation of the models into the regulatory process can only be achieved by close coordination between the transportation and the regulatory communities early in the model development process.

Travel Demand and Land Use Forecasting Models

Improvement in the ability to forecast likely behavioral responses to highway capacity additions and corresponding changes in travel service characteristics is essential to assessing environmental and other consequences of supply changes. Development of better forecasting capability requires a sound theoretical understanding of household and corporate location decisions as well as of the determinants of personal and freight travel.

Substantial new understanding of household location and passenger travel has developed during the last decade. Incorporation of this understanding into state-of-practice models requires considerable effort, both to refine the relevant behavioral linkages among the many travel and travel-related decisions made by households and to estimate the appropriate analytic relationships among them. The effort requires (*a*) collection of substantially enhanced data about the location and travel behavior of households and individuals, (*b*) estimation of enhanced models that incorporate more of the behavioral linkages among decision elements, and (*c*) test applications in one or more metropolitan regions including the development of implementation software. The data collection effort should incorporate advances from the development of activity-based travel analysis approaches. Such approaches take account of household structure and roles of household members, assignment of tasks to household members, and linkages among different aspects of travel-related decisions (e.g., the interrelationships among mode choice, destination choice, and automobile ownership).

Development of more sophisticated models for freight transportation in metropolitan areas requires a substantial effort because of the current state of freight modeling practice. The main limitations are the lack of data on freight and truck movements in metropolitan areas and the complexity of freight demand estimation and truck trip modeling. Because of these limitations, efforts should be focused at first on developing corridor-scale rather than comprehensive regional freight models.

Longitudinal studies are required to examine the long-term effects of transportation investments on land use and urban form. Although the inherent methodological and data problems are formidable, this effort is needed to understand the effects of investments that accumulate and unfold over decades. Cross-sectional comparisons of trip making as a function of different land use patterns, however, may provide partial answers more quickly as long as the analysis controls for the effects of other factors, such as automobile ownership, income, household size, and other demographic characteristics.

Support for all these activities could be provided, at least in part, from the funds granted to MPOs for their expanded planning responsibilities under the Intermodal Surface Transportation Efficiency Act of 1991. The models used by MPOs and state departments of transportation should be updated with the results of these efforts. In addition, where good historical data are available, they should be used to calibrate both travel forecasting and land use models and to "predict" current travel and land use patterns so that the models' forecasting capabilities can be validated. Finally, continued improvement in the linkages between land use and transportation forecasting models should be sought so that the long-term effects of transportation policies, such as highway capacity additions, on land use and related travel behavior can be examined comprehensively and with greater accuracy.

CONCLUDING OBSERVATIONS

Despite the considerable uncertainties in predicting the effects of expanding highway capacity on air quality and energy use, policy makers and planners must comply with current regulatory requirements and make decisions on the basis of the best available information. Thus, the committee thought it should provide its best judgment of the likely payoffs of pursuing current policies.

In its opinion, the current regulatory focus on curbing growth in motor vehicle travel by limiting additions to highway capacity is an indirect approach to achieving emission reductions in metropolitan areas that is likely to yield small changes, positive or negative, in metropolitan air quality by attainment deadlines. Historically, measures to control traffic demand or improve traffic efficiency have had limited effects (Apogee Research, Inc. 1994).[11] According to estimates from local studies using current emission models, these traditional transportation control measures (TCMs), which include traffic flow improvements among others, are likely to yield changes of 1 to 2 percent individually in regional emissions of key pollutants by current attainment deadlines (DOT and EPA 1993, 9). (The effects of traffic flow improvements could be positive or negative depending on offsetting increases in traffic.) These are small changes on a declining base; EPA projects continuing reductions of highway vehicle emissions from transportation sources over this period (Nizich et al. 1994, 5-4–5-6). Market-based TCMs—such as increased parking charges and time-of-day tolls—have greater potential for emission reductions than more traditional TCMs. However, the political feasibility of some measures is untested (Apogee Research, Inc. 1994, 43–44).

Curtailment of all highway capacity expansion that has any potential for increasing emissions risks pitting environmental against economic concerns. The conditions with the greatest potential for stimulating development and traffic and thus increasing motor vehicle emissions and energy use are likely to occur at those locations where most new capacity additions are being proposed: rapidly growing suburban areas. Yet it is precisely in these locations where the greatest need is perceived for highway capacity additions to support regional economic growth and competitiveness and where the pressures to provide highway capacity to support development are most intense.

In the past, when environmental goals have been in conflict with economic objectives, the response has been to delay or reassess environmental regulations. Given the high economic stakes associated with major highway capacity additions combined with the difficulty of determining precisely the magnitude of likely adverse effects on regional air quality, similar pressures may emerge again.

A more constructive approach in the committee's view is to look for solutions that reconcile air quality with economic goals in metropolitan areas. Historically, most reductions in motor vehicle emissions have come from changes in vehicle technology (e.g., the catalytic converter and fuel-injection technology) and fuels (unleaded gasoline) rather than from controlling motor vehicle travel. Incremental improvements in technology alone (preheated catalytic converters, engine power enrichment regulations), fuels (oxygenated fuels, alternative fuels), and maintenance and inspection programs (in-use emissions testing) should result in further emission reductions and air quality improvements over the next two decades. EPA has projected that continued fleet turnover combined with implementation of CAAA standards will result in decreases in highway vehicle emissions of VOC, CO, and NO_x of 31, 26, and 13 percent, respectively, from 1990 baseline levels by 2010 (Nizich et al. 1994, 5-4–5-6).[12]

Market solutions also have promise, although the feasibility of some approaches is untested. For example, new highway capacity could be added where congestion levels dictate, but restrictions on its use could constrain the demand-inducing potential of the capacity additions. Time-of-day tolls (i.e., congestion pricing) using electronic toll collection technologies could be introduced, traffic growth monitored, and toll levels varied to control travel demand. This managed capacity approach, if applied in a limited setting, would not require major changes in current highway finance patterns. It would allow capacity to be provided where it is most needed—that is, in highly congested corridors—but could mitigate some of the negative effects on emissions from travel growth.

Managed highway capacity additions may keep travel growth in check to meet near-term conformity requirements in some nonattainment areas. However, more aggressive measures may be necessary in the long run to reduce air pollution and conserve energy. Pricing motor vehicle travel to ensure that motorists pay the full social costs of their trips, including air pollution, could have a pronounced effect on the overall level of travel demand. Areawide time-of-day tolls could help ensure that existing metropolitan highway capacity is used more efficiently by spreading motor vehicle travel more evenly throughout the day and even eliminating some trips. A recent National Research Council report on congestion pricing (NRC 1994) has examined in depth the technical and political feasibility of this approach.

Local land use and zoning measures that increase building density and encourage mixed-use development also have the potential to reduce automobile travel and thus improve air quality, although these changes are likely to occur gradually. They should have more significant effects if they are implemented concurrently with pricing measures.

More radical technological advances—such as the "clean" car[13] that would significantly reduce pollution if not congestion from motor vehicle travel, and the automated highways and advanced vehicle control systems of the intelligent transportation system program that could dramatically improve the efficiency of existing highway facilities[14]—are on the horizon. However, these advances are at least a decade away from large-scale commercial use (TRB 1991, 33; Williams 1994, 28; PNGV 1994), and they will require massive investments and long lead times before they become widespread.[15]

Pricing strategies and major technological advances offer more direct ways of reducing motor vehicle emissions and energy consumption, but they demand a level of public acceptance that has not been evident in the past. Technology changes require massive investments, consumer acceptance of new products, and long lead times before changes are implemented in the marketplace. Pricing and land use measures require major changes in public attitudes and institutional arrangements (more coordinated regional institutions to implement areawide pricing schemes and comprehensive land use strategies) to have significant impacts. However, in the judgment of the committee, as long-run alternatives to current policy they offer far greater promise of reconciling environmental and economic interests and making significant improvements in metropolitan air quality and energy conservation.

NOTES

1. Currently the regulations apply to nonattainment and maintenance areas. However, a recent court ruling, which EPA is expected to appeal, may require the agency to issue criteria and procedures for determining conformity in attainment areas within 9 months (*AASHTO Journal* 1995).
2. EPA approval of SIPs was required by late 1993 for carbon monoxide, by late 1995 for ozone, and by late 1997 for particulates–approximately 12 months from the respective submittal deadlines for those plans, which is the maximum federal review period provided under the CAAA.
3. The final conformity regulations require a regional emission analysis for any "regionally significant" project, that is, for any facility with an arterial or higher functional classification, or any other facility that serves regional travel needs and would normally be included in the modeling for the transportation network (*Federal Register* 1993, 62,211).
4. The analysis years are the first milestone years (1995 in carbon monoxide nonattainment areas and 1996 in ozone nonattainment areas) and the attainment year for the area or, if the latter is the same as or earlier than the first milestone year, the second analysis year is at least 5 years after the first analysis year (*Federal Register* 1993, 62,244).
5. During the transition period after SIPs have been submitted but have not been approved by EPA, MPOs must demonstrate that TIPs pass the build–no-build test and also that the build scenario does not exceed the emissions budget for motor vehicle emissions contained in the submitted SIP (*Federal Register* 1993, 62,191).
6. If EPA disapproves all or portions of the SIP, states are notified, and transition period conformity regulations are in effect. If EPA finds that SIP revisions are incomplete or that states have failed to submit revisions, the conformity status of the transportation plan and the TIP will lapse 120 days after EPA's final disapproval and such a finding starts the nondiscretionary sanctions clock (*Federal Register* 1993, 62,191–62,193).
7. Route shifts can increase or decrease highway system use as measured in vehicle miles traveled by increasing or decreasing the circuity of trips to reach the new or expanded facility, but these effects are relatively minor.

8. There are no operational models, however, that formally analyze the impact of transportation improvements on aggregate regional growth, in part because of the lack of a theoretical basis for determining the relationship between transportation improvements and population and economic growth.

9. The objective of the research is a model that accurately reflects the impacts of speed, engine load, and start conditions on emissions under a comprehensive variety of driving characteristics and vehicle technologies (NCHRP 1994, 1).

10. Oak Ridge National Laboratory will collect modal emissions and fuel consumption data for a limited sample of vehicles and develop a model to estimate emissions and fuel use for alternative traffic patterns.

11. In the past, lack of funds at the local level to develop and implement competitive alternatives to automobile travel was seen as the primary impediment to achieving larger emission reductions from transportation control measures. However, the Intermodal Surface Transportation Efficiency Act of 1991 addressed this gap by expanding planning and research funds, establishing a new Congestion Mitigation and Air Quality Improvement Program, and allowing state and local governments to use traditional funding sources more flexibly to achieve air quality goals (DOT and EPA 1993, 2).

12. Although the overall level of emissions is predicted to be lower in 2010 than in 1990, highway vehicle emissions of CO are forecast to turn back up by 2005, and VOC and NO_x emissions are forecast to turn back up by 2008, because of rising emissions from growth in vehicle miles traveled (EPA 1994, 5-4–5-6).

13. The "Big Three" U.S. automobile manufacturers and the U.S. government have committed to a 10-year Partnership for a New Generation of Vehicles (PNGV) to develop a passenger vehicle with up to 3 times the fuel efficiency of today's midsized sedan. The vehicle is to cost no more to own or drive than today's comparable automobile (adjusted for economics) and is to meet or exceed current safety, emission, and performance standards. The PNGV expects to narrow the technology choices by 1997 and to develop a concept vehicle or vehicles by 2000 and a production prototype or prototypes by 2004 (PNGV 1994).

14. In the absence of other policies to control demand, advanced vehicle control systems could have the undesired effect from an air quality perspective of encouraging more motor vehicle travel and further decentralization of metropolitan areas by significantly improving the efficiency of highway transport.

15. Some low-emission vehicles (LEVs) will be introduced before the turn of the century. In California, for example, 2 percent of the light-duty vehicles marketed in 1998 must be zero-emission vehicles. EPA has approved

a similar program for the northeastern states beginning with model year 1999 (*Federal Register* 1995) but gives the states flexibility to provide emission reductions equivalent to a LEV program. The automobile makers have proposed an alternative program that would require low-emission, but not zero-emission, vehicles (i.e., electric vehicles) to be marketed in the 49 states on a phased-in approach beginning in the Northeast. EPA and state environmental officials are doubtful that the industry alternative as it is currently structured will achieve air quality objectives (*AASHTO Journal* 1994).

REFERENCES

ABBREVIATIONS

AASHTO	American Association of State Highway and Transportation Officials
DOT	U.S. Department of Transportation
EPA	Environmental Protection Agency
NCHRP	National Cooperative Highway Research Program
NRC	National Research Council
PNGV	Partnership for a New Generation of Vehicles
TRB	Transportation Research Board

AASHTO Journal. 1994. EPA Approves Low-Emission Vehicle Programs for Northeast. Dec. 30, pp. 11–12.

AASHTO Journal. 1995. Court Extends Conformity to Attainment Areas. Feb. 24, pp. 8–10.

Apogee Research, Inc. 1994. *Costs and Effectiveness of Transportation Control Measures (TCMs): A Review and Analysis of the Literature.* National Association of Regional Councils, Bethesda, Md.

Deen, T.B., and R.E. Skinner, Jr. 1994. A Paradigm for Addressing Change in the Transportation Environment. *TR News,* No. 174, Sept.–Oct., pp. 11–13.

DOT and EPA. 1993. *Clean Air Through Transportation: Challenges in Meeting National Air Quality Standards.* A joint report from DOT and EPA pursuant to Section 108(f)(3) of the Clean Air Act, Aug.

Federal Register. 1993. Criteria and Procedures for Determining Conformity to State or Federal Implementation Plans of Transportation Plans, Programs, and Projects Funded or Approved Under Title 23 U.S.C. or the Federal Transit Act. Vol. 58, No. 225, Nov. 24, pp. 62,188–62,253.

Federal Register. 1995. Final Rule on Ozone Transport Commission: Low Emission Vehicle Program for the Northeast Ozone Transport Region. Vol. 60, No. 15, Jan. 24, pp. 4,712–4,739.

Hartgen, D.T., A.J. Reser, and W.E. Martin. 1994. *State of the Practice: Transportation Data and Modeling Procedures for Air Quality Emissions Estimates.* Center for Interdisciplinary Transportation Studies, The University of North Carolina at Charlotte, Charlotte, N.C., July.

NCHRP. 1994. *Development of a Modal-Emissions Model.* Research Project Statement. NCHRP Project 25-11, Transportation Research Board, National Research Council, Washington, D.C., Oct. 6.

Nizich, S.V., T.C. McMullen, and D.C. Misenheimer. 1994. *National Air Pollutant Emission Trends, 1900–1993.* EPA-454/R-94-027. Office of Air Quality Planning and Standards, Research Triangle Park, N.C., Oct., 314 pp.

NRC. 1994. *Special Report 242: Curbing Gridlock: Peak-Period Fees to Relieve Traffic Congestion, Volumes 1 and 2.* Transportation Research Board and Commission on Behavioral and Social Sciences and Education, National Academy Press, Washington, D.C.

PNGV. 1994. *Program Plan.* U.S. Department of Commerce, July, 37 pp.

TRB. 1991. *Special Report 232: Advanced Vehicle and Highway Technologies.* National Research Council, Washington, D.C., 90 pp.

Williams, R.H. 1994. The Clean Machine. *Technology Review*, Vol. 97, No. 3, April, pp. 20–30.

Appendix A

Emission and Energy Characteristics of Heavy-Duty Diesel-Powered Trucks and Buses

K. G. DULEEP

Energy and Environmental Analysis, Inc.

Heavy-duty diesel-powered trucks are major contributors to oxides of nitrogen (NO_x) emissions and combustion-derived particulate emissions in many urban areas. This appendix provides a brief review of the energy use and emissions characteristics of heavy-duty diesel vehicles (HDDVs) and reviews the effects of expansions of highway capacity on emissions.

The structure of the HDDV fleet, which encompasses a wide range of vehicles [from 8,500 lb gross vehicle weight (GVW) to more than 80,000 lb GVW], is discussed. Data on sales, populations, and use of the HDDV fleet are presented.

Historical and future emissions regulations for HDDVs are reviewed. Since California has been the leader in new emission standards and in-use controls, particular attention is given to the California standards and the proposed low-emission truck standards. Fuel standards and in-use requirements are also discussed in detail.

The data that have been used to construct emission factors and speed correction factors for HDDVs are reviewed. In particular, U.S. Environmental Protection Agency (EPA) emission factors and speed correction factors are contrasted with the findings on these issues from other data or engineering analyses.

HDDV fuel economy data are reviewed, with emphasis on average fuel economy derived from surveys. Data on the change of fuel economy with speed derived from simulation models or on-road tests are presented. These data and their relationship to the conversion factor used to convert emissions expressed in units of work to the more familiar units of grams per mile are explored.

Finally, the findings are summarized in the context of the National Research Council's project goals of estimating the effects of expansions of highway capacity.

FLEET CHARACTERIZATION

Truck Classification

The term "heavy-duty vehicles" as defined by EPA covers trucks and buses ranging in weight from 8,501 to 80,000 lb GVW. The GVW is the total weight of vehicle with its maximum payload and is sometimes referred to as gross combination weight (GCW) for truck and trailer combinations. Trucks exceeding 80,000 lb GVW are not allowed on the Interstate highway system, although individual states permit their operation on highways. Their use in off-highway applications such as mining or logging is common. This appendix addresses only those vehicles certified for on-highway use between 14,000 and 80,000 lb GVW, largely because the 8,500- to 14,000-lb GVW class includes vehicles more similar to light-duty trucks.

These trucks and buses are also classified more commonly on the basis of a system used by industry that divides the fleet into eight classes. Classes I and II cover the 0- to 10,000-lb GVW range and include all the light-duty pickup, van, and utility vehicles that are used for personal transportation as well as in light commercial applications. Class III covers the 10,000- to 14,000-lb range and incorporates the "heavy" version of pickup trucks and vans that are used in delivery service or as motor homes. This class also incorporates some imported delivery trucks manufactured by companies such as Iveco and Isuzu (Iveco no longer sells trucks in the United States).

Class IV spans the 14,000- to 16,000-lb GVW range, and Class V spans the 16,000- to 19,500-lb GVW range. In the past, few trucks have been sold in these classes. Class IV trucks have generally been imports that are similar to the Class III imports. Class V trucks are generally the lightest versions of the Class VII trucks and are typically powered by gasoline engines. Sales in these classes account for less than 5 percent of all trucks exceeding 14,000 lb GVW. However, Ford introduced a version of its pickup truck rated at slightly more than 14,000 lb GVW in 1989–1990, which served to inflate the sales totals for this class in 1990, although the truck is really closer to a Class III truck.

Classes VI and VII span the 19,500- to 26,000-lb GVW and the 26,000- to 33,000-lb GVW ranges, respectively, and include most trucks that are referred to as medium-duty trucks. Over the last 15 years, the use of diesel engines in these trucks has increased. The extra weight of the diesel engine and related drivetrain components has caused a sales shift from Class VI to Class VII during the last decade, in parallel with increasing use of diesel engines in this market. Table A-1 gives the changing sales composition over the period from 1980 to 1990. Many import models from German and Japanese manufacturers are available in these two segments, and import penetration ranges from 10 to 15 percent.

Class VIII trucks span the range from 33,000 to 80,000 lb GVW and are sometimes incorrectly referred to as heavy-heavy duty trucks. In fact, this class is better represented as two classes, VIIIA and VIIIB. Class VIIIA spans the 33,000- to 55,000/60,000-lb range and includes trucks referred to as super-mediums and trucks used in rough applications such as construction, mining, gravel and concrete delivery, garbage hauling, and so forth. Most of these applications involve local or short-haul use. Retail sales data do not generally provide the distinction between trucks in Classes VIIIA and VIIIB. Only a few import models are sold as Class VIIIA trucks, but there are no imports in Class VIIIB.

Class VIIIB trucks, which cover the 60,000- to 80,000-lb range, are primarily for intercity or long-haul use. These trucks are correctly referred to as heavy-heavy. Table A-2 gives the factory sales by class for the United States in 1980, 1985, and 1990 and breaks out the Class VIII trucks into the two subclasses. Class VIIIB truck sales are the single largest segment of total sales and are approximately equal to half

TABLE A-1 U.S. Retail Sales by Class, All Trucks (MVMA 1981, 1986, 1991)

	1980		1985		1990		
GVW Class	Percent	Number	Percent	Number	Percent	Number	Percent Import Penetration
IV	~0	195	0	0	9.9	27,453[a]	4.6
V	0.9	2,309	1.8	5,081	1.8	5,055	66.6
VI	33.5	89,764	17.0	48,358	13.8	38,209	14.2
VII	21.8	58,434	34.2	96,973	30.8	85,343	10.6
VIII	43.8	117,270	47.0	133,581	43.7	121,324	0.15
Total	100	267,972	100	283,993	100	277,384	6.93

NOTE: Data on import penetration are not available for 1980 and 1985. GVW = gross vehicle weight.
[a] Includes a large number of Ford Super Duty Pickup Trucks.

TABLE A-2   U.S. Factory Sales and Dieselization (Excludes Imports)
(MVMA 1981, 1986, 1991)

GVW CLASS	1980		1985		1990	
	NUMBER	PERCENT DIESEL	NUMBER	PERCENT DIESEL	NUMBER	PERCENT DIESEL
IV	24	0	0	0	21,512	64.50
V	1,859	0	5,123	0	1,644	2.95
VI	51,171	21.94	27,419	59.38	16,288	71.05
VI Bus	26,084	5.90	20,530	44.26	17,853	65.17
VII	54,363	65.45	82,225	63.84	66,990	81.55
VII Bus	6,285[a]	79.70	8,756[a]	99.10	11,563	99.85
VIIIA	11,396	74.60	8,962	93.20	10,739	99.70
VIIIB	92,493	100	120,342	100	109,848	100
Total	243,675		273,357		256,437	

NOTE: GVW = gross vehicle weight.
[a]Approximately 35 percent classified as Class VIII.

of total sales. Table A-2 also indicates the increased diesel penetration
in the medium-duty classes. The data in Table A-2 exclude imports,
all of which are diesel.

Buses are generally classified into two types: school buses and
heavy-duty transit buses. School buses are generally in the 18,000- to
21,000-lb GVW category (Class V or VI), whereas transit buses are in
the 33,000- to 35,000-lb GVW range (Class VIII). Typically, school
buses are used very little, whereas transit buses and intercity buses are
used intensively. Before 1979, most school buses were gasoline powered, but the use of diesel engines in school buses increased in the
1980s. Transit and intercity buses have been powered mostly by diesel
engines for nearly two decades.

Engine Types

Unlike car and light truck manufacturers, heavy-duty truck manufacturers do not necessarily manufacture their own engines. Even the
ones who manufacture engines allow users to specify alternative

engine makes in their trucks in many cases. Engines are classified into three types: light-heavy, medium-heavy, and heavy-heavy. Manufacturers compete in the market for each segment. Table A-3 gives the U.S. factory sales by engine manufacturer in 1990, excluding imports. Data on imported engines and in domestic trucks are included in this table.

The light-heavy engine market is dominated by three models: the Navistar 7.3-L, the GM 6.2-L, and the Cummins B series engine. These engines are characterized by their relatively high rated speed of 3,000 to 3,600 revolutions per minute (RPM) and their light weight (750 to 900 lb). EPA requires that their emissions be certified to a useful life of 110,000 mi. Until 1986 the medium-duty diesel engine market was dominated by the Navistar DT-360 and DT-466, the GM 8.2-L, and the Caterpillar 3208. Ford introduced its Brazilian 6.6/7.8-L engines in the late 1980s, Caterpillar has replaced the 3208 with the 3116, and GM has discontinued the 8.2-L as of 1991. EPA rates the useful life of these engines at 185,000 mi. The heavy-heavy duty engine market for heavy-heavy duty trucks (Class VIIIB) also evolved in the 1980s. Engines are classified into those below 300 HP and those above 300 HP. Four manufacturers (Cummins, Caterpillar, Detroit Diesel, and Mack) have essentially shared these two markets. EPA rates the useful life of these engines at 285,000 mi.

Most engine models in the medium and heavy segments are offered with a variety of horsepower and RPM ratings. Typically, horsepower is changed by recalibrating the fuel system and restricting or increasing maximum fuel flow and by changing the governed speed or rated RPM. (These changes induce changes in the turbocharger size, valve timing, and injector size.) Most medium-duty engines are rated in the 2,400- to 2,600-RPM range, although ratings as low as 2,100 RPM are offered. Most heavy-duty engines are rated in the 1,800- to 2,100-RPM range, although ratings as low as 1,600 RPM are offered. In general, lower-rated RPM engines result in lower maximum truck speeds, and, as a result, low-RPM engines are less popular with truck drivers.

Diesel Truck Population, Use, and Scrappage

Details on truck use and scrappage are derived primarily from survey data. The most comprehensive survey is one conducted by the Bureau

TABLE A-3 Diesel Engines Used in Domestic Trucks, 1990 (MVMA 1991)

Engine Manufacturer	IV	V	VI	VII	VIIIA	VIIIB	Bus VI	Bus VII and Bus VIII
Caterpillar	0	0	1,184	15,575	391	33,706	0	0
Cummins	0	51	294	0	343	55,854	4	326
DDC	0	0	181	214	5	15,207	5,143	834
Ford	5	0	2,998	18,997	5,158	0	2,646	0
Mack	0	0	0	0	0	16,842	0	0
Navistar	14,820	0	7,519	25,147	5,947	0	5,526	11,117
Import Engine[a]	0	0	536	1,074	102	572	0	0
Total	14,825	51	12,712	61,007	11,946	122,181	13,319	12,277

[a] Mostly Mercedes or Volvo.

of the Census called the Truck Inventory and Use Survey (TIUS). The survey is conducted every 5 years; the most recent one (the 1987 TIUS) was conducted in early 1988. The data collected are from a sample of 104,000 trucks. Energy and Environmental Analysis, Inc. (EEA) has obtained and cleaned the 1987 TIUS data and has derived a useable sample of approximately 98,000 records. Of course, most of the trucks are light duty, since the sampling was generally according to the population distribution of trucks. Of the 98,000 trucks, 35,689 exceeded 14,000 lb GVW (that is, they were in Class IV or higher).

Truck usage is defined in TIUS on the basis of radius of operation. Local use is use within 50 mi of home base, short haul is that between 50 and 200 mi, and long haul is that exceeding 200 mi. As indicated in Table A-4, most of the Class VI through VIIA trucks are used on short-haul or local operation, whereas only Class VIIIB trucks are used in long-haul operation.

An analysis of diesel truck annual vehicle miles of travel (VMT) by vintage was also performed at the national level. The sample of diesel trucks in Classes IV and V is inadequate to provide statistically significant results. Table A-5 indicates that trucks in Classes VI, VII, and

TABLE A-4   Percent of Trucks by Area of Operation by GVW Class and Fuel Type [Based on EEA Analysis of 1987 TIUS Data (Bureau of the Census 1987)]

	AREA OF OPERATION[a]		
GVW CLASS/ENGINE TYPE	LOCAL	SHORT HAUL	LONG HAUL
Class VI Gasoline	84.4	13.8	1.8
Class VI Diesel	66.1	27.8	6.1
Class VII Gasoline	86.2	12.5	1.3
Class VII Diesel	66.4	29.0	4.7
Class VIIIA Gasoline	86.3	11.9	1.8
Class VIIIA Diesel	63.4	24.4	12.1
Class VIIIB Diesel	25.4	32.9	41.7

NOTE: GVW = gross vehicle weight.
[a]Local if greatest percentage of annual miles was accrued within 50 mi of home base. Short haul if greatest percentage of miles was accrued between 50 and 200 mi of home base. Long haul if greatest percentage of miles was accrued beyond 200 mi from home base.

VIIIA have very similar annual VMT by vintage. Annual VMT appears to be 24,000 to 26,000 mi/year for the first 4 years with a steady decline thereafter for trucks in Classes VI and VII. The same trend is apparent for Class VIIIA trucks but at slightly higher annual VMT. The VMT of Class VIIIB trucks is substantially higher, with average VMT exceeding 80,000 mi/year for the first 4 years. In an informal survey of national fleet users, EEA found that many intensive users retain a truck for about 4 years before selling it, confirming the validity of the TIUS analysis. The data in Table A-5 are an average for trucks in all types of operation including local, short, and long haul; data on long-haul Class VIIIB trucks indicate annual VMT of about 100,000 mi/year for the first 4 years.

Truck usage and scrappage are strongly interrelated. Although EPA has set useful life by engine type, engine manufacturers and truck owners both confirm that well-maintained on-road trucks not subject to severe duty cycles last substantially longer. Typically, heavy-heavy duty engines used in Class VIIIB trucks have a useful life of about 400,000 to 500,000 mi before rebuild. In long-haul use, such engines are rebuilt for the first time at the end of 4 or 5 years and undergo a second rebuild in many cases after another 300,000 to 350,000 mi.

TABLE A-5   Annual Mileage by Vintage, Diesel Trucks Only [Based on EEA Analysis of 1987 TIUS Data (Bureau of the Census 1987)]

VINTAGE (YEARS)	VI	VII	VIIIA	VIIIB
1[a]	24,049	22,183	29,819	77,957
2	23,681	26,462	33,302	86,684
3	22,308	36,186	34,974	84,475
4	24,392	26,850	39,080	82,722
5	22,541	21,220	32,937	76,912
6	19,216	21,034	28,658	66,270
7	26,082	20,051	26,503	60,169
8	20,219	20,314	27,092	55,015
9	18,028	19,478	26,238	50,600
10	16,261	17,222	24,909	45,136
11 and older	8,434	11,749	14,396	31,232

[a] Includes trucks with less than 1 year of service.

Thus, the total lifetime mileage can be 1 million to 1.2 million mi with two rebuilds, and engines and trucks can last up to 15 years. However, in many "rough use" applications such as construction and mining, the useful life can be considerably shorter.

Medium-duty engines have a typical useful life (under normal use) of 230,000 to 250,000 mi. In general, these engines are rebuilt only once, after 8 to 9 years, when used in short- or long-haul operations. Light-heavy duty diesels are not rebuilt at all, and their use in Class IV and V trucks and school buses is generally in low annual VMT applications. Light-heavy duty diesels can last about 150,000 mi in normal service, corresponding to 12 to 15 years of use, on the average.

Detailed data on registration by vintage for each of the three groups of heavy-duty trucks are not well defined because of the difficulty in classifying such trucks on the basis of available registration data. An analysis of California truck registrations by the California Air Resources Board (CARB) indicates the following approximate percentages as of 1990:

AGE (YEARS)	LIGHT AND MEDIUM-HEAVY	HEAVY-HEAVY
5 or less	25.6	64.6
6 to 10	39.3	30.0
11 to 15	25.6	5.4
16 to 20	6.5	~0
21 to 24	2.5	~0
25 or more	0.6	~0

These data indicate that virtually no heavy-heavy duty diesel trucks are older than 15 years and that about 3 percent of light/medium diesel trucks are older than 20 years. EEA believes that these data may not be correct, but the percentage of diesel trucks older than 20 years (i.e., pre-1974) that were not subject to any emission controls is small, probably less than 4 percent of all diesel trucks.

The TIUS survey also provides data on the average operating weight of trucks and the percentage of miles operated without any load (because of empty backhaul, for instance). The average loaded weights are shown in Figure A-1 by truck class. Figure A-2 shows the empty operation fraction. Surprisingly, virtually all diesel trucks report empty VMT at close to 30 percent of total annual miles.

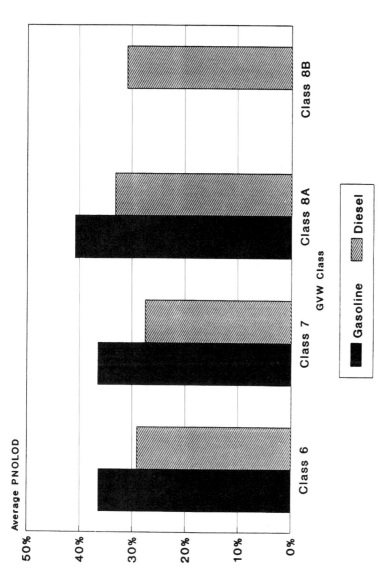

FIGURE A-1 Average percentage of annual mileage when no load was carried, by gross vehicle weight class [based on EEA analysis of 1987 TIUS data (Bureau of the Census 1987)].

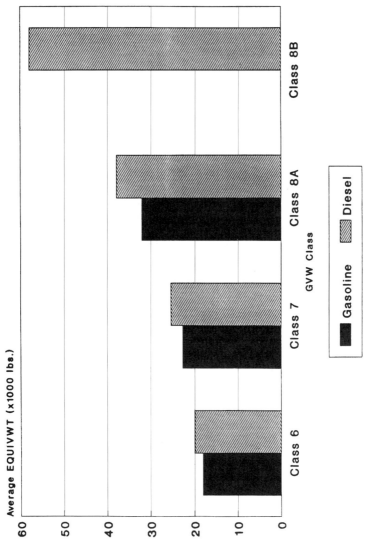

FIGURE A-2 Average operating equivalent weight by gross vehicle weight class [based on EEA analysis of 1987 TIUS data (Bureau of the Census 1987)].

The TIUS data indicate that most light-heavy and medium-heavy truck VMT is in the local area, but actual urban VMT fractions for all trucks are not well known. Heavy-heavy (Class VIIIB) trucks are used in intercity transport, which (by definition) begins and ends in urban areas, and these trucks could account for a more significant fraction of urban VMT (because of their large population and high annual VMT) than indicated by the TIUS classification. More data on and analysis of the allocation of urban VMT by truck class are desirable.

HDDV EMISSION CONTROL PROGRAMS

Introduction

HDDVs are a relatively small contributor to the national total inventory of volatile organic compounds (VOCs) and carbon monoxide (CO) emissions, but they are a significant contributor to the total NO_x emissions inventory. Diesel trucks may be a significant contributor to combustion-based PM-10 particulate, but fugitive dust dominates PM-10 emissions, so that the contribution is negligible in terms of overall PM-10. [Since 1987 EPA's particulate standard has focused on those particles with aerodynamic diameters smaller than 10 micrometers—PM-10, which are likely responsible for most of the adverse health effects of particulate matter (PM).] The National Air Pollution Emission Trends report published by EPA (Curran et al. 1994) provides some estimates of the total national contribution to emissions, although the calculation uses a number of questionable or outdated assumptions about truck emission factors, use, and scrappage. Nevertheless, these data are as follows (in thousands of short tons per year). The figures for total PM-10 do not include fugitive dust or natural source PM emissions, which can vary substantially from year to year, making trend analysis difficult.

| | *1985* | | | *1993* | | |
	HDDV	*Total*	*Percent*	*HDDV*	*Total*	*Percent*
VOC	360	25,417	1.4	298	23,312	1.3
CO	1,235	112,072	1.1	1,327	97,208	1.4
NO_x	2,389	22,853	10.5	2,014	23,402	8.6
PM-10	213	2,953	7.2	141	2,661	5.3

The ongoing federal and California regulatory efforts to reduce emissions from heavy-duty diesel vehicles are discussed in this section. Four issues that affect emissions are addressed: (*a*) emissions standards for conventional heavy-duty diesel (HDD) engines, (*b*) specifications for clean or reformulated diesel fuel, (*c*) emission standards and penetration requirements for clean-fuel and low-emitting heavy-duty vehicles, and (*d*) heavy-duty diesel vehicle inspection programs. There are currently no requirements for control of fuel economy.

HDDV Emissions Standards

EPA sets emission standards for new non-California HDD engines. CARB is responsible for setting emission standards for HDD engines that are sold as new in California. A federally certified HDDV may be registered in California as a result of relocation by the vehicle's owner or sale of the vehicle to an in-state operator. Federally certified vehicles of all types need only 7,500 mi of use before they may be registered in California.

This section discusses both federal and California emission certification standards and procedures for new HDD engines. All of the historical standards, as well as current and future standards, are presented, since some HDD engines typically remain in service considerably longer than light-duty engines and many older HDD engines are still in service. In fact, HDD engines are designed to be rebuilt and are typically rebuilt more than once, but no emission standards are currently in effect for rebuilt engines. Both EPA and CARB are developing regulations for rebuilt HDD engines.

Federal HDD Emission Standards

EPA has set standards for emissions from HDD engines since 1974. Emission standards for VOCs, CO, NO_x, and particulates have been periodically revised during the intervening years, and the emission test procedure itself was changed in 1985. EPA has recently promulgated emission standards for 1998 and subsequent model year HDD engines.

Table A-6 gives the new federal emission standards for HDD engines. All of the certification tests are performed on a diesel engine

TABLE A-6 Federal Exhaust Emission Standards for Heavy-Duty Diesel Engines (g/bhp-hr) (EPA, 40 CFR Part 86, Emission Standards for Heavy Trucks)

Model Year[a]	Volatile Organic Compounds	Carbon Monoxide	Oxides of Nitrogen	VOC + Oxides of Nitrogen	Particulates	Smoke (Opacity) (Percent)
1970–1973	—	—	—	—	—	40[b] 20[c]
1974–1978	—	40	—	16	—	20[b] 15[c] 50[d]
1979–1983	1.5 —	25 25	— —	10 5	— —	e
1984[f]	1.3 0.5	15.5 15.5	10.7 9.0	— —	— —	e
1985–1987	1.3	15.5	10.7	—	—	e
1988–1990	1.3	15.5	6.0	—	0.60	e
1991–1993	1.3	15.5	5.0	—	0.25[g]	e
1994–1997	1.3	15.5	5.0	—	0.10[g]	e
1998 and later	1.3	15.5	4.0	—	0.10[g]	e

[a] The steady-state procedure was used through 1984. The transient procedure has been used since 1985.
[b] Average opacity during acceleration.
[c] Average opacity during loaded lug down.
[d] Peak opacity during acceleration.
[e] Same as 1974–1978.
[f] Manufacturers had the option of using the 1983 procedure and standards, or standards of 1.3 VOC, 15.5 CO, and 10.7 NOx on the transient procedure, or standards of 0.5 VOC, 15.5 CO, and 9.0 NOx on the steady-state procedure.
[g] See text for discussion of urban bus emission standards.

dynamometer, but before 1985 the test consisted of measuring the emissions at 13 steady-state test points. Since 1985 the test procedure has been a transient procedure with starts, stops, and speed/load changes. The transient test is more representative of actual engine operating conditions than is the steady-state test procedure.

Table A-6 indicates that given the longevity of HDD engines, it is to be expected that the in-use heavy-duty fleet was certified to any of seven emissions standards. The table also indicates that emission standards for CO and combined VOC and NO_x were tightened considerably in steps between 1973 and 1984. The combined VOC and NO_x standards were discontinued in 1984. Particulate standards, introduced in 1988, were reduced in 1991 and again in 1994. The particulate standards may be met by averaging across all engine families (except those used in urban buses) that a manufacturer markets within each useful life category. There were no smoke opacity limits for new HDD engines until model year 1970. Since 1974 new HDD engines sold have not been allowed to exceed 20 percent average opacity during acceleration, 15 percent average opacity during loaded lug down, and 50 percent peak opacity during acceleration. HDD engines are required to meet the emission standards set forth in Table A-6 for their designated useful lives.

Emissions from urban buses are of more concern to human health than are emissions from other HDDVs because the general public is more directly exposed to urban bus emissions than to the emissions from other HDDVs. PM in diesel exhaust is the pollutant of most concern, because certain carcinogenic materials are known to be carried on the particulates. Therefore, PM emission standards for urban buses were more stringent than those for other HDDVs, at least between 1991 and 1993. Beginning in 1991, urban buses were required to meet a 0.1 g/bhp-hr particulate standard, whereas other HDDVs were required to meet that standard in 1994. The PM standards for buses are set at 0.07 g/bhp-hr for 1994 and 1995 and at 0.05 g/bhp-hr for 1996 and later years.

The emission standards that have been discussed are applicable only to new HDD diesel engines. Since HDD engines are typically rebuilt one or more times, regulators have suggested that HDD engines could be rebuilt to reduce emissions. To date, EPA has promulgated a requirement only for the rebuild or retrofit of 1993 and earlier urban buses. Operators of urban bus fleets in metropolitan areas with 1980 populations of 750,000 or more are required to choose between two options. The first sets PM emission requirements for each engine that is rebuilt or replaced. The second is a fleet average PM standard that requires an operator to meet specified annual target levels for all pre-1994 buses in the covered fleet. Although the standards are engine specific, most pre-1988 bus engines are required to meet a PM level of 0.3 or 0.5 g/bhp-hr, depending on technology feasibility, after rebuilding. Rebuild requirements for all other HDD trucks are under study.

California HDD Emissions Standards

CARB is responsible for setting HDD engine emission standards for engines sold in California. Opacity limits for smoke were initiated in 1968, and standards for VOC, CO, and NO_x were introduced in the 1973 model year. Table A-7 gives the emission standards for new HDD engines sold in California. The exhaust emissions are measured using the same test procedure that EPA uses, the only difference being that manufacturers had the option of using the transient test procedure in California beginning in 1983.

Table A-7 indicates that the California standards were generally a year or more ahead of the federal standards but that the federal and California standards for all pollutants are essentially the same between 1988 and 1997. The federal and California NO_x standard will drop to 4.0 g/bhp-hr in model year 1998, but California is considering more stringent standards for heavy-duty vehicles after 2000.

CARB was also directed by the legislature to consider emission control technology, cleaner-burning diesel fuels, and alternative fuels as methods that may be used to meet any new emission standards. One technology that has the potential for reduced emissions at relatively low cost is positive crankcase ventilation (PCV). CARB requires that all transit bus engines have PCV systems beginning in 1996. In addition, CARB has adopted the federal transit bus standards for particulate and NO_x emissions.

CARB has responded to the legislative requirements for low-emission vehicles by adopting a program that generates emission reduction credits for low-emission retrofits of existing vehicles or the purchase of low-emission transit buses. Hence, market mechanisms

TABLE A-7 California Exhaust Emission Standards for Heavy-Duty Diesel Engines (g/bhp-hr) (CARB 1993)

Model Year[a]	Total Hydrocarbons	Volatile Organic Compounds[b]	Carbon Monoxide	Oxides of Nitrogen	VOC + Oxides of Nitrogen[c]	Particulates
1973–1974	—	—	40	—	16	—
1975–1976	—	—	30	—	10	—
1977–1979	1.0	—	25	7.5	5	—
1980–1983	1.0	—	25	—	6.0	—
	—	—	25	—	5.0	—
1984	0.5	—	25	—	4.5	—
1985–1987	1.3	—	15.5	5.1	—	—
1988–1989	1.3	—	15.5	6.0	—	0.6
1990	1.3	1.2	15.5	6.0	—	0.6
1991–1993	1.3	1.2	15.5	5.0	—	0.25[d]
1994–1997	1.3	1.2	15.5	5.0	—	0.1[d]
1998 and later	1.3	1.2	15.5	4.0	—	0.1

[a] The steady-state procedure was used through 1984. The transient procedure has been used since 1985.
[b] Manufacturers may choose to certify to the total HC or the VOC standard.
[c] Manufacturers had the option of certifying to separate VOC and NO$_x$ standards or to a combined VOC + NO$_x$ standard in 1977–1979.
[d] See text for discussion of urban bus emission standards.

are being used to spur the sales of low-emission buses and to rebuild engines to lower emission standards. Low-emission engines can be certified to a range of "credit standards," which are at least 30 percent lower than the ceiling standard. The ceiling standard is the standard to which the engine was originally certified when first placed in service, or a standard indicated by CARB for pollutants if no standard existed at the time the engine was placed in service. For example, a retrofit of a 1987 HDD engine originally certified to a 6.0 g/bhp-hr NO_x standard would have to be at 4.0 g/bhp-hr or lower to obtain emission credits. California has specified a credit certification procedure and a calculation procedure to derive the credit generated by a single retrofit or purchase of a low-emission engine.

California heavy-duty truck customers would not be required to use engines that meet these low emissions standards but would be encouraged to do so by the existence of NO_x emission credit programs that would be administered by the air quality districts. Bus manufacturers have expressed concern that few customers will be willing to pay the premium for low-emission bus engines that manufacturers must charge for low sales volume engines. Consequently, little benefit may be gained from the standards.

Diesel Fuel Specifications

Both EPA and CARB have recently developed specifications for reformulated gasoline under the premise that emissions from in-use conventional vehicles can be reduced by cleaning up the fuel that they use. Research by private parties has indicated that emissions from HDD engines can indeed be cleaned up by changes in the formulation of diesel fuel. A study of diesel fuel composition on emissions (Ullman et al. 1989) is reviewed next, and federal and California requirements for diesel fuel formulations are discussed.

The 1989 study that was performed by the Southwest Research Institute (SWRI) for the Coordinating Research Council examined the effect that diesel fuel properties have on the emissions from HDD engines. The fuel properties examined were aromatics concentration, sulfur concentration, and volatility (represented by the 90 percent boiling point temperature); CO, VOC, NO_x, and particulates were the pollutants of interest. The study concluded that fuel aromatic content was most significant for PM, and PM emissions increased significantly as fuel sulfur content increased.

Section 217 of the Clean Air Act Amendments of 1990 (CAAA) contains the only federal requirements for future diesel fuel formulations. Under the CAAA, effective October 1, 1993, the concentration of sulfur in motor vehicle diesel fuel may not exceed 0.05 percent by weight, nor may the cetane number of such fuel be less than 40. The cetane requirement inhibits the dumping of low-quality fuel in domestic markets. There is currently no federal requirement on the aromatic content of diesel fuel.

CARB promulgated regulations in 1986 and 1987 that limit the sulfur and aromatic hydrocarbons content of diesel fuel to 0.05 percent by weight and 10 percent by volume, respectively. Those regulations went into effect in the South Coast Air Quality Management District only in 1988, and were in effect statewide in 1993. The low-aromatic, low-sulfur fuels caused some engine problems in California, notably with leaking fuel system gaskets. These problems have delayed the program to introduce clean diesel fuel. In reality, diesel fuel refiners in the South Coast have not been able to consistently meet the aromatics restrictions, and the aromatics limit was not enforced until 1994. There is also an exception for small refiners that permits them to produce diesel fuel with higher aromatic content up to 1997.

Section 2256(g) of the California Code of Regulations affords refiners the opportunity to develop a diesel fuel with specifications different from those of the reference fuel set forth above, but which produces NO_x and soluble organic fraction (SOF) of PM emissions from a reference engine that do not exceed the NO_x and SOF emissions (at the 90 percent confidence level) from the same reference engine using a certified reference fuel. Some refiners have been trying to develop proprietary blends that exceed the aromatics limit but meet these criteria, and at least one has been successful to date.

A law (SB 2330) was passed in 1990 that directed CARB to develop requirements for a more advanced clean diesel fuel. A second law (AB 1107) provides funds for the clean fuel research through a portion of the fines that are collected from the Roadside Heavy Duty Diesel Smoke Inspection program. As a result of these mandates, CARB has initiated its effort to develop a more advanced clean diesel fuel specification. Clean diesel fuel research is not a priority at the federal level at this time, but this may change in the near future.

Clean Fuel–Low Emission Heavy-Duty Vehicles

CARB requires the introduction of low-emission vehicles (LEVs) into the California light- and medium-duty new vehicle fleets. Some of the new LEVs may use fuels other than gasoline and diesel, such as methanol, natural gas, and liquefied petroleum gas [i.e., propane or other liquid petroleum gas (LPG)]. Consequently, CARB has developed emissions certification standards for conventional- and alternative-fuel LEVs under 14,000 lb GVW.

A similar plan for heavy-duty vehicles is under consideration, but CARB has promulgated emission standards and certification procedures for HDD diesel cycle engines that use methanol, natural gas, or LPG as fuel. The emission standards for model year 1990 and newer heavy-duty alternative-fuel engines are given in Table A-8. It can be seen that the emission standards for natural gas and LPG[1] (c.i.) engines are numerically equivalent to the standards for HDD engines as given in Table A-6. Methanol engines must meet these same standards for CO, NO_x, and particulate, and methanol engines must also meet specific formaldehyde limits and organic material hydrocarbon equivalent (OMHCE) limits. The OMHCE limits for methanol engines are designed to be as stringent as the total HC and nonmethane HC standards for nonmethanol engines.

CARB is developing an LEV program for heavy-duty (over 14,000-lb GVW) vehicles. A study assessing the technical feasibility of a heavy-duty LEV program was presented at a public workshop in September 1992. The report concluded that a low-emission truck/low-emission bus (LET/LEB) program is feasible. The study, conducted by Acurex (1992), concluded that NO_x standards for both trucks and buses could be reduced to 2.0 g/bhp-hr and PM standards could be reduced to 0.05 g/bhp-hr for diesel engines by 2002. These levels were projected on the basis of the availability of a "lean-NO_x" catalyst for diesels coupled with the use of exhaust gas recirculation. The Acurex report also concluded that by 2002, alternative-fueled (CNG/LNG/LPG) engines could attain an NO_x standard of 1.0 g/bhp-hr with ei-

TABLE A-8 California Exhaust Emissions Standards for Alternative-Fuel Heavy-Duty Diesel Cycle Engine (g/bhp-hr)

Model Year	Total HC or OMHCE[a]	Optional VOC	CO	NO_x	Particulate	Formaldehydes[b]
1985–1987	1.3	—	15.5	5.1	—	—
1988–1989	1.3	—	15.5	6.0	0.60	—
1990	1.3	1.2	15.5	6.0	0.60	—
1991–1993	1.3	1.2	15.5	5.0	0.25[c]	0.10
1994–1995	1.3	1.2	15.5	5.0	0.10	0.10
1996–1997	1.3	1.2	15.5	5.0	0.10	0.10

NOTE: New standards are under consideration for 1998 and later.
[a] The total or optional nonmethane hydrocarbon standards apply to other than methanol-fueled engines. The organic material hydrocarbon equivalent (OMHCE) standards apply to methanol-fueled engines.
[b] Methanol-fueled engines only.
[c] The particulate standard for urban bus engines in 1991–1993 is 0.10 g/bhp-hr.

ther lean burn and oxidation catalyst technology or stoichiometric burn and three-way catalyst technology. Manufacturers dispute these opinions, and CARB has not yet decided on a LET/LEB program. However, standards in the range of 2.0 NO_x/0.05 PM g/bhp-hr are under consideration for the post-2000 time frame.

There are already alternative-fuel, heavy-duty vehicles in use in California as a result of demonstration and pilot programs. Methanol, in particular, has been used in several pilot programs to demonstrate the effectiveness of alternative fuels in reducing emissions from heavy-duty engines. The Southern California Rapid Transit District, which operates transit buses in Los Angeles, has demonstrated that urban bus engines can be modified to operate on methanol. Detroit Diesel Corporation has developed and certified a methanol version of its popular 6V-92A urban bus engine.

In a requirement distinct from the California LET program, the CAAA require a clean-fuel fleet program to be implemented in non-attainment areas that meet certain population and ozone or CO design value criteria. A clean-fuel vehicle is a vehicle that has been certified to meet the clean-fuel vehicle standards that are applicable to that vehicle type and model year. Nonattainment areas with a 1980 population of 250,000 or more and either a 1987–1989 ozone design value of 0.16 ppm or greater or a 1988–1989 CO design value of 16.0 ppm are required to implement clean-fuel fleet programs beginning no later than the 1998 model year.

The clean-fuel fleet program is scheduled to begin in model year 1998. The CAAA specify that at least 50 percent of new covered heavy-duty fleet vehicles in model years 1998 and later be clean-fuel vehicles and use clean fuels when operating in the covered area. Federal exhaust standards for new heavy-duty clean-fuel vehicles (less than 26,000 lb GVW) are specified only for VOC + NO_x. Beginning in model year 1998, the VOC + NO_x limit is 3.8 g/bhp-hr.

HDDV Inspection and Maintenance Programs

California, Arizona, Colorado, Kentucky, and New Jersey currently perform exhaust smoke opacity tests on HDDVs. In addition, Maryland, Nevada, and Utah are starting pilot HDDV inspection programs. Illinois is currently developing the enabling legislation for its HDDV inspection and maintenance program. Except for California's, these programs are thought to be ineffective, since typically only 2 or 3 percent of trucks fail the inspection. This is largely due to ineffective or incorrect test procedures. Nevada and Utah have largely relied on California's program as a model for their programs.

California has implemented a heavy-duty diesel vehicle inspection program (HDVIP) to randomly inspect in-use trucks for excessive smoke. The legality of this program, which tests both California-registered and non-California heavy-duty vehicles, was challenged by the California Trucking Association (CTA). The lawsuit, referred to as the Valley Spreader case, challenged the validity of the "snap" test and the pass/fail cut points set by CARB. In May 1983 the court upheld both the test procedure and cut points and dismissed the case. Other recent court challenges by CTA, coupled with the problems from the new diesel fuel, led CARB to suspend this program in 1994, but the suspension is believed to be temporary.

The California HDVIP is designed to identify and repair the smokiest trucks on California highways (CARB 1990). The HDVIP applies to both interstate and intrastate heavy-duty vehicles and allows CARB to issue citations to vehicles that fail smoke or tampering inspections. Penalties up to $1,500 per day can be assessed against the vehicle owner, but penalties may be waived if the engine is repaired promptly. Under the HDVIP, inspections are conducted at weigh stations, fleet centers, and roadside locations. A snap-idle smoke opacity test is conducted on diesel vehicles, and an emission control system tampering check is performed on both gasoline and diesel vehicles. Peak smoke opacity of 1990 and older model year engine families must not exceed 55 percent opacity during the first year of the smoke program, and 1991 and newer model year engine families must not exceed 40 percent peak opacity.

CARB estimates that the HDVIP will reduce the number of smoking trucks by 57 percent and will produce the following emission reduction benefits by 1990:

	REDUCTION	
POLLUTANT	PERCENT	TONS/DAY
Particulate	39	32
VOC	27	22
NO$_x$	4	19

CARB has also promulgated a periodic smoke self-inspection program for heavy-duty diesel-powered vehicle fleets, as directed by Section 43701(a) of the Health and Safety Code. CARB has provided specifications for the inspection procedure, the frequency of inspections, the emission standards for smoke, and the actions vehicle owners or operators need to take to remedy excessive smoke emissions. The self-inspection program was effective as of January 1, 1995. This time was expected to be sufficient to allow adoption of any revisions to the snap test procedure suggested by the Society of Automotive Engineers, which is currently developing detailed procedures (J1667) for conducting the snap idle test and measuring smoke opacity.

The current HDVIP is primarily conducted at Interstate highway weigh stations and focuses on trucks and buses engaged in long-distance operations on major highways. The periodic smoke inspection program would provide an incentive for the owners of other heavy-duty vehicles, especially trucks and buses that rarely pass by roadside weigh stations because of localized operations, to test and repair their vehicles and thereby reduce smoke emissions. The periodic smoke inspection program is designed to complement the roadside smoke inspection program and would particularly serve to reduce smoke emissions from heavy-duty diesel trucks and buses operating on local streets and highways.

HDDV EMISSIONS AND SPEED CORRECTION FACTORS

Overview

HDD engine emissions are measured on an engine dynamometer with the engine removed from the vehicle. Emissions are measured in units of mass of emissions per unit of work over a test that simulates the loads and speeds normally encountered by the engine. As noted earlier, the engine-based test procedure was adopted because engine manufacturers are distinct from truck manufacturers and because the same engine can be used on a wide variety of trucks with different transmissions and axles. This, however, complicates comparisons between in-use vehicle emissions, engine emissions, and certification levels.

Much of the research and testing on heavy-duty truck in-use emissions was done in the early 1980s, and even these tests were done on a relatively small number of vehicles and engines. Since the mid-1980s there has been virtually no testing of in-use HDD trucks. In part, this lack of interest is traceable to the idea that diesel engine emissions are relatively stable and consistent and that additional testing may yield only marginal improvements in the quality of the emission factors.

A unique aspect of HDDV emissions is the "conversion factor," which converts emissions measured per unit of work done by the engine to the more common unit of emissions per vehicle mile. This conversion requires an understanding of the vehicle's characteristics and knowledge of its fuel economy. Predictions of future emissions, hence, require forecasts of fuel economy, and the analysis of the TIUS data presented later is particularly useful in this context.

In the next subsection, a brief overview of the steady state and transient procedures and the relationship between measured emissions in the two test procedures is provided. Next, the relationship between emissions measured from vehicle and engine tests is explored. The relationship between emission factors used by EPA and those obtained from in-use trucks is discussed. Speed correction factors and the potential for estimate errors are addressed. Finally, the emission conversion factor is documented.

Comparison Between the Steady State and Transient Test Emissions

Before 1984, EPA used the steady state test for engine certification and measurement of emissions. The steady state test involved testing the engine at various fixed points in the operating range of speed and load and was in essence a map of the engine's emissions across its speed/load range. The transient test, on the other hand, continuously varies speed and load over a broad range of engine operation and presumably reflects engine operation when driven over a New York City cycle, a Los Angeles city cycle, and a Los Angeles freeway cycle.

In the early 1980s approximately 50 engines were tested with both procedures, but some of the data were not available publicly. EEA obtained data for 33 engines and estimated the relationship between steady state and transient emissions. It was discovered that Cummins engines behaved differently from all other engine types because of their unique fuel systems. Hence, the 15 Cummins engines and the 18 other engines were separated into two groups for the regression analysis.

For the non-Cummins engines, EEA found that

$$VOC_T = 0.167 + 1.05 \ VOC_{SS} \quad (r^2 = 0.70)$$
$$(0.117) \ (0.184)$$

$$NO_{xT} = 1.70 + 0.75 \ NO_{xSS} \quad (r^2 = 0.82)$$
$$(1.04) \ (0.13)$$

The subscripts T and SS denote transient test and steady state test, respectively. For the Cummins engines, EEA found that

$$VOC_T = 0.31 + 1.77 \ VOC_{SS} \quad (r^2 = 0.79)$$
$$(0.04) \ (0.25)$$

$$NO_{xT} = 1.03 + 0.81 \ NO_{xSS} \quad (r^2 = 0.84)$$
$$(1.04) \ (0.13)$$

The NO_x relationships are similar, but the VOC relationships are quite different for the two groups. Nevertheless, good correlation was obtained between two very different test methods over a broad range of emissions performance (VOC ranging from 0.3 to 2.2 g/bhp-hr and NO_x from 3.6 to 10.8 g/bhp-hr on the transient test). It is particularly significant that the correlation was obtained between two tests, one using a cold start and the other starting with an engine that was fully warmed up. Many in the industry believe that these correlations could be further improved by reweighting the different modes on the steady state test.

No data on particulates were available from the steady state tests, but EPA believes that the correlation between steady state and transient test particulate emissions is poor. (This is disputed by some manufacturers.) However, there are a number of engineering reasons suggesting that it may be possible to obtain good correlations for all emissions of concern between steady state engine maps and transient cycle emissions:

- Diesel engines do not require acceleration enrichment, and the air-fuel ratio during a transient acceleration/deceleration is more carefully controlled than in a gasoline engine.
- Diesel engines require very little cold start enrichment, and the effect of cold starts on emissions is small.
- Diesel engines do not yet use any exhaust aftertreatment, and modeling their emissions does not, therefore, require the difficult prediction of catalyst efficiency.

The most important conclusion is that it is possible to develop emission estimates for almost any arbitrary driving cycle with reasonable accuracy from a steady state VOC, CO, and NO_x emissions map of the engine. This has not been attempted to date largely because of lack of interest rather than technical obstacles. Opinions about the potential to model particulate emissions from steady state maps vary, and it is possible that such an approach is inadequate to model particulate emissions accurately.

Vehicle Versus Engine Emissions

Thirty in-use 1979 diesel heavy-duty trucks and buses were tested by SWRI in the early 1980s (Dietzmann et al. 1983). The heavy-duty trucks were tested on a chassis dynamometer over a transient cycle test that was not exactly identical to the New York and Los Angeles urban cycles and the Los Angeles freeway cycle used to simulate the engine test. Nevertheless, the chassis test was similar in average speed and loading to the engine test procedure.

Three of the engines in the vehicles were removed and tested on the engine test procedure, providing a reference for comparison of emissions from the two test procedures. On the basis of the fuel consumption data from the three engines tested on both procedures, EEA developed a method to calculate the work done, in bhp-hr, for an engine driven over the chassis dynamometer cycle given the dynamometer settings of inertia weight and absorption horsepower.[2]

In two of the three cases, the match between emissions in g/bhp-hr was extremely close, within ±2 percent. In the third case, the match was much poorer (+20 percent) because the vehicle was equipped with a high-horsepower engine, which was very lightly loaded on the chassis dynamometer test but loaded normally on the engine test.

A more comprehensive analysis of the dependence of emissions on distance traveled was attempted from the chassis dynamometer data by converting the emissions to units of g/bhp-hr using the calculation described previously. It was obvious that the emissions (in g/bhp-hr) were radically different for buses compared with trucks (2 to 3 times higher on the average). Therefore, the two vehicle types were treated separately. For the 23 trucks, inspection indicated that there was a strong trade-off between VOC and NO_x emissions. This trade-off is well known in engineering circles, and since the 1979 emissions requirements specified only a VOC + NO_x standard, manufacturers often set different goals for VOC and NO_x. Only one vehicle had both very high NO_x and very high VOC emissions. Because of this uncharacteristic behavior and because it was the first vehicle tested by SWRI on the chassis procedure, EEA believes that the data are erroneous and discarded them for the remainder of the analysis.

The remaining emissions data on 22 trucks were then analyzed to provide emission factors as a function of use, that is, a 0-mi rate and an odometer-dependent rate of the following form:

$$\text{Brake-specific emissions} = C + D \times \text{odometer}$$

The results for VOC, CO, NO_x, particulates, and VOC + NO_x are summarized in Table A-9. The data for all 22 trucks indicate that the odometer dependence of the emission factor (i.e., deterioration rate) is not statistically significant at the 90 percent confidence level for VOC, NO_x, and VOC + NO_x emissions. On the other hand, the deterioration rates for the CO and particulate emission factors are significant at the 90 and 95 percent confidence level, respectively.

The number of Cummins engines tested was the largest of any manufacturer. All were of the same displacement (855 CID) but had different horsepower ratings. Because of the physical similarity of the engines, EEA believed that a regression of emissions from these engines against odometer readings might provide a better indicator of

TABLE A-9 Results of Emission Factor Analysis (Emissions in g/bhp-hr) (EEA 1985)

	Intercept	Standard Error of Intercept	Deterioration Rate[a]	Standard Error of Deterioration Rate	Sample Mean
All 22 Trucks					
VOC	0.765	0.125	2.73×10^{-3} [b]	$8.7 \ \times 10^{-3}$	0.798
CO	1.954	0.652	8.35×10^{-2} [c]	4.55×10^{-2}	2.971
NO$_x$	7.131	0.521	-5.59×10^{-3} [b]	3.64×10^{-2}	7.064
Particulate	0.475	0.081	1.36×10^{-2} [d]	5.70×10^{-3}	0.640
VOC + NO$_x$	7.897	0.477	-2.86×10^{-3} [b]	3.33×10^{-3}	7.862
Cummins Only (12 Trucks)					
VOC	0.732	0.081	1.850×10^{-2} [c]	1.22×10^{-6}	0.940
CO	1.555	0.753	1.721×10^{-1} [d]	5.60×10^{-2}	3.492
NO$_x$	7.146	0.552	-2.950×10^{-2} [b]	4.10×10^{-2}	6.814
Particulate	0.397	0.089	2.133×10^{-2} [d]	6.60×10^{-3}	0.637
VOC + NO$_x$	7.878	0.494	-1.102×10^{-2} [b]	3.67×10^{-2}	7.754
All Others (10 Trucks)					
VOC	0.750	0.083	-9.232×10^{-3} [b]	5.50×10^{-3}	0.628
CO	2.249	0.825	7.171×10^{-3} [b]	5.40×10^{-2}	2.315
NO$_x$	7.216	1.007	1.106×10^{-2} [b]	6.59×10^{-2}	7.363
Particulate	0.577	0.148	5.071×10^{-3} [b]	9.70×10^{-3}	0.644
VOC + NO$_x$	7.966	0.972	1.828×10^{-3} [b]	6.36×10^{-2}	7.991

NOTE: bhp = brake-horsepower.
[a] In g/bhp-hr/10^4 mi.
[b] Not significant at the 0.10 level.
[c] Significant at the 0.10 level.
[d] Significant at the 0.05 level.

the deterioration factors. Regression analysis of the data from the 12 Cummins engines indicated large improvements in the significance of the 0-mi and deterioration rates for all pollutants except the deterioration rate for NO_x. The values of the 0-mi emissions rate from Cummins engines were not significantly different from those of all trucks; however, the deterioration rate for VOC emissions was significant at the 90 percent confidence level, whereas the deterioration rates for CO and particulate were significant at the 95 percent confidence level. As expected, regression analysis of the data from all non-Cummins engines resulted in loss of significance for all of the deterioration rate estimates. This is because of the wide range of manufacturers and engine sizes in the sample of 10 trucks. The results of the analysis of Cummins- and non-Cummins-powered vehicles are also given in Table A-9. Data from Cummins engines indicate that VOC emissions increase by 72 percent[3] relative to 0-mi emissions at the end of the engine's useful life of 285,000 mi, whereas particulate emissions increase by 153 percent. The Cummins engines display high deterioration rates for particulate emissions relative to the overall average deterioration for all engines of 82 percent, partly because of low 0-mi emissions.

The emission estimates from the brake-specific emission analysis were compared with the only other source of equivalent data on HDD emissions. SWRI had previously tested 19 new engines on engine dynamometer tests to provide a 1979 baseline emissions value (EPA 1981). The results of those tests are compared with the estimated 0-mi emissions (because those engines were new) from the chassis test data in Table A-10. The comparison indicates remarkable agreement between the two values for all pollutants, especially considering the differences in test procedures. For all pollutants, the engine-test-based averages were within one standard error of the chassis-test-based averages.

Bus emission factors did not have significant deterioration rates because the sample tested was too small for meaningful analysis, but average bus emissions were a factor of two higher for all pollutants compared with truck emissions.

On the basis of these data, one can conclude that the measured emissions from vehicle and engine tests agree well even if the test cycles are not quite identical, as long as the load factor on the engine on the two tests is similar.

TABLE A-10   Comparision of 1979 Baseline Emissions with Intercept of Emission Factors (g/bhp-hr) (EEA 1985)

	BASELINE (ENGINE TEST)	INTERCEPT (CHASSIS TEST)
VOC	0.83	0.765 ± 0.125
CO	2.28	1.954 ± 0.652
NO$_x$	7.04	7.131 ± 0.521
Particulate	0.49	0.475 ± 0.081

HDDV Emission Factors

Because of the limited testing of in-use HDDVs, EPA has largely assumed the emission factors from certification standards. MOBILE5, the EPA mobile source emission inventory model, incorporates emission factors for all HDDVs but treats all HDDVs as a single group, so that differences between light-heavy, medium-heavy, and heavy-heavy duty vehicles cannot be observed from the emission factors (EPA 1992). More important, the emission factors for VOC and NO$_x$ are based solely on certification standards and have zero deterioration rates for all diesel trucks since 1984. Whereas detailed documentation of the EPA emission factor derivation was not provided, it is apparent that the emission factor is set approximately equal to an assumed certification level, which is 20 to 30 percent below the certification standard, for 1984 and later HDDs. EPA does not have separate emission factors for buses, and the available data suggest that bus emissions are significantly higher than truck emissions. CARB's model, EMFAC7, also treats all HDDVs as a single group, although inputs to the model were derived from more disaggregate analysis of the three subgroups.

Surveys conducted by CARB have established that many diesel truck VOC emissions increase with use because of component deterioration, poor maintenance, or intentional maladjustment (tampering) in the field. Many types of malperformances give rise to high smoke levels, and smoky trucks are widely observed on the road. Random samples of HDDVs have indicated that about one-third of the population have smoke well in excess of certification standards, especially during acceleration. Hence, EPA's assumption of zero deterioration appears unjustifiable for VOC and particulate emissions. However, the inverse relationship between NO_x and VOC suggests that NO_x emissions deterioration with age or use may be zero or even negative. CARB's model incorporates the effects of malperformance to derive a nonzero deterioration rate.

Surveys of diesel engines in the field and the expertise of the manufacturers' service organizations have allowed a comprehensive compilation of the typical malperformances leading to high smoke or gaseous emissions in diesels. In general, malperformances in the intake air system or the fuel system are the most common causes of high smoke and VOC emissions, although an engine in very poor mechanical condition can have sufficient loss of lubricating oil or compression to cause high smoke and gaseous emissions. The data developed by EEA in Table A-11, which is based on discussions with manufacturers, are a comprehensive description of malperformance in diesel engines and their frequency of occurrence as measured in a qualitative form. In the air intake system, dusty air filters and leaky turbocharger oil seals are relatively common. More serious turbocharger damage or problems with the intercoolers are quite rare. Valve system timing and valve leaks are also less frequently observed; if a valve leak is significant, the cylinder can stop functioning completely because of loss of compression. The resulting vibration will quickly make the engine undriveable.

On the fuel system side, tampering with the governor and the air-fuel ratio control (also known as throttle delay) are widely acknowledged as the most common forms of tampering, although even these have been declining in recent years. Advancing the maximum fuel stop or the injection timing is more rare because these are not easily accomplished, but advancing the injection timing for the 1977 to 1984 engines (when the California engines were designed to meet NO_x standards by injection timing retard) may occur in the field.

Problems with injectors vary in severity, because most injectors are replaced only once between rebuilds, if at all. Fouling of injectors or spray hole erosion may be common in older trucks, but serious injector problems, if uncorrected for a long time, will lead to serious engine damage. An incorrect injector size could be used during replacement or rebuild, but this may simply raise the maximum fuel delivered to another certified rating level (i.e., it may result in the engine producing more horsepower, but with no increase in emissions

TABLE A-11 Effect and Frequency of Component Malperformances in Heavy-Duty Diesel Engines (EEA 1993)

Components	Effect on Emissions	Frequency
Air filter (dirty)	Can increase full throttle smoke considerably	Extent of blockage varies but is common
Turbocharger seals worn	Can leak oil and cause smoke/VOC	Minor oil leaks are common in older engines
Turbocharger damage	Significant damage is catastrophic, but minor damage has little effect on emissions	Minor nicks on turbocharger are common
Intercooler internal leaks	Coolant induction can cause white smoke	Rare
Intercooler plugged	High heat will increase smoke and NO_x	Unknown
Valve timing	Incorrect timing can have minor emissions effect	Rare
Valve leaks	Loss of compression and high smoke; engine is hard to start	Rare, self-correcting due to poor startability
Governor RPM setting	Increased RPM setting can increase VOC/smoke in some trucks	Common among independent trucks
Maximum fuel stop setting	Increased VOC/smoke at full throttle	Rare
Injection timing	Advance causes increased NO_x, retard causes increased VOC/smoke	Rare
Throttle delay/air-fuel ratio control	Causes excessive smoke during acceleration	Common among independent trucks
Worn injector spray holes	Increased smoke/VOC	Occurs in older trucks
Injector plugging	Asymetric spray can cause increased smoke/VOC	Occurs in older trucks
Injector tip cracking	Excessive smoke, but is catastrophic to engine	N/A
Incorrect injector size	Effect can vary, but VOC and smoke increase with increasing injector size	Could be common in replacement of injectors
Worn piston rings	High smoke from low compression/oil leak	Rare because vehicle is hard to start
Leaking valve seals	Blue smoke from oil consumption, VOC increased	Unknown
Wrong part numbers	Minor effects if mismatch is not severe	Unknown, but could be a problem with after-market parts

per horsepower produced). However, in some cases, the mismatch between the existing turbocharger/intake system and the upsized injector may be so severe that high emissions result.

The use of wrong parts (i.e., incorrect size or part number) during repair or rebuild can similarly result in higher emissions in some cases, but this is believed to be rare. Very worn engines with leaky valve guides or worn piston rings are likely to be found near the end of the engine's useful life. A certain fraction of engines on the road are always in this range of their useful life.

A qualitative estimate of the effect of these malperformances in diesel engines on air quality can be obtained by combining the frequency of occurrence and the emissions effect. This suggests that the biggest impact on air quality is caused by dirty air filters, worn or plugged injectors, and incorrect fuel injection system setting for the governor and throttle delay. A survey of repairs on 100 trucks that failed the CARB inspection provided detailed data on 81 trucks (19 had minimal repairs or contested the CARB citation). The following table, the source of which is the CARB Northern Heavy Duty Diesel Section, gives the distribution of repairs observed (many trucks had more than one type of repair):

REPAIR TYPE	PERCENTAGE OF TRUCKS
Air filter	43.2
Turbocharger	6.2
Air-fuel ratio control	35.8
Injectors	43.2
Injection pump settings (may include governor setting and injection timing)	22.2
Valves	22.2
Worn engine (rebuild)	8.6
Injection timing	2.2

Of course, the observed distribution is also based on CARB's use of the snap idle test, which may preferentially fail certain types of malperformances.

Under contract to CARB, Radian (1988) developed a model to estimate in-use emission factors by associating each malperformance type (e.g., disabled puff limiter) with an increase or decrease in emissions of VOC, NO_x, and particulate. Radian estimated these emission effects and malperformance rates for 19 types of malperformances to derive a composite emission factor for all in-use HDDVs grouped by certification standard. The analysis did not estimate emissions as a function of mileage but simply as an average for each vintage class (e.g., 1984–1988). The accuracy of this model depends on

- The completeness of the list of malperformances modeled,
- The estimated emission impact, and
- The estimated rate of occurrence of each malperformance type.

The limited data on these issues suggest that the Radian model is reasonable, and it has been updated by EEA with more recent and complete data on malperformances rates. On the basis of this updated version, the "average" emissions increases over the useful life by pollutant type for the California fleet in 1995 are 34 percent for VOC, 6.6 percent for NO_x, and 43.7 percent for particulate. These percentages indicate the fraction of total emissions associated with trucks emitting above the certification level.

Interestingly, the analysis of the 22 trucks from model year 1979 described in the previous subsection leads to similar estimates of increased emissions. The analysis of the Cummins engine data provided statistically significant coefficients of deterioration for each pollutant. Estimating the deterioration at the midpoint of an HDDV's life (150,000 mi) leads to the following increases in emission estimates from the regressions given in Table A-9: VOC, 36 percent (based on Cummins engines); NO_x, approximately 0 percent; and particulate, 41 percent (based on all engines).

These data suggest that the Radian model's predictions of excess emissions are correct, at least in the order of magnitude sense. On the basis of these data, one can conclude that the current EPA HDDV emission factors underestimate VOC emissions by about 30 percent and particulate emissions by about 45 percent for pre-1988 trucks.

The advent of particulate standards in 1988 and 1991 and improvements in engine technology have brought about dramatic reductions in VOC emissions levels, even though the VOC emission standards have not been changed from the 1.3 g/bhp-hr level set in 1984. In the early and mid-1980s, actual certification VOC levels were in the 0.7- to 0.9-g/bhp-hr range. More recently, certification levels have declined to the 0.3- to 0.5-g/bhp-hr range, indicating a 50 percent reduction in emissions. Some engines have certification VOC levels of less than 0.2 g/bhp-hr, a level approaching 10 percent of the standard! These reductions have not been taken into account in the EPA emission factors or the Radian model, and both models are probably overestimating VOC emissions from HDDVs by as much as a factor of two for 1991 and later engines.

Speed Correction Factors

Speed corrections for emissions of HDDVs have been based on the different cycles that comprise the total transient test. Current speed correction factors embodied in MOBILE5 have used the 22-vehicle chassis dynamometer tests of 1979 engines that were described earlier. Since they are derived from vehicle data, no additional conversion of g/bhp-hr to g/mi, which may not be constant with respect to speed, is required.

Speed correction factors for emissions are specified in EPA's MOBILE5 model as multipliers of basic emission rates. They predict emissions at speeds other than the speed for which the basic emission rate is derived. This can be expressed as

Emissions at speed S = Correction factor (S) × basic emission rate

If the basic emission rate is valid for a particular speed, S_1, it is obvious that

$$\text{Correction factor } (S_1) = 1$$

Speed correction factors are decoupled from the effects of cold start by considering only hot-start data. Thus all of the data used to derive speed correction factors are from the "hot" cycles only.

As described earlier, the EPA transient cycle for heavy-duty trucks comprises four segments, two of which are identical. They are the Los Angeles Freeway, the Los Angeles Nonfreeway (labeled 2 LANF and 3 LANF), and two New York Nonfreeway (1 NYNF and 4 NYNF) cycles, one from a cold start and the second from a hot start. These cycles are not similar to the FTP test for light-duty vehicles because of the different acceleration capabilities of heavy trucks compared with light-duty vehicles. Only the 1 NYNF cycle was excluded for the speed correction factor derivation to eliminate any cold-start-related emission effects. Each of the three cycles used to derive the speed correction factors has a unique speed, as follows: 2 LANF, 16.82 mph; 3 LAF, 46.91 mph; and 4 NYNF, 7.31 mph. Data for VOC, CO, and NO_x are available on a cycle specific basis, but such data are not available for particulate emissions.

The composite cycle, which has an average speed of 18.79 mph, is not a separate cycle but an average of the cycles described above. Emissions for the composite cycle, which are used to derive the basic emission rate, represent a distance-weighted average of the four cycles described above. In comparison, the basic emission rate for light-duty vehicles is derived from an actual cycle whose speed corresponds to the speed for the basic emission rate. This has important ramifications for the speed correction for heavy-duty vehicles, as discussed in this section.

The speed correction factor (SCF) for emissions is generally expressed as a polynomial of speed in miles per hour. Since there are only three speeds at which emission data are available, a maximum of three constants can be solved for, restricting the polynomial in speed to second order. It is well known that emissions per unit distance rise steeply at low speeds—in fact, it is infinite at idle, but the SCF is not used at idle—and therefore exponential forms of the equations are generally used. The two forms normally used are

$$E/E_o = \exp(A_1 + B_1 S)$$

or

$$E/E_o = \exp(A_2 + B_2 S + C_2 S^2)$$

where

$$\begin{aligned}
E &= \text{emission rate of VOC, CO, or } NO_x \text{ at speed } S; \\
A, B, \text{ and } C &= \text{regression constants; and} \\
E_o &= \text{emission rate of VOC, CO, or } NO_x \text{ at a reference speed.}
\end{aligned}$$

This form of the equation allows the SCF to be used as a multiplier of the base emission rate. An advantage of this form is that emission rates for each speed are normalized by the composite emission rate, and hence vehicle-specific effects are removed. Since trucks are geared so that they reach 70 to 75 mph at rated power and speed, a check of emissions is possible at 70 to 75 mph by theoretically converting the g/bhp-hr emissions of engines at full load/rated speed to g/mi. This is used to check the derived SCFs for consistency with expected results at higher speeds, especially if a second-order polynomial is used to construct the factor.

The approach used by EPA to determine the regression constants was to fit the equations, by pollutant, for each vehicle and then average the constants over all vehicles. As with the emission factor analysis, the buses were removed from consideration because of their unique behavior. Models were selected for each pollutant depending on their relative accuracy as measured by the variance of the estimated values for each coefficient as well as their ability to behave correctly outside the range of speeds for which there are data. Correct behavior is defined on the basis of engineering analysis of directional trends for emissions at speeds higher than the range encountered in the data.

The following values (standard errors are in parentheses) were determined by EEA for the SCFs, using the first-order model: $E/E_o = \exp(A_1 + B_1 S)$ or, equivalently, $\ln E/E_o = A_1 + B_1 S$. The results of regression analysis of the data were as follows:

$$\ln VOC/VOC_o = 0.9450 - 0.0351S$$
$$(0.2134)\ \ (0.0096)$$

$$\ln CO/CO_o = 0.6594 - 0.0244S$$
$$(0.1403)\ \ (0.0050)$$

$$\ln NO_x/NO_{xo} = 0.1859 - 0.0063S$$
$$(0.1247)\ \ (0.0039)$$

EPA used the second-order relationships in MOBILE5 (EPA 1992) derived from the same sample and obtained the following:

$$\ln (VOC/VOC_o) = 0.924 - 0.055S + 0.00044S^2$$

$$\ln (CO/CO_o) = 1.396 - 0.088S + 0.00091S^2$$

$$\ln (NO_x/NO_{xo}) = 0.676 - 0.048S + 0.00071S^2$$

The EPA relationships are plotted in Figure A-3. It can be seen that VOC and CO decrease continuously over the range of speeds (up to 47 mph) for which data are available. NO_x emissions increase at high speeds, since NO_x is dependent on engine load and load continues to increase with speed above 40 mph. Simulations provided by engine manufacturers also suggest a minimum for NO_x in the 35- to 40-mph range, consistent with the EPA NO_x SCF, which has a minimum at 34 mph. The EPA SCF predicts minimum VOC emissions at 62.5 mph and minimum CO emissions at 48.3 mph. CARB also has used the same correction factors in its EMFAC model, although new factors are under development.

A check of these relationships with speed for speeds up to 70 to 75 mph is based on emissions data from steady state tests, where the engine is tested at intermediate (peak torque) and rated (maximum horsepower) speeds. In top gear, truck drivetrains are usually designed to achieve a speed of 70 to 75 mph at rated RPM. Class VIIIB diesel trucks typically have engines with ratings of 1,800 to 1,900 RPM, whereas trucks in Classes VI and VII typically have engines with ratings of 2,400 to 2,600 RPM. Typical intermediate ratings are 1,300 to 1,400 RPM for Class VIIIB truck engines and 1,600 to 1,800 RPM for Class VI/VII truck engines, corresponding to a speed of about 50 mph.

Emission factors from the steady state test conducted at the two engine speeds indicate that the brake-specific NO_x emissions (in g/bhp-hr) were nearly constant for the engines built in the 1970s and the early 1980s. In addition, the bhp-hr/mi (or work done per mile) increases by 27 percent for a truck traveling at 70 mph compared with the work required for the same truck traveling at 50 mph (a more detailed discussion of work done is given later). Since

$$g/mi = g/bhp\text{-}hr \times bhp\text{-}hr/mi$$

NO_x emissions should increase by only 27 percent from 50 to 70 mph. In contrast, the SCF predicts an increase of more than 100 percent. Newer truck engines are calibrated to operate leaner at rated speed/maximum horsepower than older engines, and the brake-specific emissions could increase, but even in this case a doubling of emissions between 50 and 70 mph is not supported.

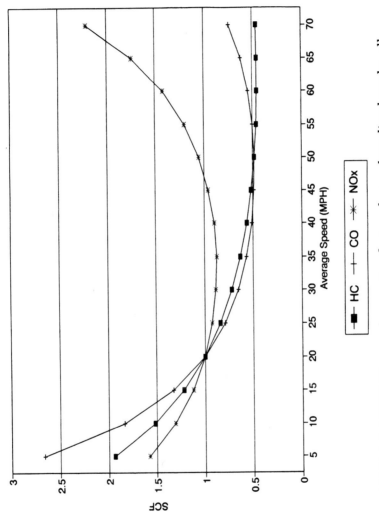

FIGURE A-3 MOBILE5a speed correction factors, heavy-duty diesel trucks, all model years (EPA 1992).

The steady state test data on VOC emissions indicate significant variability between engines in brake-specific emission rates from 50 to 70 mph. Most engines have an increase in brake-specific VOC emission rates ranging from 30 to 100 percent, and the average increase is about 60 percent. The increase, coupled with the 27 percent increase in bhp-hr/mi, suggests that VOC emissions should increase by 90 percent between 50 and 70 mph. In contrast, the SCFs predict no increase. EEA is not aware of any detailed particulate emissions data as a function of speed, but trends in particulate emissions tend to follow those for VOC emissions, since similar mechanisms are responsible for their formation.

In summary, it appears that the current EPA SCFs are probably accurate for speeds up to 55 mph but incorrect for higher speeds. The SCFs overpredict NO_x at 70 mph by 50 to 60 percent and underpredict VOC emissions by nearly 100 percent.

A separate issue is that the "composite" base emission factor is derived from a linear weighting of emissions on the three cycles and is the factor used for a speed of 18.79 mph. Unfortunately, a nonlinear SCF fit to the data points at the three speeds does not pass through unity at 18.79 mph, and EPA adjusted the calculated coefficients by changing the intercept term to force the SCF to be 1 at 18.79 mph. In EEA's opinion, this is incorrect because the base emission factor does not actually represent emissions from an 18.79-mph average speed cycle. This methodology introduces an error in the SCF and overstates emissions at 18.79 mph by 10 to 15 percent.

Observers have argued that the SCFs are based on a sample of vehicles that are now 15 years old. Although a more modern sample would benefit the analysis, the engines tested in 1979 displayed a wide range of emission levels (some would meet 1990 standards for gaseous emissions). Second, and more important, the observed range of SCFs did not vary substantially across the group. In general, the SCF varied by a factor of two for individual trucks, which is not large with compared with order of magnitude variations observed for light-duty vehicles, and most of the sample was clustered around the average value. Hence, there is reason to believe that a more recent sample of trucks tested over a range of speeds will not result in large changes in the SCF up to 55 mph. Of course, "large" is relative only to the light-duty vehicle case, where the uncertainties in the SCF are much larger in spite of the availability of test data.

HEAVY-DUTY TRUCK FUEL ECONOMY

Average Fuel Economy

Truck fuel economy is a function of several variables, including

- Truck size or class,
- Engine type,
- Payload,
- Driving cycle, and
- State of technology.

In contrast to the situation for cars and light-duty trucks, whose fuel economy is measured on a specific cycle and advertised, no standardized data source exists for heavy-duty truck fuel economy. This is because most trucks are custom built with owner choice of engine type, gearbox, and axles within any specific weight class. In addition, truck uses and payloads vary widely; many trucks that carry large but light objects rarely operate at full weight capacity, whereas others such as oil tankers may operate at maximum payload frequently.

Given the wide variations in use, it is meaningful to address average fuel economy only in some defined category of trucks. Fortunately, good fuel economy data are available from TIUS. Truck fuel economy by weight class and vintage was computed from the most recent (1987) data.

Figures A-4 to A-7 show the results of computing the average fuel economy by weight class and vintage for Classes VI, VII, VIIIA, and VIIIB, respectively. The standard error of the estimate is displayed as an "error bar" and is typically less than ±0.2 mpg because of the large sample size. It is immediately obvious that truck fuel economy has improved steadily with newer models. The increases are in the range of 1.4 ± 0.2 percent per year across all classes as an average for the 1977 to 1987 period. The actual average values decline with increasing truck weight, as expected, although the differences between classes are not as large as would be expected from the total weight difference (i.e., the Class VII truck is only 45 percent better in fuel economy, even though its weight is less than half that of a Class VIIIB truck).

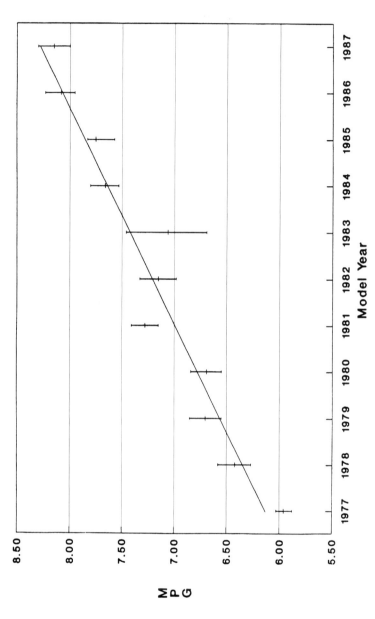

FIGURE A-4 Average MPG (miles per gallon) by vintage, Class VI diesel trucks [based on EEA analysis of 1987 TIUS data (Bureau of the Census 1987)]. Model year 1977 includes 1977 and pre-1977 models.

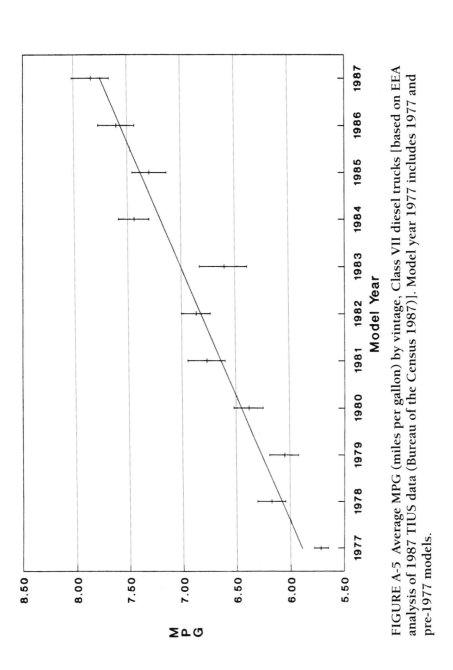

FIGURE A-5 Average MPG (miles per gallon) by vintage, Class VII diesel trucks [based on EEA analysis of 1987 TIUS data (Bureau of the Census 1987)]. Model year 1977 includes 1977 and pre-1977 models.

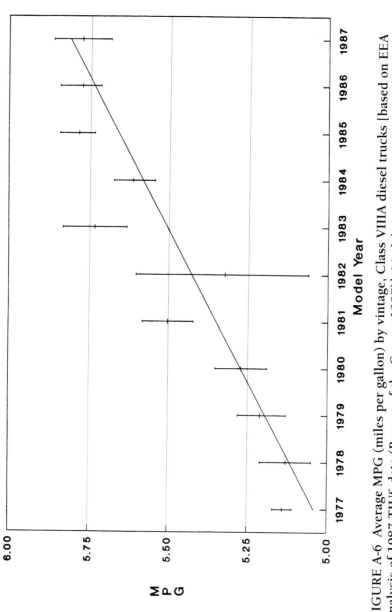

FIGURE A-6 Average MPG (miles per gallon) by vintage, Class VIIIA diesel trucks [based on EEA analysis of 1987 TIUS data (Bureau of the Census 1987)]. Model year 1977 includes 1977 and pre-1977 models.

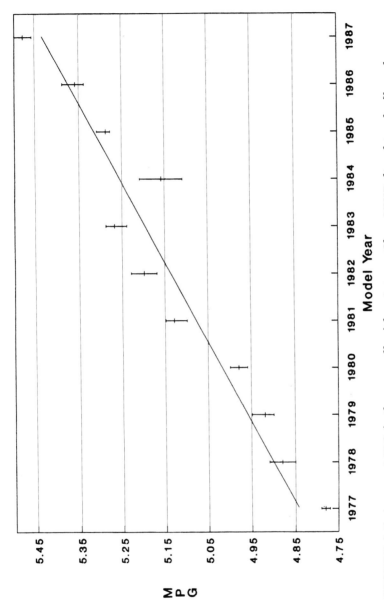

FIGURE A-7 Average MPG (miles per gallon) by vintage, Class VIIIB diesel trucks [based on EEA analysis of 1987 TIUS data (Bureau of the Census 1987)]. Model year 1977 includes 1977 and pre-1977 models.

The data in TIUS do not permit a detailed disaggregation of the effect of weight or driving cycle on fuel economy because only a reported average over the previous year is available. TIUS also reports on average payload and "area of operation" (divided into local, short haul, or long haul, depending on where the greatest percentage of annual miles was accrued). Regression analysis of the data indicated that the ratio of average payload to maximum weight and the area of operation had significant influence on the fuel economy of medium-duty trucks, whereas horsepower and area of operation were most significant for Class VIIIB trucks (average payloads did not vary as much across the sample for Class VIIIB trucks). On the basis of these regressions, for medium-duty truck (Classes VI, VII, and VIIIA), predominantly local operation reduced fuel economy by 5 ± 1.5 percent compared with trucks in short- or long-haul operation, whereas a 10 percent change in operating weight resulted in a 2.2 ± 0.2 percent change in fuel economy. For a Class VIIIB truck, predominantly local operation causes a 2.5 ± 0.3 percent change in fuel consumption compared with trucks in predominantly long-haul use, whereas a 10 percent increase in horsepower results in a 1.1 ± 0.1 percent decrease in fuel economy. However, these broad averages may mask differences in truck types for those in local use and in average payload over the entire cycle of operation.

Fuel Economy Dependence on Speed

Few data are publicly available on fuel economy from tests of HDDVs conducted under controlled conditions on a chassis dynamometer. Data from on-road tests are principally at highway speeds. However, truck manufacturers have developed simulation models for fuel economy that are used as a marketing tool to educate their customers about the effect of truck component specification on fuel economy. In particular, Navistar's TCAPE model is well documented (1990), and its representatives claim that the model has been validated to within ±5 percent in field tests. The model has three built-in cycles to represent city, suburban, and highway driving conditions with average speeds of 20, 40, and 55 mph, respectively.

Figure A-8 shows the change in fuel economy as computed by TCAPE for two trucks at the three speed cycles. The first is a Class VIIIA super medium truck of 48,000-lb GVW loaded to 40,000 lb. The second is a 78,000-lb Class VIIIB truck loaded to maximum weight. These cases are illustrative, because most medium-duty vehicles are rarely loaded to maximum weight.

Figure A-8 shows that both trucks display relatively small fuel economy changes with speed between the 40 and 55 mph cycles, but fuel economy falls off in the city cycle. The Class VIIIB truck experiences a larger percentage loss in fuel economy in the city partly because of its higher payload and partly because Class VIIIB trucks are more highly optimized for highway use.

At speeds higher than 55 mph, fuel economy drops, largely because of the rapid rise of aerodynamic drag. Studies conducted by the U.S. Department of Transportation (DOT) in the mid-1970s in response to the enactment of the 55-mph speed limit indicated the horsepower required to move a Class VIIIB truck at the following steady speeds (DOT 1974):

	HORSEPOWER		
SPEED (MPH)	ROLLING RESISTANCE	AERODYNAMIC DRAG	TOTAL
50	144	57	201
60	172	97	269
70	200	157	357

Truck engines of that era were typically in the 360- to 400-HP range to allow speeds of up to 70 mph in addition to powering accessory drive loads. Low-rolling-resistance radial tires and improved truck aerodynamics have reduced both loads by about 20 percent, so a modern truck would require only 285 HP to cruise at 70 mph; today's trucks are often powered by 300- to 325-HP engines.

Using these data, it can be seen that driving at 70 mph requires 5.1 bhp-hr/mi,[4] whereas driving at 50 mph requires only 4.02 bhp-hr/mi, so the speed increase from 50 to 70 mph increases power consumption by 27 to 28 percent. (The increase is similar for modern trucks.) Engine efficiency in terms of brake-specific fuel consumption also can

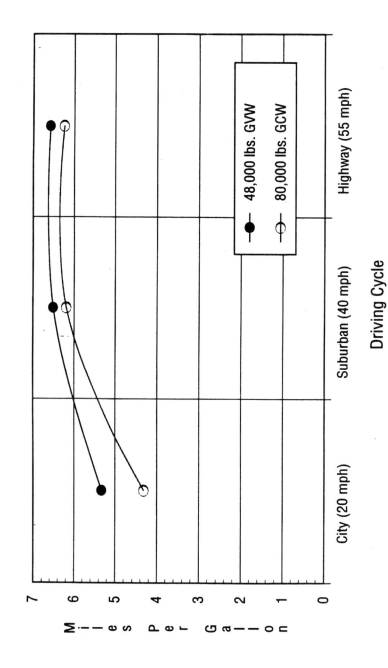

Driving Cycle

FIGURE A-8 Fuel economy of heavy-duty trucks as a function of driving cycle (Navistar, TCAPE outputs).

decrease with increased engine speed, so a net decrease in fuel economy of more than 30 percent can be expected for a speed increase from
50 to 70 mph. Table A-12 indicates the fuel economy decrease observed from actual trucks in the 50- to 65-mph range. Although there
is considerable variation between trucks due to the choice of engines,
axle ratios, and gear ratios, the fuel economy loss with speeds over
50 mph is directionally consistent on all trucks tested.

Emission Conversion Factor

The emission conversion factor provides a link between engine emissions per unit of work (g/bhp-hr) to vehicle emissions per mile. The
conversion factor is based on the following identity:

$$g/mi = g/bhp\text{-}hr \times bhp\text{-}hr/mi$$

The conversion factor, bhp-hr/mi, is the work required to move a
vehicle 1 mi; obviously the larger and heavier the truck, the greater
the work and the larger the conversion factor. The conversion factor
can be further decomposed into the following:

$$bhp-hr/mi = \frac{bhp-hr}{lb\ fuel} \times \frac{lb\ fuel}{gal} \times \frac{gal}{mi}$$

$$= \frac{fuel\ density}{bsfc \times MPG}$$

where bsfc is the engine brake-specific fuel consumption expressed in
pounds of fuel consumed per brake horsepower-hour produced, fuel
density is a constant, and MPG is the fuel economy of the truck.

Detailed knowledge about MPG is available from the TIUS data, as
presented earlier. The bsfc of HDD engines is available from the emissions test. Once these variables are known, the conversion factor can
be obtained with good accuracy. Only one aspect of the estimating procedure could lead to inconsistencies: the fuel economy is an on-road
average and is not tied to the specific driving cycle and speed of the
base emission factor. The average speed of many medium-duty vehi-

TABLE A-12   Effect of Speed on Fuel Consumption Rates (DOT 1974)

VEHICLE NO.	FUEL CONSUMPTION RATE (MILES PER GALLON) FOR INDICATED SPEED (MPH)				PERCENTAGE INCREASE IN FUEL CONSUMPTION CAUSED BY INDICATED INCREASE IN SPEED (MPH)				
	50	55	60	65	50 TO 55	55 TO 60	60 TO 65	50 TO 60	50 TO 65
1	5.12	5.06	4.71	a	1.2	7.4	a	8.7	a
2	5.41	5.02	4.59	4.08	7.8	9.4	12.5	17.9	32.6
3	5.45	4.97	4.52	a	9.7	10.0	a	20.6	a
4	5.21	4.90	4.88	4.47	6.3	—	9.2	6.8	16.6
5	4.49	4.40	4.14	3.72	2.0	6.3	11.3	8.5	20.7
6	4.97	4.51	4.42	a	10.2	0.2	a	12.4	a

NOTE: Each figure is the average of more than 20 timed runs on roadways with less than 1 percent grade.
[a] The governor setting that controls fuel injection did not permit this vehicle to be operated at 65 mph.

cles in urban and short-haul routes may, indeed, be close to 20 mph, making the conversion factor derivation approximately consistent with the base emission factor. The average fuel economy of the heavy-duty Class VIIIB truck is likely to be more heavily weighted to highway speeds, leading to some degree of inconsistency in the derived conversion factor. EPA has derived a composite conversion factor for all heavy-duty trucks that is a sales- and travel-weighted average for all diesel trucks exceeding 8,500 lb GVW. This average was found to be 2.60 in 1982.

Projections of the conversion factor require the MPG and bsfc of future vehicles and engines. Engine efficiency improvements translate into bsfc improvements that are inversely proportional to MPG improvements. Hence, the term bsfc $\times$ MPG does not change with increased engine efficiency. Changes in the conversion factor depend only on the vehicle technology improvements that improve fuel economy, including

- Weight reduction,
- Aerodynamic improvements,
- Reduction in tire rolling resistance,
- Improved lubricants,
- Transmission and axle improvements, and
- Use of electronic speed control.

EPA has developed a forecast of these technology improvements. On the basis of the expected changes in MPG, the conversion factor will decrease from 2.60 in 1982 to 2.30 in 1997, a 14 percent reduction. This translates into a 0.88 percent per year MPG improvement from non-engine-related improvements.

The TIUS data indicated that HDDV fuel economy has increased between 1.2 and 1.5 percent per year depending on class. Given that engine bsfc has decreased by about 0.5 percent per year over the last decade, the EPA forecast appears reasonable, since the total forecast change is 0.88 + 0.5, or about 1.4 percent per year, consistent with the observed MPG change. Studies conducted by EEA for EPA suggest that annual improvements of 1.2 to 1.5 percent in fuel economy are likely to continue over the next decade, with the conversion factor also continuing to decrease at approximately 0.9 percent per year to 2000.

In conclusion, the conversion factor estimates are well grounded in data, and the only source of error is the absence of a direct link of MPG and bsfc to vehicle speed. The total estimation error is not likely to be large (about 5 percent of the estimate), and the conversion factor is not a source of major concern in estimating HDDV emissions. Conversion factors for buses are included in the EPA weighted average but can easily be calculated separately.

SUMMARY

The discussion in the preceding four sections is the basis for the following conclusions.

In addressing HDDVs, it is useful to divide transit buses and trucks into two weight classes. For heavy-duty trucks the categories are medium-heavy and heavy-heavy, and for buses the categories are transit buses and school buses. The annual use, operating radius, useful life, and fuel economy vary dramatically across these classes. Light-heavy duty diesels, which are more similar to light-duty vehicles, are not covered in this appendix.

Unfortunately, EPA does not maintain these distinctions in modeling emissions from heavy-duty diesels, but aggregates emissions from all subcategories of diesels. These distinctions are probably important in the analysis of emissions associated with increases in urban highway capacity, since light-heavy and medium-heavy trucks are more likely to be used in urban areas than are heavy-heavy duty trucks.

Emissions data on heavy-duty diesel engines suggest that emissions over a transient driving cycle can be correlated with emissions from a steady state engine "map" for VOC, CO, and NO_x and even possibly for particulates. EPA and engine manufacturers differ in their assessment of the correlation for particulates. Although the development of "modal" models to calculate emissions from any arbitrary driving cycle has not been pursued, there are no significant technical obstacles to their development to estimate VOC, CO, and NO_x emissions.

The data also indicate good correspondence between emissions measured on an engine test and emissions measured from a vehicle test. The representativeness of an engine dynamometer test has been

questioned in some quarters, but EEA believes that the errors introduced by this type of test are not large. Part of the reason is that trucks
and buses are so power limited that accelerations are usually conducted at wide-open throttle, so that errors in acceleration rates between engine and vehicle tests have no significant effect on engine
load and emissions.

EPA's approach to emission factors has been to group all subclasses
of heavy-duty diesel trucks and buses into one class, making it difficult to model the differential deterioration rates in emissions between
subclasses. EPA's approach to deriving heavy-duty diesel emission factors are simplistic and are based on assumed certification levels. In
particular, EPA's assumption of zero deterioration rates cannot be
justified. Hence, the EPA estimates of absolute emissions are almost
certainly in error. Improved models, such as the one developed by
Radian for CARB, appear to give more defensible estimates of emission
factors for older trucks. Both the EPA and CARB estimates of VOC
emissions from newer HDDVs are probably in error since they pre-
suppose a relationship between VOC standards and certification
levels, whereas actual VOC certification levels have declined to values far below standards as a result of technology improvements. Urban
buses have received little attention, but limited data suggest that they
are particularly high emitters.

SCFs derived by EPA, on the other hand, appear to be reasonable
up to 55 mph and conform to engineering expectations. At speeds
above 55 mph, there are no data available on emissions for HDDVs,
and engineering analysis must be used to gauge the correctness of the
SCFs. The analysis indicates that NO_x emissions at 70 mph are probably overstated by 50 to 60 percent, whereas VOC emissions at 70 mph
are understated by nearly 100 percent. Although the SCFs were derived from limited data on older trucks, engineering analysis suggests
the low speed factors are unlikely to change significantly even if newer
data become available. The emission conversion factor to convert
g/bhp-hr to g/mi is estimated from relatively good data and is not likely
to be in significant error. (This conversion factor does not affect the
SCF.) In the case of both factors, there are some issues that could
change their absolute magnitude by 20 to 30 percent if the issues are
resolved correctly. However, trends with speed up to 55 mph in the

case of the SCF or with time in the case of the conversion factor are not likely to be affected much.

In summary, there are probably significant errors in the absolute magnitude of emissions predicted by current methods, but not in the trends with time or speed up to 55 mph. In general, average speed is a good surrogate for the drive cycle encountered for heavy-duty trucks simply because acceleration rates of trucks are so limited. As noted, virtually all accelerations of heavy-duty diesels are conducted at wide-open throttle, and the acceleration rate (an important determinant of emissions for light-duty vehicles) is not a significant source of error in this analysis.

On the basis of EEA's analysis, it appears that emissions of all pollutants decline with speed up to 35 to 40 mph. Beyond that speed, NO_x and VOC emissions increase, with VOC emissions increasing more sharply at speeds exceeding 50 mph. Anecdotal information from industry experts suggests that particulate emissions follow the same trend as VOC emissions up to about 50 mph, but the behavior at higher speeds is not well understood. These trends should provide some guidelines for most traffic conditions except those where high speeds (over 50 mph) are encountered for heavy-duty trucks.

The lack of good particulate emissions data as a function of speed is a major drawback, since HDDVs are a major source of combustion particulate, and particulate emissions are known to increase the most of all regulated pollutants under in-use conditions. The use of the VOC SCF for estimating the change of particulate emissions with speed can be considered a very rough approximation, which may not hold good as the engine approaches the "smoke limit" at full load. More research in this topic could be fruitful.

Fuel economy is a function of truck size, vintage, load, and speed. Good data are available on average truck fuel economy by weight class and by area of operation from surveys conducted by the Bureau of the Census. Fuel economy as a function of speed is dependent on truck design and load; light-heavy and medium-heavy vehicle fuel economy is less sensitive to speed change than over-the-road heavy-heavy truck fuel economy. Nevertheless, it appears that speed increases to about 50 mph have favorable effects on fuel economy for all vehicles. Beyond 50 mph, fuel economy declines sharply, falling by as much as 30 percent from 50 to 70 mph.

NOTES

1. Most CNG/LPG engines are of the spark ignition type.
2. The method relied on engineering analysis to develop a model to link the dynamometer inertia weight and power absorption setting to cycle bhp-hr using field consumption data.
3. The percentages can be calculated from the deterioration rate and intercept in Table 4-1 as follows for VOC: 0.0185 * 28.5/0.732.
4. From the table at 70 mph, bhp-hr/mi $= \dfrac{357}{70} = 5.1$.

REFERENCES

ABBREVIATIONS

CARB	California Air Resources Board
DOT	U.S. Department of Transportation
EEA	Energy and Environmental Analysis, Inc.
EPA	Environmental Protection Agency
MVMA	Motor Vehicle Manufacturers Association

Acurex Environmental Corp. 1992. *Technical Feasibility of Reducing NO_x and Particulate Emissions from Heavy Duty Engines*. Draft Final Report. California Air Resources Board.

Bureau of the Census. 1987. *Truck Inventory and Use Survey*.

CARB. 1990. *Technical Support Document: Proposed Roadside Smoke Test Procedures and Opacity Standards for Heavy Duty Diesel Trucks*. June.

CARB. 1993. *Mobile Source Emission Standards Summary*. June.

Curran, T., T. Fitz-Simons, W. Freas, J. Hemby, D. Mintz, S. Nizich, B. Parzygnat, and M. Wayland. 1994. *National Air Quality and Emissions Trends Report, 1993*. 454-R-94-026. U.S. Environmental Protection Agency. Research Triangle Park, N.C., Oct., 157 pp.

Dietzmann, H.E., et al. 1983. *Emissions from In-Use Trucks by Chassis Version of 1983 Transient Procedure*. U.S Environmental Protection Agency, June.

DOT. 1974. *The Effect of Speed on Truck Fuel Consumption Rates*. Aug.

EEA. 1985. *Mobile Source Emissions Analysis for California: Vol. II*. June.

EEA. 1993. *Feasibility Study for an I/M Program for Heavy Duty Vehicles*. California Bureau of Automotive Repair, Jan.

EPA. 1981. *Emissions from Heavy Duty Engines Using the 1984 Transient Test Procedure: Vol. II*. South West Research Institute report to EPA. PB83-142067, July.

EPA. 1992. *MOBILE5 Emission Factor Model*. Washington, D.C.

MVMA. 1981, 1986, 1991. *Factor Sales of Trucks and Buses*. FS-3 and FS-5 monthly reports, Jan.

Navistar. 1990. *Truck Computer Analysis of Performance and Fuel Economy (TCAPE)*. Brochure PSM 15200.

Radian. 1988. *Heavy-Duty Vehicle I/M Study*. CARB, Sacramento, Calif., May.

Ullman, T.L., et al. 1989. *Investigation of the Effects of Fuel Composition on Heavy-Duty Diesel Engine Emissions*. Paper 892072. Society of Automotive Engineers.

Appendix B

Review of Empirical Studies of Induced Traffic

HARRY S. COHEN
Cambridge Systematics, Inc.

The results of empirical studies of the effects of expanding highway capacity on highway system use are reported in this appendix according to the following categories:

- Studies of specific facilities,
- Studies of areawide measures of highway supply, and
- Studies of the travel behavior of individuals or households that can be used to estimate changes in highway system use.

FACILITY-SPECIFIC STUDIES

The travel forecasting literature includes a number of facility-specific studies of the traffic-generating effects of highway improvements. Jorgensen (1947) studied the effects of the construction of the Merritt and Wilbur Cross parkways on traffic in the corridor between New York City and New Haven, Connecticut. To estimate normal traffic growth in the corridor, Jorgenson examined traffic counts in the corridor for several years before the opening of the new facilities and found that they were closely correlated with gasoline sales in Connecticut. Consequently, he used information on the growth in gasoline sales after the opening of the parkways to estimate the normal growth in traffic. Using this approach, Jorgenson concluded that the parkways generated 20 to 25 percent more traffic in the corridor than would have been expected from the normal rate of growth.

Lynch (1955) analyzed traffic in the Maine Turnpike/U.S. Route 1 corridor to estimate the traffic effects of opening the turnpike. He used information on the growth of traffic on major roads in Maine outside the corridor to estimate normal growth in the corridor. He concluded that 5 years after the opening of the turnpike, traffic in the corridor was 30 percent greater than would have been expected as a result of normal growth.

Both the Connecticut parkways and the Maine Turnpike serve high volumes of intercity trips, and both provided significant reductions in both peak and off-peak travel times.

Frye (1964a, 1964b) examined the traffic effects of the construction of the Dan Ryan and Eisenhower expressways in Chicago on the basis of a review of traffic counts and origin-destination survey data collected before and after the opening of the expressways. He found that traffic through a 5-mi screenline centered on the Dan Ryan Expressway increased by 11 percent after the expressway opened, but concluded that almost all of the increase was a result of route diversion. He found a 21 percent increase in traffic for the Eisenhower Expressway, versus a 14 percent increase in three control areas. Frye identified four factors contributing to the exceptional growth rate in the Eisenhower Expressway corridor:

- Natural growth: the increase in traffic in the study area that would have occurred regardless of whether the new expressways were constructed.
- Adverse traffic: an increase in vehicle miles of travel (VMT) on local and arterial streets that is necessary to get to or from expressway on- or off-ramps.
- Diverted traffic: traffic diverted from routes outside the study area to the new expressway or to local streets and arterials for which travel conditions have improved.

- Induced traffic: additional trips in the study area made because of the improved level of service on both the new facility and old competing facilities.

Noting the difficulty in separating the four factors, Frye expressed the opinion that little of the observed increase was due to induced traffic.

Holder and Stover (1972) studied the traffic generation impacts of eight urban highway projects in Texas. They identified six components of traffic on new highways:

- Diverted traffic from other roads,
- Converted traffic from other modes,
- Growth traffic from increases in population,
- Developed traffic from changes in land use,
- Cultural traffic from changes in the propensity to travel resulting from socioeconomic changes, and
- Induced traffic from new trips made because of added convenience.

For each of the eight projects, the authors compared corridor traffic growth before project opening with either regional trends or corridor growth before project completion, referring to the difference as "apparent induced traffic." For six of the projects, estimates of apparent induced traffic ranged from 5 to 21 percent. For the other two, no evidence of apparent induced traffic was found, a finding the authors attributed to the availability of other routes offering comparable travel times in the project corridors. On the basis of their analysis, Holder and Stover made the following general conclusions:

- Apparent induced traffic can represent a significant portion of the traffic on a new facility;
- Most induced traffic occurs during off-peak hours; and
- If a substantial amount of induced traffic is to occur on a new facility, then the off-peak travel time must be reduced significantly or the existing facilities must be congested.

Pells (1989) examined user responses to new highways in the greater London area. The methodology included measurement of traffic in the corridors in which the new highways were built before and after construction and comparison of the percentage growth in traffic with the percentage growth in control corridors. Three facilities examined by Pells are discussed in the following paragraphs.

- A40 Westway, a 2.5-mi elevated highway in West London, was opened in July 1970 and has undergone several improvements since then. A before-and-after study conducted in May, September, and October 1970 to test the initial effects of the road revealed a 14 percent increase in traffic in the Westway corridor, versus a 2 percent increase in a control corridor during the same period. Over the long term, the differences between Westway and the control corridor were much greater. From 1970 (before the opening of Westway) to 1984, traffic in the Westway corridor grew by 87 percent, versus 10 percent for the control corridor. Pells did not discuss reasons for the low traffic growth rate in the control corridor traffic, nor did he provide any justification for why such a low growth rate should have been expected in the Westway orridor if the new highway had not been opened.
- A316, a major radial route in southwest London, was widened from four to six lanes in 1976. From 1974 to 1980, 24-hr two-way flows in the A316 corridor increased by 57 percent, versus 30 percent for the control corridor. From 1980 to 1983, flows in the A316 corridor increased by 3 percent, versus a decline of 2 percent in the control corridor. No reason was given for the decrease in control corridor traffic. Land use effects in West London and Heathrow Airport were noted as contributors to the high levels of growth in the A316 corridor.
- The two Blackwell tunnels are located in east London. One tunnel was built at the end of the last century and the second was built in 1969. From 1962 to 1982, traffic in the Blackwell corridor increased by 153 percent, versus 64 percent for the control corridor.

According to Pells, the differences measured represent the combined effects of the following factors:

- Wide area reassignment, involving rerouting of trips from corridors external to the study area;
- Redistribution of trips to different destinations;

- Attraction of trips from other modes;
- Retiming of trips; and
- Generation of trips (trips that are entirely new or are made more frequently).

Pells also reported on a survey of motorists using the Rochester Way Relief Road, a major new radial route in southeast London. A total of 770 questionnaires was distributed, of which 184 (24 percent) were returned. The questionnaire asked about the trip that drivers were in the course of making and how the introduction of the new route affected their behavior. Most respondents indicated that they were just changing their route. However, 3.3 percent reported a change in destination, 2.7 percent reported a change in mode, and 9.8 percent reported that they made the trip more frequently.

In September 1990, the final part of M10 Amsterdam Beltway, the Zeeburger Tunnel, was opened. The Rijkswaterstaat Transportation and Traffic Research Division conducted an extensive before-and-after study (Bovy et al. 1992) of the consequences of this project for travel and traffic patterns. The research period extended from March 1990 to September 1991.

The Zeeburger Tunnel crosses under the North Sea Canal, which cuts through Amsterdam in the east-west direction. North Sea Canal crossing points had been subject to growing congestion in recent years, with many drivers commuting from their homes north of the canal to workplaces south of the canal. Opening of the Zeeburger Tunnel provided a 25 percent increase in capacity across the North Sea Canal.

The study included traffic counts, interviews with members of 12,000 households north of the North Sea Canal, and roadside origin-destination interviews with 50,000 road users crossing the canal.

The study revealed that the opening of the Zeeburger Tunnel caused a 4.5 percent increase in automobile traffic across the North Sea Canal, broken down as follows:

- A 1.5 percent increase from route diversion,
- A 1.0 percent increase from diversion from transit, and
- A 2.0 percent increase from changes in destinations or travel frequency.

Notwithstanding the relatively small increase in total traffic due to the tunnel opening, a significant increase in peak-period traffic was found. In the 7 to 9 a.m. time period, the number of canal crossings increased by 16 percent, primarily as a result of drivers changing their travel times.

Ruiter et al. (1979, 1980) used transportation planning models to estimate the effects on VMT of two highway improvement projects in California. The models used by Ruiter differed from those used in conventional travel forecasting in that trip generation rates were sensitive to travel times. However, land use patterns were fixed, so that changes in VMT associated with changes in land use patterns were not incorporated in the model outputs.

The first project involved the construction of 5 mi of a new 8-lane freeway, which constituted a 0.855 percent increase in capacity in the study area. This increase in capacity was found to cause a 0.379 percent increase in VMT in the study area. Dividing the percent increase in VMT by the percent increase in capacity produces an estimated elasticity of VMT with respect to capacity of 0.4.

The second project examined by Ruiter et al. involved widening a 12-mi section of freeway from 4 lanes to 6 or 8 lanes (depending on the location), which constituted a 0.647 percent increase in study area capacity. This increase in capacity was found to produce a slight decrease in VMT, with added VMT from new trips offset by reduced circuity of travel for existing trips.

A key distinction between the two projects studied by Ruiter is that the first project was a new freeway that would provide significant time savings in both the peak and off-peak periods, whereas the second project was the widening of an existing freeway that would provide significant time savings in the peak period only. The primary effect on VMT of the second project was a shift in VMT from the off-peak to peak periods.

Hansen et al. (1993) examined before-and-after traffic volumes for 18 California highway projects involving capacity additions to existing highways. They used pooled time series and cross-sectional data to estimate elasticities of traffic volumes with respect to highway capacity (i.e., the percentage increase in volumes divided by the percentage increase in capacity). For individual segments, the elasticities were found to increase somewhat over time. Elasticities of 0.3 to 0.4

were found during the first 10 years after the capacity increase. This means that if a segment's capacity is increased by 10 percent, traffic on that segment will increase by 3 to 4 percent during the first 10 years. After approximately 20 years, the elasticities were found to increase to 0.4 to 0.7.

The authors noted an important limitation of the study of individual segments: only traffic levels on the improved segments were studied. They stated " ... clearly, any additional traffic on the improved segment must also use other links on the roadway network as well. Further, a large proportion of the additional traffic may have diverted from other routes. These complement-substitute relationships between different links in a road network imply that if a change to one link has a substantial traffic impact on that link, other links are likely to be significantly affected as well" (Hansen et al. 1993, 3,4).

Elasticities such as those developed by Ruiter et al. and Hansen et al. provide a simple means for summarizing study findings regarding the effects of increases in highway capacity on travel. Hansen et al. measured changes in capacity in terms of lane miles, and Ruiter et al. measured changes in capacity in terms of vehicle miles of capacity.[1] One advantage of using the changes in lane miles or vehicle miles of capacity to represent improvements in capacity is that these measures can often be compiled for a given area directly from highway system inventories maintained by state departments of transportation.

However, these measures also have a number of limitations that greatly affect the transferability of elasticities to other areas or capacity improvements. Most important, the amount of time savings produced by a given change in lane miles or vehicle miles of capacity is highly variable, depending on such factors as preexisting levels of congestion and bottlenecks. Consider, for example, a congested bridge that is a traffic bottleneck during peak periods. Widening the bridge could provide large peak-period time savings with a small increase in lane miles or vehicle miles of capacity. Conversely, adding lanes to a facility that is not currently congested will have a small effect on travel time, even though the addition may represent a significant increase in lane miles. In addition, the construction of new limited-access highways (with much higher free-flow speeds than the facilities they replace) will have travel time effects that are not well represented by the change in capacity. Finally, the use of elasticities must take into account the types of traffic effects that are and are not reflected in the elasticities (i.e., the elasticities developed by Ruiter et al. represent the net effects on total highway system use, whereas the elasticities developed by Hansen et al. represent the effects on the improved facilities and include diversion from other facilities).

A recently released report for the Department of Transport of the United Kingdom (SACTRA 1994) reviewed the evidence for the existence of induced traffic. As in many metropolitan areas in the United States, the Department of Transport uses transportation models that assume fixed trip patterns (but allow for the effect of general economic growth on traffic growth) in assessing new road projects or major highway capacity additions (SACTRA 1994, iv).

The Standing Committee's review of case studies of major European highway projects, as well as of the Department of Transport's own monitoring studies of before-and-after traffic flows on road improvement projects, found that traffic increases on newly expanded road segments more than exceeded traffic reductions on unimproved segments. This finding provides evidence of induced traffic, that is, of growth in traffic beyond route shifts (SACTRA 1994, 80). However, the Standing Committee indicated that the studies are not helpful in identifying the components of this traffic growth (SACTRA 1994, 76, 77). It is not possible, for example, to distinguish changes in the time-of-day of travel or separate travel growth attributable to improved economic conditions from growth attributable to the road improvement itself, nor is it possible to rule out as a source of traffic growth broader shifts in travel routes than are captured by study control corridors and screenlines (SACTRA 1994, 76).

The Standing Committee also reviewed the evidence for induced traffic using transportation models that allow demand to vary. Predicted estimates of induced traffic from major highway capacity additions in congested urban areas were found to be small when viewed at the network level; the effects were more significant in the corridors directly affected by the road projects (SACTRA 1994, 160). Because the scale of effects depends on the size of the study area modeled the scale of the project, and the behavioral responses modeled, among other factors, the Standing Committee noted the circumstances in which induced traffic is most likely to be large (SACTRA 1994, 169, 170):

- When the network is operating, or is expected to operate, close to capacity,
- Where elasticity of demand with respect to travel cost is high, and
- Where implementation of a project causes large changes in travel costs.

Two other areas of interest to this study were mentioned in the report. First, with respect to freight travel, the Standing Committee noted the limited studies of the effects of road improvements on the distribution of freight (SACTRA 1994, 158). The available research suggests that the impact of new road capacity on freight is likely to be greater where transport costs constitute a large share of the total distribution expenditures of a company (SACTRA 1994, 159). However, the researchers caution that the role of highway improvements should not be "exaggerated" because other factors also have a considerable impact on distribution system costs (SACTRA 1994, 159).

Second, new travel resulting from development induced by highway capacity additions is identified in the report as a major source of induced travel. However, the Standing Committee notes the considerable difficulty of separating development that can be attributed to the accessibility provided by the new or improved facility from development that would have occurred anyway because of other economic conditions (SACTRA 1994, 25). It also acknowledges the difficulty of distinguishing development that has simply been transferred from elsewhere in the region (thus resulting in a decline in traffic in those areas) from development that represents net new growth (and thus net new travel) in the region (SACTRA 1994, 25).

AREAWIDE STUDIES

A number of researchers have used data for entire metropolitan areas (or large districts within them) to obtain models that predict vehicle miles of travel within these areas as a function of transportation system supply. Ruiter et al. (1979, 2-34) summarized results from several of these studies in the form of elasticities (see Table B-1).

TABLE B-1   Estimated Elasticities of VMT with Respect to
Transportation Supply Measures (Ruiter et al. 1979, 2-34)

TRANSPORTATION SUPPLY MEASURE	ELASTICITIES	SOURCES
Average highway speed	+0.58, +1.76	A.M. Voorhees & Assoc. (1971), Zahavi (1972)
Total lane miles of highway	+0.13, +0.15	Kassoff and Gendell (1972), Koppelman (1972)
Lane miles of Interstate	+0.0056	Mellman (1976)
Lane miles of freeways	+0.05	A.M. Voorhees & Assoc. (1971)
Miles of rail transit service	−0.033	Mellman (1976)
Vehicle miles of transit service	−0.09	EIC Corporation (1976)
Seat miles of transit service	−0.0098	A.M. Voorhees & Assoc. (1971)
Fraction of driving surface on freeways	+0.16	Koppelman (1970)

For most of the supply measures, the elasticities are small, indicating small expected changes in areawide VMT as the supply measures change. The exception is average highway speed, with estimated elasticities of 0.58 and 1.76.

In addition to the study of specific facilities discussed previously, Hansen et al. (1993) conducted an areawide analysis in which they compiled data on VMT, lane miles, population, density, personal income, and gasoline prices for 32 urban counties in California from 1973 to 1990. Pooled time series and cross-sectional data were used to estimate several VMT models. Results from the areawide studies were reported as elasticities of VMT with respect to lane miles. These elasticities were found to be 0.5 to 0.6, implying that a 10 percent increase in lane miles would result in a 5 to 6 percent increase in VMT.

The authors noted a significant data limitation in conducting the areawide analysis: whereas data for VMT for state highways were available over a sufficient period to include significant temporal variation in lane miles, data for total VMT (including local roads) were available for a considerably shorter span of years. Consequently, the main focus of their study was on how changes in lane miles on state highways affect traffic on state highways. However, to account for the possibility that the effect of increases in lane miles on state highways was merely to divert traffic from nonstate highways, the authors conducted some limited analyses using total VMT data; they tentatively concluded that the increases in traffic observed on state highways primarily represented new traffic and not diverted traffic.

One potential problem, which was not discussed by the authors, is the possibility that estimates of the effects of changes in lane miles on VMT might have been affected by reclassification of nonstate highways as state highways or conversely.

The authors discussed the problem of direction of causality in relating capacity increases and VMT. They noted that their analysis assumes that "road supply is the cause and traffic the effect, whereas in fact, traffic levels affect road supply as well. While we concede that the causality is bidirectional, we do not believe that this substantially affects our results. State and regional planning processes are subject to imperfect information, lumpiness of investment, fluctuations in costs and revenues, politically motivated allocation formulas, and other 'exogenous' factors that significantly loosen the coupling between road supply and road traffic" (Hansen et al. 1993, 6-2).

The regression equations developed by Hansen et al. show that, of all the factors affecting VMT growth, population growth, with an elasticity in the range of 0.7 to 0.8, is the most important (Hansen et al. 1993, 6-29). Hence, during the study period, growth in population contributed much more to the growth in VMT than did growth in lane miles. Other factors cited by the authors as affecting VMT were declining gasoline prices, increased two-worker commuting, and increases in per capita car ownership (Hansen et al. 1993, 6-31).

TRAVEL TIME ELASTICITIES

Several researchers have estimated highway travel time elasticities (defined as the percentage change in travel between two areas divided by the percentage change in travel time)

- Domencich et al. (1968) estimated the in-vehicle travel time elasticities of -0.82 for automobile work trips and -1.02 for automobile shopping trips. Their analysis used cross-sectional data on zone-to-zone travel volumes, times, and costs from the Boston area. These elasticities overstate the systemwide effects of travel time improvements because only part of the observed increase in zone-to-zone travel is composed of completely new trips (i.e., some of the observed increase is from changes in trip destinations).

- Chan and Ou (1978) reported the travel time elasticity for automobile work trips as -0.4 for Louisville.
- Groenhout et al. [1986 (in Industry Commission 1993)] estimated the elasticity of automobile travel with respect to in-vehicle travel time as -0.17 for Sydney, Australia.
- Burright (1984) estimated the elasticity of vehicle miles with respect to travel time as -0.27 without land use changes and as -0.51 when the indirect effects of land use changes were taken into account.

Numerous studies of travel time elasticities were also reviewed for the SACTRA report (1994). On the basis of these studies and calculations using the Department of Transport's own estimates of the cost of travel (i.e., direct fuel costs and travel time costs), the Standing Committee concluded that a travel time elasticity of -0.5 in the short term and -1.0 in the long term were reasonable estimates (SACTRA 1994, 45, 46). The long-term estimate, which implies that all of the travel time savings would be spent in additional travel, is high compared with studies reviewed for this and other recent reports (Dowling et al. 1994). These studies suggest that travel time elasticities are nearly always less than one. The Standing Committee notes that the higher estimate is consistent with the concept of stable travel time budgets promoted by Zahavi and others (SACTRA 1994, 40). The notion is based on empirical evidence that, despite differences in travel conditions and opportunities even across countries, travelers tend to spend the same amount of time, on average, in daily travel. According to this concept, savings in travel time and costs will be used for more travel. However, the Standing Committee itself points out (SACTRA 1994, 40) that the concept of constant travel time budgets has been the subject of considerable debate (Gunn 1981; Kitamura 1991, 24, 25), calling into question the notion that all travel time savings are spent in additional travel.

The estimation and application of travel time elasticities is also subject to many practical problems, which are described in this report in Chapter 4. Notwithstanding these problems, travel time elasticities have been used to estimate potential induced traffic from highway capacity increases. In response to questions about the potential induced traffic effects of Westway, a highly controversial 4-mi Interstate segment proposed for the lower west side of Manhattan, project staff developed modifications to traffic forecasting software that allowed the direct application of travel time elasticities for individual pairs of traffic analysis zones. Specifically, zone-to-zone travel times in Manhattan with and without Westway were compared, and the number of trips between zones was adjusted on the basis of time savings. For example, with an elasticity of −0.25, a 10 percent travel time reduction between two zones from the new highway would result in a 2.5 percent increase in travel between the zones. Separate analyses were performed for a.m. peak, p.m. peak, and off-peak periods; however, no attempt was made to account explicitly for shifts of travelers among time periods or the substitution of longer trips for shorter trips. Thus, the analytical procedure can be regarded as a reasonable way of developing rough estimates of the induced traffic and associated impacts from highway improvements.

The fact that travel time elasticities generally fall between 0.0 and −1.0 means that only part of the time savings resulting from highway improvements is used for additional travel. For example, with an assumed travel time elasticity of −0.5, a 10 percent decrease in travel time per trip will result in a 5 percent increase in the number of trips. Hence, total travel time (calculated as travel time per trip multiplied by the number of trips) will decrease.

NOTE

1. For a highway segment, vehicle miles of capacity is calculated as the product of the segment length (in miles) and its capacity (in vehicles per hour). Vehicle miles of capacity is a more accurate measure of areawide capacity than lane miles because it accounts for the fact that highways with signalized intersections or stop signs have much less capacity per lane than freeways.

REFERENCES

ABBREVIATION

SACTRA   The Standing Advisory Committee on Trunk Road Assessment

Bovy, P.H.L., A.L. Loos, and G.C. De Jong. 1992. *Effects of the Opening of the Amsterdam Orbital Motorway. Final Report Phase I*. Ministry of Transport and Public Works, Transportation and Traffic Research Division, Rotterdam, Netherlands, 83 pp.

Burright, B.K. 1984. *Cities and Travel*. Garland Publishing, New York, N.Y.

Chan, Y., and F.L. Ou. 1978. Tabulating Demand Elasticities for Urban Travel Forecasting. In *Transportation Research Record 673*, TRB, National Research Council, Washington, D.C., pp. 40–46.

Domencich, T.A., G. Kraft, and J.P. Valette. 1968. Estimation of Urban Passenger Travel Behavior: An Economic Demand Model. In *Highway Research Record 238*, HRB, National Research Council, Washington, D.C., pp. 64–78.

Dowling, R., S.B. Colman, and A. Chen. 1994. *Effects of Increased Highway Capacity on Travel Behavior*. Prepared for California Air Resources Board. Dowling Associates, Oakland, Calif., Oct.

EIC Corporation. 1976. *Refinement to the AEEP Fleet Model*. Prepared for the Transportation Systems Center, Cambridge, Mass.

Frye, F.F. 1964a. Redistribution of Traffic in the Dan Ryan Expressway Corridor. *CATS Research News*, Vol. 6, No. 3, June 26, pp. 6–14.

Frye, F.F. 1964b. Eisenhower Expressway Study Area-1964. *CATS Research News*, Vol. 6, No. 4, June 24, pp. 7–13.

Groenhout, R., D. Madan, and M. Ranjbar. 1986. Mode Choice for Urban Travellers in Sydney. *Transport and Planning*, Vol. 13, Part 8, pp. 52–62.

Gunn, H.F. 1981. Travel Budgets: A Review of Evidence and Modelling Implications. Transportation Research, Vol. 15 A. No. 1.

Hansen, M., D. Gillen, A. Dobbins, U. Huang, and M. Puvathingal. 1993. *The Air Quality Impacts of Urban Highway Capacity Expansion: Traffic Generation and Land Use Change*. UCB-ITS-RR-93-5. Institute of Transportation Studies, University of California, Berkeley, April.

Holder, R.W., and V.G. Stover. 1972. *An Evaluation of Induced Traffic on New Highway Facilities*. Texas A&M University, College Station, March.

Industry Commission. 1993. Appendix B: Determinants of Demand for Urban Travel. *Urban Transport, Vol 2: Appendices*. Australia, Oct. 14.

Jorgensen, R.E. 1947. Influence of Expressways in Diverting Traffic from Alternate Routes and in Generating New Traffic. *HRB Proc.*, Vol. 27, pp. 322–330.

Kassoff, H., and D.S. Gendell. 1972. An Approach to Multiregional Urban
    Transportation Policy Planning. In *Highway Research Record 348*, HRB,
    National Research Council, Washington, D.C., pp. 76–93.
Kitamura, R. 1991. The Effects of Added Transportation Capacity on Travel:
    A Review of Theoretical and Empirical Results. *Proc., The Effects of
    Added Transportation Capacity*, Bethesda, Md., pp. 21–37.
Koppelman, F.S. 1970. A Model for Highway Needs Evaluation. In *Highway
    Research Record 314*, HRB, National Research Council, Washington,
    D.C., pp. 123–134.
Koppelman, F.S. 1972. *Preliminary Study of Development of a Macro Urban
    Travel Demand Model*. Prepared for U.S. DOT, Assistant Secretary of Pol-
    icy and International Affairs. Department of Civil Engineering, MIT,
    Cambridge, Mass, Dec.
Lynch, J.T. 1955. Traffic Diversion to Toll Roads. *Proceedings 702*, American
    Society of Civil Engineers, June, Washington, D.C., pp. 1–27.
Mellman, R.E. 1976. *Aggregate Auto Travel Forecasting: State of the Art
    and Suggestions for Future Research*. Transportation Systems Center,
    Cambridge, Mass, June.
Pells, S.R. 1989. *User Response to New Road Capacity: A Review of Published
    Evidence*. Working Paper 283, Institute for Transport Studies, The Uni-
    versity of Leeds, Yorkshire, England, Nov.
Ruiter, E.R., W.R. Loudon, C.R. Kern, D.A. Bell, M.J. Rothenberg, and T.W.
    Austin. 1979. *The Relationship of Changes in Urban Highway Supply to
    Vehicle Miles of Travel*. Final Report (Preliminary Draft). Cambridge
    Systematics, Inc., Cambridge, Mass.; JHK & Associates, Alexandria, Va,
    March.
Ruiter, E.R., W.R. Loudon, C.R. Kern, D.A. Bell, M.J. Rothenberg, and T.W.
    Austin. 1980. The Vehicle-Miles of Travel-Urban Highway Supply Re-
    lationship. *NCHRP Research Results Digest 127*. TRB, National Research
    Council, Washington, D.C., Dec.
SACTRA. 1994. *Trunk Roads and the Generation of Traffic*. Conducted for the
    Department of Transport, London, England, Dec.
Alan M. Voorhees & Associates, Inc. 1971. *A System Sensitive Approach for
    Forecasting Urbanized Area Travel Demands*. FH-11-7546. FHWA, U.S.
    Department of Transportation, Dec.
Zahavi, Y. 1972. Traffic Performance Evaluation of Road Networks by the
    Alpha-Relationship. *Traffic Engineering and Control*, Vol. 14, Nos. 5,6.

Appendix C

Impact of Changes in Highway Capacity on Truck Travel

LANCE R. GRENZEBACK
Cambridge Systematics, Inc.

The impact of changes in highway capacity on truck travel in metropolitan areas is discussed in this appendix. At issue is whether highway capacity improvements induce truck travel and, conversely, whether restricting highway capacity dampens truck travel. The answers are needed to inform the debate about the impact of changes in highway capacity on congestion, air pollution, and energy consumption.

Changes in highway capacity include the addition of physical capacity to existing facilities (e.g., more lanes), the addition of operational capacity (e.g., better management of traffic flow through traffic engineering or road pricing), and the addition of new facilities to the highway network (e.g., construction of new highways or bridges).

For the truck driver, these improvements result in changes in travel time (i.e., faster trips), changes in travel reliability (i.e., more predictable trip times), or changes in accessibility (i.e., the ability to physically reach new areas and new markets). Where highway capacity is reduced, the changes result in slower trips, less predictable travel times, and restricted access to markets.

310

Over time, the truck driver, the motor carrier firm, and eventually the shipper will react to these changes by adjusting their travel behavior and changing their use of the highway system. They may reallocate their trips—shifting the hour or day that a trip is made, changing the route, and changing the destination; or they may make new trips, take longer trips, and shift freight between truck and rail or truck and air. By altering the total truck miles of travel and its allocation between congested and uncongested roads, changes in highway capacity can increase or decrease congestion, engine emissions, and energy consumption.

The general impact of changes in highway capacity on truck traffic is examined in the first section of this appendix. The author argues that, in the short term, changes in highway capacity are not likely to result in significant changes in truck travel. The three major reasons for this argument are the marginal nature of most changes in highway capacity today, the moderate exposure of trucks to severe congestion, and the overriding influence of low freight transportation costs.

Reviewed in the second section is the fragmentary evidence on the specific responses of motor carriers to changes in highway capacity, the primary ones being changes in the time of travel, route, and mode.

Structural changes in the economy, freight logistics, and trucking that may make truck travel more sensitive to changes in highway capacity in the future are discussed in the third section. These trends include a shift toward longer and more time-sensitive supply chains and distribution networks that leave trucks exposed to congestion and a countervailing shift toward the use of information technology to improve the productivity and flexibility of freight transportation.

In the fourth section research findings are reviewed on the relationship between truck accidents and congestion, which suggest that reducing peak-period congestion may reduce the frequency of common accidents, but will have little effect on the frequency of major truck accidents, which tend to occur during uncongested off-peak periods.

The state of truck travel modeling and the data available to transportation planners and engineers to analyze trucking issues are reviewed in the fifth section.

In the final section the author's conclusions are summarized and the implications for highway capacity planning, air quality, and energy use are discussed.

The conclusions rely heavily on empirical data from planning and policy studies and on anecdotal information from the freight and motor carrier industries. Although a large body of academic and applied research on many aspects of freight logistics and trucking exists, there is little on the topic of induced truck travel. Almost all of the work on travel demand forecasting and induced traffic has been focused on automobiles and transit.

Finally, the information that exists on truck travel usually pertains to large trucks, typically heavy five-axle tractor-semitrailers. There are 45.5 million trucks registered in the United States; however, 39.5 million of these trucks, or about 88 percent of that fleet, are pickup trucks, panel trucks, and minivans, many of which are used for personal transportation. For traffic and congestion management purposes, these light trucks are indistinguishable from automobiles and are seldom accounted for as trucks in urban transportation studies. The balance of the trucks in the U.S. fleet, approximately six million, or about 12 percent of all trucks, are medium and heavy trucks, ranging from local delivery trucks with two axles and six tires to large over-the-road tractor-semitrailers with five axles and 18 tires (BTS 1994, 64). (The size classes used to categorize trucks are presented in Table C-1.) In the medium and heavy truck categories, the heavy and heavy-heavy trucks (Classes 7 and 8) are the focus of most truck transportation studies. These large trucks, an estimated 2.5 million trucks, or about 5 percent of the total fleet, are thought to account for more than three-fourths of all truck miles of travel and most of the ton miles and revenue miles of travel in urban areas (Blower and Campbell 1988).[1]

GENERAL IMPACT OF CHANGES IN HIGHWAY CAPACITY

In the short term, changes in highway capacity are not likely to result in significant changes in truck travel for three major reasons.

Extensiveness of Existing Highway Network

The first reason is the extensiveness of the existing highway network in the United States. The aggregate contribution of the highway ca-

TABLE C-1 Large Trucks : 3+ Axles, Straight, or Combination (Grenzeback et al. 1988, 2).

Size Class	Weight Class	Gross Vehicle Weight (lb)	Axles/Tires	Examples
Heavy-Heavy	8	>33,000	7/22+ 6/18+ 5/18	Multitrailer trucks Tractor-semitrailers and doubles
			4/14 3/10	Concrete mixers and dump trucks
Heavy	7	26,000–33,000	3/10	City tractor with 28-ft pup trailer
Light-Heavy	6	19,500–26,000	2/6	Beverage truck Home-heating fuel truck
	5	16,000–19,500	2/6	Stake truck
	4	14,000–16,000	2/6	Flatbed
Medium	3	10,000–14,000	2/6	Metro van (UPS)
	2	6,000–10,000	2/4	Step van (mail)
Light	1	<6,000	2/4	Pickup truck, van

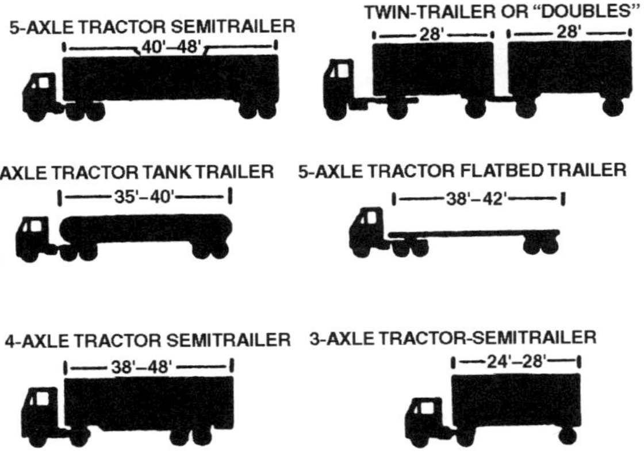

Illustration labels:
TWIN-TRAILER OR "DOUBLES" — 28' — 28'
5-AXLE TRACTOR SEMITRAILER — 40'–48'
5-AXLE TRACTOR FLATBED TRAILER — 38'–42'
5-AXLE TRACTOR TANK TRAILER — 35'–40'
4-AXLE TRACTOR SEMITRAILER — 38'–48'
3-AXLE TRACTOR-SEMITRAILER — 24'–28' 
STRAIGHT TRUCK — 25'–40'

NOTE: Includes four- and five-axle trucks, weight Classes 7 and 8, greater than or equal to 26,000 lb gross vehicle weight.

pacity improvements planned for the next two decades will be marginal, at best, to the overall capacity of the existing system. The highway system is composed of 3.9 million mi of roads and streets and supports a highly developed truck freight system. The 45,500-mi Interstate highway system and the 200,000 mi of other expressways and principal arterial highways (together about 6 percent of the total system) are the economic backbone of the highway system and carry the bulk of the truck traffic. Urban highways—composed of 12,500 mi of Interstates, 6,500 mi of freeways and expressways, and 52,200 mi of other principal arterials, for a total of 71,200 mi—account for 30 percent of the truck network and about 1.8 percent of all roads (FHWA 1993, 146).[2] The size of this urban system has been relatively static for the past two decades as highway funds have shifted from construction of new roads to the repair and replacement of existing roads. This pattern is expected to continue through the next two decades.

From a historical perspective the highway capacity improvements being debated today will be occurring at the end of the truck era, not the beginning. When trucks were introduced at the beginning of this century, they freed industry and workers from the need to locate near rail lines, just as the introduction of railroads in the early 1800s freed industry and workers from the need to locate within dray horse–hauling distance of ports, rivers, and canals. In both cases the new transportation technologies led to sharp drops in the cost of moving goods and contributed to profound changes in the structure and dynamics of cities.

The push to improve farm-to-market roads in the 1930s and the decision to build a full intercity-Interstate highway network in the 1950s and 1960s provided the basic highway capacity that supports the trucking industry today. None of the highway capacity improvements currently planned are comparable to these programs and none will significantly reduce the average cost of truck freight movement. They will make marginal improvements to specific corridors and relieve critical bottlenecks; however, they will not fundamentally restructure the economics of trucking.

Limited Exposure of Trucks to Congestion

The second reason that changes in highway capacity are not likely to result in significant changes in truck travel is the modest exposure of trucks to congestion. Most truck travel is not exposed to severe congestion and therefore is not highly sensitive to marginal changes in travel time and travel reliability. Truck travel is spread more evenly across the day than commuter traffic, with relatively more truck trips than automobile trips made during uncongested off-peak hours. Changes in highway capacity designed to facilitate or restrict peak-period automobile travel will have little effect on off-peak truck travel.

A 1988 study of truck traffic in Los Angeles, San Diego, and San Francisco, California, found that large trucks accounted for less than 5 percent of vehicles on the freeways during the peak periods (Grenzeback et al. 1988, 1).[3] The percentage and the absolute number of large trucks on the freeways were highest during the midday off-peak period (see Table C-2 and Figure C-1). A subsequent study of large-truck traffic on city streets in Los Angeles resulted in similar findings (JHK & Associates 1989).[4]

A parallel analysis of California Department of Transportation annual average daily traffic data for all freeway segments in Los Angeles, San Diego, and San Francisco found that the "worst" freeway segments (i.e., those with high traffic volumes, high injury rates,

TABLE C-2   Large Trucks as a Percentage of Total Vehicles (One Direction) (Grenzeback et al. 1988, 8)

	LOS ANGELES	SAN DIEGO	SAN FRANCISCO
MORNING PEAK (7:00 TO 9:00 A.M.)			
Weighted Average[a]	3.8	1.8	4.2
Observed Range	0.5–17.2	0.7–5.7	0.8–13.2
MIDDAY OFF-PEAK (11:00 A.M. TO 1:00 P.M.)			
Weighted Average[a]	5.5	2.5	5.4
Observed Range	0.7–16.2	0.6–4.8	0.6–12.1
EVENING PEAK (4:00 TO 6:00 P.M.)			
Weighted Average[a]	2.6	0.8	2.4
Observed Range	0.2–13.2	0.1–1.9	0.3–6.8

[a] Average traffic volumes during the evening peak period were slightly higher than average traffic volumes during the morning peak period. Midday traffic volumes were 10 to 15 percent lower than the peak-period volumes.

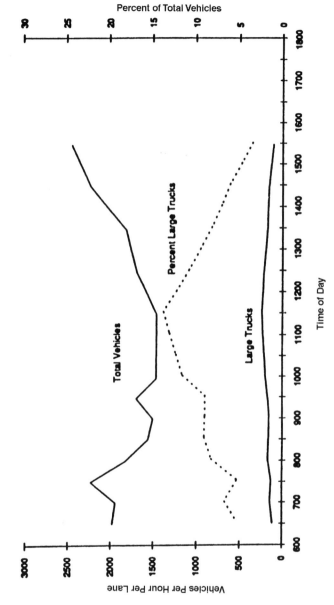

FIGURE C-1 Large truck and total traffic volumes on I-5 northbound at Los Feliz Boulevard, Los Angeles (Grenzeback et al. 1988, 8).

and severe congestion) tended to have a lower percentage of large trucks (2.86 percent on average in Los Angeles) than all other freeway segments (4.0 percent on average in Los Angeles) (Grenzeback et al. 1988, 5).

A 1992 count of truck traffic on the Capital Beltway in the Washington, D.C., metropolitan region found that large trucks (three or more axles) averaged 3.0 percent of all vehicles during the morning peak period (6:00 to 9:00 a.m.) and 2.3 percent during the evening peak period (4:00 to 7:00 p.m.). The range of observed percentages was 1.5 to 4.5 percent during the morning peak and 1.25 to 4.0 percent during the evening peak (Zilliacus 1993).

Two reasons account for the lower percentages and lower absolute numbers of trucks on the road during the morning and evening peak periods. The first is cost: it costs $20 to $60 per hour to operate a large truck in an urban area (Grenzeback and Warner 1994, 4–9).[5] When possible, truck drivers and motor carrier firms schedule and route trips to minimize congestion delays, which result in increased travel time and cost. The pressure to minimize costs is especially strong in the for-hire motor carrier industry, for which interstate operations were deregulated in 1980, triggering strong price and service competition.

The second, and usually dominant, factor determining truck exposure is the business cycle of the clients—the shippers and receivers of goods. The business operations of many industries work to insulate trucks from the morning and evening peak traffic periods. For example, consider the operation of a downtown retail department store. The primary market for a downtown department store is midday walk-in shoppers. Because the peak business time is the midday, sales employees start later in the morning than office workers and therefore tend to commute later in the morning peak period. Truck deliveries are usually made during the evening and at night when parking space is available at loading docks and store staff are free to handle new merchandise. Likewise, maintenance, cleaning, restocking, and display are done late at night or early in the morning so that they do not interfere with daytime sales.

Suburban department stores operate on a different cycle. Their primary market is evening drive-in traffic, usually split around the afternoon commute and dinner hours. Sales staff work overlapping shifts, but tend to commute outside peak traffic hours. As with down-town stores, maintenance, cleaning, and restocking are done late at night or early in the morning, but truck deliveries are made during the midday off-peak period so that they do not interfere with the af-ternoon or evening sales periods. As a consequence of these business cycles, only a fraction of all truck movements serving major depart-ment stores at downtown and suburban locations is likely to be exposed to substantial congestion.

Similar patterns are evident in other trucking operations, includ-ing petroleum distribution. Tank trucks delivering gasoline and home-heating fuel account for a large number of local truck movements in urban areas. Home-heating fuel trucks are loaded at tank farms dur-ing the midday or evening, and deliveries are made the next morning or afternoon to comply with local noise ordinances that restrict truck deliveries in residential areas to daylight hours. Gasoline tankers serv-ing metropolitan areas tend to be loaded at tank farms during the afternoon, and deliveries are made in the evening or at night when business slacks off at local service stations. In both cases exposure to severe congestion is minimized, but primarily because of client needs, not travel time or cost considerations that would be affected by improvements in highway capacity.

By contrast, couriers, parcel services, and less-than-truckload car-riers, such as Federal Express, United Parcel Service, and Roadway, operate in a much different business environment, which leaves their pick-up and delivery operations exposed to peak-period traffic con-gestion. These carriers distribute inbound freight during the morning peak period as offices and retail stores open and pick up outbound freight during the afternoon peak period as their clients close out the business day. This pattern persists because few offices and retail stores ship or receive sufficient volumes of freight to justify the cost of employing a night shipping clerk, dock worker, and security officer. As a consequence, these carriers operate during the peak periods and are very sensitive to local highway capacity changes.

For businesses that are open at night, some firms and their motor carriers make nighttime deliveries. Hotel and restaurant provisioners, including bakery, dairy, meat, and produce truckers, sometimes de-liver at night; however, the primary incentive is often uncongested parking and open docks, not lack of traffic congestion per se. A study of United Parcel Service operations found that the cost of the parking tickets that its trucks received in downtown Boston during the day was five times greater than the cost the firm incurred on those routes because of traffic congestion (Warner and Wilson 1989).

In summary, the trucking industry is highly fragmented. The exposure of trucks to congestion and their response to highway capacity improvements is determined by the industries they serve, their geographic range, whether they operate fixed or variable routes, the time sensitivity of their shipments, and the size and sophistication of the fleet. This diversity has tended to spread truck travel more evenly across the day than automobile travel, making trucks generally less sensitive to changes in highway capacity.

Low Freight Transportation Costs

The third reason for the limited impact of highway capacity changes on truck travel is the overriding influence of low freight transportation costs. Changes in highway capacity result primarily in changes in travel time and reliability. For a motor carrier these changes are accrued directly as increased (or decreased) labor and vehicle operating costs and indirectly as changes in the level of service that can be offered to shippers and receivers. Carriers are sensitive to changes in travel time, and therefore driver time, because labor costs [payroll, benefits, and purchased transportation (i.e., leased owner-operators)] account for almost 60 percent of operating expenses. Fuel purchases account for a smaller proportion of operating expenses, about 8 percent, but both labor and fuel costs have escalated rapidly during the past decade. In the for-hire trucking industry, which accounts for a large share of truck miles of travel and for which statistics are available, labor costs rose 40 percent and fuel costs rose 50 percent between 1986 and 1991 (BTS 1994, 115).

Despite these cost increases, overall freight transportation costs have dropped relative to the gross national product (GNP) and other producers' prices (BTS 1994, 58). Because transportation costs typically account for 1 to 4 percent of total production costs in the manufacturing and retail industries, low freight costs have made it more attractive for shippers and receivers to substitute transportation for higher cost labor, materials, and land.[6] The outsourcing of manufacturing and assembly work to Asia and Mexico and other Latin American countries depends on long, but relatively inexpensive, transportation supply lines to realize large savings on labor. Just-in-time manufacturing and distribution substitute more frequent truck deliveries to factories and retail stores to reduce the cost of carrying extra inventory. Similarly, the emergence of exurban distribution and warehousing centers reflects business decisions to increase expenditures on truck, rail, and air transportation to obtain access to low-cost and easily developed land, which is more available on the periphery of metropolitan areas.

In general highway capacity improvements have played a small role in driving down transportation costs and making such substitutions possible. The dominant factors are discussed in the following paragraphs.

- Evolution of air freight services using all-cargo air freighters and the belly-freight capacity of commercial wide-body passenger airliners. Air freight service has captured and expanded the market for very-high-value and time-sensitive shipments, outperforming trucking. Since the 1950s the air freight share of national freight ton miles has grown tenfold from 0.03 to 0.37 percent, for which the air freight industry now receives 4 percent of national freight revenues. By comparison, trucks account for 25 percent of the national ton miles and receive 79 percent of national freight revenues (BTS 1994, 58,59). The trucking industry percentages are expected to remain stable or decrease slightly during the next decade and the air freight share of tonnage and revenues is expected to increase.
- Introduction of containerization and very large container ships (i.e., post-Panamax container ships). Containerization has reduced damage and pilferage of goods in transit and reduced the cost of labor required to load and unload shipments. Automation and economies of scale in ship design have sharply reduced the cost of moving a container across the Atlantic or Pacific oceans.
- Development of double-stack rail service on unit trains. Double-stack service has halved the cost of long distance (i.e., greater than 1,200 mi) intermodal rail container shipments. Rail rates per ton

for intermodal container movements reportedly fell from $75 in 1980 to $47 in 1990, reflecting increases in productivity and strong competition among rail carriers for market share (*21st Century Trucking: Profiles of the Future* 1994, IV-1 and Figure IV-3).

- Deregulation of the transportation industry, especially deregulation of the motor carrier industry in 1980. The abolishment of most business entry and exit barriers to interstate trucking and the effective abandonment of pricing, service, and route restrictions precipitated a major restructuring of the motor carrier industry. (A second wave of restructuring is expected to follow recent congressional deregulation of intrastate motor carrier operations.) From the restructuring are emerging cost-competitive integrated and intermodal transportation companies that work closely with shippers and receivers. These firms have been successful in reducing the costs of organizing, managing, and administering freight services. Truckload motor carriers working with the railroads and air freight forwarders have been especially effective at developing integrated transportation services, which were once provided at higher cost by third-party brokers.

The net effect of these changes has been to make changes in highway capacity less visible and important to the shippers and receivers who determine the overall demand and logistics strategies for freight transportation. Changes in highway capacity are important to individual motor carriers, but are a secondary factor in determining the general level of demand for freight transportation and truck miles of travel.

SPECIFIC RESPONSES TO CHANGES IN HIGHWAY CAPACITY

The fragmentary evidence on the specific responses of motor carriers to changes in highway capacity is examined in this section. Two types of travel responses are of interest: those that involve reallocation of truck travel, such as changes in travel hour, route, and destination, and those that involve induced travel, such as changes in the number, length, or mode of trips.

Reallocation of Truck Travel

Changes in Travel Hour

There is a paucity of data on truck travel by hour of the day. State departments of transportation and metropolitan planning organizations take frequent vehicle and truck counts on major arterials, but this information is usually aggregated to the daily or annual level because the primary users of truck count data have been pavement and bridge design engineers who must estimate total axle-loadings on a yearly, not an hourly, basis. As a proxy for more comprehensive data, truck crossings at toll facilities provide some indication of truck travel patterns by time of day and their response to changes in highway capacity.

In 1985 and 1991, the Port Authority of New York and New Jersey conducted origin and destination and commodity surveys of all trucks at its eastbound Hudson River bridge and tunnel toll plazas. Figure C-2 shows the distribution of truck crossings by hour for those years (Cambridge Systematics, Inc. 1992).[7] The data show a pronounced shift in the distribution of truck trips away from the morning and midday hours and toward the early morning and late evening hours.

Anecdotal information from motor carriers using the George Washington Bridge, which carries more than 50 percent of the truck traffic crossing the Hudson River, suggests that increasing congestion has been the major factor in this shift. At least three groups of motor carriers have shifted the time of their trips: long-haul interstate carriers serving New England from warehouses in New Jersey, produce haulers moving fruits and vegetables from the New Jersey rail yards and the South to the Hunt's Point Market in the South Bronx, and local provisioners serving restaurants and hotels in Manhattan. Toll pricing did not influence their decisions because the Port Authority's truck tolls are based solely on the number of axles; no discounts are offered for off-peak travel.

The scale and level of congestion in New York make it atypical of metropolitan areas, but similar, although less pronounced, shifts in peak-period travel patterns have been observed at locations (such as San Francisco's Bay Bridge) where highway capacity is severely restricted. In these situations highway capacity improvements will likely result in a shift of truck traffic back to the peak period. Those most

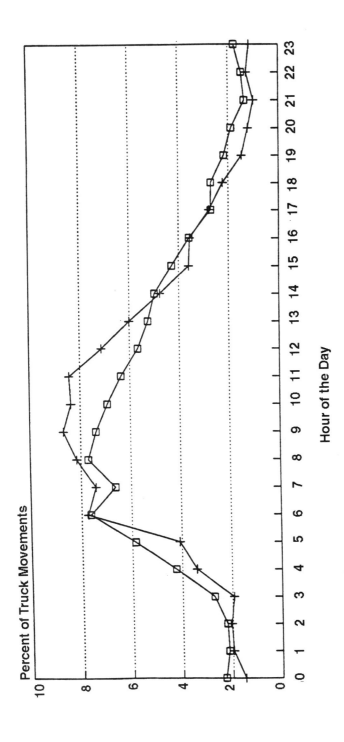

Percent of Truck Movements

Hour of the Day

+ **1985 All Commodities**   □ **1991 All Commodities**

FIGURE C-2 Truck trips by hour for all eastbound crossings, 1985 and 1991, all commodities (Cambridge Systematics, Inc. 1992)[7].

affected would be carriers serving firms that have early morning delivery windows.

Changes in Route

Large trucks operate on a small number of routes in most metropolitan areas. Figure C-3 shows the regional truck freightways in the New York and New Jersey metropolitan area. New York is particularly constricted because interstate-standard trucks, which are 13 ft 6 in. high and 102 in. wide, cannot use the Lincoln and Holland tunnels. Similar bridge and tunnel clearance restrictions exist in Boston, Chicago, San Francisco, Seattle, and other cities. These physical clearance restrictions limit the ability of truck drivers to avoid congestion and incidents and introduce considerable circuitry to urban truck routes. A network analysis of truck routes in Chicago by Chicago Area Transportation Study staff showed that truck route restrictions in the metropolitan Chicago area added significantly to the truck miles of travel in that area (Reilly and Hochmuth 1990).

The trend toward the use of larger, interstate-standard trucks, as shown in Figure C-4 by the increase in five-axle trucks at the expense of four-axle trucks, concentrates large-truck traffic into those few corridors that can safely accommodate it.[8] This shift, which has occurred nationwide, makes large-truck travel sensitive to bridge and tunnel improvements that restrict or provide access to specific corridors.

Small trucks, particularly vans and two-axle, six-tire delivery trucks, face fewer route restrictions. Many urban carriers allow their drivers considerable latitude in picking local routes and delivery sequences. Federal Express, for example, provides its drivers with a list of delivery points and deadlines, but lets the drivers determine the specific route to minimize traffic delays. However, less-than-truckload carriers, such as Roadway, Yellow Freight, and Consolidated Freightways, can seldom take advantage of this flexibility. Because they carry heavier shipments packed for a specific sequence of deliveries, the last shipment into the trailer must be the first shipment out.

Changes in Destination

A study of the impacts of urban congestion on service-sector industries found that congestion and highway capacity were a con-

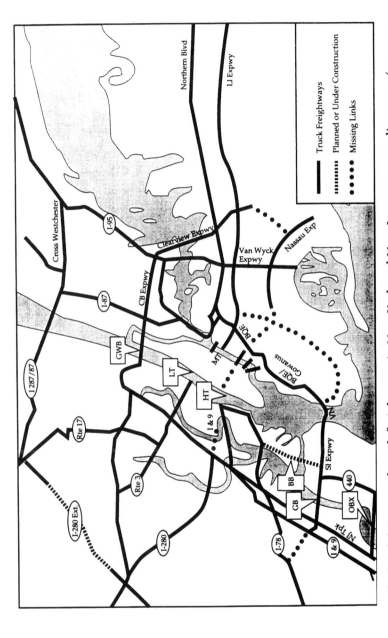

FIGURE C-3 Regional truck freightways in New York and New Jersey metropolitan area (source: Port Authority of New York and New Jersey).

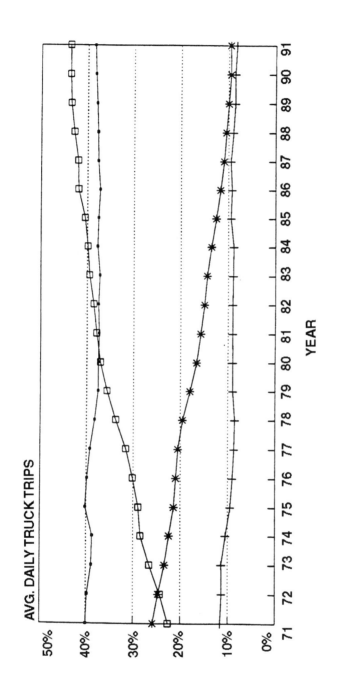

FIGURE C-4 Truck trips by truck type for all eastbound crossings, 1971–1991 (Cambridge Systematics, Inc. 1992)[7].

tributing, but not major, factor in corporate relocation decisions (Grenzeback and Warner 1994). Although relocation may significantly reduce a firm's exposure to congestion, the dominant factors driving decisions to relocate were the availability and cost of labor and housing, tax rates, and perceived levels of crime. Service-sector industries generally are not as transportation dependent as manufacturing or wholesale firms, but service-sector firms are the primary source of jobs and growth in most urban areas today.

Studies of trends in warehousing and truck terminal locations also suggest that congestion and highway capacity are contributing, but not major, factors in relocation decisions. A study of warehousing in the New York metropolitan region by Port Authority of New York and New Jersey staff (Strauss-Wieder et al. undated) found that land, tax, and labor costs were the primary factors determining warehousing and truck terminal location decisions. These factors were important because of structural changes in the warehousing and distribution industry that forced warehouse operators to reorganize their operations and physical plants. Those changes included consolidation, computerization, automation, introduction of value-added services, and growth in public and contract warehousing.

Interviews with major truck terminal operators in Los Angeles and New York revealed that the decision to relocate a terminal was usually triggered by the inability to expand operations at an existing location because of encroaching residential development and restrictive noise regulations.[9] When truck terminals are relocated, most are moved to the periphery of the metropolitan area, along existing nterstate highways. In almost all cases this relocation leads to an increase in truck miles of travel for the carrier; however, the savings in land costs and inability to locate closer to the urban core make this trade-off financially acceptable. Such relocation would not be possible without the access provided by previous investments in Interstate and metropolitan highway capacity.

Induced Travel

Changes in the Number of Trips

The high cost of labor makes adding trips to compensate for congestion less attractive than shifting travel times and routes. Most motor carriers rely on overtime and temporary drivers (i.e., leasing trucks and using owner-operator drivers) to deal with short-term and seasonal congestion. Research attempting to relate fleet size and truck miles of travel to urban congestion levels have been stymied by a lack of reliable data on congestion levels and the inability to adequately distinguish the impacts of congestion, economic growth, and improved routing and dispatching techniques by motor carriers.

In urban areas some service-delivery firms have been able to minimize truck travel by establishing satellite branches and consolidation terminals. By using a satellite base the firm avoids sending its staff and vehicles between the service area and a more distant central facility during the day. An office machine repair firm that has small bases throughout its service area is a good example of this logistics strategy. Its satellite offices, usually one or two small rooms in an office or strip commercial building, have inventory and parts rooms that are restocked at night. The technicians assigned to the satellite offices travel locally to work on clients' machines, returning to the central office only once or twice or week. In central business districts where there is a heavy concentration of office machines, the bases are numerous enough so that the technicians can walk to the customers' offices in their territories. In some cases couriers or less-than-truckload carriers are used to deliver parts directly from a central warehouse to the clients' offices. The clear limitation to this strategy is the size and weight of the goods being moved.

Changes in Trip Length

National freight statistics show an increase in the total number of ton miles moved in the United States during the last 20 years, but a decline in the number of ton miles per unit of GNP. The implication of these statistics is that lighter, higher-value goods are being moved over longer distances. This is consistent with the trend, discussed earlier, toward substitution of low-cost transportation for high-cost production factors, such as labor, inventory, and land. There are numerous examples of individual firms, as well as metropolitan areas and regions, that have taken advantage of lower transportation costs to develop warehousing and distribution centers.

One of the more successful examples has been the emergence of an "inland port" in Columbus, Ohio. Because of its central location in the eastern half of the United States and the freight capacity of the highways, rail lines, and airports serving the region, Columbus has developed into a centralized warehousing and distribution center for such major retailers as The Limited, Spiegel's, and Consolidated Stores. These firms bring much of their inventory into central warehouses in Columbus and then distribute them, primarily by truck, to individual retail stores across the United States. This logistics strategy generates longer individual truck trips, but there are no readily available statistics to determine whether the net effect is to increase or decrease total truck miles of travel compared with more localized distribution strategies.

As with the relocation of metropolitan warehouses, the development of major distribution centers depends on previous investments in air, rail, and highway capacity, but in most cases the emergence of such distribution centers has lagged behind the transportation investments by decades. It is therefore difficult to determine how much additional truck travel is the result of increased highway capacity and how much is the result of broader structural changes in the economy.

Changes in Mode

A significant change in the past decade has been the accelerating integration of truck and rail service to provide intermodal freight service. Freight movements by intermodal containers have been growing rapidly. The number of intermodal containers coming into and going out of the United States has been growing at an average annual rate of just over 7 percent. The use of domestic containers, which is a new, small, and rapidly growing market, is expected to increase at an average annual rate of about 25 percent. The use of roadrailers (truck trailers equipped with retractable road wheels and removable rail wheels) and similar flexible equipment is expected to grow at about 10 percent per year, cutting into the volume of piggyback trailers (truck trailers that have fixed wheels and are carried on railroad flatcars), which are projected to decline about 10 percent annually.[10]

Changes in highway capacity have played a role in making intermodal and domestic containers more attractive to shippers and carriers, but the major consideration has been pressure to cut total transportation costs. The introduction of intermodal stack trains, especially double-stack trains, has cut the cost of moving a container long distance (more than 1,200 mi), approximately in half, making them competitive with long-haul truckload service. It is likely that intermodal service will become competitive with truckload service over distances as short as 500 to 600 mi during the next decade; however, this will occur only in high-volume rail corridors with sufficient capacity to provide timely, high-speed service.

The shift to intermodal rail will free up highway capacity on the major cross-country truck lanes, but few of these corridors experience significant congestion except in metropolitan areas. As the volume of intermodal freight increases, railroads will improve or convert existing rail yards to intermodal service. This action will result in reallocation of truck travel, both long haul and short haul, but no research studies have yet attempted to document the net impact on truck miles of travel.

There are fewer opportunities to shift freight from truck to rail within metropolitan areas. The demand for intra-metropolitan movement of heavy and bulky freight has dropped as heavy industry has relocated away from metropolitan areas, and most of the rail distribution networks that flourished in the late 1800s have been removed to make way for other land uses. The industries that are growing today in urban areas—business services, government, distribution, research and development, education, health, light manufacturing, and the like—generate smaller, lighter, higher-value shipments that railroads cannot handle cost-effectively over short distances.

Rail transportation is cost-effective at moving large volumes of freight over long distances where it can achieve economies of scale that offset the high cost of maintaining locomotives, track, and control systems; however, it cannot achieve the necessary economies of scale when shuttling two or three carloads or container-loads of freight at a time across a metropolitan area. Trucking, with its lower equipment and control costs and greater flexibility, is cost-effective at serving such local distribution and intra-metropolitan plant shipments. Because of the substantial cost differences, trucking will continue to dominate the metropolitan freight market even if highway congestion, and therefore intra-metropolitan distribution costs, increase substantially during the next decades. Rail will continue to be the carrier of choice for the delivery of bulk products, such as coal to metropolitan power plants, and the intercity movement of low-value commodities, such as sand and gravel. Rail will capture a larger share of long-haul shipments of produce and manufactured goods through intermodal containerization, and there will be greater integration of rail for long-haul moves and trucks for short-haul distribution, but there will be little modal shift within metropolitan areas.

TRENDS

Freight transportation is in the early stages of another major shift, comparable to those that occurred with the introduction of railroads in the 1800s and trucks in the 1900s. This time the shift is being driven by structural changes in the economy and the application of information technology to transportation. The direction and dimensions of the new transportation system are not clear, but two countervailing trends may make truck transportation more sensitive to highway capacity changes in the future.

The first trend is the structural movement in the economy toward service-intensive industries. The U.S. economy requires fewer tons of freight to produce a unit of GNP today than it did 20 years ago. Manufacturing and assembly are being done in smaller factories that employ fewer people and are more widely dispersed over metropolitan areas. For transportation this has meant a demand for faster, more reliable, and higher quality transportation services tailored to the needs of widely dispersed individual manufacturers, retailers, and consumers. This demand has been met by the rapid expansion of trucking, air freight, and now intermodal rail services. The result has been the development of long, time-sensitive supply chains and distribution networks that leave trucks exposed to congestion.

In air freight operations, for example, the truck is the first and last link in a long, high-cost trip. The total truck miles of travel involved is a small fraction of the total ton miles, but truck movements into and out of congested metropolitan airports are quickly becoming the least reliable links in the total move. The same type of problem may arise as the number of intermodal and domestic container movements increases during the next decade. Access to and from intermodal rail yards by truck will be the least predictable link in the total trip. In each case local decisions about highway capacity and truck access will have a multiplier effect on freight travel times, costs, and economic activity far beyond the immediate roadway because they will affect an extended and, in most cases, time- and cost-sensitive shipment.

The second trend is toward the use of information technology to improve the productivity and flexibility of freight transportation. Two information systems are evolving, somewhat independently, today. The first system consists of fleet management technologies that provide motor carrier managers with the ability to route, track, and communicate with trucks on the road. The first generations of computerized routing and dispatching software have proved to be an effective competitive weapon for long-haul truckload carriers operating nationally and urban couriers operating locally. Both are realizing considerable costs savings by minimizing truck miles of travel and driver time per shipment.

The second system is composed of urban automated traffic management systems, which are an outgrowth of traffic signal engineering intended to improve the flow of vehicles through city streets; automated traveler information systems, which are an attempt to influence driver route and travel time choices by providing near-real-time information on traffic, weather, and road conditions; and commercial vehicle regulatory systems, which are targeted at improving the speed and quality of truck size, weight, and safety inspections.[11] These intelligent transportation systems (ITS) programs are evolving slowly, but offer the promise of feeding better highway capacity information to motor carrier fleet management systems. In the short term these systems are likely to improve the productivity of motor carriers and reduce truck miles of travel. In the long term they are likely to provide the flexibility and redundancy to operate long supply chains and distribution networks, supporting the continued dispersion of businesses and housing across metropolitan areas. As with just-in-time transportation strategies, the net effect of these changes on truck miles of travel is unknown.

TRUCKS, CONGESTION, AND SAFETY

Research on highway incidents suggests that reducing peak-period congestion may reduce the frequency of common accidents (typically, a multi-vehicle, rear-end or sideswipe collision with minor to moderate injury and property damage), but may have little effect on the frequency of major truck accidents, which tend to occur during uncongested off-peak periods. General knowledge about the accidents on metropolitan highways and the relationship between accidents and congestion are reviewed in this section. Specific knowledge about truck accidents and their relationship to congestion are then examined.

It is estimated that 70 percent of all highway incidents in metropolitan areas are recorded by police and highway agencies; the other 30 percent go unreported and, as such, are assumed to be minor incidents having little impact on traffic.[12] (Figure C-5 is a composite profile of reported highway incidents by type that shows typical incident duration and congestion impact for metropolitan highways.) Of the incidents recorded by police and highway departments, the vast majority, some 80 percent, are vehicle disablements—cars and trucks that have run out of gas, had a flat tire, or been abandoned by their drivers. During off-peak periods when traffic volumes are low, these disabled vehicles have little or no impact on traffic flow. When traffic volumes are high, however, the presence of a stalled car or a driver changing a flat in the breakdown lane can slow traffic in the adjacent traffic lane, causing significant delay to other motorists.

Accidents account for only 10 percent of reported incidents. Most are the result of collisions, such as sideswipes and slow-speed rear-end collisions. Few of these accidents, variously estimated to make up 5 to 15 percent of accidents, are major incidents (typically single-vehicle or head-on collisions with fatalities or severe injuries and extensive property damage). Major incidents are relatively rare, but may last 3 to 10 hr and trigger thousands of hours of vehicle delay to other motorists on a congested urban highway. The remaining 10 percent of reported incidents are most often blockages and slowdowns caused by debris on the roadway.

Studies of the relationship between accident rates and congestion levels suggest that accident rates are lowest when traffic volumes are moderate (i.e., at Levels of Service B and C). Accident rates appear to increase as traffic volumes drop (i.e., at Levels of Service A and B) and as traffic volumes and congestion increase (i.e., at Levels of Service D and E). This u-shaped curve is composed of two accident patterns:

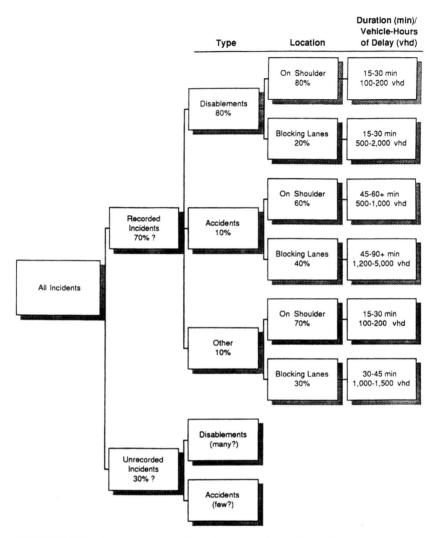

FIGURE C-5 Composite profile of reported incidents by type (Cambridge Systematics, Inc. 1990).

high accident rates at low traffic volumes that are typically the result of single-vehicle, often fatal, involvements that occur at night and high accident rates at high traffic volumes that are typically the result of common accidents that occur during the day. As highways approach saturation levels with stop-and-go traffic conditions, the accident rate is thought to drop as travel speeds fall.[13]

The distribution of truck accidents and the relationship between truck accident rates and congestion levels appear to follow the general patterns just described with some significant variations: trucks are involved in more common accidents than cars because they are less maneuverable in congested conditions; they are involved in more accidents during the midday than cars because relatively more trucks operate during that time; and they are involved in more fatal accidents than cars because of their greater size and weight.

[The nationwide accident rate for trucks has dropped during the past decade. The fatal accident rate for medium and heavy trucks dropped by 39 percent despite a 42 percent increase in truck miles of travel during that period, but trucks are still involved in a disproportionately high percentage of fatal accidents (*21st Century Trucking: Profiles of the Future* 1994; BTS 1994, 138).]

An analysis of truck incidents on Los Angeles freeways found that 50 percent of all reported truck incidents were caused by breakdowns, stalls, broken fan belts, flat tires, and the like, whereas 30 percent of truck incidents were common accidents, typically involving sideswipes and rear-end collisions (Recker et al. 1988). Five to 10 percent of truck incidents were found to be major incidents, which were defined as truck-involved accidents or spills requiring the closing of two or more lanes of freeway for 2 hr or longer. The remaining 10 percent of reported incidents were attributed to debris on the roadway.

Major truck accidents were most often the result of overturns, spills, and shifted loads; they were usually fatal and caused extensive property damage. They tended to occur on freeway ramps, the primary cause being excessive speed on the curve. Most major accidents occurred during off-peak periods—at dawn when traffic volumes are low and trucks travel at full speed, or at midday when trucks and other vehicles operate at full freeway speeds. By contrast, common accidents, usually involving sideswipes and rear-end collisions, tended to occur during peak periods. Overall, it was estimated that 90 to 95 percent of truck incidents occurred on weekdays, 70 to 80 percent during the daytime, and about 50 percent during the midday period when truck volumes, and therefore truck exposure on the freeways, were highest.

These findings suggest that increasing highway capacity and smoothing traffic flow during congested peak periods may reduce the rate of common accidents for both cars and trucks and the substantial delay and economic costs of these incidents; however, the findings also suggest that increased highway capacity alone may do little to reduce the frequency of major truck accidents, both because fewer trucks operate during peak periods and because most major accidents occur at night or at midday when trucks operate at full speed.

MODELING TRUCK TRAVEL

There are many approaches, all relatively simple, to truck trip modeling. Some regional travel demand models, particularly in smaller urban areas, do not differentiate between trucks and automobiles. The current models are descended from the urban transportation planning system suite of models developed during the 1960s and 1970s to help size new highway, and later, transit, projects. The forecast horizon for these models was typically 20 years, and a substantial margin of error was expected because of the difficulty of accurately anticipating underlying land use and socioeconomic trends. Trucks (especially large trucks) were known to account for a relatively small proportion of all traffic (e.g., 5 to 10 percent of total vehicles). Because this is well within the margin of error of the models, transportation modelers did not push to develop separate or accurate truck forecasts.

Many regional model systems today estimate vehicle trips from person trips, usually based on observed behavior. After total vehicle trips are estimated and assigned to roadways on the metropolitan network, the link traffic volumes are apportioned among trucks and automobiles. The more detailed models use current traffic counts by functional class of roadway as the basis for estimating the percentage of trucks in the traffic stream; less developed models use a single estimated percentage for major roads only, largely disregarding local and small truck travel. To account for the size difference among trucks and cars, most traffic assignment programs perform calculations in passenger-car-equivalents (PCEs), then convert these units to vehicles by equating an automobile to one PCE, small or medium trucks to two PCEs, and large trucks to three PCEs.

A few of the larger and more advanced metropolitan areas have refined this process by developing separate trip tables for trucks and automobiles. Chicago, for example, has developed a separate truck trip table for its regional model on the basis of extensive surveys of shippers and motor carriers in the region. This permits the Chicago Area Transportation Study, the metropolitan transportation agency, to model the impact of major changes in highway capacity (e.g., new roads, major widenings, truck access restrictions) on truck miles of travel and to approximate the subsequent air quality and energy impacts. Phoenix has recently developed a similar truck modeling capability, and other metropolitan areas have developed partial truck trip tables for corridor or area analyses, but these are the exceptions rather than the rule. The overall state-of-practice with respect to truck travel modeling is very modest.

The two major hurdles to development of more sophisticated truck travel models are the general lack of data on freight and truck movement and the complexity of freight demand estimation and truck trip modeling. The lack of data reflects the historic focus of metropolitan transportation agencies on automobiles and passenger transit and the difficulty of collecting the data. Local transportation agencies have had no mandate or funding to deal with trucks, except as they affect downtown parking and loading zones. For the most part, truck travel has been viewed as a private-sector responsibility that is of concern to state agencies primarily for revenue, safety, and size and weight regulation.

The Intermodal Surface Transportation Efficiency Act of 1991 mandates greater attention to freight transportation and more private-sector involvement in the planning and programming of highway improvements; over time this will lead to a more sophisticated understanding of freight movement and truck travel, which will be reflected in better data collection programs and regional travel models. In the interim, however, current and reliable data on commodity movements and truck travel patterns at the metropolitan level are scarce. (At the national level there are good aggregate data on commodity and freight movement and sophisticated analytical models for economic policy issues such as size and weight regulation, but again, only limited data and modeling capability to analyze the impact of freight system capacity changes.)

The second hurdle is the complexity of freight movement and truck travel modeling relative to passenger and automobile travel modeling.

- Freight modeling lacks a definable common unit, such as a traveler, that can be used across all freight demand analyses. Freight is measured and forecast variously in tons, units, and value, forcing transportation and logistics planners to develop separate (and usually incompatible) models by commodity and carrier.

- Freight does not aggregate well for travel demand and behavior modeling purposes, as can be done by using households or commuters for passenger transportation modeling.
- Freight mode choice modeling is complex and must often be modeled at the commodity, industry, and sometimes firm level to produce acceptable results.
- Freight trips, especially local truck pick-up and delivery trips, are often chained trips, with trucks making dozens of stops across a metropolitan area during an 8- to 10-hr work day. Such trips can be described and modeled individually (e.g., using routing and dispatching software), but the techniques for effectively handling thousands of chained trips within a regional model are not yet available. (This problem is common to activity-based passenger modeling as well.)
- Freight trips typically extend beyond the geographic scope of metropolitan transportation agencies. One area may see the container as it lands at a seaport, a second as it moves through on a rail car, and a third as it moves by truck from a rail terminal to a warehouse. Few agencies have the resources to track and represent such multimodal trips into regional travel models.

Overall, regional travel models are not well equipped to forecast changes in truck travel as a result of changes in highway capacity within metropolitan areas, except by treating trucks as automobiles. This is adequate to evaluate the impact of limited highway capacity changes, such as lane widenings, on general travel times, but the changes cannot be tied back to specific types of trucks, industries, or commodities. The models are not capable of anticipating the impact of economic demand management techniques, such as road pricing or emission pricing schemes, on trucks because the models do not incorporate shipper demand or motor carrier behavior models. Where the highway capacity changes studied are modest in scale and limited to a single definable corridor, the shortcomings of the models can be compensated for by direct interviews with industries and motor carriers. For larger projects in complex metropolitan areas, planners must develop truck trip tables or forego detailed analysis of the impacts of highway capacity on truck travel.

CONCLUSIONS AND RECOMMENDATIONS

In the short term changes in highway capacity are not likely to result in significant changes in truck travel. With a well-developed highway system in place, the demand for truck travel is determined primarily by the overall level of economic activity in a metropolitan area and the area's role in the national and global economy. Deregulation of the transportation industry and technological innovations outside trucking have pushed down the cost of transportation relative to labor and materials, making shippers less sensitive to changes in highway capacity at a metropolitan scale. Moreover, the business cycles of many industries work to insulate trucks from the morning and evening peak traffic periods, resulting in truck travel that is spread more evenly across the day than is the case with automobile travel. This leaves trucks less exposed to peak-period congestion and less sensitive to changes in highway capacity designed to facilitate or restrict peak-period travel. This pattern makes it unlikely that air quality and energy conservation goals for trucks can be achieved solely by manipulating highway capacity.

Internal economic pressures within the trucking industry may achieve what changes in highway capacity cannot: relative reductions in truck miles of travel, engine emissions, and energy consumption. Deregulation of the trucking industry has induced shippers to expand their use of trucking, but it has also triggered strong competitive pressures within the trucking industry to reduce costs and improve productivity. During the next decade trucking will carry more freight with fewer trucks and fewer truck miles of travel relative to the past decade and the years before deregulation. The productivity improvements will come in vehicle and engine design, vehicle and driver use, and administration. The effects of these improvements will be most pronounced in long-haul intercity truck traffic where freight can be shifted to rail and less pronounced in short-haul metropolitan distribution operations where rail is not, and will not be, a cost-effective competitor.

The public sector should take advantage of these internal economic pressures to accelerate the trucking industry's move toward more productive operations. Effective programs might include removal of physical and regulatory barriers within metropolitan areas that result in circuitous truck routes and excessive truck miles of travel, tax incentives to retire high-emission trucks, and training programs to introduce automated routing and dispatching programs to small trucking fleets as part of urban ITS programs. The great majority of trucking firms in metropolitan areas are in small fleets of 5 to 25 trucks; like many small businesses, they have the flexibility to innovate quickly, but seldom have the sophistication or resources to explore and transfer new concepts and new technologies. For these programs to be effective, they must be targeted and designed for specific industry and motor carrier groups, and they must involve the shippers who buy trucking services as well as the motor carriers who provide them. These efforts must be coupled with aggressive enforcement programs aimed at putting unsafe truck drivers and firms out of business.

Working against these programs will be long-term pressures on the trucking industry to increase truck miles of travel, absorbing much of the remaining capacity of today's highway system. The key forces will be continuing dispersion of business and housing across metropolitan areas, which will expand the service area that trucking firms must cover; changing land values, which will push warehouses and truck terminals toward the periphery of metropolitan areas; adoption of just-in-time manufacturing and retailing practices, which will generate more truck trips; and globalization of trade, which will produce growing demand for long, time-sensitive supply chains and distribution networks.

To address these forces, metropolitan areas must develop a more integrated approach to freight transportation planning. Basic research is needed to describe and forecast the following:

- Freight generation rates by industry and commodity that can be tied to specific land uses and industrial facilities. Which industries generate freight and how much?
- Trip patterns by industry and commodity across carriers. Where does the freight come from and where is it going? Who carries it and where is it transferred from one mode to another?

- Economic behavior of trucking firms. How do motor carriers make truck routing and dispatching decisions and terminal location decisions?
- Engine emissions and energy consumption by engine, body type, and duty cycle. Many more combinations of engines, body types, and duty cycles exist within the truck fleet than the passenger car and light truck fleets. What are the most prevalent combinations in urban areas and what are their emission patterns?

This basic research will not immediately produce models that forecast the impact of changes in highway capacity on truck travel, but it will provide planners and policy makers with a better understanding of the interrelationship of economic development, land use, freight transportation, and environmental quality. This understanding is necessary for informed decisions about the appropriateness and effectiveness of land use, tax, and regulatory policies.

Concurrent research is needed to develop more sophisticated regional travel models, particularly corridor-scale models, that can accommodate multiple truck trip tables and truck networks. However, focused models with the potential for practical application should be encouraged over comprehensive models because of the complexity of freight transportation.

NOTES

1. Using data from the National Truck Trip Information Survey (Blower and Pettis 1988), this study estimates that large trucks account for 79 percent of all truck travel (excluding travel by light trucks, such as pickups and panel trucks) within the 15 large urban areas that were surveyed.
2. Under the provisions of the Intermodal Surface Transportation Efficiency Act of 1991, about 155,000 mi of Interstate and other economically critical arterials will be designated as the National Highway System.
3. For the purposes of the study, a large truck was defined as having three or more axles and a gross vehicle weight rating of 26,000 lb or more. Truck counts and classifications were made from video tapes of traffic flows at 78 urban freeway sites across the three cities. Counts were made of two-axle, six-tire trucks, but not reported because the California legislature had specified a study of large, three-or-more-axle trucks. The distribution of two-axle, six-tire trucks was similar to the distribution of the large trucks.

4. This follow-on study used the same sampling, video-taping, and classification methodology as the *Urban Freeway Gridlock Study* (Grenzeback et al. 1988).

5. The average value of time for truck drivers is estimated to be approximately $20.00 per hour ($15.65 per hour for four-tire trucks, $21.54 per hour for six-tire trucks, $16.99 per hour for three- to four-axle trucks, and $19.63 per hour for combination trucks). The cost estimates, in 1990 dollars, include hourly wage rates, fringe benefits, an allowance for overtime, and adjustments for vehicle occupancy. American Trucking Associations officials have suggested that the cost of operating a truck may be as high as $60 per hour when union wages and depreciation of the tractor and trailer are taken into account. None of these estimates include the opportunity cost of time lost to receivers because of congestion delays.

6. Cambridge Systematics, Inc., estimates based on national and state input-output tables. See also *21st Century Trucking: Profiles of the Future* 1994, VI-3 and Figure VI-2. In this report, Mercer Management, a contributing author, estimates that transportation accounts for 6.4 percent of the 1992 U.S. gross domestic product (GDP). Total logistics costs, including warehousing, administration, and other inventory carrying costs are estimated to be 10.9 percent of GDP.

7. Data are available for eastbound truck crossings only; the Port Authority does not charge drivers traveling westbound across the Hudson River.

8. The federal Surface Transportation Assistance Act of 1982 (STAA) established a de facto interstate-standard truck by declaring that trucks meeting specified size and weight standards could operate without restriction on the national system of designated truck routes (i.e., Interstate highways, specified arterials, and access roads). The STAA effectively preempted the states' rights to regulate the size and weight of trucks in interstate commerce as long as those trucks operated on the Interstate and designated access routes. The net effect of the STAA and the economic pressures felt by motor carriers to improve the productivity of their drivers and tractors has been to push carriers toward larger capacity five-axle trucks or smaller, more maneuverable three-axle trucks, reducing the demand for midsize four-axle trucks. States still regulate the size and weight of trucks operating in intrastate commerce and may authorize the use of heavier or larger trucks within a state under special permit arrangements.

9. Cambridge Systematics, Inc., field interviews conducted for the Port Authority of New York and New Jersey and the California Department of Transportation under various projects, 1987 through 1990.

10. Estimates prepared by Dr. Paul O. Roberts of Transmode Consultants, Inc., for Cambridge Systematics, Inc., and reported in work by Cambridge Systematics, Inc. (1994, 3–7).

11. The intelligent transportation systems (ITS) commercial vehicle operations (CNO) programs involve automated clearance and verification of

truck credentials (e.g., registration, operating authority, fuel tax permits, oversize-overweight permits), automated weighing (weigh-in-motion), and may eventually incorporate automated roadside safety inspection technology and on-board vehicle diagnostics and driver-fatigue monitoring systems. Most size, weight, and safety inspections are done on rural Interstates and state highways. ITS CVO systems will improve state productivity and minimize delays and congestion for motor carriers at weigh stations and ports-of-entry, but will have little impact on urban congestion and urban truck movements.

12. These estimates are drawn from *Incident Management*, a study of metropolitan traffic and highway incident management programs prepared for the Trucking Research Institute of the American Trucking Associations by Cambridge Systematics, Inc. (1990). The estimates are based on interviews with police and highway officials; case studies of traffic and incident management programs in Chicago, Fort Worth, Los Angeles, Minneapolis, and New York; incident management program records; and available studies, including *Incident Characteristics, Frequency, and Duration on a High Volume Urban Freeway (I-10, Los Angeles)* (Giuliano 1988).

13. For a summary of the literature, see work by Campbell et al. (1994) and Hall and Pendleton (1989). Hall and Pendleton discuss urban freeway accident rates and congestion in Appendix C (pp. 22, 23) of their study.

REFERENCES

ABBREVIATIONS

BTS   Bureau of Transportation Statistics
FHWA   Federal Highway Administration

Blower, D.F., and K.L. Campbell. 1988. *Analysis of Heavy-Duty Truck Use in Urban Areas.* UMTRI-88-31. Transportation Research Institute, The University of Michigan, Ann Arbor, June 30, 76 pp.

Blower. D., and L.C. Pettis. 1988. *National Truck Trip Information Survey.* UMTRI-88-11. Transportation Research Institute, The University of Michigan, Ann Arbor, March, 88 pp.

BTS. 1994. *Transportation Statistics Annual Report.* U.S. Department of Transportation, Jan.

Cambridge Systematics, Inc. 1990. *Incident Management.* Prepared for Trucking Research Institute, American Trucking Associations. Cambridge, Mass., Oct.

Cambridge Systematics, Inc. 1992. *Interstate Goods Movement—Trends and Issues.* Prepared for Interstate Transportation Division, Port Authority of New York and New Jersey. Cambridge, Mass., May.

Cambridge Systematics, Inc. 1994. *Transportation Infrastructure Improvement Study for the Greater Columbus Inland Port Program.* Prepared for Mid-Ohio Regional Planning Commission. Cambridge, Mass.

Campbell, B.J., R.G. Hughes, and C. Zegeer. 1994. *A Discussion of Some Aspects of the Potential Impact of IVHS on Traffic Safety.* Draft. April.

FHWA. 1993. *Highway Statistics 1992.* FHWA-PL-93-023. U.S. Department of Transportation, Oct.

Giuliano, G. 1988. *Incident Characteristics, Frequency, and Duration on a High Volume Urban Freeway (I-10, Los Angeles).* Institute of Transportation Studies, University of California at Irvine, June (reprinted May 1989).

Grenzeback, L.R., W.R. Reilly, P.O. Roberts, and J.R. Stowers. 1988. *Urban Freeway Gridlock Study.* Prepared for California Department of Transportation. Cambridge Systematics, Inc., Cambridge, Mass.

Grenzeback, L.R., and M.G. Warner. 1994. *Impact of Urban Congestion on Business.* NCHRP Project 2-17(5). Final Report. Cambridge Systematics, Cambridge, Mass., June.

Hall, J.W., and O.J. Pendleton. 1989. *Relationship Between Volume/Capacity Ratios and Accident Rates.* FHWA-HPR-NM-88-02. Prepared for New Mexico State Highway and Transportation Department, Department of Civil Engineering, The University of New Mexico, Albuquerque, June.

JHK & Associates. 1989. *Los Angeles: Large Truck Study.* Prepared for the South Coast Air Quality Management District, Calif., May.

Recker, W., T. Golob, C. Hsueh, and P. Nohalty. 1988. *An Analysis of the Characteristics and Congestion Impacts of Truck-Involved Freeway Accidents.* FHWA/CA/UCI-ITS-RR-88-2. Institute of Transportation Studies, University of California at Irvine, Dec.

Reilly, J.P., and J.J. Hochmuth. 1990. Effects of Truck Restrictions on Regional Transportation Demand Estimates. In *Transportation Research Record 1256,* TRB, National Research Council, Washington, D.C., pp. 38–48.

Strauss-Wieder, A., G. Pfeffer, K. Kang, M.H. Yokel, R. Codd, and J.C. Nelson. undated. *Warehousing in the NY/NJ Region.* Business Analysis Division, Office of Business Development, The Port Authority of New York and New Jersey, New York, N.Y.

21st Century Trucking: Profiles of the Future. 1994. American Trucking Associations Foundations, Alexandria, Va.

Warner, M, and N. Wilson. 1989. *The Potential for Traffic Restraint Techniques in Major U.S. Cities.* Progress Report Number 2. Center for Transportation Studies, Massachusetts Institute of Technology, Cambridge, Nov.

Zilliacus, C.P. 1993. *1992 Count of Heavy Truck Traffic on the Capital Beltway and Other Major Highways in the Washington Region: Final Draft.* Prepared for the Metropolitan Washington Council of Governments, National Capital Region Transportation Planning Board, Washington, D.C. Jan.

Appendix D

Review of Studies of Transportation Investments and Land Use

Key studies that attempt to link the effect of transportation investment on land use and urban form are reviewed in this appendix. The studies include major highway and rail investments in the United States and Canada.

MAJOR HIGHWAY INVESTMENTS

Beltways

During the 1970s considerable controversy arose about the potentially negative effects of beltways on the economic fortunes of central cities. A major evaluation performed for the U.S. Department of Transportation and the U.S. Department of Housing and Urban Development compared economic indices in metropolitan areas with and without beltways to help guide future national and local policy decisions (Payne-Maxie and Blayney-Dyett 1980). To enable the reader to appreciate the difficulty of assessing the effects of transportation investments on land use, the results of and problems with this study are summarized in detail in this section.

Statistical techniques such as analysis of variance and multiple regression were used in the study to compare the presence or absence of beltways on a variety of measures of economic impact within metropolitan areas. Results from a sample of 27 metropolitan areas with beltways were compared with results from a sample of 27 metropolitan areas without beltways. The measures were tracked over 10 years or more (depending on the availability of data and the length of time since construction of the beltways). In an attempt to determine the effect of beltways on the distribution of growth within metropolitan areas, central-city population growth was compared with that of the suburbs, and the location of housing development, manufacturing activity, wholesale employment, and retail sales was examined. In general this analysis found few statistically significant differences in development patterns in beltway and nonbeltway metropolitan areas, and the differences that were found were not large or consistent over time.

The study findings on the possible land use effects of beltways can be summarized as follows.

- *Central-city population*: It proved hard to deduce any effect of beltways on central-city population. Regional effects (growth in Sun Belt versus Frost Belt metropolitan areas) appeared to swamp other effects.
- *Retail sales*: The comparative increase in retail sales between central cities and suburbs was not significantly different in areas with beltways compared with areas without beltways.
- *Suburban housing development*: The presence of beltways did not determine the rate of suburban housing development. Cities without beltways had more suburban than urban housing development, which made it difficult to argue that beltways induced residential development in the suburbs at the expense of the central city.
- *Manufacturing employment*: For the 1967 to 1972 period, the study found that in cities with beltways, manufacturing employment in the central city lagged, whereas it grew in the suburbs.

In cities without beltways, suburban and central-city employment in manufacturing grew at a comparable rate. However, no significant differences between beltway and nonbeltway cities were apparent during the 1972 to 1977 period.

- *Wholesale employment*: No significant difference was found between beltway and nonbeltway cities in the rate of wholesale employment growth outside central cities.

Many methodological problems were encountered in the Payne-Maxie and Blayney-Dyett (1980) study. Most notably, because older metropolitan areas in the Northeast and Midwest were more likely to have partial or full beltways than cities in the Sun Belt, it was difficult to establish a meaningful comparison group. In addition, even though the comparison cities may not have had beltways, they surely had extensive arterial road networks in existence or under construction. It would be difficult with aggregate statistics to separate the effects of beltways on the location of development within a region from those of a good or rapidly expanding arterial road system.

Significant measurement problems were also encountered during the study. Census data classify many economic measures on the basis of jurisdiction. However, to measure the effects of beltways on the location of growth and economic activity as required by location theory, the study needed to measure the effect on central business districts, which in many cases are considerably smaller than the census-defined jurisdictions. The necessary data were unavailable. There were also a limited number of years of data available for several economic impacts of interest.

A major difficulty encountered was the degree of correlation (multicollinearity) among the explanatory variables. In other words, the measures of variables thought to independently affect an outcome, such as the location of central-city employment or economic activity, were found to be interrelated. It was not possible in many instances to separate the effects of beltways within a metropolitan area from national shifts in population and economic growth toward Sun Belt cities, shifts in manufacturing activity to suburbs and exurbs, and other trends.

Major Capacity Expansions

Recent analysis has suggested that expansion of major arterial highway capacity of several routes in California has induced additional traffic (Hansen et al. 1993). Estimates from this study suggest that after approximately 15 to 20 years, a 10 percent expansion in highway capacity results in a 4 to 7 percent increase in traffic. The traffic-inducing effects of capacity expansion estimated in this study were discussed in Chapter 4. The study did not attempt to estimate the percentage increase in traffic attributable to changes in land use. Included as part of the study, however, were separate analyses of the effects of capacity expansion on increased development and interviews with real estate developers and local planners to determine whether their decisions were influenced by highway capacity expansions.

The study used pooled time-series and cross-sectional data collected from 26 communities potentially affected by eight freeway-widening projects. All the freeways were Interstates or state highways of near-Interstate quality. Three projects were in the San Francisco Bay area, one was in the Sacramento area, two were in greater Los Angeles, and two were in San Diego. Most of the affected communities were small jurisdictions on the edge of or outside the urbanized area. Many could be viewed as bedroom communities for residents who commute to jobs in the urbanized area. All the projects occurred in or near metropolitan areas that have experienced rapid population growth and extensive highway construction during the last 30 years or more.

Development Patterns

The study analyzed the changes in residential and commercial development in the corridors in which capacity had been increased relative to development in the same region, while controlling for gasoline prices, regional income, and other variables. Statistically significant relationships were found between expanded highway capacity and increased residential construction in the same corridors relative to residential construction in the region. The capacity expansions were correlated with an increased rate of single-family home construction initially, but the rate of increase slowed with time. This finding could indicate that the highway projects accelerated the point in time at which construction occurred, but did not cause an aggregate increase in development. For multifamily housing, the capacity expansions were associated with a one-time spurt in development, which then dissipated. Commercial development also accelerated with the completion of capacity expansions, but industrial development did not. Although the authors of the study concluded that the intensification of land uses may have been caused by capacity expansions in the same corridors, they could not determine whether this development was offset by decreased development elsewhere in the same region. They also did not know whether the increased development would increase traffic because the intensification of residential and commercial land uses in the corridors may have resulted in shorter trips.

Development Decisions

In a separate phase of the study, researchers selected seven cities as case studies and interviewed developers and land use planners to determine whether their decisions were influenced by or depended on highway capacity expansion projects. The interviews indicated that developers and planners viewed the capacity expansions to have been of minor importance. Many developers indicated that the highway projects had not been considered in their decision making at all. The consensus among developers and planners was that development would have occurred without the capacity expansion projects. The attractiveness of the quality of life and the moderate housing prices were believed to be much more important than individual highway capacity expansion projects.

The study authors were surprised to find that developers and planners placed such little importance on the capacity expansions, especially given that the statistical analyses suggested that they had been important in at least accelerating the rate of development. On the other hand, highway capacity expansion, population growth, and residential development had been occurring in these areas for 30 years or more. The minor impact of individual highway projects on development decisions could be explained by the expectations of both developers and planners that growth would occur and that new development would be served by highway capacity eventually, if not initially.

MAJOR RAIL INVESTMENTS

Studies of the impact of large investments in transit, which are often viewed as encouraging denser development patterns, may also shed light on the land use impacts of major transportation investments. Several evaluations have been conducted on the development impacts of new rail transit lines and new rail systems in the United States. Major evaluations have also been conducted of the development impacts of large-scale investments in rail systems for Toronto and Montreal, Canada, which provide for an interesting comparison with the evaluations of rail system investments in the United States.

U.S. Rail Transit Impacts

The impact of the San Francisco Bay Area Rapid Transit (BART) system investment on land use has been the subject of many studies.[1] The consensus is that development in the downtown area may have been redirected and residential development in the outlying areas served by BART may have been accelerated (Meyer and Gomez-Ibanez 1981). The overall impact of the investment, however, is perceived as quite small. Potential increases in development density around some transit stations were blocked in some instances by community opposition, and the existence of a built environment around other stations hindered or precluded more dense development. In cases in which office buildings have been built near BART stations in suburban communities such as Walnut Creek and Concord, surveys indicate that few of the workers actually use BART (Garrison and Deakin 1992). Oakland, which has been struggling to attract development to the downtown area, has had little success in luring development to its BART stations.

Early analyses of the development impact of the rail system in the Washington, D.C., area provided conclusions similar to those reached in analyses of BART (Meyer and Gomez-Ibanez 1981). In a summary of development impacts through 1982, the Metropolitan Washington Council of Governments (MWCOG) concluded that the Metro system had little impact on the demand for building development in the newer areas of downtown, which was already high, and had little effect in the declining areas of the old downtown (MWCOG 1983). The presence of Metro facilitated development around some stations in suburban communities, particularly in Arlington County, Virginia, and Montgomery County, Maryland, but the development depended heavily on local acceptance of changes in zoning densities. Increased development near other suburban stations was blocked by residents who feared the consequences for low-density neighborhoods. Metro was not able to attract development to stations in declining or low-income residential areas of the region. The MWCOG analysis indicated that Metro had mixed effects on development, but less than half the mileage of the system had been built by the time the study was completed. In the areas in which Metro was judged to have a positive impact, no attempt was made to estimate whether the system had induced new development or shifted development that would have otherwise occurred.

The extension of the Lindenwold line from Philadelphia to Camden County, New Jersey, has been studied extensively. Few land use impacts could be discerned. One study judged that the investment had improved the attractiveness of downtown Philadelphia (Gannon and Dear 1972), but did not address whether the increased investment around transit stations diverted investment from other parts of the downtown (Garrison and Deakin 1992). Boyce et al. (1972) found that residential housing values near the line were enhanced, but found other evidence to suggest that some of the increased value was transferred from decreased housing values for residences located farther from the new line. The line may have enhanced the attractiveness of multifamily and commercial development near the suburban stations in Camden County, but the availability of developable land and local zoning and growth policies appeared to be the primary determinants (Boyce et al. 1972).

Canadian Rail Transit Impacts

Major investments have been made in rail transit systems for Toronto and Montreal, and Toronto's experience has been the subject of many studies. Case studies tend to find a substantial impact of the rail investment on land use, but the results from more sophisticated statistical analyses that control for other influences on development are mixed (Meyer and Gomez-Ibanez 1981). In their extensive review of the studies, Knight and Trygg (1977) concluded that the Toronto system did have a substantial impact on land use. The land use consequences were in part due to a variety of influences that stimulated demand for downtown office space in Toronto and by coordinated land use planning by local governments in the area.

Analyses of the impact of the rail system investment in Montreal showed less impact. The rail system was believed to have enhanced the attractiveness of downtown, but limited land for development and lack of special high-density zoning around the stations appeared to have mitigated the potential impact on density (Meyer and Gomez-Ibanez 1981).

NOTE

1. See work by Knight and Trygg (1977) for a bibliography of the studies.

REFERENCES

ABBREVIATION

MWCOG   Metropolitan Washington Council of Governments

Boyce, D.E., B. Allen, R.R. Mudge, P.B. Slater, and A.M. Isserman. 1972. *Impact of Rapid Transit on Suburban Residential Property Values and Land Development: Analysis of the Philadelphia-Lindenwold High-Speed Line.* Regional Science Department. University of Pennsylvania, Philadelphia.

Gannon, C., and M. Dear. 1972. *The Impact of Rail Rapid Transit Systems on Commercial Office Development: The Case of the Philadelphia-Lindenwold High-Speed Line.* University of Pennsylvania, Philadelphia, June.

Garrison, W., and E. Deakin. 1992. Land Use. In *Public Transportation*, 2nd ed. (G. Gray and L. Hoel, eds.). Prentice-Hall, Inc., Englewood Cliffs, New Jersey, pp. 527–550.

Hansen, M., D. Gillen, A. Dobbins, Y. Huang, and M. Puvathingal. 1993. *The Air Quality Impacts of Urban Highway Capacity Expansion: Traffic Generation and Land Use Change.* UCB-ITS-RR-93-5. Institute of Transportation Studies, University of California at Berkeley, April.

Knight, R., and L. Trygg. 1977. *Land Use Impacts of Rapid Transit: Implications of Recent Experience.* Prepared by DeLeuw, Cather & Co. for the U.S. Department of Transportation.

Meyer, J., and J. Gomez-Ibanez. 1981. *Autos, Transit, and Cities.* Harvard University Press, Cambridge, Mass.

MWCOG. 1983. *Metrorail Area Planning: Metrorail Before-and-After Study.* Washington, D.C., Aug., 169 pp.

Payne-Maxie and Blayney-Dyett, Urban and Regional Planners. 1980. *The Land Use and Urban Development Impact of Beltways*, Final Report. DOT-OS-90079. U.S. Department of Transportation and U.S. Department of Housing and Urban Development. Oct.

Appendix E

Minority Statement of Michael A. Replogle

The committee charged with evaluating the effects of added highway capacity on the environment and energy use has reviewed extensive literature and conducted numerous meetings in pursuit of consensus. Although I concur with many of the report's findings, some of the findings and much of the report's tone are based on judgments or opinions I must reject on the basis of my 18 years of experience as a transportation planning engineer and modeling professional. The committee report is correct in identifying the need to improve our analysis tools, but it errs by asserting that we cannot adapt these tools to meet current regulatory requirements without substantial delay. The problem is not a lack of good science to support analysis, but institutional resistance to the use of good science in transportation analysis that would challenge entrenched and powerful pro-highway expansion interests. One might hope that the report will contribute to increased investment in improved analysis and transportation/environmental monitoring systems. It would be unfortunate if the report's conclusions are misread as an excuse for inaction, regulatory rollback, and a resurgence of business-as-usual highway policies on the basis that we just do not know what the future might bring. Citizens need no experts to know that one does not cure obesity by loosening one's belt nor cure traffic-related problems by simply expanding highways.

Readers of this report should consider two closely related reports issued in 1994 by high-level study commissions in the United Kingdom. These considered a wider range of evidence and drew conclusions and judgments that contrast with the committee report and are generally more consistent with this minority statement. The Standing Advisory Committee on Trunk Road Assessment (SACTRA) report, *Trunk Roads and the Generation of Traffic*, is focused specifically on the strong evidence that highway capacity expansion spurs increased motor vehicle travel demand (SACTRA 1994). In the Royal Commission on Environmental Pollution (RCEP) report, *Transport and the Environment*, an overview is given of the broader challenge of making transportation more sustainable, including extensive discussion and recommendations regarding the role of road investment in contributing to environmental degradation (RCEP 1994).

The committee report does not give appropriate consideration to evidence related to the effects on energy use and the environment caused by a reduction of highway capacity—for example the effects of traffic calming and traffic cells—although such evidence is highly relevant to the issue at hand. While asserting that transportation pricing strategies are more important than changes in highway capacity in determining environmental performance, the report gives only limited consideration to evidence from outside the United States that might isolate the effects of highway capacity changes from the effects of transport pricing, levels of public transportation provision, and alternative land use and urban design patterns. Excluding this evidence, and in a tone that appears to subtly play to one side of current contentious domestic policy debates, the report concludes that our state of knowledge is insufficient to evaluate the effects of added highway capacity to support current federal environmental regulations.

It is intellectually inconsistent for the report to argue that on the one hand, current models cannot evaluate the effects of changes in highway capacity on the environment, while on the other hand asserting that alternative strategies, such as time-of-day tolls, will have known and larger effects on air pollution emissions. If we lack the ability to develop reasoned estimates of likely effects of changes in highway capacity, we are unlikely to have the ability to estimate the effects of changes in pricing, technology, or other system attributes. However, the report's lead finding in the Executive Summary concludes that "analytic methods in use are inadequate for addressing regulatory requirements [to assess the effects of added highway capacity on air quality]. The accuracy implied by the interim conformity regulations issued by EPA [the Environmental Protection Agency], in particular, exceeds current modeling capabilities. . . . The current regulatory requirements demand a level of analytic precision beyond the current state of the art in modeling."

Current traffic and emission models need expeditious improvement and substantially higher levels of research, data collection, development, and dissemination of best-practices techniques. However, significant and steady improvement in operational regional models for evaluating the likely emission, system performance, travel behavior, and development impacts of changes in highway capacity, pricing, and policy is possible in both the short and mid-term to meet current regulatory requirements. State-of-the-art modeling methods, if applied with common sense (e.g., considering likely effects of transportation capacity on land development patterns), are adequate to judge the probable direction and approximate magnitude of regionally significant highway capacity additions in transportation plans.

Unfortunately, in the 5 years since passage of the Clean Air Act Amendments of 1990 (CAAA), metropolitan planning organizations (MPOs) that are typically responsible for evaluating transportation conformity have made only slow progress in improving their analytic tools to respond to new policy requirements. Ironically, much of the resistance to improved transportation and air pollution modeling practices in the past has come from the same parties that have most strongly resisted Clean Air Act implementation and that now seek to weaken or overturn its provisions requiring transportation plans and programs to contribute to air quality attainment. Inappropriate use of the models can be addressed by recognizing their shortcomings and devising incremental improvements (Replogle 1993a; Cambridge Systematics, Inc. 1994; Harvey 1993; U.S. District Court 1990). Rather than devoting adequate resources and methods to accomplish this, many state and regional transportation agencies prefer to question the requirements of the regulatory process, citing the small differences they find between "build–no-build" scenarios when these are analyzed using deeply flawed models.

The Intermodal Surface Transportation Efficiency Act of 1991 (ISTEA) gave states unprecedented flexibility to use federal transportation capital assistance funds for planning, data collection, model development, and investments in different modes of travel. However, many states have been slow to flex funds from traditional highway construction to support improved performance measurement, modeling, and management systems. CAAA and ISTEA require a positive demonstration that transportation plans and programs contribute to public health and other goals, with the potential to cut off federal transportation funds to jurisdictions that fail to address persistent health-threatening air pollution problems related to motor vehicle use. Our scientific knowledge is more than adequate to support the CAAA mandate that transportation spending be consistent with health-based air pollution control plans.

Despite its assertions to the contrary and statement that "the complex and indirect relationship between highway capacity [and] air quality . . ., which is heavily dependent on local conditions makes it impossible to generalize about the effects of added highway capacity on air quality . . . even with improved models," this report concludes that "limiting highway capacity . . . is likely to have relatively small effects, positive or negative, on metropolitan air quality by current attainment deadlines." Whether highway capacity will affect emissions over the 20-year life of transportation plans and for the duration of a region's maintenance period, as required by the CAAA, is not judged. The report strays from its assigned scope in implying that current regulations represent a collision of environmental goals and economic objectives likely to lead to delay and reassessment of environmental regulations, and to error and manipulation of the policy process (Executive Summary). The assertions of the report's conclusions ignore strong evidence that restraints on motor traffic growth can be highly supportive of economic development (Hook and Replogle 1995) and reveal the challenge faced by those who would defend the CAAA's mandates for transportation planning. Although the report recommends "a more constructive approach" toward adding new highway capacity, with congestion pricing to mitigate emissions growth, the report does not discuss the likely effects of restraining road capacity within a road pricing context. It is nonetheless arguable that higher motorist user fees and investments in public transportation and other alternatives would encourage earlier and greater energy and air pollution emissions reductions in a policy environment that limited, rather than accommodated, new highway capacity.

KEY FINDINGS

The effects of added highway capacity on energy use and the environment are complex and vary over time. Although we cannot determine with great precision the effect of an individual project, we can with some confidence determine the general direction and relative magnitude of changes that are likely to accompany substantially different investment programs and policies. We now know that trying to reduce emissions by emphasizing supply-side high-occupancy vehicle (HOV) and single-occupancy vehicle (SOV) highway capacity expansion strategies is at best uncertain and temporary. It often makes the problem worse by spurring greater motor vehicle travel demand and lower-density, automobile-dependent land use patterns and by reducing the relative attractiveness of alternatives to automobile travel. Although technological improvements to vehicles, fuels, and vehicle maintenance promise further cost-effective reductions in air pollution emissions, action is needed to manage the growth of traffic demand to reduce emissions of greenhouse gases and air pollution, curb noise pollution, manage traffic congestion, reduce dependence on foreign energy supply, boost the sustainability of our local and regional economies, and enhance community livability.

Limiting further highway capacity expansion, reducing highway capacity, and calming traffic (especially in central areas) can be effective strategies for reducing energy use, air pollution, and other environmental problems, particularly when done in a context of regional growth management that encourages revitalization of urban and suburban centers instead of further sprawl. Smoothing traffic flows to reduce sharp acceleration and deceleration also offers significant promise for reducing emissions when done within a balanced multimodal transportation policy framework that includes effective demand management tools, such as road and parking pricing. Automated vehicle speed limitation using intelligent transportation systems may also offer a promising future strategy and merits further investigation.

The best way to ensure that transportation plans and programs contribute to improved air quality is to ensure that they provide expanded opportunities to meet daily needs for access to jobs, shops, services, and recreation with less forced dependence on petroleum-fueled motor vehicles. This means promoting accessibility instead of mobility, using information and communications more effectively to manage community and mobility systems and to provide virtual access, and integrating land use and transportation planning and development with sound urban design for more livable, walkable, and efficient communities. It means explicating the hidden subsidies and tax expenditures that now spur inefficient consumption and investment patterns, charging motorists for these costs, and encouraging a new sense of values about transportation and the responsibilities of individuals in communities.

Much more research, data collection, and model development are necessary to support local and regional planning and policy evaluation and to better ascertain the effects of alternative investments and policies on energy use and the environment. This research, data collection, and development of decision-support systems should be undertaken as a partnership involving local, regional, state, and federal agencies within the ISTEA planning systems framework. The creativity and initiative of the private and nonprofit sectors should be encouraged in developing these new management systems for sustainable regional economies and healthy communities. Special attention should be paid to developing modal motor vehicle emission models and activity-based microsimulation models of travel behavior and surface transportation system performance. The federal government could play an important role by developing an information-based National Transportation System in cooperation with states and regions to strengthen strategic management systems for monitoring transportation system performance against key benchmarks, in addition to the factors that affect travel demand and transportation service quality. These systems are necessary to ensure that transportation investments will contribute to wise expenditure of scarce taxpayer dollars, improved air quality, safety, productivity, and more livable communities. Performance-oriented federal funding for transportation could also play a useful role.

INDUCED TRAFFIC EFFECTS: FINDINGS FROM A MAJOR UNITED KINGDOM STUDY

The committee's conclusions regarding induced traffic are an improvement over earlier official studies, but are so heavily modified and hedged as to have little meaning. The recent British SACTRA study commission offers more useful guidance on the effect of major road projects (which it calls "schemes") and has far greater confidence than this report in the ability of current scientific knowledge to evaluate these impacts. SACTRA found that

> ... induced traffic is of greatest importance in the following circumstances:
>
> • where the network is operating or is expected to operate close to capacity;
> • where traveller responsiveness to changes in travel times or costs is high, as may occur where trips are suppressed by congestion and then released when the network is improved;
> • where the implementation of a scheme causes large changes in travel costs.

This suggests that the categories of road where appraisal needs to be most careful are improvements to roads in and around urban areas, estuary crossing schemes, and strategic capacity-enhancing interurban schemes, including motorway widening. . . . [Studies] we have reviewed demonstrate convincingly that the economic value of a scheme can be overestimated by the omission of even a small amount of induced traffic. We recommend that variable demand methods should now become the normal basis of trunk road forecasts, and these forecasts must be carried through into the operational, economic, and environmental evaluation of schemes in a systematic way. In particular, where networks are operating close to capacity, suitable procedures must be used to represent the constraint of traffic in the base case and the release of traffic growth in the do-something case as additional capacity is provided. . . . We do not think that continuing to appraise solely at the scheme level using the fixed demand approach is, either intellectually, or in practical terms, acceptable. It is this central conclusion which has led us to make the recommendations in this Report. (SACTRA 1994, iii-iv)

The report continues as follows:

Results of published research demonstrate the following important findings, to a reasonable level of confidence: (a) there is an effect of fuel prices on traffic levels, and a larger effect on fuel consumption; (b) the quality and/or price of public transport can have a small effect on car ownership or use, or perhaps both; (c) the length of the motorway network is one of the influences on the amount of traffic using it; (d) some but not all of the time saved on travel when journey speed increases is likely to be used for additional travel; (e) car users do in fact trade off time and money to an extent and a measure of this trade-off is given by the empirical estimation of the value of time savings; (f) journey times can have an influence on depot location and length of haul of freight operations; (g) the land-use changes consequent on improved access are likely, in turn, to lead to changes in the patterns of travel, car dependence, and the volume of travel. (SACTRA 1994, 45)

SACTRA concluded that in the short term, "about half the time saved through speed increases might be used for additional travel . . . the longer-term effect is likely to be greater, with a higher proportion (perhaps all) of the time saved being used for further travel" (SACTRA 1994, 47).

These conclusions are more comprehensive and succinct than the committee report and differ in some key respects, particularly with regard to the potential impact of highway expansion on freight travel, the elasticity of travel demand with respect to time savings, and the prospects for improving plan and project appraisal. It is the position of this minority statement that SACTRA has better stated the current state of scientific knowledge in this area. The "fixed demand" approach (i.e., assuming that building new highway capacity will ave no effect on land use and time-of-day of travel or other components of travel demand), which SACTRA finds unacceptable, is the same approach that in the United States produces differences between scenarios smaller than the error term of the models of which this report is critical. SACTRA prescribes the use of currently available improved analytical methods for project appraisal instead of questioning our ability to perform such analysis to meet regulatory requirements.

DETERMINANTS OF TRAVEL DEMAND

Effects of Subsidies

The committee report implies that growth in traffic is an inevitable function of income and economic growth (Chapter 4) and indeed these are important factors in traffic growth. However, the report generally avoids discussing the effects of hidden subsidies and transport pricing systems in explaining the growth of motor vehicle use, although these too are key determinants that reinforce automobile-dependent lifestyles, consumption trends, and land use patterns. In the United States a major share of the costs of highway construction and maintenance continues to be paid for out of general tax revenues, mostly at the local government level. The large past investment in highway capacity by taxpayers imposes a stream of current and future costs that affect the provision of added capacity.

The recent report by the U.S. Congressional Office of Technology Assessment (OTA), *Saving Energy in Transportation*, provides a good accounting of these elements (OTA 1994, 91–111). OTA identifies $76.5 billion in 1990 public spending on highway construction, maintenance, and services covered by payments by motor vehicle users, along with hidden private sector expenditures related to motor vehicle use of $150 to $400 billion a year in 1990 for parking. OTA estimates that U.S. taxpayers provided $33 to $64 billion in subsidies for highway construction and motor vehicle infrastructure and services in 1990, after accounting for total costs and deducting payments by motor vehicle users. Nonmonetary externality costs related to motor vehicle use are estimated at $325 billion to $580 billion per year in 1990. According to OTA, "Approximately 49 to 61 percent of the total monetary and nonmonetary costs of motor vehicle use, excluding the value of time, are efficiently priced [i.e., paid and recognized by motor vehicle users]" (OTA 1994, 109–110). The report continues,

"Motor vehicle users paid openly for 53 to 69 percent of the social (public plus private) costs of motor vehicle use, both monetary and nonmonetary, excluding the value of time . . . if subsidies were withdrawn, externalities 'internalized,' and hidden costs brought out into the open and directly charged to motor vehicle users, the perceived costs of motor vehicle use would increase substantially (by 14 to 89 percent, depending on whether nonmonetary costs and other factors are included), and people would drive less." Such factors play a major role in influencing the effects of highway capacity changes on energy and the environment, as this committee report implies in its closing discussion of "managed capacity" strategies.

Effects of Added Highway Capacity on Freight Travel Demand

The RCEP report states, "It is clear that where an alternative is available, moving freight by road takes more space, uses more energy, produces more pollution, and is more likely to lead to an accident" (RCEP 1994, 166). The short-term potential to switch freight from road to rail, water, or pipeline transportation is limited by the specialized functional requirements for many types of shipments, as this committee report correctly notes. However, over a period of two or more decades, alternative transportation investment choices could produce profound differences in freight travel demand. Contrast, for example, a program of significant further public investment in freeway capacity expansion with a program of minor highway capacity expansion, conversion of existing HOV and SOV freeway lanes to privately managed toll facilities, and a combination of policies promoting more aggressive private development of intermodal transfer facilities, railways, water- and pipeline-based freight systems, and intelligent intermodal freight management systems. Highway capacity expansion will clearly affect the use of just-in-time shipping, and in the longer term, the location of commercial, warehouse, and industrial activities.

Effects of Added Highway Capacity in Built-Up Areas

The committee report asserts, "Within developed areas, traffic flow improvements such as better traffic signal timing and left-turn lanes that alleviate bottlenecks may reduce some emissions and improve energy efficiency by reducing speed variation and smoothing traffic flows without risking large offsetting increases from new development and related traffic growth." In Chapter 6 the report states, "In central cities and other built-up areas these longer-term impacts [of stimulated travel demand] are likely to be small because the potential for development is limited." Although small capacity-expanding projects individually may have positive short-term effects on emissions, when many such projects are combined, the effects on latent traffic generation are likely to be significant, as the report acknowledges.

Alleviating bottlenecks with new highway capacity frequently leads to the greatest release of latent or suppressed travel demand, especially in more densely developed areas. In many cases traffic flow improvements are taken at the expense of pedestrians, bicyclists, and users of public transportation. These investments often make it more dangerous to travel in the community except by motor vehicle, or represent lost opportunities to restore a walkable streetscape and near-road environment. In many older urban and town centers, such "improvements" have contributed to the decline of old shopping districts, which have lost their amenity and charm, often sacrificing traffic slowing and pedestrian-enhancing on-street parking in the interests of faster and greater traffic throughput to spur the driver on to the nearby shopping mall, where pedestrian space is privatized and controlled and accessible only by car. Areawide traffic signal control systems that significantly boost average travel speeds across many streets and corridors can spur induced traffic and thus may more than fully offset any short-term emission reductions due to traffic smoothing and speed change effects, unless accompanied by effective and ongoing travel demand management programs (TDM), such as pricing, parking management, and street space reallocation for transit and nonmotorized travelers.

Consideration of Alternatives to Highway Capacity Expansion

Consideration of alternative scenarios is vital to answering the question, "What is the effect of added highway capacity on energy use and the environment?" Alternatives will produce different patterns of travel demand and transportation system performance, emissions, and energy use. The report's discussion of the consequences of alternative scenarios (Chapter 6), however, focuses mostly on alternatives that expand transportation system supply. The key example given assumes that demand and congestion will inevitably grow without considering the potential for demand management strategies. Yet there are many ways of reallocating investment, street space, subsidies, and land activities, and of reshaping urban design and pricing systems; it is not just a choice of highway investment or transit investment.

A major study sponsored by private foundations and the Federal Highway Administration (FHWA), Making the Land Use-Transportation-Air Quality Connection (LUTRAQ), considered this question by evaluating the proposed Western Bypass highway around the west side of Portland, Oregon, versus a transit- and pedestrian-oriented development alternative. The lessons from LUTRAQ are that transit- and pedestrian-oriented urban design and infill development and the retrofit of pedestrian improvements to automobile-oriented suburbs can have significant effects on travel behavior sufficient to eliminate the need to build new ring freeways, particularly when reinforced by sensible economic and pricing incentives, such as modest parking charges and reduced transit fares that begin to level the playing field between travel modes. Total vehicle trips per household in the transit-oriented developments (TODs) were 6.05 per day, compared to 7.09 outside the TODs under the LUTRAQ scenario and 7.7 with either the bypass or no-action alternative. The LUTRAQ scenario reduced vehicle miles traveled (VMT) in the study area by almost 14 percent compared with the bypass alternative and reduced vehicle hours of travel in the evening peak hour by almost 8 percent. Even greater effects on travel behavior can be expected when these measures are combined with bicycle improvements, stronger economic incentives, more effective parking management, introduction of neighborhood vehicles, and further shifts in land use policies to favor infill housing and commercial development.

The committee report discusses but misreads the LUTRAQ study (in Chapter 5) and the selection of LUTRAQ study data presented may mislead some readers. Instead of presenting data on travel demand changes in the specific areas subject to policy intervention, the report cites regional data in which the effects of LUTRAQ policy interventions are much diluted. Instead of presenting LUTRAQ data on total travel or nonwork travel, which constitutes the vast majority of all trips, the report draws its conclusions principally from changes estimated for work trips. Thus, the report incorrectly states that "The travel demand measures [employee commuter subsidy programs that support transit and charges for parking] increase both transit use and carpooling more than the land use and design measures." In fact, the LUTRAQ analysis indicated that TDM measures accounted for only about 30 percent of the increase in nonautomobile driver mode shares for all trips and about 55 percent of the increase in nonautomobile work trip mode shares, not counting the corrections for under-estimated walking trips, which would further increase the effects of the design measures (T. Ross, Cambridge Systematics, Inc., correspondence, February 8, 1995; LUTRAQ working documents, summer 1992).

The LUTRAQ model incorporated measures of pedestrian friendliness but underestimated the potential to shift short car trips to pedestrian trips. This was due to acknowledged underreporting of walking trips in the 1985 Portland household travel survey data (Cambridge Systematics, Inc., et al. 1992), the assumption that nowhere in the region would pedestrian friendliness be better than it is today in downtown Portland, and the insensitivity of the pedestrian mode choice model to pricing and other TDMs. Clearly Portland neighborhoods could become far more pedestrian friendly than observed today. Market-based pricing strategies and other TDMs would also increase the propensity to satisfy travel needs by walking and bicycling. Despite these shortcomings, the LUTRAQ analysis showed that modest improvement in the quality of the pedestrian environment alone could reduce the VMT in suburban zones by about 10 percent. Variation in building orientation at the zonal level was also found to account for changes of 10 percent or more in VMT per household (Parsons Brinckerhoff Quade and Douglas 1994).

Key LUTRAQ performance measures cited in this report (Table 5-5) do not reflect adjustments made by Cambridge Systematics to correct for known undersampling of pedestrian trips in the 1985 Portland travel survey. Data on travel demand changes estimated for the much larger study region are emphasized instead of the significant travel demand reduction effects noted in relation to TODs versus conventional highway-oriented development. LUTRAQ did not attempt to modify urban design patterns in the entire study area, but only in selected neighborhoods near new transit lines. The LUTRAQ assumptions for the composition and mix of building types for development was also constrained by a market demand forecast that assumed that the housing preferences of recent decades for different demographic segments would persist into the future, which implies continued tax subsidies for housing and automobile transportation, rising real household incomes, and continued high levels of consumer and public debt to finance housing and transportation consumption. Moreover, the LUTRAQ model was unable to reflect potential improvement of bicycle friendliness, bicycle access to transit, or encouraging bicycle use, due to the lack of available local empirical data. However, experience in cities such as Davis, California, and Copenhagen, Denmark, shows that reallocation of street space and development of comprehensive cycling networks can have a profound effect in diverting car trips to bicycles and that bicycle access can promote dramatic expansion of transit catchment areas (Replogle 1993b, Replogle 1994, Replogle and Parcells 1993). Indeed, the Portland regional government (Metro) is moving forward to develop methods for incorporating these additional factors into its long-range planning analyses.

London

Portland, Oregon, is being joined by a growing number of other regions considering such alternatives. A study by the United Kingdom Department of Transport for the greater London region found that a combination of car restraint and improved public transport—with a cordon charge, reduced parking provision, and light rail construction—would likely reduce carbon dioxide emissions by 23 percent compared with the base case for 2000. It was estimated that this combined strategy would reduce traffic entering the central area of London and increase peak period traffic speeds in the central area from 23 to 30 kph (14 to 19 mph). Approximately 15 percent of this increase was projected to be due to the effects of the light rail network and the remainder due to measures to restrain traffic (RCEP 1994, 194).

Copenhagen

Some regions have made these kinds of changes real. In Copenhagen, a city of 1.7 million people, road building was abandoned in the early 1970s, large numbers of bus priority lanes were introduced, and a comprehensive network of segregated cycle paths was built. The result was a 10 percent decrease in traffic since 1970 and an 80 percent increase in the use of bicycles since 1980. Approximately one-third of commuters now use cars, one-third public transport, and one-third bicycles. Had Copenhagen embarked on major highway expansions in recent decades, surely energy use and emissions would be far higher than they are today. Is this not relevant evidence that highway capacity expansion in metropolitan regions promotes environmental degradation?

EFFECT OF REDUCED HIGHWAY SPEED AND CAPACITY

Since the 1970s in Europe, Japan, Australia, and increasingly in the United States, traffic calming and traffic cell systems have been and continue to be developed to reduce traffic speed and capacity in central areas and residential neighborhoods. There is empirical evidence that these highway capacity reduction strategies typically also reduce air pollution emissions, noise, and energy use. Although mentioned in the report (Chapter 3), this evidence is not well-considered in the report's findings.

Reducing Road Speed and Capacity with Traffic Calming

Traffic calming encompasses a wide range of techniques for slowing down motor vehicle traffic to provide an environment more supportive of walking and bicycling and safer for children, the elderly, and others. Traffic calming measures include narrowing roadways, reducing speed limits, introducing curvilinear elements in formerly straight streets to slow traffic, and changing the vertical profile of the street with elements such as raised intersection tables for pedestrian and bicycle path crossings. Although the EPA MOBILE model would indicate that slowing down traffic typically increases emissions, empirical research indicates the opposite in many cases. Research in Germany has shown that the greater the speed of vehicles in built-up areas, the higher is the incidence of acceleration, deceleration, and braking, all of which increase air pollution. German research indicates that traffic calming reduces idle times by 15 percent, gear changing by 12 percent, brake use by 14 percent, and gasoline use by 12 percent (Newman and Kenworthy 1992, 39–40). This slower and calmer style of driving reduces emissions, as demonstrated by an evaluation in Buxtehude, Germany. Table E-1 shows the relative change in emissions and fuel use when the speed limit is cut from 50 kph (31 mph) to 30 kph (19 mph) for two different driving styles. Even aggressive driving under the slower speed limit produces lower emissions (but higher fuel use) than under the higher speed limit, although calm driving produces greater reductions for most emissions and net fuel savings (Newman and Kenworthy 1992, 39–40).

Moreover, by encouraging more use of walking and bicycling and reducing the advantage offered by the automobile for short trips relative to these alternatives, traffic calming usually reduces the number of trips, trip starts, and VMT. Applied on a widespread basis in conjunction with transit improvements and transportation pricing changes, traffic calming may contribute as well to a reduction in household automobile ownership levels, further reducing emissions and travel demand. Thus, even under circumstances in which indi-

TABLE E-1 Percentage Change in Vehicle Emissions and Fuel Use with Speed Change from 50 kph (31 mph) to 30 kph (19 mph) (Newman and Kenworthy 1992)

| | DRIVING STYLE | |
EMISSION TYPE	2ND GEAR AGGRESSIVE	3RD GEAR CALM
Carbon monoxide	−17	−13
Volatile organic compounds	−10	−22
Oxides of nitrogen	−32	−48
Fuel use	+7	−7

vidual vehicle emissions per mile traveled increase due to more aggressive acceleration, braking, and use of second gear, traffic calming will likely lead to overall emission reductions due to its influence on travel demand (see Table E-1).

A recent FHWA report discusses the German experience with traffic calming in six cities and towns in the early 1980s:

> The initial reports showed that with a reduction of speed from 37 km/h (23 mph) to 20 km/h (12 mph), traffic volume remained constant, but . . . air pollution decreased between 10 percent and 50 percent. The German Auto Club, skeptical of the official results, did their own research which showed broad acceptance after initial opposition by the motorists. Interviews of residents and motorists in the traffic calmed areas showed that the percentage of motorists who considered a 30 km/h (18 mph) speed limit acceptable grew from 27 percent before implementation to 67 percent after implementation, while the percentage of receptive residents grew from 30 percent to 75 percent. (Project for Public Spaces 1992)

This experience of initial skepticism of traffic calming, followed by its widespread popularity after implementation, has been experienced in hundreds of communities across Europe, Japan, and Australia, along with the few U.S. communities that have adopted such strategies, such as Palo Alto, California, and Seattle, Washington.

Reducing Road Capacity with Traffic Cells for Environmental Benefit

Many places in Europe and Japan—cities such as Göteborg, Sweden, Hannover, Germany, and Osaka, Japan; suburban new towns such as Houten, Netherlands; and established automobile-oriented suburban centers such as Davis, California—have successfully implemented traffic cell systems. These typically consist of a set of radial pedestrian, bicycle, and transit-only streets focused on a central area. Whereas pedestrians, bicyclists, and public transportation can freely cross these streets, automobile traffic cannot, but must instead use a ring road around the center. Traffic cell systems are very effective at eliminating through-traffic in central areas and shifting short automobile trips in the central area to walking, bicycling, and public transportation, significantly reducing cold start and evaporative emissions. Reducing central area traffic and increasing street space dedicated to walking, bicycling, and public transportation makes these alternatives more attractive and diminishes parking requirements in the central area. Success in reducing environmental impacts depends on curbing automobile-oriented peripheral development.

Göteborg, Sweden, introduced traffic cells in the mid-1970s together with priority for public transportation at traffic signals, new suburb-to-downtown express bus service, and central area parking controls. Noise was cut from 74 to 67 dB in the main shopping street, peak carbon monoxide levels dropped 9 percent, 17 percent fewer cars entered the center city, weekday transit trips to the center were up 6 percent, traffic on the inner ring road was up 25 percent, and the costs of running public transport went down 2 percent. Nagoya, Japan, introduced traffic cells in residential areas in the mid-1970s, together with a computer-managed signal system, bus lanes, bus priority at traffic signals, staggered work hours, and parking regulation. This resulted in a 17 percent increase in traffic speeds on main roads covered by the signal system, and a 3 percent increase in bus ridership. Fifteen percent fewer cars entered the central area in the morning peak, and automobile-related air pollution decreased by 16 percent (National League of Cities 1979).

The Downtown Crossing pedestrian zone in Boston, Massachusetts, is a limited traffic cell serving a core area with 125,000 employees. Eleven blocks of the central business district were closed to traffic in 1978 while steps were taken to improve transit service and parking management. In the first year, there was a 5 percent increase in visitors to the area, a 19 percent increase in weekday shop purchases, a 30 percent increase in weeknight purchases, an 11 percent increase in Saturday purchases, a 21 percent increase in walking trips to the area, a 6 percent increase in transit trips to the area, a 38 percent decrease in automobile trips to the area, and no increase in traffic congestion on adjacent streets, thanks to the elimination of on-street parking and stricter parking enforcement on nearby traffic streets.

Davis, California, a town of 50,000 people near Sacramento, illustrates a successful full traffic cell system that has cut highway capacity significantly in the vicinity of the University of California (UC Davis) and the town center to increase walking and bicycle use. Bicycle use grew sharply in the 1960s, leading to election of a pro-bikeway city council in 1966. Demonstration bikelanes proved popular and were quickly extended. In addition to the UC Davis traffic cell and bicycle network, the city of Davis now has 59 km (37 mi) of bicycle lanes and 46 km (29 mi) of bicycle paths in an interconnected network. Parking is limited and costs drivers on the UC Davis campus. Bus, van, and commuter rail services offer other alternatives to the automobile. Davis has prohibited development of shopping centers near the freeway, retaining a vibrant pedestrian-oriented downtown commercial area. As a result, 27 percent of UC Davis employees and 53 percent of UC Davis students use bicycles as their primary commute mode; among those who live and work in Davis, 44 percent bicycle to work. The City Planning Department estimates that 25 percent of all person trips in the city are by bicycle. Walk shares in the city are also high—on the order of 10 to 20 percent. Clearly air pollution has been reduced by restricting and reducing highway capacity in Davis.

EFFECT OF HIGHWAY CAPACITY ADDITIONS ON METROPOLITAN FORM

The report is correct in asserting, "Major highway capacity additions in less developed parts of metropolitan areas, where most growth is occurring, pose a greater risk of increasing emission levels and energy use in those areas. If developable land is available and other growth conditions are present, new capacity is likely to attract more development and related traffic to the location of the improvement. Corresponding increases in emission levels and energy use in these areas are likely" (Chapter 6). Yet the report notes, "Because of the large investment implicit in current metropolitan spatial patterns, it may be years before changes in land use and related traffic patterns induced by the added capacity make a significant difference in regional emission levels and air quality" (Executive Summary), downplaying this potential effect in relation to conformity analysis by following with the statement, "In comparison, . . . EPA predicts further emission reductions for major pollutants on the order of one-quarter to one-third from 1990 baseline levels by attainment deadlines simply from continued vehicle fleet turnover and implementation of CAAA-required vehicular and fuel standards and enhanced vehicle inspection and maintenance programs. Market-based TCMs [transportation control measures], such as increased parking charges and time-of-day tolls, have greater potential for emission reductions. . . ."

Most new highway development is likely to have a significant emission-increasing effect within the 20-year planning horizon for conformity analysis unless the region is experiencing no net economic growth or the region's highway access-dependent periphery is not growing at the expense of its older urban neighborhoods. It is irrelevant whether the highway expansion redistributes growth that would have occurred elsewhere in the region or whether it stimulates productivity gains that result in net new growth (Executive Summary). Most new highway capacity will eventually foster automobile-oriented growth. In either case, increased emissions may break an emissions budget and work against attainment and maintenance of health standards.

In regions undergoing rapid development and significant infrastructure investment, major regional impacts on motor vehicle emissions have been observed in relatively short time horizons. Substantial economic growth has not always been accompanied by proportional growth in traffic. Restrained investment in highways accompanied by enhancements of pedestrian, bicycle, and transit access; economic incentives encouraging alternatives to the automobile; and supportive land use policies have resulted in slower growth of traffic despite rising motorization and dramatic economic growth in many European and Asian metropolitan areas, most notably in cities such as Copenhagen, the Randstadt (Amsterdam-Hague-Rotterdam-Utrecht, Netherlands), and in Japanese and Chinese cities. Indeed, there is evidence that such policies enhance growth and economic development (Replogle 1991).

This evidence is given no mention in the report, which instead emphasizes that accessibility and generalized travel cost changes are only one factor shaping metropolitan development. However, the report appears to overgeneralize its conclusions regarding the 20-year effects of highway capacity changes on land use patterns, drawing evidence primarily from land use model projections that can be called into question. For example, the committee report discusses the relatively small changes (plus or minus a few percentage points) in regionwide locations of employment and households in built-up metropolitan areas over a 20-year forecast period from systemwide changes in travel time of as much as 20 percent, predicted using commercially available but less-than-state-of-the-art land use models. This is cited as evidence that added highway capacity will have small impacts on regional air quality. However, the land use models cited were generally calibrated on very short time-series data, often 1980–1985 or 1985–1990, when substantial "hot" savings and loan money was diverted into highly speculative and often not economically viable real estate development, leading to drastic over-building in many markets. Indeed, the models used in the United States have mostly failed to represent land and rent values, the variable quality of key public services (education, public safety), and the potential for mixed-use cluster development around nodes of high public transportation accessibility. Moreover, the results of model evaluations have usually been predicated on exogenous constraints related to zoning and limitation of redevelopment, giving little room for differences between transportation investment scenarios to express themselves.

In short, the SACTRA report offers more effective statements of our current state of knowledge in these matters, indicating that added highway capacity indeed frequently leads to changes in development patterns that reinforce motor vehicle dependence and use.

DATA COLLECTION, MODEL DEVELOPMENT, AND RESEARCH NEEDS

There is broad agreement with this report's conclusions regarding the need for improved emission and travel-related data collection and model development. Cost-effective resolution of some of the central questions posed by this study would be well-supported by a cooperative effort of states, local governments, and regions, with federal leadership, to develop broader standards for traffic and travel data collection, the coding of networks and spatial data bases, and transportation-land use monitoring and performance measurement systems. Dozens of uncoordinated, incompatible data systems now hinder the development of effective benchmarks and comparative evaluation frameworks for local and national strategic planning and for theoretical research. The externality costs of transportation and land use investments, such as hidden subsidies, pollution and congestion costs, and accident and health effects, need to be more widely appraised through local measurement and monitoring. A national household travel panel survey is needed to better comprehend the dynamics of travel and activity patterns, vehicle acquisition and use, residential location choice, and commercial development. States should be encouraged to allocate an increased share of surface transportation capital resources to system management and monitoring, planning, and forecasting, to promote long-term, least-cost strategies for community and regional development. The alternative is to continue to pursue costly taxpayer-subsidized, pork-barrel spending unsuited to an era demanding lean government.

THE BUILD–NO-BUILD TEST AND REGULATORY BACKLASH

New Scientific Uncertainty or Just a New Backlash?

This report challenges the "build–no-build" test that has been a key part of transportation conformity under the federal Clean Air Act. This challenge would respond to the distress expressed by many individuals involved in highway development at EPA's November 1993 final transportation conformity rule. Supporters of highway development were generally satisfied with the science of emission speed factor adjustments during the era of EPA's interim conformity rule 1991–1993 and under earlier versions of conformity. During this era, the conformity rule and the emission speed factor adjustments worked together to ensure that new road capacity would be found to increase average motor vehicle travel speeds and reduce vehicle miles traveled and hence reduce air pollution emissions of carbon monoxide (CO) and volatile organic compounds (VOCs) at least by a slight amount (based on EPA's official models), thus sustaining business as usual. However, in 1994, with the final transportation conformity rule, the build–no-build test was extended to also apply to oxides of nitrogen (NO_x). NO_x generally increase with higher engine speed and efficiency of combustion, thus rising with the higher traffic speeds that usually accompany highway capacity expansion (based on EPA's official models). The final rule thus questioned the wisdom of massive road expansion, especially in areas where NO_x controls will be needed to reduce ozone problems. Only now, when emission speed adjustment factors in EPA's emission model have regulatory implications for the addition of new high-speed roadway capacity, are major issues being raised about their scientific basis. There were few complaints when transportation plans passed the test by less than a fraction of 1 percent. Now there is a widespread outcry over transportation plans failing the test by equivalent amounts, although most agencies doing modeling have thus far been able to get around these problems with "just-in-time model enhancements" and the addition of mitigation TDM programs.

Now, as this report states about the effects of added highway capacity on the environment and energy use, "No definitive and comprehensive conclusions can be reached . . . the conformity tests . . . will themselves change as the build–no-build test is phased out . . ." (Executive Summary). Indeed, proposals have been introduced in the 104th Congress to repeal part or all of the Clean Air Act including transportation conformity. As the report notes, under current regulations states only need to show that their transportation plan produces emissions less than their adopted transportation emission budget which is part of an acceptable air quality attainment plan. A challenge to the way EPA's build–no-build test has been applied by regional agencies may be deserved. However, millions of Americans with serious respiratory problems that are worsened by motor vehicle-related air pollution breathe unhealthful air 25 years after the first Clean Air Act despite cleaner tailpipes and significant but inadequate progress toward attainment. Our science is adequate to tell us that large-scale highway expansion, even with congestion pricing on new facilities, will not contribute to attainment and maintenance of healthful air compared to alternative investments and policies. This report has gone too far in asserting scientific uncertainty.

Real Problems with Build–No-Build

As typically applied, the build–no-build test assumes that building major new highways will have no effect on land use patterns, time of day of travel, and often even travel mode or choice of destinations. This is the "fixed demand" approach to analysis decried by SACTRA. A computer simulation is performed that assumes a fixed pattern of vehicle trip making in a region and two alternative transportation networks: the region's road system with and without a set of road improvements. The predictable result is that the computer simulation shows that adding lanes or new roads will alleviate congestion; provide shorter, faster travel routes; and reduce the number of miles of driving compared to not building the improvements. Average travel speeds will go up at least slightly with the improvements. And if one believes the speed adjustment factors of EPA's MOBILE emissions model, with the road improvements VOC and CO emissions will go down and NO_x emissions will go up, in most cases by much less than 1 percent. It is predictable that most agencies have found "very small differences between the two alternatives [confirming that] current forecasting models cannot reliably estimate differences to that degree of accuracy (Hartgen et al. 1994)" (Chapter 6).

Highlight Near-Term Model Reform Needs

Indeed, most transportation models in use are little changed in architecture or policy sensitivity from those of the 1970s and 1980s and are generally designed to overestimate the benefits of both highway and transit investment. They ignore urban design, walking and bicycling, hidden transportation subsidies and user costs, the way people plan trip itineraries and make decisions about travel and vehicle use, and the time of day of travel effects. Although some agencies have made improvements to travel models in the past several years on their own, many more have moved only slowly in response to pressure from local and national environmental groups or federal agencies. Few agencies are expeditiously moving toward best practices in the field, such as Portland, Oregon, which is undertaking new activity-based surveys, stated preference surveys, and development of yet more policy-sensitive analysis tools.

The committee report might have highlighted the short- and mid-term fixes available to support better conformity analysis. Good discrete choice models based on recent surveys—including total personal travel rather than just motor vehicle trips, with formal or informal accounting for the effects of highway capacity increases on land development, time of day of travel, mode and destination choice—can be developed in any metropolitan region in the span of a year or two with an investment representing a fraction of the cost of a single freeway interchange. Such "better practices" analysis tools can be used to perform far more policy-sensitive build–no-build tests in the near term, which will not be highly accurate or certain, but at least will be more likely to point in the right direction than current analyses. The state-of-the-art of modeling is advancing rapidly in this area, and data collection and research are warranted today for most metropolitan transportation planning agencies to prepare for the next generation of microsimulation-based analysis tools. The SACTRA panel offers useful recommendations for modeling and analysis, including issuance of general advice on good practice in developing models, the auditing of strategic transport demand models to ensure their satisfactory sensitivity "to estimate all the important demand responses to road provision, including trip frequency and choice of time of travel" (SACTRA 1994, 191).

Emission models are in critical need of redevelopment with support for research at the national level. Recent EPA and California Air Resources Board (CARB) research shows that the federal test procedure and other drive-cycle based emission estimation approaches do not well match current driving conditions. Significant variability exists in emissions between vehicles undergoing similar speed changes and in the same vehicle under different load conditions. There is consensus within the committee that modal-based emissions models need to be developed to improve the evaluation of the effects of changes in speed, acceleration, and traffic system management, such as ITS, and some work is under way, but could be accelerated. As this report notes, "current models significantly underpredict emissions of some pollutants" (Executive Summary). This is yet further reason to place greater emphasis on the analysis of the emissions impacts of growth in travel demand likely to be induced by highway investment, instead of continuing to focus analysis solely or primarily on emissions impacts related to harder to estimate changes in vehicle speeds that are modified by highway investments.

Performance-based funding that gives states flexibility in expending federal funds contingent on meeting key objectives is in place under CAAA and ISTEA with the transportation conformity and management system requirements. Although evaluation tools like MOBILE 5.1 are imperfect, they should continue to be used with caution as the best analysis models currently available to support ongoing public policy making. When needed, ad hoc project-specific methods should be used to complement these tools until better data and software are available. Sound transportation and environmental policy making should focus air pollution control strategies on cost-effective technological controls, such as inspection and maintenance of vehicles and reformulated gasoline, in addition to strategies that reduce the growth in vehicle trip starts, VMT, and motor vehicle dependence. Until we get our emission models more refined, we should focus less on strategies that depend on demonstrating emission reductions on the basis of changes in traffic speed. We should not abandon the analysis of the emissions impacts of alternative transportation investments and policies because of uncertainties about emission changes with respect to speed, accelerations, and other factors. We should improve the quality of performance measurement, analysis, and forecasting systems and expand the range of alternatives considered in the evolving new regional transportation planning process.

REFERENCES

ABBREVIATIONS

OTA	Office of Technology Assessment
RCEP	Royal Commission on Environmental Pollution
SACTRA	Standing Advisory Committee on Trunk Road Assessment

Cambridge Systematics, Inc., et. al. 1992. *The LUTRAQ Alternative/Analysis of Alternatives: Interim Report.* 1000 Friends of Oregon, Portland, Oreg., Oct., pp. 82, 97–101.

Cambridge Systematics, Inc. 1994. *Short-Term Travel Model Improvements.* FHWA, U.S. Department of Transportation.

Harvey, G. 1993. *A Manual of Improved Modeling Practice.* Environmental Protection Agency Region IX, Sacramento, Calif.

Hook, W., and M. Replogle. 1995. Motorization and Non-Motorized Transportation in Asia: Transport System Evolution in China, Japan, and Indonesia. *Land Use Policy* (forthcoming).

National League of Cities. 1979. *Transportation and the Urban Environment.* Washington, D.C., p. 32.

Newman, P., and J. Kenworthy. 1992. *Winning Back the Cities.* Pluto Press, Leichhardt NSW, Australia, pp. 39–40. Quoting C. Hass-Klau (ed.), New Ways of Managing Traffic, *Built Environment*, 12 (1/2), 1986 and T. Pharoah and J. Russell, *Traffic Calming: Policy Evaluation in Three European Countries*, Occasional Paper 2/89, Department of Planning, Housing, and Development, South Bank Polytechnic, London.

OTA. 1994. *Saving Energy in Transportation.* U.S. Congress, July.

Parsons Brinckerhoff Quade and Douglas, Inc. 1994. *Making the Land Use Transportation Air Quality Connection: Vol. 4B, Building Orientation.* 1000 Friends of Oregon, Portland, Oreg., May.

Project for Public Spaces. 1992. *The Effects of Environmental Design on the Amount and Type of Bicycling and Walking.* National Bicycling and Walking Study. FHWA Case Study 20. FHWA-PD-93-037. FHWA, U.S. Department of Transportation, Oct., p. 15.

Replogle, M. 1991. Sustainability: A Vital Concept for Transportation Planning and Development. *Journal of Advanced Transportation*, Vol. 25, No. 1, Spring, pp. 3–18.

Replogle, M. 1993a. *Improving Transportation Models for Air Quality and Long Range Planning.* Presented at 72nd Annual Meeting of the Transportation Research Board, Washington, D.C.

Replogle, M. 1993b. *Bicycle and Pedestrian Policies and Programs in Asia, Australia, and New Zealand.* National Bicycling and Walking Study. FHWA Case Study 17. FHWA, U.S. Department of Transportation.

Replogle, M. 1994. *Transportation Conformity and Demand Management: Vital Strategies for Air Quality Attainment.* Environmental Defense Fund. Washington, D.C.

Replogle, M., and H. Parcells. 1993. *Improving Bicycle/Pedestrian Linkage to Transit.* National Bicycling and Walking Study. FHWA Case Study 9. FHWA, U.S. Department of Transportation.

RCEP. 1994. *Transport and the Environment.* London, United Kingdom, Oct.

SACTRA. 1994. *Trunk Roads and the Generation of Traffic.* Department of Transport, London, United Kingdom, Dec.

U.S. District Court for the District of Northern California. 1990. *Declaration of Dr. Peter R. Stopher in Support of Sierra Club's Objections to MTC's Proposed Conformity Assessment.* Civil No. C-89-2044-TEH and C-89-2064-TEH (consolidated), Aug. 20, San Francisco, Calif.

Study Committee
Biographical Information

Paul E. Peterson, *Chairman*, is Henry Lee Shattuck Professor of Government and Director of the Center for American Political Studies at Harvard University. Dr. Peterson received his bachelor's degree from Concordia College and his master's degree and Ph.D. from the University of Chicago. He previously was a Professor in the Department of Political Science at Johns Hopkins University, Director of Governmental Studies at The Brookings Institution, Research Associate for the National Opinion Research Center, and Professor in the Departments of Political Science and Education at the University of Chicago. Dr. Peterson is a member of the U.S. Advisory Commission on Intergovernmental Relations, the American Political Science Association, the Association for Public Policy and Management, and the National Academy of Education. He served on the Transportation Research Board (TRB) Study Committee on Urban Transportation Congestion Pricing and has been a member of numerous committees of the National Research Council.

Paul E. Benson is a Supervising Materials and Research Engineer for the California Department of Transportation and a registered civil engineer in California. He received his bachelor's and master's degrees in civil engineering at the University of California, Davis. Mr. Benson has worked in the field of air quality modeling since 1977 and has developed a nationally implemented model and published a number of papers in the field. He is Chair of the TRB Committee on Transportation and Air Quality and a member of the Committee on Energy and Environmental Aspects of Transportation of the American Society of Civil Engineers.

Robert G. Dulla is a Senior Partner at Sierra Research, Inc., an air pollution consulting firm, which he joined in 1986. Before coming to Sierra Research, he held positions of increasing responsibility at Energy and Environmental Analysis, Inc., as an Analyst, Project Manager, Director of Transportation Studies, and Partner. Before that, he was an Information Specialist with the Highway Research Board. Mr. Dulla studied mechanical engineering at Clemson University and is the author of numerous reports and technical papers on motor vehicle emissions and fuel economy. He is a member of the Air and Waste Management Association and the Society of Automotive Engineers, where he serves on the Readers Committee for papers on fuels.

Genevieve Giuliano is an Associate Professor of Urban and Regional Planning and Director of the Lusk Center Research Institute in the School of Urban and Regional Planning at the University of Southern California (USC). She received her bachelor's degree from the University of California, Berkeley, and her Ph.D. in social science from the University of California, Irvine. Before joining USC in 1988, Dr. Giuliano served as Assistant Director of the Institute of Transportation Studies at the University of California, Irvine. Her research interests include transportation policy evaluation, land use and transportation relationships, and travel behavior. She is coeditor of the international journal *Urban Studies*, a member of the Editorial Board of *Transportation Research*, and a research fellow at the Lincoln Institute of Land Policy.

David L. Greene is a Senior Research Staff Member and Manager of the Energy Policy Research Programs of the Center for Transportation Analysis at Oak Ridge National Laboratory, which he joined in 1977. Dr. Greene received his bachelor's degree at Columbia University, his master's degree at the University of Oregon, and his Ph.D. in geography and environmental engineering at Johns Hopkins University. He is a member of the Association of American Geographers, the American Statistical Association, the Society of Automotive Engineers, the Operations Research Society of America, the American Association for the Advancement of Science, and the Editorial Advisory Board of *Transportation Research*. He chairs TRB's Section F, Energy and Environmental Concerns, is a member of the Group 1 Council, and served on the TRB Committee for the Study of High-Speed Surface Transportation in the United States.

Frank S. Koppelman is Professor in the Department of Civil Engineering and the Transportation Center at Northwestern University. He received his bachelor's degree in civil engineering from the Massachusetts Institute of Technology (MIT), his M.B.A. from Harvard University, and his Ph.D. in transportation systems analysis from MIT. Dr. Koppelman was a Research Assistant at MIT and a Manager at the Tri-State Regional Planning Commission. An expert on travel behavior analysis and forecasting, Dr. Koppelman is an Associate Editor of *Transportation Research*, is a member of the TRB Committee on Passenger Travel Demand Forecasting, and served on the TRB Committee for the Study of High-Speed Surface Transportation in the United States.

Kenneth J. Leonard is Director of the Bureau of Strategic Planning in the Division of Planning and Budget at the Wisconsin Department of Transportation. The bureau is responsible for developing departmental strategies concerning urban, land use, environmental, and economic development issues. Mr. Leonard received his bachelor's degree from the University of Wisconsin at LaCrosse and his master's degree in city and regional planning from the University of Southern Illinois. He chairs the Air Quality Subcommittee of the Standing Committee on the Environment of the American Association of State Highway and Transportation Officials.

Edwin S. Mills is Gary Rosenberg Distinguished Professor of Real Estate and Finance and Director of the Center for Real Estate Research in the Kellogg Graduate School of Management at Northwestern University. Dr. Mills received his bachelor's degree in economics from Brown University and his Ph.D. from the University of Birmingham, England. He was previously Professor of Economics, Professor of Economics (and Public Affairs), and Gerald L. Phillippe Professor of Urban Studies in the Department of Economics and the Woodrow Wilson School at Princeton University; Professor, Associate Professor, and Assistant Professor in the Department of Political Economy at Johns Hopkins University; and Instructor in the Department of Economics at MIT. Dr. Mills is a Fellow of the Urban Land Institute, elected member of the Board of Directors of the American Real Estate and Urban Economics Association, coeditor of the *Journal of Real Estate Finance and Economics*, and member of numerous editorial boards, including the *Review of Urban and Regional Development Studies*. He also has served on several committees of the National Academy of Sciences, including the Committee on Motor Vehicle Emissions, the Committee on Nuclear and Alternative Energy Systems, and the Motor Vehicle Nitrogen Oxide Standard Committee.

Stephen H. Putman is Professor of City and Regional Planning and Associate Dean for Graduate Programs in the Graduate School of Fine Arts at the University of Pennsylvania. He is also Director of the Urban Simulation Laboratory. Before coming to the University of Pennsylvania, Dr. Putman was a Systems Analyst with CONSAD Research Corporation. He received his bachelor's degree in electrical engineering at the Carnegie Institute of Technology and his M.B.A. and Ph.D. at the University of Pittsburgh. Dr. Putman is the author of numerous articles and books on integrated transportation and land use models. He is a member of the Regional Science and the Urban and Regional Information Systems Associations.

William R. Reilly is a Principal with Catalina Engineering, Inc., an engineering consulting firm. Mr. Reilly received his bachelor's and master's degrees in civil engineering from the University of California, Berkeley, and the University of Arizona, respectively. He spent 23 years with JHK & Associates, Inc., as Executive Vice President, Senior

Vice President, and Senior Associate and Transportation Engineer. Before that he was a Lecturer at the University of Arizona; Highway Engineer with the Highway Department in Santiago, Chile; Junior Traffic Engineer in Alameda, California; and Teaching Assistant at the University of Arizona. Mr. Reilly is a registered civil engineer in several states and past President of the Arizona Section of the Institute of Transportation Engineers. He is a member of the American Society of Civil Engineers, the National Society of Professional Engineers, the American Planning Association, and the TRB Committee on Highway Capacity and Quality of Service.

Michael A. Replogle is Co-Director of the Transportation Project at the Environmental Defense Fund. Before that, he was Transportation Coordinator for the Montgomery County, Maryland, Planning Department; Founder and President of the Institute for Transportation and Development Policy—a nonprofit corporation that promotes low-cost sustainable global transportation strategies; and Transportation Research Associate with Public Technology, Inc. Mr. Replogle received a bachelor's degree in sociology and bachelor's and master's degrees in civil and urban engineering from the University of Pennsylvania. He is a member of the TRB Committee on Bicycling and Bicycle Facilities and the Global Task Force on Nonmotorized Transportation.

Gordon A. Shunk is a Research Engineer and Manager of the Urban Analysis Program at the Texas Transportation Institute (TTI), Texas A&M University System. He received a bachelor's degree in engineering science at DePauw University and bachelor's and master's degrees in civil engineering and a Ph.D. in urban planning and engineering at Purdue University. Before coming to TTI, Dr. Shunk was Director of Transportation and Energy at the North Central Texas Council of Governments, Chief Transportation Planning Engineer at DeLeuw Cather & Company, Program Manager for the Bay Area Rapid Transit Impact Program at the San Francisco Metropolitan Transportation Commission, and Senior Associate Engineer at Alan M. Voorhees & Associates. He is a member of the American Society of Civil Engineers and the Institute of Transportation Engineers and is a registered professional engineer in California. Dr. Shunk chairs the TRB Committee on Transportation Planning Applications.

Kenneth E. Sulzer is Executive Director of the San Diego Association of Governments (SANDAG) and Chief Executive Officer of Source-Point, a nonprofit public benefit corporation chartered by SANDAG. Mr. Sulzer received his bachelor's degree in geography from Valparaiso University and his master's degree in urban planning from the University of Illinois. Before coming to SANDAG as Deputy Executive Director, he was Deputy Director of Planning and Program Coordination for the County of San Diego; Urban Planner and Director for District Planning at the National Capital Planning Commission in Washington, D.C.; and Senior Project Planner with the Boston Redevelopment Authority. Mr. Sulzer is a member of the board of directors of the National Association of Regional Councils; member of the American Institute of Certified Planners and the American Planning Association; member emeritus of the California Planning Roundtable; board member of Partners for Liveable Places, San Diego; and associate member of the International City Managers Association.

George V. Wickstrom retired in 1992 from the Metropolitan Washington Council of Governments where he was Deputy Director and Manager of Technical Services. Before that, he was Executive Director of the New Castle County Land Use and Transportation Study, Deputy Director of Transportation Planning for the Penn-Jersey Transportation Study, Senior Traffic Engineer at Edwards and Kelsey, and Chief of Arterial Planning at the New York City Department of Traffic. Mr. Wickstrom received his bachelor's degree in civil engineering from Cooper Union College and his graduate certificate in highway traffic from Yale University. He is a Fellow of the Institute of Traffic Engineers and member of the TRB Committee on Transportation Planning Applications.

Catherine Witherspoon is the Legislative Director for the South Coast Air Quality Management District in Southern California. Previously, she worked as an Expert Consultant for the U.S. Environmental Protection Agency in San Francisco on air quality planning issues. Between 1981 and 1994, Ms. Witherspoon held positions of increasing responsibility at the California Air Resources Board, including Legislative Representative, Chief of Air Quality Planning, and Assistant Executive Officer. Ms. Witherspoon received her bachelor's degree in politics at the University of California at Santa Cruz. She is a member of the Air and Waste Management Association.

Julian Wolpert is Henry G. Bryant Professor of Geography in the Public Affairs and Urban Planning Department at the Woodrow Wilson School of Public and International Affairs at Princeton University. He received his bachelor's degree in economics and geography from Columbia University and his master's degree and Ph.D. in geography from the University of Wisconsin. Before coming to Princeton, Dr. Wolpert was Professor of Regional Science and Geography, Associate Professor, and Assistant Professor at the University of Pennsylvania. He was elected to the National Academy of Sciences in 1977 and has chaired several activities for the National Research Council. Dr. Wolpert is a past member of the TRB Executive Committee and the Subcommittee for NRC Oversight and is a Fellow of the American Association for the Advancement of Science (elected in 1985) and the American Institute of Certified Planners (appointed in 1986).